Sport, Leisure and Ergonomics

Edited by

Greg Atkinson
and
Thomas Reilly

School of Human Sciences
Liverpool John Moores University,
Liverpool, UK

Proceedings of the Third
International Conference on Sport,
Leisure and Ergonomics
12th–14th July 1995

E & FN SPON
An Imprint of Chapman & Hall

London · Glasgow · Weinheim · New York · Tokyo · Melbourne · Madras

Published by E & FN Spon, an imprint of
Chapman & Hall, 2–6 Boundary Row, London SE1 8HN, UK

Chapman & Hall, 2–6 Boundary Row, London SE1 8HN, UK

Blackie Academic & Professional, Wester Cleddens Road, Bishopbriggs, Glasgow
G64 2NZ, UK

Chapman & Hall GmbH, Pappelallee 3, 69469 Weinheim, Germany

Chapman & Hall USA, 115 Fifth Avenue, New York, NY 10003, USA

Chapman & Hall Japan, ITP-Japan, Kyowa Building, 3F, 2-2-1 Hirakawacho, Chiyoda-ku,
Tokyo 102, Japan

Chapman & Hall Australia, 102 Dodds Street, South Melbourne,
Victoria 3205, Australia

Chapman & Hall India, R. Seshadri, 32 Second Main Road, CIT East,
Madras 600 035, India

First edition 1995

© 1995 E & FN Spon

Printed in Great Britain by Hartnolls Ltd, Bodmin, Cornwall

ISBN   0 419 20600 0

∞ Printed on permanent acid-free text paper, manufactured in accordance with
ANSI/NISO Z 39.48-1992 and ANSI/NISO Z 39.48-1984 (Permanence of Paper).

Publisher's note
This book has been produced using camera ready copy provided by the individual
contributors.

Third International Conference on Sport, Leisure and Ergonomics
12th–14th July 1995

A conference of the Ergonomics Society organised from Liverpool John Moores University and held at Burton Manor, The Wirral

Organisers
Thomas Reilly, Greg Atkinson and Tony Shelton

Co-sponsors
World Commission for Sport Biomechanics
International Society for Advancement of Kinanthropometry
British Association of Sport and Exercise Sciences

Contents

Contributors

G. **Adamson,** Centre for Sport and Exercise Sciences, School of Human Sciences, Liverpool John Moores University, Byrom Street, Liverpool L3 3AF, England

. L. **Allen,** School of Science, Sheffield Hallam University, Pearson Building, 27 Broomgrove Road, Sheffield S10 2NA, England

. **Atkins,** Centre for Physical Education and Dance, Liverpool John Moores University, Mountford Building, Byrom Street, Liverpool L3 3AF, England

G. **Atkinson,** School of Human Sciences, Liverpool John Moores University, Mountford Building, Byrom Street, Liverpool L3 3AF, England

G. **Barton,** Centre for Sport and Exercise Sciences, School of Human Sciences, Liverpool John Moores University, Mountford Building, Byrom Street, Liverpool L3 3AF, England

W. **Bell,** Cardiff Institute of Education, Cyncoed, Cardiff CF2 6XD, Wales

. **Borms,** Department of Human Biometry, Vrije Universiteit Brussel, Laarbeeklaan 103, B-1090 Brussel, Belgium

A. **Borrie,** Centre for Sport and Exercise Sciences, Liverpool John Moores University, Mountford Building, Byrom Street, Liverpool L3 3AF, England

L. **Broomhead,** All England Netball Association, 9 Paynes Park, Hitchin, Hertfordshire SG5 lEH, England

V. **Bunc,** Faculty of Physical Education and Sports, Charles University, J. Martiho 31, CZ-162 52 Prague 6, Czech Republic

C. N. **Burton,** Centre for Sport and Exercise Sciences, School of Human Sciences, Liverpool John Moores University, Mountford Building, Byrom Street, Liverpool L3 3AF, England

L. **Burwitz,** Division of Sports Science, The Manchester Metropolitan University, Crewe and Alsager Faculty, Alsager Campus, Hassal Road, Alsager, Stoke on Trent ST7 2HL, England

N. T. Cable, Centre for Sport and Exercise Sciences, School of Human Sciences, Liverpool John Moores University, Mountford Building, Byrom Street, Liverpool L3 3AF, England

D. Caboor, Department of Experimental Anatomy, Vrije Universiteit Brussel, Laarbeeklaan 103, B-1090 Brussel, Belgium

E. Campbell, Division of Sport Science, The Manchester Metropolitan University, Crewe and Alsager Faculty, Hassall Road, Alsager, Stoke on Trent ST7 2HL, England

I. G. Campbell, Division of Sport Science, The Manchester Metropolitan University, Crewe and Alsager Faculty, Hassall Road, Alsager, Stoke on Trent ST7 2HL, England

J. H. Chapman, School of Science, Sheffield Hallam University, Pearson Building, 27 Broomgrove Road, Sheffield S10 2NA, England

J. P. Clarys, Department of Experimental Anatomy, Vrije Universiteit Brussel, Laarbeeklaan 103, B-1090 Brussels, Belgium

M. A. Cooke, Health Research Institute, Sheffield Hallam University, Pearson Building, 27 Broomgrove Road, Sheffield S10 2NA, England

S. Cooper, Centre for Sport and Exercise Sciences, School of Human Sciences, Liverpool John Moores University, Byrom Street, Liverpool L3 3AF, England

S.-M. Cooper, Centre for Sport, Physical Education and, Leisure, Cardiff Institute of Higher Education, Cyncoed Centre, Cardiff CF2 6XD, Wales

K. Craig, Centre for Sport and Exercise Sciences, School of Human Sciences, Liverpool John Moores University, Byrom Street, Liverpool L3 3AF, England

A. D. Crocombe, Department of Mechanical Engineering, University of Surrey, Guildford, Surrey GU2 5XH, England

P. Dabnichki, Division of Sport Science, The Manchester Metropolitan University, Crewe and Alsager Faculty, Hassall Road, Alsager, Stoke on Trent ST7 2HL, England

A. L. Dallmeijer, Faculty of Human Movement Sciences, Vrije Universiteit, Van der Boechorststraat 9, 1081 BT Amsterdam, The Netherlands

G. W. N. Dalzell, Regional Medical Cardiology Centre, Royal Victoria Hospital, Belfast, Northern Ireland

. **S. Davies,** Department of Medicine, University of Wales College of Medicine, Heath Park, Cardiff CF4 4XW

. Davies, Department of Public Health Medicine and Epidemiology, Medical Faculty, Queen's Medical Centre, Nottingham NG7 2UH, England

. Davies, School of Human Sciences, Liverpool John Moores University, Mountford Building, Byrom Street, Liverpool L3 3AF, England

. Dlouha, Faculty of Physical Education and Sports, Charles University, Martiho 31, CZ-162 52 Prague 6, Czech Republic

. D. Dobbins, Centre for Sport, Physical Education and Leisure, Cardiff Institute of Higher Education, Cyncoed Centre, Cardiff CF2 6XD Wales

. Doggart, Centre for Sport and Exercise Sciences, School of Human Sciences, Liverpool John Moores University, Mountford Building, Byrom Street, Liverpool L3 3AF, England

. I. Dreyer, Institute for Biokinetics, Potchefstroom University for CHE, Potchefstroom 2520, Republic of South Africa

. Dugdill, Centre for Health Studies, Liverpool John Moores University, Trueman Street, Liverpool L3 2ET, England

. Duquet, Department of Human Biometry, Vrije Universiteit Brussel, Laarbeeklaan 103, B-1090 Brussel, Belgium

. D. Evans, Department of Medical Physics and, Bioengineering, University Hospital of Wales, Heath Park, Cardiff CF4 4XW, Wales

. M. Fothergill, Naval Medical Research Institute, Bethesda, Maryland 0889-5607, USA

. E. Fowler, Division of Sport Science, The Manchester Metropolitan University, Crewe and Alsager Faculty, Hassall Road, Alsager, Stoke on Trent T7 2HL, England

. L. Fysh, School of Science, Sheffield Hallam University, Pearson Building, 7 Broomgrove Road, Sheffield S10 2NA, England

. E. Gates, Division of Sport Science, The Manchester Metropolitan University, Crewe and Alsager Faculty, Hassall Road, Alsager, Stoke on Trent ST7 2HL, England

K. P. George, Division of Sport Science, The Manchester Metropolitan University, Crewe and Alsager Faculty, Hassall Road, Alsager, Stoke on Trent ST7 2HL, England

N. Gleeson, Division of Sport, Health & Exercise, School of Sciences, Staffordshire University, Leek Road, Stoke on Trent ST4 2DF, England

V. L. Goosey, Division of Sport Science, The Manchester Metropolitan University, Crewe and Alsager Faculty, Hassall Road, Alsager, Stoke on Trent ST7 2HL, England

D. W. Grieve, Department of Anatomy, Royal Free Hospital, School of Medicine, Pond Street, London NW3 2QG, England

A. Grootaers, Department of Experimental Anatomy, Vrije Universiteit Brussel, Laarbeeklaan 103, B-1090 Brussel, Belgium

D. R. Jarvis, School of Leisure and Food Management, Sheffield Hallam University, Pearson Building, 27 Broomgrove Road, Sheffield S10 2NA, England

G. Jones, Department of PE, Sports Science and Recreation Management, Loughborough University, Loughborough, Leicestershire LE11 3TU, England

G. Juras, Department of Theory of Motor Behaviour, Academy of Physical Education, 72 Mikolowska, 40-065 Katowice, Poland

H. K. A. Lakomy, Department of Physical Education, Sports Science and Recreation Management, Loughborough University of Technology, Loughborough, Leics LE11 3TU, England

J. Langfort, Department of Applied Physiology, Medical Research Centre, Polish Academy of Sciences, 17 Jazgarzewska str., 00-730 Warsaw, Poland

A. Lees, Centre for Sport and Exercise Sciences, School of Human Sciences, Liverpool John Moores University, Mountford Building, Byrom Street, Liverpool L3 3AF, England

B. D. Levine, Institute for Exercise and Environmental Medicine, Presbyterian Hospital of Dallas, and the University of Texas Southwestern, Medical Center, 7232 Greenville Avenue, Dallas, Texas 75231, USA

D. Maclaren, Centre for Sport and Exercise Sciences, School of Human Sciences, Liverpool John Moores University, Mountford Building, Byrom Street, Liverpool L3 3AF, England

R. McIlhagger, Engineering Composites Research Centre, University of Ulster, Co Antrim BT37 0QB, Northern Ireland

F. A. Meenan, Northern Ireland Bioengineering Centre and School of Leisure and Tourism, University of Ulster, Co Antrim BT37 0QB Northern Ireland

T. H. Mercer, Division of Sport, Health & Exercise, Staffordshire University, Leed Road, Stoke on Trent, Staffordshire ST4 2DF, England

A. Miles, School of Sciences, Worcester College of Higher Education, Henwick Grove, Worcester WR2 6AJ, England

J. Mitchell, Division of Sport, Health & Exercise, Staffordshire University, Leed Road, Stoke on Trent, Staffordshire ST4 2DF, England

N. Mullan, Division of Sport Science, The Manchester Metropolitan University, Crewe and Alsager Faculty, Alsager Campus, Hassall Road, Alsager, Stoke on Trent ST7 2HL, England

C. Palmer, Division of Sport Science, The Manchester Metropolitan University, Crewe and Alsager Faculty, Alsager Campus, Hassall Road, Alsager, Stoke on Trent ST7 2HL, England

R. Phillips, Centre for Physical Education and Dance, Liverpool John Moores University, Barkhill Road, Liverpool L17 6BD, England

T. Pilis, Department of Physical Education, Pedagogical University of Czêstochowa, 4/8 Waszyngton str., 42-200 Czêstochowa, Poland

W. Pilis, Department of Physical Education, Pedagogical University of Czêstochowa, 4/8 Waszyngton str., 42-200 Czêstochowa, Poland

A. D. J. Pinder, Department of Anatomy, Royal Free Hospital, School of Medicine, Pond Street, London NW3 2QG, England

J. Raczek, Academy of Physical Education, 72a Mikolowska str., 40-065 Katowice, Poland

S. Rakowski, Division of Physics, School of Sciences, Staffordshire University, Leek Road, Stoke on Trent ST4 2DF, England

D. Rees, Department of Orthopaedics, Leighton Hospital, Mid-Cheshire Hospitals Trust, Middlewich Road, Crewe, Cheshire CW1 4QJ, England

T. Reilly, Centre for Sport and Exercise Sciences, School of Human Sciences, Liverpool John Moores University, Mountford Building, Byrom Street, Liverpool L3 3AF, England

H. Roberts, Department of Public Health Medicine and Epidemiology, Medical Faculty, Queen's Medical Centre, Nottingham NG7 2UH, England

A. H. Rouard, Centre de Recherche et d'Innovation sur le Sport, Université Claude Bernard Lyon (UCBL), UFRSTAPS, 27–29 Boulevard du 11 Novembre 1919, 69632 Villeurbanne Cédex, France

T. Springate, Division of Sport, Health & Exercise, Staffordshire University, Leed Road, Stoke on Trent, Staffordshire ST4 2DF, England

H. S. Steyn, Department of Human Movement Science, Potchefstroom University for Christian Higher Education, Private bag x6001, Potchefstroom 2520, Republic of South Africa

G. Stratton, Centre for Physical Education and Dance, Liverpool John Moores University, Barkhill Road, Liverpool L17 6BD, England

G. L. Strydom, Department of Human Movement Science, Potchefstroom University for CHE, Potchefstroom 2520, Republic of South Africa

M. Szpalski, Department of Orthopaedic Surgery, Molière-Longchamp Hospital, Rue Marconi 142, B-1 180 Brussels, Belgium

R. J. Tong, Centre for Sport, Physical Education and Leisure, Cardiff Institute of Higher Education, Cyncoed Centre, Cardiff CF2 6XD, Wales

S. Van der Merwe, Institute for Biokinetics, Potchesfstroom University for CHE, Potchefstroom 2520, Republic of South Africa

D. C. Van der Westhuizen, S. A. Medical Services, S. A. National Defence Force, PO Box 1896, Potchefstroom 2520, Republic of South Africa

L. H. V. Van der Woude, Faculty of Human Movement Sciences, Vrije Universiteit, Van der Boechorststraat 9, 1081 BT Amsterdam, The Netherlands

P. Van Roy, Department of Experimental Anatomy, Vrije Universiteit Brussel, Laarbeeklaan 103, B-1090 Brussel, Belgium

H. E. J. Veeger, Faculty of Human Movement Sciences, Vrije Universiteit, Van der Boechorststraat 9, 1081 BT Amsterdam, The Netherlands

E. S. Wallace, Northern Ireland Bioengineering Centre and School of Leisure and Tourism, University of Ulster, Co Antrim BT37 0QB Northern Ireland

Z. Waskiewicz, Department of Human Motor Behaviour, Academy of Physical Education, 40-065 Katowice, Mikolowska 72A, Poland

D. Weller, Department of Public Health Medicine and Epidemiology, Medical Faculty, Queen's Medical Centre, Nottingham NG7 2UH, England

D. Whitby, Centre for Sport and Exercise Sciences, School of Human Sciences, Liverpool John Moores University, Mountford Building, Byrom Street, Liverpool L3 3AF, England

J. A. White, Department of Public Health Medicine and Epidemiology, Medical Faculty, Queen's Medical Centre, Nottingham NG7 2UH, England

C. Williams, Department of Physical Education, Sports Science and Recreation Management, Loughborough University of Technology, Loughborough, Leics LE11 3TU, England

J. P. Wyse, Division of Sport, Health & Exercise, School of Sciences, Staffordshire University, Leed Road, Stoke on Trent, Staffordshire ST4 2DF, England

R. Zarzeczny, Department of Physical Education, Pedagogical University of Czêstochowa, 4/8 Waszyngton str., 42-200 Czêstochowa, Poland

E. Zinzen, Department of Experimental Anatomy, Vrije Universiteit Brussel, Laarbeeklaan 103, B-1090 Brussel, Belgium

Preface

Constant mass participation in sport, exercise and recreational activities necessitates a reappraisal of human factors in these domains. In parallel with the growth in leisure and recreation activity, has been the development of systematic approaches towards the analysis of sports and the stresses on participants. There are also major thrusts in optimising the preparation of individuals and teams for competitions, improving the design of sports equipment and facilities, and fitting the performer for outdoor leisure sports. Conventional ergonomics criteria – e.g. safety, efficiency, comfort and so on are recognised as important in these developments, whilst the array of analytical techniques used in the sports sciences overlaps with those of industrial ergonomics.

The Third International Conference on Sport, Leisure and Ergonomics was held at Burton Manor, July 12th–14th, 1995. The conference was organised under the aegis of the Ergonomics Society and followed the previous International Conferences held in 1987 and 1991. The conference provided up-to-date information on current applications of ergonomics in sport, leisure and recreation and offered opportunity for cross fertilisation of ideas between leisure and industrial ergonomics researchers from 15 different countries.

In addition to those working in sport, leisure and ergonomics research, these Proceedings should be of interest to a wide range of practitioners. These include individuals working in health and fitness centres, sports and recreation centres, professional sports clubs, the sports leisure industry, manufacturers of sports clothing and equipment, sports information technology and human–machine sports.

Greg Atkinson and Thomas Reilly

Sport, leisure and ergonomics: an introduction
G. Atkinson and T. Reilly

The proceedings of Sport, Leisure and Ergonomics provide a record of the peer-reviewed communications to the Third International Conference on Sport, Leisure and Ergonomics. This event was held at Burton Manor College (July 12-14 1995) and is now integrated in a four-year cycle into the calendar of international sports science meetings. The Conference is organised on behalf of the Ergonomics Society and previous Proceedings were published in special issues of its journal Ergonomics Vol. 31 (November) 1988, and Volume 37 (January) 1994. These issues helped to underline the common ground between the sports sciences and ergonomics by highlighting the contemporary applications of ergonomics techniques to sport, exercise and leisure contexts.

One difficulty that editors of Conference Proceedings are faced with is the lag between the formal communication of research work and its appearance in the press. Researchers frequently complain that their material is out of date by the time others read about it. Consequently, we adopted a different approach to this conference and attempted to have the material published at the time of this meeting. That we succeeded in doing so was due to the thoroughness with which authors prepared their papers and the speed with which they responded to queries from referees. It was also due to the support for our plans given by staff at the publisher's office.

The field of sports ergonomics is now recognised as an interdisciplinary area in its own right (Reilly and Ussher, 1988; Reilly and Shelton 1994). This is recognised by the co-sponsorship for the Conferences from the World Commission of Sports Biomechanics, the International Society for Advancement of Kinanthropometry and the British Association of Sport and Exercise Sciences. Their involvement is reflected in the range of topics that come within the scope of the conference theme. The main topics are organised into sections of this book and provide a testimony of the progress in sports ergonomics since the previous meetings.

The 'disabled athlete' is now a focus of attention in sports science research. The problem of harmonising the machine and the capabilities of the individual is a classical ergonomics one and the collection of papers in this volume demonstrates the range of interest in this special population. There is also a forceful research thrust directed towards the able-bodied non-athlete. Seemingly, the benefits of a well-structured exercise regimen for the health of a work-force is acknowledged in industry though its implementation is not always realised.

Whilst fitness programmes for the work-force at large place a heavy emphasis on safety, the training programmes of elite athletes operate within a narrower zone. Elite performers invariably tread a thin line between 'training' and 'straining' in their attempt to optimise their competitive efforts. Consequently many seek their winning edge by means of nutritional strategies in preparation for, during and recovery from both training and competing. There are also environmental factors, such as altitude and the biological disruptions due to international travel that can provide obstacles towards reaching maximal performance. This concept of there being limits to performance capability cuts across a number of sections in this book. It is not surprising that in a sports context researchers strive to perfect valid and reliable methods of measuring biological and psychological limits and to find ways of pushing them further back.

References

Reilly, T. and Shelton, T. (1994). Ergonomics in sport and leisure. Ergonomics, 37, 1-3.

Reilly, T. and Ussher, M. (1988). Sport, leisure and ergonomics. Ergonomics, 31, 1497-1500.

Part One

Ergonomics and Disabled Athletes

1 The ergonomics of wheelchair sports
L.H.V van der Woude, H.E.J. Veeger and A.J. Dallmeijer

1 Introduction

Success in wheelchair sports is highly dependent upon the
performance capacity of the athlete and the wheelchair.
From an ergonomics research perspective three areas within
the wheelchair-athlete combination are relevant in order to
maximize performance capacity: (1) vehicle mechanics of the
wheelchair, (2) work capacity and propulsion technique of
the human engine, and (3) the wheelchair-user interface
(Woude et al., 1994a). Apart from mere maximum performance,
power production, speed and manoeuvrability are the prime
wheelchair sports-related task aspects, which must be
considered within the current framework. A special focus
will be on the wheelchair-user interface paper.

2 Vehicle mechanics

The mechanical characteristics of the wheelchair - in close
relation with the environmental aspects - will clearly
influence performance. Rolling friction can be as low as 2
- 5 N for racing wheelchairs due to their weight, weight
distribution, proper alignment and wheel characteristics.
Internal friction in a well maintained wheelchair will only
be a fraction of rolling resistance (Frank and Abel, 1993),
whereas air drag will become relevant at speeds over ±3
$m.s^{-1}$, as is shown by wind tunnel experiments of Coe
(1979). Air drag may be reduced through wheelchair design:
reduction of frontal plane area and improvement of
streamline (see Coe, 1979; O'Reagan et al., 1981; Frank and
Abel, 1993).

3 Human Engine

The human engine will determine endurance and maximum work
capacity as well as the technique of propulsion. Work
capacity can be trained, but its magnitude clearly depends
upon the overall functionality of the athlete (Veeger et
al., 1991a; 1992a). Aerobic power will generally range
between 20 W and 100 W, but may even reach up to 150 W, as
measured in a wheelchair exercise test. Clearly it depends
on functionality. Anaerobic power may range within similar

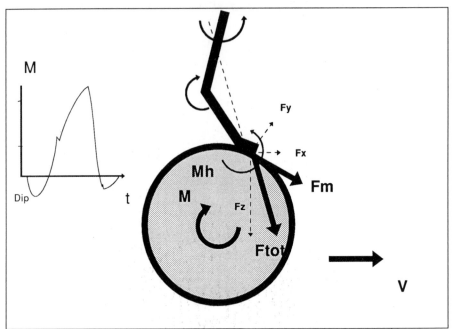

Figure 1. Forces and torques generated during handrim wheelchair propulsion.

boundaries in a 30 s sprint test (Veeger et al., 1992a; Woude et al., 1994b), but is highly susceptible to the level of resistance (Veeger et al., 1991b). Again variation due to differences in disability, training status or age will lead to considerable inter-individual differences.

Propulsion technique is characterised by timing, kinematics, muscle activity and force production (Veeger et al., 1991b; 1992a,b; Vanlandewijck et al., 1994). Seemingly ineffective forces, i.e. low fraction effective force [Fm/Ftot] and 'twisting torque' [Mh] (Veeger and Woude, 1994), appear functional and dominated by both the guided motion during the push phase and the functional-anatomy of the upper extremity (Figure 1). The complex hand-to-rim coupling leads to a braking torque at start and end of the push phase (Dip: Figure 1) – which will generally be avoided in the 'butterfly' wheelchair racing technique. Conventional hand-to-rim coupling – as in basketball and tennis wheelchairs – is based upon a sufficiently high friction between hand and rim which originates from considerable vertical [Fz] and medio-lateral [Fy] forces and Mh. As a consequence, forceful activity of finger flexors and possibly of wrist stabilising lower arm muscles is seen, while the wrist travels through extreme radial and ulnar deviation. This may stimulate repetitive strain injuries (as in the carpal-tunnel), which are also seen in the shoulder region (McCormack et al., 1991; Burnham et al., 1993, 1994). These health problems are not specific for athletes (Bailey et al., 1987).

4 Wheelchair-athlete interface

The wheelchair-athlete interface will influence performance: the interaction of the musculo-skeletal system with
the form and geometry of the propulsion mechanism and the
seat configuration has been shown to influence the energy
cost, physical strain and the gross mechanical efficiency
as well as propulsion technique: propulsion mechanism
(Woude et al., 1986, 1993), seat height (Woude et al.,
1990), rim size (Woude et al., 1988) and rim tube diameter
(Lesser, 1986; Traut, 1989; McLaurin and Brubaker, 1991).
It is suggested that in general the interface must be
finely tuned to the physical characteristics of the
individual in order to optimize or maximize performance.

4.1 Lever and crank propulsion
Other than hand rim propulsion mechanisms are not allowed
in regular wheelchair track events. This is rather
unfortunate. In general hand rim propelled wheelchairs are
inefficient as is shown for instance in Figure 2, where a
comparison between a three-wheeled synchronous lever, a
conventional crank propelled wheelchair and two hand rim
propelled wheelchairs (a daily-active and sports wheelchair) has been made with respect to oxygen uptake (mean
values of N=10 non-disabled subjects, treadmill speed =
0.96 m.s^{-1}; slope of 0-3°). Despite the higher power output
of the quite heavy tricycles, heart rate and oxygen cost
(and minute ventilation) were significantly lower. Gross

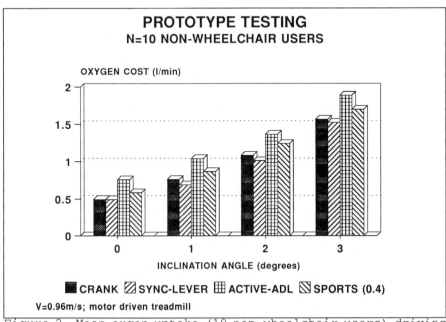

Figure 2. Mean oxgen uptake (10 non-wheelchair users) driving
4 different propulsion mechanisms on a motor driven
treadmill.

mechanical efficiency was just over 11% for the tricycles whereas values for hand rim wheelchairs remained below 9%.

The comparison was made purely on basis of the existing designs (prototype evaluation): differences in hand velocity, segment trajectories and magnitude and direction of force differed as such and may explain the differences in physiology. Other factors in crank and lever propelled wheelchairs are: continuity of the motion, effective use of backrest and probably the larger muscle mass involved. The crank and lever propulsion mechanisms seem appropriate for outside use at relatively high velocities, as well as for longer distances. Optimization of gear ratio, lever length, hand grip and spatial orientation of the lever must receive attention (Lesser, 1986; McLaurin and Brubaker, 1991; Woude et al., 1986, 1993). Currently, a strong development in contemporary lever and crank propelled wheelchairs for (open category) sports events and recreational purposes is seen (Crase et al., 1987).

4.2   Hubcrank
A less well-known propulsion mechanism is the hubcrank, a device which allows a continuous motion of the hand around the wheelhub of the rear wheels of a track or racing wheelchair. Thus, hubcranks allow 'continuous' force exertion onto the wheelhubs. The hubcrank has a well-fitted handgrip which rotates freely around an axle perpendicular to the crank and adapts itself to the orientation of the hand. The crank has a freewheel. It is typically used in training of athletes, in open-competition sports events and in recreation. To study the possible beneficial aspects of the hubcrank over the handrim, a group of ten non-wheel-chair users were tested during two submaximal wheelchair exercise tests on a Sopur[e] (Sopur, Heidelberg, Germany) roller-based ergometer (Meijs et al., 1993). The subjects propelled the wheelchair at a speed of 1.39 m.s^{-1} and with an increasing simulated slope (+0.5% every 3 minutes), starting at -0.5 up to 3.0%. The handrims and hubcranks had a similar diameter (0.26 m) and were mounted to separate sets of wheels which were mounted to a Speedy Wheely Marathon wheelchair (Veldink Techniek[e], The Netherlands). The order of the exercise tests was random. Oxygen uptake, minute ventilation, heart rate, power output and mechanical efficiency were determined every third minute of each exercise block. The results showed significantly lower strain for the hubcrank (Figure 3) and higher gross mechanical efficiency which was up to 3% higher for the hubcrank. More or less similar trends were seen in a pilot study for a small group of trained wheelchair athletes propelling the same configurations on a motor driven

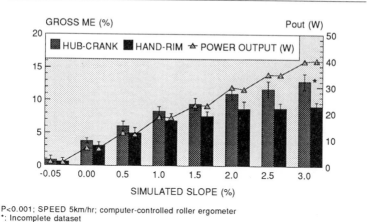

Figure 3. Mean and standard deviation for gross mechanical efficiency during handrim and hubcrank propulsion on a roller ergometer.

treadmill (Woude et al., 1995). The positive effects - using the hubcrank - may be explained with the following notions:
I) a continuous circular motion, allowing both push and pull actions, spreading the effort over both flexors and extensors of elbows and shoulders, thus reducing the average power contributions of the individual muscles and subsequently reducing the tendency to muscular fatigue.
II) a more natural orientation of the hand and wrist to the lower arm (the handgrip adapts to the spatial hand orientation) and a less strenuous coupling of the hand to the propulsion mechanism (the forces will be directed to the axis of the grip, which generally will be in line with the lower arm), reducing grip force of the finger flexors. This may lead to a reduction of strain in the carpal tunnel.
III) finally the natural coupling of the hand to the crank will prevent a possible negative gripping torque [Mh] - as is seen in hand rim wheelchair propulsion (Veeger et al., 1992a,b; Veeger and Woude, 1994). Also the braking torque at the start/end of the push phase (Veeger et al., 1991b, 1992b) will be absent in the hubcrank condition (see Figure 1). The hubcrank has advantages over the handrim. Its use to date has been restricted to track wheelchairs, outdoor use, and to proficient wheelchair users. The wheelchair is hard to steer, braking is more complicated and its increased width (+0.15 m) complicate indoor use.

4.3 Gear ratio
The hand rim wheelchair is an inefficient means of ambulation, but has general advantages in everyday use: its size and steering characteristics allow manoeuvring in

small spaces. Different applications may require different gearing levels: groups of well-trained subjects may want a gearing which enables them to compete at high velocities, whereas a steep incline for physically less able subjects will demand a low gear. A variable gear is easily implemented in a lever or crank propelled wheelchair (Crase et al., 1987). In hand rim wheelchairs this is technically much more complicated. Bachl et al. (1989) evaluated a prototype gear system for handrims with physiological parameters. The relevance of different gear ratios in hand rim wheelchairs is stressed by the results of different experimental studies (Traut, 1989; McLaurin and Brubaker, 1991; Veeger et al., 1992b).

In general the physical strain as a consequence of a certain external power output is dependent upon mechanical advantage (input force/output force) or gear ratio as is shown in results of experiments on a computer controlled wheelchair ergometer (Veeger et al., 1992b; Figure 4). At equal submaximal power output, a higher mechanical advantage (0.43 -> 0.87) i.e. a higher hand velocity - and simultaneously a lower mean resisting force - during the push phase led to a higher cardio-respiratory response (oxygen cost, heart rate; P<0.05) in a group of 9 non-wheelchair users propelling on the ergometer at rim velocities up to 1.67 m.s^{-1}. Simultaneously, a lower mechanical efficiency is seen.The increase in linear hand velocity during the push phase led to a decrease in effective force is seen. This is represented in Figure 4 by FEF-peak, the ratio between the peak effective force [Fm] - tangent to the rim - and the total force vector [Ftot], which decreased from 71 to 58%. The amount of negative work (or Dip) at the beginning and end of the push phase increased with mechanical advantage. In other words gear ratio influences propulsion technique and (subsequently)

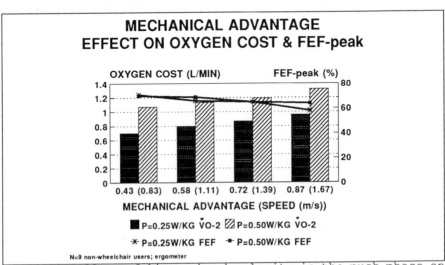

Figure 4. Effect of linear hand velocity in the push phase on oxygen uptake and fraction effective force [FEF].

leads to significant changes in the cardio-respiratory responses possibly as consequence of co-ordination of muscle activity in arms, shoulders and trunk.

Application of a variable gearing in hand rim wheelchairs is worth considering. However, the choice of ratio will be dependent on power and velocity.

4.4 Rim diameter

Although different gear ratios are not common in hand rim wheelchairs, different rim diameters are often seen in track wheelchairs. In wheelchair sports athletes tend to individualize their choice of hand rim size, tube diameter and profile. As a consequence much experimentation is currently going on. To study the physiological effects of rim size an experiment was conducted with a racing wheelchair (Speedy Wheely; Veldink Techniek[e], The Netherlands) and five different rim diameters. Eight track athletes conducted five subsequent exercise tests on a motor driven treadmill, each with a different rim diameter (diameter 0.3 - 0.56 m; tube diameter 0.03 m; wheel diameter 0.66 m; five 3-minute exercise blocks at speeds of 0.83 to 4.17 m.s^{-1}; slope 0.5°; Woude et al., 1988). The results showed a significant effect of rim size on the cardio-respiratory parameters. Generally the largest rim led to the highest physiological strain and lowest efficiency level, which overall was not high: a mean maximum of somewhat less than 8% (gross) for the smallest rim (Figure 5). Heart rate showed a mean difference of 20% (10-20 beats.min^{-1}) between the smallest and the largest rim size. Again the linear speed of the hand rim limited performance: five out of eight athletes were unable to perform at V=4.17 m.s^{-1} (power output did not exceed 50 W!). Muscle co-ordination, acceleration and deceleration of

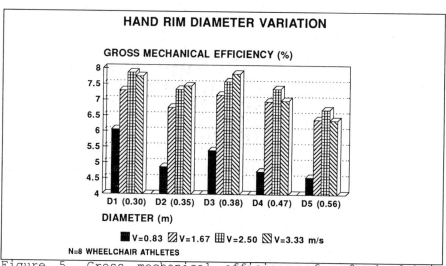

Figure 5. Gross mechanical efficiency for 8 wheelchair athletes using a racing wheelchair on a motor driven treadmill with 5 different handrim diameters.

segments, direction of effective force will influence efficiency. Mechanical advantage increased from 0.43 to 0.77 with rim size and apparently largely determines the cardio-respiratory responses. However the shoulder-rim distance also is relevant as was shown with multiple regression analysis ($R^2=0.71$; $p<0.001$):
$\dot{V}_{O_2}= -1.3 + 0.03$ Power $+ 2.68$ Shoulder-rim $+ 3.89$ Diameter.

Systematic study should be conducted with respect to the effects of the rim size, tube diameter, form and profile in a physiological and biomechanical context for different groups of wheelchair confined subjects.

4.5 Camber

The majority of sports wheelchairs is equipped with cambered rear wheels. Wheelchairs with cambered wheels are generally thought to perform better in track events than wheelchairs without. There seems to be a biomechanical rationale for the suggested better performance with cambered wheels: with the top of the wheels as near as possible to the trunk the rims are in a plane more or less passing through the shoulder joint. This would prevent the upper arms from abducting in the frontal plane, thus reducing static effort of the shoulder muscles. The effective force vector can also be directed as closely as possible to the shoulder joint.

Whether these assumptions are valid was studied by Veeger et al. (1989) for a basketball wheelchair during propulsion at speeds of 0.56 to 1.39 m.s^{-1} on a motor driven treadmill (N=8 non-wheelchair users). During four subsequent exercise tests the camber angle varied randomly from 0 to 3, 6 and 9°. The cardio-respiratory parameters indicated no positive or negative effect of camber angle in this wheelchair model. Similar findings were seen for the kinematics: no change in abduction angle was evident with camber angle. The electromyographic signal even showed an absence of activity of the m.deltoideus pars medialis, the major shoulder abductor, during the push phase. The explanation for this phenomenon is that the major active shoulder muscles - mm.pectoralis major and the deltoideus pars anterior - lead both to anteflexion as well as abduction and endoration, because of the closed system which exists between the hand and the shoulder in the push phase. No active abduction is required under the given testing condictions.

In conclusion, camber in the above test conditions does not influence the functional load. However, the practical advantages of cambered rear wheels are relevant: a better stability, protection of hands on the rim when passing along objects and the ease of turning. No extra rolling resistance is to be expected on the basis of the results of O`Reagan et al. (1981).

5 Conclusions

In conclusion, systematic study of the wheelchair-athlete combination helps understand and identify determinants of performance in wheelchair athletes and may help to increase

performance in sports. Presented and other interface
characteristics (seat height/orientation) require further
detailed analysis in relation to functional use. Thus, also
long-term ailments of the musculo-skeletal system - related
to a wheelchair dependent lifestyle - may be prevented.

6 References

Bachl, N., Ziegler, J.W., Baron, R., Liebeberger, S.,
   Kirsten, H., Prokop, L. (1989) Verhalten leistun-
   gsphysiologischer Parameter bei Rollstuhlfahrern unter
   Verwendung von verschiedene Uebersetzungsnaben zum
   Rollstuhlantrieb **Medizinische Orthopaedie Technik**, 6,
   235-238
Bayley, J.C., Cochran, T.P., Sledge, C.B. (1987) The weight
   bearing shoulder: the impingement syndrome in paraple-
   gics **Journal of Bone & Joint Surgery (AM)** 69, 676-678.
Burnham, R.S., May, L., Nelson, E., Steadward, R., Reid,
   D.C. (1993) Shoulder pain in wheelchair athletes: the
   role of muscle imbalance **American Journal of Sports
   Medicine** 21, 238-243.
Burnham, R., Chan, M., Hazlett, C., Laskin, J., Steadward,
   R. (1994) Acute median nerve dysfunction from
   wheelchair propulsion: the development of a model and
   study of the effect of hand protection **Archives of
   Physical Medicine & Rehabilitation**, 75, 513-518.
Coe, P.L. (1979) **Aerodynamic characteristics of wheelchairs**
   NASA Technical Memorandum 80191, Langley Research
   Center, Virginia.
Crase, N., Schmid, R., Robbins, S. (1987) Pedal power hand
   cycle survey **Sports `n Spokes** 12, 43-49.
Frank, T.G., Abel, E.W. (1989) Measurement of the turning,
   rolling and obstacle resistance of wheelchair cas-tors
   Journal of Biomedical Engineering 11,462-466.
Lesser, W. (1986) **Ergonomische Untersuchung der Gestaltung
   antriebsrelevanter Einflussgroessen beim Rollstuhl mit
   Handantrieb** Duesseldorf: Fortschrittberichte VDI Verlag
   Reihe 17: Biotechnik nr28,pp265
McCormack, D.A.R., Reid, D.C., Steadward, R.D., Syrotuik,
   A. (1991) Injury profiles in wheelchair athletes:
   results of a retrospective study **Clinical Journal of
   Sport Medicine** 1, 35-40.
McLaurin, C.A., Brubaker, C.E. (1991) Biomechanics and the
   wheelchair **Prosthetics & Orthotics International**, 15,
   24-37.
Meijs, P.J.M., Michels, K.J., Woude, L.H.V. van der, Veen-
   baas, R., Rozendal, R.H. (1993) Technical require-ments
   **"Ergonomics of manual wheelchair propulsion: state of
   the art"** (Woude et al.), IOS, Amsterdam 61-71.
O'Reagan, J.R., Thacker, J.G., Kauzlarich, J.J., Mochel,E.,
   Carmine, D.,Bryant, M. (1981) Wheelchair dynamics In:
   Wheelchair Mobility 1976-1981, REC, University of
   Virginia (p33-41)
Traut, L.(1989) **Ergonomische Gestalltung der Benutzer
   schnittstelle am Antriebssystem des Greifreifenroll-
   stuhls** Berlin, Springer Verlag
Vanlandewijck, Y.C., Spaepen, A.J., Lysens, R.J. (1994)

Wheelchair propulsion efficiency: movement pattern adaptations to speed changes **Medicine and Science in Sport   and Exercise** 26, 1373-1381.

Veeger, HEJ, Woude, LHV van der & Rozendal, RH (1989) The effect of rear wheel camber in manual wheelchair propulsion **Journal of Rehabilitation Research & Development** 26, 37-46.

Veeger, H.E.J., Hadj Yahmed, M., Woude, L.H.V. van der, Charpentier, P. (1991a) Peak oxygen uptake and maximal power of Olympic wheelchair athletes **Medicine and Science in Sport and Exercise**, 23, 1201-1209.

Veeger, H.E.J., Woude, L.H.V. van der, Rozendal, R.H. (1991b) Within-cycle characteristics of the wheel-chair push in sprinting on a wheelchair ergometer **Medicine and Science in Sport and Exercise,** 23, 264-271.

Veeger, H.E.J., Lute, E.M.C., Roeleveld, K., Woude, L.H.V. van der (1992a) Differences in performance between trained and untrained subjects during a 30-s sprint test in a wheelchair ergometer **European Journal of Applied Physiology**, 64, 158-164.

Veeger, H.E.J., Woude, L.H.V. van der, Rozendal, R.H. (1992b) Effect of handrim velocity on mechanical efficiency in wheelchair propulsion **Medicine and Science in Sport and Exercise**, 24, 100-107.

Veeger, H.E.J., Woude, L.H.V. van der (1994) Force generation in manual wheelchair propulsion In: **Biomedical Engineering Recent Developments (Vossoughi, J.),** Proc South Biom Eng Conf, Washington, 779-782.

Woude, L.H.V. van der, Groot, G.de, Hollander, A.P., Ingen Schenau, G.J. van, Rozendal, R.H. (1986) Wheelchair ergonomics and physiological testing of prototypes **Ergonomics**, 29, 1561-1573.

Woude, L.H.V. van der, Veeger, H.E.J., Ingen Schenau, G.J. van, Rozendal, R.H., Nierop, P.van, Rooth, F. (1988) Wheelchair racing: effect of hand rim diameter variation on physiology and technique **Medicine and Science in Sport and Exercise**, 20, 492-500.

Woude, L.H.V. van der, Veeger, H.E.J., Rozendal, R.H. (1990) Seat height in hand rim wheelchair propulsion: a follow-up study **Journal of Rehabilitation Sciences**, 3, 79-83.

Woude, L.H.V. van der, Veeger, H.E.J., Boer, Y.A. de, Rozendal, R.H. (1993) Physiological evaluation of a newly designed lever mechanism for wheelchairs **Journal of Medical Engineering & Technology**, 17, 232-240.

Woude, L.H.V. van der, Janssen, T.W.J., Meijs, P.J.M., Veeger, H.E.J., Rozendal, R.H. (1994a) Physical stress and strain in active wheelchair propulsion: an overview of a research programme **Journal of Rehabilitation Sciences**, 7, 18-25.

Woude, L.H.V. van der, Drexhage, D., Veeger, H.E.J. (1994b) Peak power production in wheelchair propulsion **Clinical Journal of Sport Medicine**, 4, 14-24.

Woude, L.H.V.van der, Maas, K., Rozendal, R.H., Veeger, H.E.J. (1995) Physiological responses during hubcrank and handrim wheelchair propulsion: a pilot study **Journal of Rehabilitation Sciences**, in press.

2 Development of a treadmill test to examine the physiological responses of wheelchair athletes to submaximal exercise

V.L. Goosey, I.G. Campbell and N.E. Fowler

1 Introduction

Various authors have examined the physiological and metabolic responses to wheelchair propulsion on a motorised treadmill (Gass and Camp, 1984; Lakomy *et al.*, 1987; McConnell *et al.*, 1989; Pohlman *et al.*, 1989; Campbell, 1992; Hartung *et al.*, 1993; Rasche *et al.*, 1993). In addition several studies have also been concerned with the effects of wheelchair design upon cardiorespiratory responses and propulsion techniques, whilst pushing on a motorised treadmill (Veeger *et al.*, 1988; Woude *et al.*, 1988; Woude *et al.*, 1988b; Veeger *et al.*, 1989). Typically these studies have employed low propulsion speeds and a standardised wheelchair. However, there is a need from both a physiological and technical standpoint, to examine the physiological and wheelchair propulsion techniques at race speeds with athletes using their own racing chair.

Recent treadmill developments have allowed athletes to be examined at realistic propulsion speeds in their own racing wheelchair (Lakomy *et al.*, 1987; Campbell 1992; Campbell *et al.*, in press). Campbell (1992) has reported the physiological and metabolic responses of wheelchair athletes of speeds upto 7 m.s^{-1}. The propulsion speeds being achieved during races now exceed the top speed of many motorised treadmills (e.g. Woodway ELG2; speed range 0-7 m.s^{-1}). In fact Hatung (1993) suggested that a treadmill protocol using only increments of speed may be unsatisfactory for athletes in order to elicit maximal responses for safety reasons. This has meant that those treadmill tests originally devised by Campbell (1992) need to be modified in order to test athletes at high relative exercise intensities.

This study was concerned with whether an increase in gradient, sufficient to increase physiological stress, affected the kinematic responses to wheelchair treadmill exercise.

2 Methods

2.1 Subjects
Eleven wheelchair athletes; 7 paraplegic and 4 spina bifida (Paralympic Racing Classifications: T3 (n=5) and T4 (n=6)) volunteered to participate in this study. All subjects trained for, and competed regularly in endurance races.

2.2 Exercise Test Protocol

An incremental exercise test was performed on a motorised treadmill (Woodway ELG2; speed range 0-34.3 $km.h^{-1}$; gradient range 0-22%) adapted for wheelchairs (Campbell *et al.*, in press). Each athlete performed the test in his own racing chair at realistic race propulsion speeds.

Prior to the main test, skinfolds were taken from the subscapular, supra-iliac, biceps and triceps sites (Durnin and Womersley, 1974) using skinfold callipers (John Bull, St Albans, England). In addition, body mass for each athlete was recorded using Seca seated beam balanced scales.

Each subject completed an incremental exercise test which comprised of five, four minute stages on the motorised treadmill. The initial speed for each athlete, based on previous visits to the laboratory was set at a level comfortable for the athlete, and was found to be between 20-50% $\dot{V}O_2$ peak. The first stage was performed at 0% gradient. At the end of the first stage the grade was increased to 0.7% and the speed remained the same. For the subsequent stages the gradient remained at 0.7% but the speed was increased by 0.5 $m.s^{-1}$. During the last minute of each stage, a mouthpiece with a two-way value connected to low-resistance wide bore tubing allowed the collection of expired air in 150 l Douglas Bags. Subjects stopped pushing and a small capillary blood sample was obtained from the earlobe, and analysed for blood lactate concentration using a YSI 1500 Sport (Yellow Springs, USA). After one minute of recovery subjects commenced pushing again. Heart rate was monitored using a short range telemetry system (Polar PE4000 Sports Tester).

Peak oxygen uptake ($\dot{V}O_2$ peak) was also determined for each athlete using a continuous incremental gradient protocol (Campbell *et al.*, in press).

2.3 Technique Analysis

A stationary Panasonic F15 video camera was positioned perpendicular to the treadmill and recorded the sagittal view. One complete unobstructed stroke cycle was digitised and analysed for each athlete for the first three stages. Each sequence was digitised at a sampling frequency of 50 Hz (50 fields / s) using an Arvis video captive board interfaced with an Acorn Archimedes 440 microcomputer.

The athlete was modelled as five rigid segments, defined by seven bony landmarks, the head, neck, shoulder, elbow, wrist, fingers and hip (Figure 1). The digitised data were smoothed and differentiated using cross-validated quintic splines. Angle of lean (towards the horizontal), elbow angle and the cycle time, defined as the time to complete one push cycle, were calculated.

2.4 Statistical Analysis

All data have been expressed as mean and standard deviation. To assess differences between the 0% grade and 0.7% gradient of the treadmill for the selected variables, independent t-tests were performed. Differences across the stages were identified through performing one-way analysis of variance (ANOVA) with repeated measures. When differences were revealed using ANOVA, then a Tukey post-hoc test was applied in order to identify where the differences lay. Values at the $P<0.05$ level were accepted as being statistically significant.

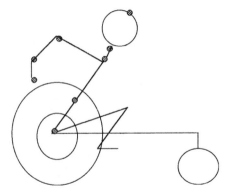

Figure 1. Kinematic model of an athlete, defined by seven bony landmarks.

3 Results

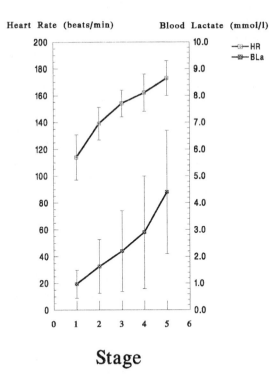

Figure 2. Heart rate (HR) and blood lactate (BLa) responses of the wheelchair athletes (n=11) during the incremental treadmill test (mean ±SD).

Table 1. Cycle dynamics and displacement data for stages 1 to 3

Variable		Stage 1 - 0% grade	Stage 2 - 0.7% grade	Stage 3 - 0.7% grade (+ .5m/s)
Pushing Rate (push/min)		33 ± 15	62 ± 14	65 ± 15
Cycle Time (s)		1.1 ± 0.4	0.7 ± 0.1	0.8 ± 0.4
Elbow Angle (degrees)	Min	91 ± 11	97 ± 10	95 ± 8
	Max	176 ± 3	176 ± 3	175 ± 4
Angle of Lean (degrees)	Min	38 ± 10	37 ± 9	33 ± 9
	Max	42 ± 15	43 ± 12	44 ± 11

The mean peak $\dot{V}O_2$ of the eleven athletes was 2.2 ± 0.7 l.min^{-1}; range $1.2 - 3.4$ l.min^{-1}, sum of 4 skinfolds was 34 ± 7.5 mm and body mass was 59.4 ± 14.7 kg.

Figure 2 shows that the incremental exercise test was sufficient to increase the physiological stress. There was a curvilinear relationship between heart rate and blood lactate concentrations during the stages of the test. This resulted in a mean blood lactate concentration of 4.4 ± 2.3 mmol.l^{-1} being reached.

When the grade was increased from 0 to 0.7% there was an increase ($P<0.01$) in both heart rate and oxygen consumption and a tendency for blood lactate to increase (Figure 2). There was also an increase in cycle time ($P<0.05$) and strokes per minute ($P<0.01$). However, the displacement data showed no change between the level and 0.7% grade increase (Table 1). When the velocity was increased by 0.5 m.s^{-1} (stage 3), there was a tendency for the physiological parameters to increase (N.S.). The cycle time and strokes per minute remained similar (Table 1). Furthermore, there was no change in the displacement data (Table 1). Between the first and third stage there was a tendency ($P=0.08$) for greater forward lean to occur as a result of a grade and speed increase. Finally, the combined effect of the grade and speed (stages 1 to 5) resulted in an increased heart rate, blood lactate and oxygen uptake ($P<0.01$).

4 Discussion

This study was primarily undertaken to determine whether a 0.7% grade increase was suitable to increase the physiological demands of the task, without significantly affecting the kinematics of wheelchair propulsion.

The increase in grade resulted in an increase in heart rate ($P<0.01$), oxygen consumption ($P<0.01$) and a tendency for an increased blood lactate concentration. This indicates that the physiological demands of the task were increased by the increase in grade. Despite this, kinematically the effects of an increase grade resulted in adaptations in the temporal data rather than the displacement data. Consequently, the demands of the exercise were met by an increase in the rate of movement rather than any change in the movement pattern. The cycle dynamics that include cycle time and the number of pushes per minute were higher when the grade of the treadmill was increased ($P<0.05$ and

P<0.01, respectively). The grade increment was found to be accompanied by a mean reduction of 0.4 s to complete a full cycle and an increase of 29 pushes per minute. In accordance with the present data, Veeger *et al.* (1989) showed that a decrease in cycle time is predominantly attained by a reduction in push time. This implies that with increasing velocity an increased amount of work per cycle must be generated in a shorter time period. Hence, either a grade or speed increment which are sufficient to increase the physical demands of the task will subsequently affect the cycle dynamics.

When the grade remained constant and speed increment of 0.5 m.s^{-1} occurred (stage 2), there was a moderate increase in the physiological parameters (n.s). Also, only negligible differences could be found between the second and third stage in both the cycle time, strokes per minute and the displacement data. This is probably because the athletes found this particular increment less demanding than the initial 0.7% grade increments, this can be supported by only marginal changes in the physiological parameters.

The combined effect of a 0.7% gradient and an increase in speed of 0.5 m.s^{-1} was adequate to increase the physiological demands of the task. Kinematically, the movement pattern of propulsion technique was not affected by this 0.7% grade increment. Nevertheless, there was a tendency for increased forward lean (P=0.08) between stages 1 and 3. This is consistent with other studies; for example, Veeger *et al.* (1989), found that trunk flexion was strongly related to changes of belt speed. It was suggested that these changes were the result of the higher output demands of the task. In this instance, they can be attributed to the combined effect of the gradient and speed increment.

The athletes in the present study were found to have a mean peak $\dot{V}O_2$ of 2.2 ± 0.7 l.min^{-1} which ranged from 1.2 - 3.4 l.min^{-1}. These values were found to be consistent with those previously reported by Campbell (1992) which suggests that the group was endurance trained. The results of the study also showed large variability between athletes, in both the propulsion styles and blood lactate responses to the incremental exercise test. These results may have been due to a number of factors, in particular, the wide range of lesion levels within the group, nature and length of disability. It is also possible that the variability found, may have been the result of the athletes' training status. Furthermore, each athlete may have been working at slightly different relative exercise intensity during the five stages of the incremental exercise test.

In conclusion, the results from the incremental exercise test suggest that the physiological demands of the task were increased, and were sufficient to develop a physiological profile from which training programmes could be recommended.

5 Summary

In summary, the physiological responses and the propulsion techniques of eleven wheelchair athletes were examined in this study. Each athlete performed an incremental exercise test, on a motorised treadmill adapted for wheelchairs (Campbell *et al.,* in press). The findings suggest that the use of a 0.7% gradient is sufficient to stimulate an increased physiological demand without significantly affecting the movement pattern of wheelchair propulsion. Therefore, the results of the study suggest that this exercise test protocol may be recommended to examine the physiological and wheelchair propulsion techniques of the athletes in their own racing wheelchair at realistic race speeds.

6 References

Campbell, I.G. (1992) The influence of spinal cord injury on the physiological and metabolic responses to exercise and performance. **Ph.D. Thesis,** Loughborough University of Technology, England.

Campbell, I.G. Lakomy, H.K.A. and Williams, C. (in press) A comparison of two wheelchair treadmill exercise test protocols for determination of peak oxygen uptake (VO$_2$ peak): gradient versus speed. In proceedings: **Third International Medical Congress on Sports for the Disabled.** Laval University. Quebec. 1994.

Durnin J.V.G.A. and Womersley, J. (1974) Body fat assessed from total body density and its estimation from skinfold thickness: measurements on 481 men and women aged from 16 to 72 years. **British Journal of Nutrition**, 32, 77-97.

Gass, G.C. and Camp, E.M. (1984) The maximum physiological responses during incremental wheelchair and arm cranking exercise in male paraplegics. **Medicine and Science in Sports and Exercise**, 16, 355-359.

Hartung, G.H. Lally, D.A. and Blancq, R.J. (1993) Comparison of treadmill exercise testing protocols for wheelchair users. **European Journal of Applied Physiology**, 66, 362-365.

Lakomy, H.K.A. Campbell, I.G. and Williams, C. (1987) Treadmill performance and selected physiological characteristics of wheelchair athletes. **British Journal of Sports Medicine,** 21(3), 130-133.

McConnell, T.J. Horvat, M.A. Beutel-Horvat, T.A. and Golding, L.A. (1989) Arm crank versus wheelchair treadmill ergometry to evaluate the performance of paraplegics. **Paraplegia.** 27, 307-313.

Pohlman, R.L. Gayle, G.W. Davis, G.M. and Glaser, R.M. (1989) Metabolic responses to maximal arm crank and wheelchair ergometry in male paraplegics. **Clinical Kinesiology.** 43, 89-95.

Rasche, W. Janssen, T.W.J. Van Oers, C.A.J.M. Hollander, A.P. and Woude, L.H.V. van der. (1993) Responses of subjects with spinal cord injuries to maximal wheelchair exercise: comparison of discontinuous and continuous protocols. **European Journal of Applied Physiology**, 66, 328-331.

Veeger, H.E.J. Woude, L.H.V. van der, and Rozendal, R.H. (1988) Wheelchair hand rim diameter on stroke and technique of wheelchair sportsmens. In L. Larson (Ed.), **Biomechanics XI**, (pp. 519-523). Champaign, IL: Human Kinetics.

Veeger, H.E.J. Woude, L.H.V. van der, and Rozendal, R.H. (1989) Wheelchair propulsion technique at different speeds. **Scandinavian Journal of Rehabilitation Medicine**, 21, 197-203.

Woude, L.H.V. van der, Veeger, H.E.J. Hendrich, K.M. Rozendal, R.H. and Ingen Schenau, G.J. van, (1988) Manual wheelchair propulsion: Effects of power output on physiology and technique. **Medicine and Science in Sports and Exercise**, 20, 70-78.

Woude, L.H.V. van der, Veeger, H.E.J. Rozendal, R.H. Ingen Schenau, G.J. van, Rooth, P. and Nierop, P.van (1988b) Wheelchair racing: Effect of rim diameter and speed on physiology and speed. **Medicine and Science in Sports and Exercise**, 7, 94-98.

3 A dynamic model of wheelchair propulsion during racing and the relevant pressure distribution
P. Dabnichki, V.L. Goosey and I.G. Campbell

1. Introduction

Wheelchair racing places high physical and physiological demands on the bodies of athletes and the interaction between the athlete and the wheelchair has been identified as an area of critical importance (Cooper, 1990). Developing mathematical models based upon laws and actual experience are ways of gaining further insight into the interaction of the athlete, chair and environment. Recent wheelchair modelling work has focused on the efficiency of the human-racing wheelchair interaction (Cooper, 1990; Hofstad and Patterson, 1994).

This study builds upon the modelling based around standard wheelchairs and was designed to model wheelchair propulsion at race speed. This model has a broad range of applications as the final goal is to establish a thermodynamical model for the calculation of the pushing technique efficiency and evaluation of the body balance in differently constructed wheelchairs. The application presented in this study is the seating comfort of the athlete which has been evaluated on the base of proper pressure distribution. The proper pressure distribution of people with a spinal cord injury has been well documented (Zacharkow, 1984). Furthermore, the danger of extreme pressure in the tissues below the tuberosity have been recognised (Dabnichki *et al.*, 1994).

The purpose of this study was to create a model of an athlete who regularly participates in endurance races, and to estimate the relevant pressure distribution.

2. Methods

2.1 Subject
The model was based around one paraplegic athlete (Lesion level L2), body mass of 52.2 kg and a peak oxygen uptake of 2.25 l.min^{-1}.

2.2 Physiological Characteristics of the athlete
The athlete performed an incremental exercise test which comprised of five, four minute stages on a motorised treadmill (Woodway ELG2) adapted for wheelchairs (Campbell *et al.*, in press) with a one minute recovery period between stages (Table 1). During the last minute of each stage, a mouthpiece with a two-way value connected to low-resistance wide bore tubing allowed the collection of expired air in 150l Douglas Bags. Following

this test peak oxygen uptake ($\dot{V}O_2$ peak.) was determined using a continuous incremental gradient protocol (Campbell *et al.*, in press).

Various anthropometric measurements of the athlete were taken along with measurements of the athletes racing wheelchair (Table 2).

Table 1. Oxygen uptake over a range of propulsion speeds

Propulsion Speed (m.s^{-1})	5.50	6.0	6.5	7.00	7.7
Oxygen Uptake (l.min^{-1})	1.43	1.60	1.80	2.10	2.20

Table 2. Design parameters of the wheelchair

Wheel diameter (mm)	670
Wheel inclination (deg.)	7
Seat length (mm)	325
Seat width (mm)	165
Push rim diameter (mm)	390

2.3 Video Analysis

A stationary Panasonic F15 video camera was positioned perpendicular to the treadmill and recorded the sagittal view. The athlete was modelled as five rigid segments, defined by seven bony landmarks, the head, neck, shoulder, elbow, wrist, fingers and hip. Straight line of motion was regarded so the forces applied by both arms were equal. This means that full symmetry was preserved throughout the whole pushing cycle. Angle of body inclination, displacement data including arm position and the cycle time, defined as the time to complete one push cycle, were calculated. One push cycle was modelled at race propulsion speed (6.5 m.s^{-1}), which corresponded to 80% of the athletes $\dot{V}O_2$ peak.

2.4 Dynamic computer model of wheelchair athlete

The model of the athlete was created using ADAMS/ Android (MDI Co.) programme. The anthropometric data taken from the athlete were input into the programme. The model is presented in Fig. 1. The model included the kinematic constraints of the human body. The kinematic input data for the movement of the trunk and the upper limbs were taken as described in 2.3. The inertia moments of the different body parts were calculated using inertial ellipsoids relevant to the anthropometric data of the subject. The pushing force was used as dynamic input to the model. Its magnitude in real time was calculated using inverse dynamics (known accelerations, unknown forces in the second law of Newton) based on the kinematic data for the body acceleration. Two main assumptions were made:

i) the efficiency of the pushing was 0.9;
ii) the symmetry was preserved throughout the pushing.

This model allowed the forces acting on the athlete's body and the resultant torque in the joints to be obtained. The contact forces between the body and the seat were necessary input data for the finite element model.

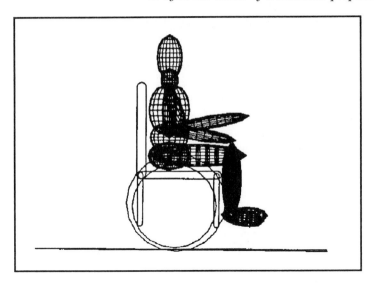

Fig.1. Saggital view of Android model of a disabled athlete in a wheelchair.

2.5 Finite element model

The finite element mesh is shown on Fig.2. It is based on earlier works (Dabnichki and Crocombe, 1992; Dabnichki *et al.*, 1994). The mesh consisted of 4-noded quadrilateral hyperelastic elements, specified in ANSYS 5.0A as HYPER-56. The ishial tuberosity was modelled as a rigid body and the top part of the mesh was also undeformable. This model allowed of a high level of pressure to be generated under the ishial tuberosity and simulated an existent experimental setting (Reddy *et al.*, 1982). The rationale for this was that the magnitude of a possible bone deformation is in the range of microns which

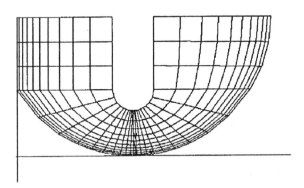

Fig.2. Finite element mesh of the buttock tissue under the ishial tuberosity

compared to tissue displacement of 30 mm is negligible. The soft tissue part was divided into 260 elements. Only the right half of the buttock was modelled as full symmetry was presumed. The contact interface was modelled using CONTACT-26 3-noded node to rigid surface type contact elements. These elements provide excellent and speedy convergence despite the large deflection occurring in the soft tissue. Contact elements were placed vertically in the middle of the buttock to reflect the symmetry preservation.

The ground was modelled i) as a rigid plane and ii) as a circular rigid base. The rationale for this is the lack of cushioning and the very high Young modulus (elastic constant of elongation) of the seat material. When the cloth is not stretched it could be modelled as a plane and when the strip is elongated we can assume that the seat is a rigid body with an arch form.

The resultant load obtained from the dynamic model was applied using automatically optimised load stepping and this allowed very fast convergence in only 104 load steps.

3 Results

From the dynamic model described in 2.4 a profile of the ground reaction force was derived (Figure 3). This force represents the total reaction force acting on the seating parts assuming that the athlete's body is rigid. The force profile has not been experimentally validated because mounting a force platform on a racing wheelchair, at present, is impossible. A special pressure gauge has been designed and very soon experimental results will be obtained. The task is highly demanding and such data have not been published yet. The origin of the complication is the dynamic nature of wheelchair racing.

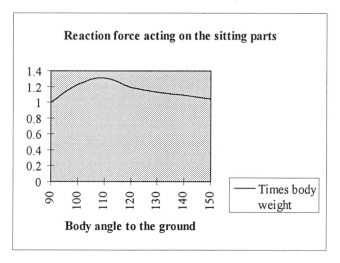

Fig.3. Reaction force as function of the angle of inclination

The pressure distribution on the buttock-cushion interface and the internal tissue stresses were obtained using the profile from Fig.3 as input data. They were calculated and transferred to a finite element model of the buttock as boundary conditions (nodal forces). The other additional assumption made was that no ground reaction forces were acting on the legs.

Figure 4 represents the stress distribution data when the seat is not stretched. The time distribution without considering viscous effects shows that a sustained very high level of pressure occurs under the ishial tuberosity and this carries potential hazard to the health of the athlete.

A feature of the results is their high computational accuracy - very strict convergence limit of 0.01% of the load applied per load step was sustained. So the absolute value of the sum of the out of balance forces (the difference between the integral internal forces and the applied external force) was less than 0.001 N.

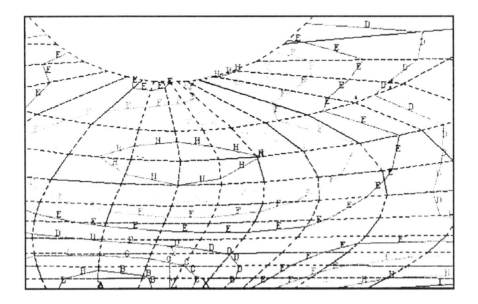

Fig.4.   Stress intensity contours in the deformed shape of the tissue under the ishial tuberosity.

4 Discussion

This work presents the first stage of an interdisciplinary study of wheelchair propulsion. The study addressed the evaluation of the efficiency of pushing and combined physiological monitoring with dynamic and finite element modelling. The model is closely linked to the conditions of wheelchair racing and reflects the existing pattern of motion. Further improvement will be achieved after physiological validation.

A time animation of the stress state throughout the pushing interval was produced. The duration of the push cycle and its subintervals measured during the tests allow reproduction of the stress state in real time. The results provide a good basis for estimation of a maximum training duration for particular individuals without risking sore formation or other tissue damage caused by overload. It is recommended that the wheelchair producers should modify the seats of the racing chairs using light foam materials as these chairs are used for prolonged training and this could cause long term health damage.

The study presents one particular application (seating comfort in close to race conditions) but its potential is much broader. The model will be utilised for a general analysis during training and competition of wheelchair athletes the major goal being to help the athletes choose an optimal construction of their wheelchair for best results and comfort. It is intended to help the athletes avoid potential health hazards such as joint overloading and bad posture. The initial results from the study are to be carefully validated in controlled physiological experiments. It is deemed necessary to combine the advantages of physiological and biomechanical approaches in order to provide further insight into the athlete-wheelchair interaction.

5 References

Campbell, I.G. Lakomy, H.K.A. and Williams, C. (in press) A comparison of two wheelchair treadmill exercise test protocols for determination of peak oxygen uptake (VO_2 peak): gradient versus speed. In proceedings: **Third International Medical Congress on Sports for the Disabled.** Laval University. Quebec. 1994.

Cooper, R. A. (1990) A system approach to the modelling of racing wheelchair propulsion, **Journal Rehabilitation Research**, 27, 151-162.

Dabnichki, P.A., Crocombe, A.D. and Hughes, S.C. (1994) Deformation and stress analysis of supported buttock contact, **Proceedings of the Institution of Mechanical Engineers, Part H: Journal of Engineering in Medicine**, 9-17.

Dabnichki, P.D. and Crocombe, A.D. (1994) The non-linear contact of seating and the resultant tissue stress analysis, **Proceedings of the Second World Congress of Biomechanics**. Amsterdam, Netherlands.

Dabnichki, P.D. and Crocombe, A.D. (1992) Finite element model of the buttock - cushion interaction, **Proceedings of the XXVIII World Congress of Theoretical and Applied Mechanics**, Haifa, Israel.

Engel, P. (1991) Aspects of wheelchair seating comfort, **Preliminary Proceedings of an International Workshop, Ergonomics of Manual Wheelchair Propulsion: State of the Art,** Amsterdam, Netherlands.

Hofstad, M. and Patterson, P.E. (1994) Modelling of the propulsion characteristics of a standard wheelchair, **Journal of Rehabilitation Research and Development**, 31, 129-137.

Reddy, N.P., Himanshu, P. and Cochran G.V.B. (1982) Model experiment of study the stress distribution in a seated buttock, **Journal of Biomechanics**, 15, 493-504.

Zacharkow, D., (1984), **Wheelchair Posture and Pressure Sores**. Charles Thomas Publ., Springfield, Illinois, pp. 18-69.

4 Physiological characteristics of wheelchair athletes determined from arm crank ergometry and wheelchair treadmill exercise

I.G. Campbell, H.K.A. Lakomy and C. Williams

1 Introduction

Over the past decade a number of different forms of exercise have been used to determine the peak exercise responses of individuals with a spinal cord injury (Shephard, 1988). The methods used for the determination of $\dot{V}O_2$ peak in the laboratory have included arm crank ergometry (Nilsson et al., 1975), wheelchair ergometry (Pohlman et al., 1989) and wheelchair treadmill exercise (Gass and Camp, 1979; Lakomy et al., 1987; Campbell et al., in press).

Using arm crank ergometry (ACE) to examine the physiological responses of wheelchair users has the advantage that it is relatively cheap, commercially available and portable. It is also attractive because it is a task which is easily standardised (Shephard, 1990), and also accurate and reproducible (Zwiren and Bar-Or, 1975). In addition a number of authors have chosen to examine the physiological responses to arm exercise using an arm crank ergometer because the conversion of cycle ergometers, for the use of the arms, is relatively easy and thus cost effective.

The main advantage of systems employing wheelchairs is that the exercise mode is realistic to everyday life for wheelchair users and thus more ecologically valid. Indeed it has been suggested that the biomechanics and neuromuscular recruitment patterns for wheelchair versus arm crank ergometers are very different (Glaser, 1985). This suggests that wheelchair propulsion should be employed to examine the physiological and metabolic responses to exercise.

While it may appear logical that wheelchair exercise should be used to examine the physiological responses of wheelchair users to exercise, there are problems with this. A survey of the literature indicates that most wheelchair ergometers have been specifically designed by researchers and as a consequence they have their own special characteristics (Campbell, 1992). In this respect the wide array of wheelchair ergometer designs have included: platforms mounted with rollers upon which the wheelchair of the subject is mounted (Coutts et al., 1983), a standardised wheelchair on rollers (Pohlman et al., 1989), standard wheelchairs with fitted push rims , and a wheelchair linked to a cycle ergometer flywheel (Glaser et al., 1980).

Rather than develop a wheelchair ergometer some researchers have adapted motorised treadmills for the use of wheelchairs (Gass and Camp, 1979; Lakomy et al., 1987; Campbell et al., in press). These devices, like the wheelchair ergometers, have been specifically designed by researchers to examine the physiological and metabolic responses of wheelchair athletes to exercise (Lakomy et al., 1987; McConnell et al., 1989). A limitation of many of the treadmill systems developed has been the maximum speed at which they can be safely used (Gass and Camp, 1979). However, the most recent developments have overcome these problems, and allowed wheelchair athletes to perform safely at race speeds using their own racing wheelchair (Lakomy et al., 1987; Campbell et al., in press). This has the advantage that meaningful propulsion speeds can be used to test wheelchair athletes. Furthermore, a protocol for determining $\dot{V}O_2$ peak has been developed using this system which is both accurate and reproducible (Campbell, 1992).

The purpose of the present study was therefore to determine whether it was more appropriate to determine the peak exercise responses of wheelchair athletes with spinal cord injuries using arm crank ergometry or wheelchair treadmill exercise.

2 Methods

2.1 Subjects

Twenty wheelchair athletes gave their informed consent and volunteered to participate in the study. All the subjects were fully informed of the requirements of the study, and familiar with the experimental procedures to be employed. All the wheelchair athletes in this study trained regularly for, and competed regularly in, endurance races. Each athlete had at least 4 years racing experience and 7 of the subjects were of international standard. The group comprised of 2 tetraplegics and 18 paraplegics. The range of lesion levels within the group was from C7 to L4. The age of group (mean ±SD) was 28 ±7 years and the body mass was 65.8 ±7.9 kg.

2.3 Protocols

Each athlete was required to perform an arm crank exercise (ACE) and wheelchair treadmill exercise (WTE) test protocol for the determination of $\dot{V}O_2$ peak approximately one week apart. Which of the tests was performed first was decided at random. Prior to any testing all subjects were fully familiarised with ACE and WTE. Before each test started the subjects followed their usual warm up procedures which were all submaximal in nature. Both protocols were continuous incremental exercise tests. Wheelchair treadmill exercise (WTE) was performed on a motorised treadmill (Woodway ELG2; speed range 0-7.00 m.s^{-1}; elevation 0-20% grade)adapted for wheelchairs (Campbell et al., in press), This system allowed the athletes to use their own racing wheelchairs at realistic propulsion speeds. Arm crank exercise (ACE) was performed on a wall mounted arm crank ergometer (Monark Rehab Trainer 881, Varberg, Sweden.). This arm crank ergometer (ACE) was similar in design to the Monark cycle ergometer, being mechanically braked by a belt passing around the wheel rim. For the test, the subject was seated so that when the hand grip had reached its maximum horizontal displacement the arm was slightly flexed at the elbow.

Wheelchair treadmill exercise test protocol: During this test the speed of the treadmill remained constant and the treadmill gradient was increased at 3 minute intervals until volitional exhaustion. As a result of pilot work, for the paraplegics (n=18) the gradient was increased by 0.7% every 3 minutes and for the tetraplegics (n=2) by 0.5%. The treadmill speed was selected for each subject on the basis of previous visits to the laboratory and remained constant throughout. Expired air was collected for 60 s from 1 min 45 s to 2 min 45 s of each exercise period via a lightweight respiratory valve and wide bore tubing into 150 l Douglas Bags. The test protocol was open-ended and continued until the subjects indicated that they could only continue the test for a further minute when a final collection of expired air was obtained.

Arm Crank Exercise Test protocol: During this test the loading remained constant throughout but the cranking rate was increased by 10 rev. min^{-1} every 3 minutes until volitional exhaustion. The initial work rate was selected on the basis of previous visits to the laboratory. Expired air was collected for 60 seconds from 1 min 45 s to 2 min 45 s of each exercise period. The test protocol was open-ended and continued until the subjects indicated that they could only continue the test for a further minute, when a final collection of expired air was obtained.

Fractional concentrations of oxygen and carbon dioxide in the samples of expired air were measured using a paramagnetic oxygen analyser (Servomex, OA570, Crowborough, Sussex) and infrared carbon dioxide analyser (Mine Safety Appliances, Lira 303, Crowborough, Sussex) respectively. From this information the oxygen uptake was determined

2.4 Statistical analysis

The descriptive statistics reported in the text and the tables refer to group means and standard deviations (±SD). The strength of a relationship between two variables was evaluated using a Pearsons Product Moment correlation. A Student t-test for correlated means was employed for testing the significance of the difference between two means. Values at the 0.05 level were accepted as being statistically significant.

3 Results

In general, higher peak values were achieved during wheelchair treadmill exercise than during arm crank ergometry (Table 1).When the group was divided into paraplegics (n=18) and tetraplegics (n=2), the 2 tetraplegics obtained the lowest values for each characteristic for both ACE and WTE (Table 2). It was also found that those athletes who achieved the highest values on the ACE test also did so on the WTE test with high correlation coefficients (r) being found (Table 1). The relationship found between $\dot{V}O_2$ peak determined from arm crank ergometry and wheelchair treadmill exercise is shown in Figure 1 (r=0.93; P<0.01).

Table 1. Physiological characteristics (mean ±SD) of the wheelchair athletes (n=20) determined from arm crank ergometry (ACE) and wheelchair treadmill exercise (WTE).

Test	$\dot{V}O_2$ peak (l/min)	$\dot{V}O_2$ peak (ml/kg/min)	$\dot{V}E$ peak (l/min)	HR peak (beats/min)	RER
ACE	1.96 ±0.67	28.6 ±8.7	78.6 ±29.8	176 ±36	1.07 ±0.08
WTE	2.16 ±0.64*	33.4 ±9.3*	80.8 ±27.3	188 ±28**	1.10 ±0.03

* P<0.05 from ACE; ** P<0.01 from ACE

r	0.93	0.90	0.85	0.93	0.14
P	P<0.01	P<0.01	P<0.01	P<0.01	

Table 2. Physiological characteristics of the paraplegic group (n=18) and the 2 tetraplegic athletes determined from arm crank ergometry (ACE) and wheelchair treadmill exercise (WTE).

Test	$\dot{V}O_2$ peak (l/min)	$\dot{V}O_2$ peak (ml/kg/min)	$\dot{V}E$ peak (l/min)	HR peak (beats/min)	RER
Paraplegics (n=18)					
ACE	2.10 ±0.55	30.6 ±6.6	84.3 ±26.5	188 ±12	1.08 ±0.07
WTE	2.27 ±0.58*	35.1 ±7.9*	84.5 ±26.4	197 ±11*	1.10 ±0.03

* P<0.05 from ACE.

Tetraplegic subjects

Subject 1					
ACE	0.70	9.8	25.3	79	0.94
WTE	1.13	15.9	43.3	108	1.09
Subject 2					
ACE	0.79	12.0	26.1	75	0.92
WTE	1.26	19.2	55.1	115	1.08

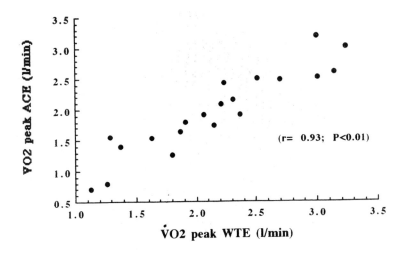

Figure 1. The relationship between $\dot{V}O_2$ peak determined from arm crank ergometry (ACE) and wheelchair treadmill exercise (WTE) for the 20 wheelchair athletes.

4 Discussion

The main finding of this study was that there were physiological differences between wheelchair treadmill exercise and arm crank ergometer exercise to maximal exercise. For each physiological characteristic examined the peak value achieved during wheelchair treadmill exercise was either higher or had a tendency to be higher than for arm crank exercise.

The finding that a higher $\dot{V}O_2$ peak was elicited during wheelchair treadmill exercise when compared with arm crank exercise is consistent with two previous studies (Gass and Camp, 1984; McConnell et al., 1989). It is suggested that the reason for this result and the other higher peak responses found during wheelchair treadmill exercise may be due to an increased activated muscle mass due to the task specificity, and also due to the fact that the treadmill test allowed athletes to use their characteristic methods of wheelchair propulsion. It should be noted that the present finding is not supported by several other studies which have compared arm crank exercise with wheelchair exercise (Glaser et al., 1980; Pitetti et al., 1987; Pohlman et al., 1989) The reason for the differences between the results of various studies may relate to the subject sample selected. In this respect the present study and those which have reported higher peak responses during treadmill exercise compared with arm crank exercise have employed trained wheelchair athletes (Gass and Camp, 1984; McConnell et al., 1989). All the other studies have used a variety of subject populations such as untrained able-bodied subjects or untrained wheelchair users or a mixture of both (Glaser et al., 1980; Pitetti et al., 1987; Pohlman et al., 1989).

The finding that those athletes who achieved the highest values on the treadmill also did on the treadmill indicates that arm crank ergometry does differentiate between subjects in a similar way and could be used to determine $\dot{V}O_2$ peak of groups of wheelchair athletes. However, because values were in the order of 10% higher during wheelchair treadmill exercise, which is consistent with previous work employing trained subjects (Gass and Camp, 1984; McConnell et al., 1989), it would appear to be more appropriate to use wheelchair treadmill exercise for trained athletes.

The wide range of $\dot{V}O_2$ peak values in the group, evident from Figure 1, for both tests may be explained largely by the wide range of lesion levels and differences in training status' within the group. It was particularly noticeable that the two tetraplegics recorded the lowest $\dot{V}O_2$ peak and heart rate values for both test protocols. This is consistent with the results from previous studies on tetraplegic athletes (Gass and Camp, 1979; Coutts et al., 1983; Lakomy et al., 1987; Eriksson et al., 1988). This group has the least recruitable muscle mass available for exercise and therefore the least potential for oxygen utilisation during exercise (Coutts et al., 1983) and this may partly explain the reason for the lower $\dot{V}O_2$ peak values of these athletes. In addition to the least recruitable muscle mass available for exercise, tetraplegics also have the greatest loss of sympathetic neural control. In support of this, the athletes had the lowest peak heart rates of around 115 beats.min^{-1}, which is characteristic of this level of spinal cord injury (Coutts et al., 1983; Lakomy et al., 1987; Eriksson et al., 1988) and occurs because of complete transection of the spinal cord in the cervical region severs the sympathetic nerve supply to the heart (Knuttson et al,, 1973). This means that the peak heart rate is determined by the intrinsic sinoatrial rhythm and therefore peak heart rates will be between 100-125 beats.min^{-1} (Knuttson et al., 1973). In the present study the peak heart rate of the paraplegic group was comparable with that achieved by able-bodied subjects during uphill treadmill running to exhaustion (Ramsbottom et al., 1989). The result of tetraplegics achieving lower $\dot{V}O_2$ peak values than the paraplegic athletes was not influenced by the protocol although it should be mentioned that tetraplegics find arm crank exercise particularly difficult due to their disability.

In conclusion, the results of this study suggest that wheelchair treadmill exercise is a more appropriate way of determining the peak physiological responses of wheelchair athletes with a spinal cord injury than using arm crank exercise. Furthermore, the results may emphasise the importance of examining the physiological responses of wheelchair athletes to exercise in their own racing wheelchairs.

5 References

Campbell, I.G. (1992) The influence of level of spinal cord injury on the physiological and metabolic responses to exercise and performance. **Ph.D. Thesis**, Loughborough University of Technology, England.

Campbell, I.G. Lakomy, H.K.A. and Williams, C. (in press) A comparison of two wheelchair treadmill exercise test protocols for the determination of peak oxygen uptake (VO2 peak): gradient versus speed. In proceedings: **Third International Medical Congress on Sport for the Disabled**, Laval University. Quebec. 1994.

Coutts, K. D. Rhodes, E. C. and McKenzie, D. C. (1983) Maximal exercise responses of tetraplegics and paraplegics. **Journal of Applied Physiology**, 55, 479-482.

Eriksson, P. Loftstrom, L. and Ekblom, B. (1988) Aerobic power during maximal exercise in untrained and well-trained persons with quadriplegia and paraplegia. **Scandinavian Journal of Rehabilitative Medicine**, 20(4)141-147.

Gass, G.C. and Camp, E.M. (1979) Physiological characteristics of trained Australian paraplegic and tetraplegic subjects. **Medicine and Science in Sports and Exercise**, 11, 256-259.

Gass, G.C. and Camp, E.M. (1984) The maximum physiological responses during incremental wheelchair and arm cranking exercise in male paraplegics. **Medicine and Science in Sports and Exercise**, 16, 355-359.

Glaser, R.M. (1985) Exercise and locomotion for the spinal cord injured. **Exercise and Sports Science Reviews**, 13, 263-303. R.J. Terjung, ed. New York:MacMillian.

Glaser, R.M. Sawka, M.N. Brune, M.F. and Wilde, S.W. (1980) Physiological responses to maximal effort wheelchair and arm crank ergometry. **Journal of Applied Physiology**, 48, 1060-1064.

Knuttson, E. Lewenhaupt-olsen, E. and Thorsen, M. (1973) Physical work capacity condition in paraplegic patients. **Paraplegia**, 11, 205-216.

Lakomy, H.K.A. Campbell, I.G. and Williams, C. (1987) Treadmill performance and selected physiological characteristics of wheelchair athletes. **British Journal of Sports Medicine**, 21, 130-133.

McConnell, T.J., Horvat, M.A., Beutal-Horvat, T.A. & Golding, L.A. (1989) Arm crank versus wheelchair treadmill ergometry to evaluate the performance of paraplegics. **Paraplegia**, 27, 307-313.

Nilsson, S. Staff P.H. and Pruett, E.D.R. (1975) Physical work capacity and the effect of training on subjects with long-standing paraplegia. **Scandinavian Journal of Rehabilitative Medicine**, 7, 51-56.

Pitetti, K H Snell, P G and Stray-Gunderson (1987) Maximal response of wheelchair confined subjects to four types of arm exercise. **Archives of Physical Medicine and Rehabilitation**, 68, 10-13.

Pohlman, R.L. Gayle, G.W. Davis, G.M. and Glaser, R.M. (1989) Metabolic responses to maximal arm crank and wheelchair ergometry in male paraplegics. **Clinical Kinesiology**, 43, 89-95.

Ramsbottom, R. Williams, C. Boobis, L. and Freeman, W. (1989) Aerobic fitness and running performance of male and female recreational runners. **Journal of Sports Sciences**, 7, 9-20.

Shephard, R.J. (1988) Sports medicine and the wheelchair athlete. **Sports Medicine**, 4, 226-247.

Shephard, R.J. (1990) **Fitness in Special Populations.** Human Kinetics, Champaign, III.

Zwiren, L.D. and Bar-Or, O. (1975) Responses to exercise of paraplegics who differ in conditioning level. **Medicine and Science in Sports and Exercise**, 7, 94-98.

5 Relationship between anaerobic power of arms and legs in untrained men

W. Pilis, J. Langfort, R. Zarzeczny, J. Raczek and T. Pilis

1 Introduction

The Wingate test has often been used for determination of anaerobic power of the lower limbs (Bar-Or, 1980; Bar-Or et al., 1980; Dotan and Bar-Or, 1983; Inbar and Bar-Or, 1986; Nakamodo et al., 1986). The relationships between the level of anaerobic power evaluated by this method and variables such as blood lactate, percentage composition of FT muscle fibres, and the average FT/ST area ratio (Bar-Or et al., 1980), as well as the activity of serum CK have been established (Pilis et al., 1988).

The anaerobic power of the upper limbs is less than that of the lower limbs and has only seldom been investigated (Dotan and Bar-Or, 1983). It is evident that the main source of ATP resynthesis for both all-out anaerobic tests lasting 30 seconds or more is breakdown of phosphocreatine and muscle glycolysis with lactate (La) production (di Prampero, 1981). Data on differences in blood lactate concentration in response to anaerobic tests of the upper and lower limbs and that relation to physical performance are insufficient.

The aim of this study was to determine the level of anaerobic power and blood lactate concentration during 30s all-out ergocycle tests of the upper and lower limbs. Also investigated were the relationships of mechanical variables of anaerobic power and blood lactate concentration obtained in both tests.

2 Methods

Nine male students participated in the study after they familiarized themselves with the laboratory tests. The mean±SD age of the subjects was 23±1.5 years while the mean±SD body height and mass were 175±5.1 cm and 71.2±4.3 kg, respectively. All of the subjects performed two, all-out ergocycle tests of maximal intensity lasting 30 seconds. The lower limb cycling test was performed on a "Monark" ergometer during the first day, while the arm cranking test was conducted on the second day on the same ergometer where one pedal was substituted for a handle. According to our previous (unpublished) data a period of 24 h of rest following 30 s Wingate test is sufficient for full recovery. The handle was connected to the pedal at one end and to the frame at the other. The base of the ergometer was fixed to the same steel frame. The 80 cm long handle was placed in the horizontal position in front of the sitting subject with both feet placed on the floor. The arm crank axle was at about 20 cm below heart level. During the test the subject kept both hands on the handle at the same level.

The pre-test warm-up consisted of 5 min pedalling at 60 rev/min with the resistance set at 2.5 W/kg B.W. for the lower limbs and of 5 min cranking for the upper limbs with the resistance set at 1.25 W/kg B.W.. Two minutes after the warm-up, subjects performed the all-out exercise tests. The resistance used in the lower limb test equalled 0.075 kp/kg B.W. and 0.040 kp/kg B.W. for the upper limbs. During both tests the following mechanical variables were determined: total external work (W_t), maximal power (P_{max}), minimal power (P_{min}), mean power (P_m) and the fatigue index (FI). They were expressed in the absolute and relative values. Arterial blood samples were taken from the fingertips before the warm-up and in the third and fifth minutes after the exercise. In these samples lactate concentration was determined in 0.05 ml of blood, deproteinized with perchloric acid by an enzymatic procedure with the use of commercial kits (Boehringer, Mannheim).

The differences in the results for the upper and lower limb tests were assessed for statistical significance by the Student's t-test for paired data. To evaluate the relationship between the variables, the Pearson correlation coefficients were calculated. The level of statistical significance was set at $P<0.05$.

3 Results

The absolute and relative values of anaerobic power of the upper and lower limbs are presented in Table 1. All absolute as well as relative indices of the upper limbs were lower than those of the lower limbs ($P<0.001$).

The level of blood lactate during the third and fifth minute following the exercise was significantly higher ($P<0.005$) in the lower-limb test than in the upper-limb test. The respective blood lactate concentrations were as follows: 2.04 ± 0.49 mmol/l at rest, 7.42 ± 0.99 and 7.67 ± 0.85 mmol/l in the third and fifth minute of recovery, respectively of the upper-limb test as well as 8.20 ± 0.78 and 8.67 ± 1.37 mmol/l in the same period of recovery after the lower-limb test.

Significant correlation coefficients were obtained between the following absolute anaerobic indices in the lower and upper limb tests: W_t($r=0.72$, $P<0.02$), P_{max} ($r=0.82$, $P<0.01$), P_m($r=0.71$, $P<0.05$) and FI($r=0.78$, $P<0.001$).

Moreover there were significant relationships between blood lactate concentration obtained in the third minute as well as in the fifth minute of the recovery period and relative values of W_t($P<0.001$; $P<0.001$), P_{max}($P<0.02$; $P<0.001$), P_m($P<0.001$; $P<0.001$), P_{min}($P<0.01$; $P<0.01$) calculated for the lower-limb test. A significant correlation was also obtained between FI in the upper-limb exercise and blood lactate concentration measured in the fifth minute after work ($P<0.05$ - Table 2).

Table 1. Values of anaerobic indices obtained during the ergocycle tests of the upper and lower limbs (n=9)

Anaerobic indices	Upper limbs mean ± SD	Lower limbs mean ± SD	p
W_t[J/30s]	7784.6±1253.1	16529.6±994.7	0.001
W_t[J/30s/kg]	109.3±16.2	233.5±11.2	0.001
P_{max}[W]	295.4±59.1	683.4±34.7	0.001
P_{max}[W/kg]	4.1±0.7	9.6±0.5	0.001
P_m[W]	259.4±55.2	550.9±48.7	0.001
P_m[W/kg]	3.6±0.5	7.7±0.5	0.001
P_{min}[W]	231.9±46.9	449.8±45.2	0.001
P_{min}[W/kg]	3.2±0.5	6.3±0.5	0.001
FI[W/s]	3.0±1.8	11.6±1.7	0.001

Table 2. Relationships between anaerobic indices and blood lactate concentration (n=9)

Anaerobic indices	Post-exercising blood lactate concentration			
	Upper limbs		Lower limbs	
	3 min	5 min	3 min	5 min
W_tAb.	0.16	-0.37	0.17	0.11
	n.s.	n.s.	n.s.	n.s.
W_tRel.	0.47	-0.04	0.90	0.88
	n.s.	n.s.	0.001	0.001
P_{max}Ab.	0.10	-0.42	-0.09	0.01
	n.s.	n.s.	n.s.	n.s.
P_{max}Rel.	0.44	-0.07	0.76	0.89
	n.s.	n.s.	0.02	0.001
P_mAb.	0.16	-0.37	0.17	0.11
	n.s.	n.s.	n.s.	n.s.
P_mRel.	0.47	-0.03	0.90	0.88
	n.s.	n.s.	0.001	0.001
P_{min}Ab.	0.17	-0.36	0.29	0.23
	n.s.	n.s.	n.s.	n.s.
P_{min}Rel.	0.45	-0.05	0.83	0.80
	n.s.	n.s.	0.01	0.01
FI	-0.43	-0.72	-0.52	-0.28
	n.s.	0.02	n.s.	n.s.

Ab.-absolute values; Rel.-relative values; n.s.-not significant

4 Discussion

Maximal power in anaerobic ergocycle tests is developed when resistance values are optimal. According to Bar-Or (1980), the optimal resistance for lower-limb exercise is 0.075 kp/kg B.W.. According to Dotan and Bar-Or (1983) the optimal values for legs and arms of young men were as follows: 0.0872 and 0.0615 kp/kg B.W., respectively. During the anaerobic upper-limb test lasting 40 s performed by Lutos³awska et al. (1994), the resistance was set at 6.5% of body mass. In this paper we used resistance equal to 0.075 and 0.040 kp/kg B.W., for the lower- and upper-limb tests, respectively. The results for anaerobic power obtained in our investigation are similar to those presented by Bar-Or (1980), Bar-Or et al. (1980), Dotan and Bar-Or (1983), Hakkinen et al. (1984) and Nakamodo et al. (1986) in relation to the lower-limb test, and correspond to results of Dotan and Bar-Or (1983) and Inbar and Bar-Or (1986) in the case of the upper-limb test. Some authors obtained much higher results for the upper-limb anaerobic indices than in our study. For instance maximal power output has been reported as 10.7±1.4, 9.7±1.2 (Mercier et al., 1993) and 9.9±1.0 (Lutos³awska et al. 1994) W/kg B.W. for sprint and middle-distance swimmers, as well as for elite kayakers, respectively. The differences of the anaerobic indices between the upper and lower limbs presented in our study are related primarily to the muscle mass engaged in both tests.

The blood lactate concentration measured in our study after the lower-limb test (8.20± 0.78 mmol/l in the third and 8.67±1.37 mmol/l in fifth minute of recovery) was much lower than that measured by Bosco et al. (1983) - 15.4±2.1 mmol/l and Lutos³awska et al. (1994) - 15.8±1.3 mmol/l. The primary reason for such differences is probably due to the subjects that participated in our study which consisted of untrained students. Data presented by other researchers related to elite athletes, whose pedalling technique was far better from that of the students. In our study the blood lactate concentration obtained during the lower-limb test was significantly higher (P<0.001) than in the upper- limb exercise. It is probably connected with the higher power output performed during the lower-limb test. Some researchers have shown greater increase in blood lactate concentration during arm than leg exercise at the same $\dot{V}O_2$ (Hooker et al., 1990; Koz³owski et al., 1983; Pimental et al., 1983; Sawka et al., 1982). It is probably caused by a higher adrenaline concentration during the lower-limb test compared to the upper-limb test at an equivalent $\dot{V}O_2$ (Astrand et al., 1965; Bevegard et al., 1966; Koz³owski et al., 1983; Sawka et al., 1982) so this amine is a potent stimulant of muscle glycogenolysis, with lactate being a major end-product of this metabolic pathway (Richter et al., 1981). The data in the literature about the relationships between catecholamines and blood lactate concentrations during physical exercise of supramaximal intensity are not sufficient to draw definite conclusions.

The significant relationships which were observed between absolute values of W_t, P_{max} and P_m of the upper- and lower-limb anaerobic indices indicate the importance of the muscle mass engaged in the generation of anaerobic power. Similar correlations were observed between isokinetic strength of elbow flexors, knee flexors and knee extensors and the cross-sectional area of those muscle groups (Kanehisa et al., 1994). The lack of significant correlations between relative anaerobic indices of the upper and lower limbs is probably connected with different muscle fibre type composition and with different proportions of muscle, fat and bone in the above mentioned limbs (Kanehisa et al., 1994).

The physiological differences in hormonal and metabolic responses, for instance adrenaline and lactate accumulation during arm and leg exercise (Hooker et al., 1990) do not explain why in our investigation significant relationships were observed between post-exercise blood lactate accumulation and relative anaerobic indices only in relation to the lower-limb test. A higher proportion of FT muscle fibres in the lower and upper limbs of the subjects could be the explanation.

Concluding, it must be stated, that present data indica-te that higher values of anaerobic power of the lower limbs are related to greater muscle mass engaged during exercise. We are suggesting that the relationships between absolute values of anaerobic power of the lower and upper limbs are connected with the quality component of the active muscles; however, muscle fibre composition was not measured in our study. The explanation of why significant relationships between relative anaerobic indices and post-exercise blood lactate accumulation existed only in the case of the lower-limb test is difficult.

5 References

Astrand, P.O. Ekblom, B. Messin, R. Saltin, B. and Stenberg, J. (1965) Intra arterial blood pressure during exercise with different muscle groups. **Journal of Applied Physiology,** 20, 253-256.

Bar-Or, O. (1980) Um novo teste de capacidade anaerobica - characteristica e applicabilidade. **Medicina Dello Sport - Porto Alegre**, 5, 73-82.

Bar-Or, O. Dotan, R. Inbar, O. Rothstein, A. Karlsson, J. and Tesch, P. (1980) Anaerobic capacity and muscle fiber type distribution in man. **International Journal of Sports Medicine,** 1, 82-85.

Bevegard, S. Freyschuss, U. and Strandell, T. (1966) Circu-latory adaptation to arm and leg exercise in supine and sitting position. **Journal of Applied Physiology**, 21, 37-46.

Bosco, C. Luthanen, P. Komi, P.V. (1983) A simple method for measurement of mechanical power in jumping. **European Journal of Applied Physiology**, 50, 273-281.

di Prampero, P.E. (1981) Energetics of muscular exercise. A review. **Physiological and Biochemical Pharmacology**, 89, 143-149.

Dotan, R. and Bar-Or, O. (1983) Load optimalization for the Wingate anaerobic test. **European Journal of Applied Physiology**, 51, 409-417.

Hakkinen, K. Alen, M. and Komi, P.V. (1984) Neuromuscular anaerobic and aerobic performance characteristics of elite power athletes. **European Journal of Applied Physiology**, 53, 97-105.

Hooker, S.P. Wells, Ch.L. Manore, M.M. Philip, S.A. and Martin, N. (1990) Differences in epinephrine and substrate responses between arm and leg exercise. **Medicine and Science in Sports and Exercise**, 6, 779-784.

Inbar, O. Bar-Or, O. (1986) Anaerobic characteristics in male children and adolescents. **Medicine and Science in Sports and Exercise**, 18, 264-269.

Kanehisa, H. Ikegawa, S. Fukunaga, T. (1994) Comparision of muscle cross-sectional area and strength between untrained women and men. **European Journal of Applied Physiology**, 68, 148-154.

Kozlowski, S. Chwalbińska-Moneta, J. Vigas, M. Kaciuba-Uscilko, H. and Nazar, K. (1983) Greater serum GH response to arm than to leg exercise performed at equivalent oxygen uptake. **European Journal of Applied Physiology**, 52, 131-135.

Lutoslawska, G. Sitkowski, D. Krawczyk, B. (1994) Plasma uric acid response in elite kayakers to 40 s arm cranking before and after training. **Biology of Sport**, 4, 233-240.

Mercier, B. Granier, P. Mercier, J. Trouquet, J. and Prefaut, Ch. (1993) Anaerobic and aerobic components during arm-crank exercise in sprint and middle-distance swimmers. **European Journal of Applied Physiology**, 66, 461-466.

Nakamodo, F. Tanaka, K. Watanabe, H. and Fukuda, T. (1986) Feasibility of using modified Wingate and Evans-Quinney methods to measure maximal anaerobic power output. **Journal of Physical Fitness Japan**, 35, 161-167.

Pilis, W. Langfort, J. Pilœniak, A. Pyzik, M. and Bᵌasiak, M. (1988) Plasma lactate dehydrogenase and creatine kinase after anaerobic exercise. **International Journal of Sports Medicine**, 9, 102-103.

Pimental, N.A. Sawka, M.N. Billings, D.S. and Trad, N.A. (1983) Physiological responses to prolonged upper-body exercise. **Medicine and Science in Sports and Exercise**, 16, 360-365.

Richter, E.A. Galbo, H. and Christensen, N.J. (1981) Control of exercise-induced muscular glycogenolysis by adrenal medullary hormones in rats. **Journal of Applied Physiology**, 50, 21-26.

Sawka, M.N. Miles, D.S. Petrofsky, I.S. Wilde, S.W. and Glaser, R.M. (1982) Ventilation and acid-base equili-brium for upper body and lower body exercise. **Aviation Space and Environmental Medicine**, 53, 354-359.

6 Cardiac dimensions in spinal cord injured athletes
P.E. Gates, K.P. George and I.G. Campbell

1 Introduction

Previous research has shown that chronic exercise training results in an adaptation of the heart that is specific to the nature of the training stimulus (Morganroth et al., 1975). Resistance training has been reported to induce a concentric hypertrophy of the left ventricle attributable to increased wall thicknesses (Menapace et al., 1982) whilst endurance training has produced an eccentric hypertrophy of the left ventricle attributable to increased chamber dimensions (Ehsani et al., 1978). Grossman et al. (1975) suggested that training-specific haemodynamics, volume overload during endurance training and pressure overload during resistance exercise, accounted for different structural changes.

Huonker et al. (1994) reported significantly larger cardiac dimensions in trained paraplegics compared to untrained paraplegics. However, they did not state the nature of training in their population. Haemodynamically, spinal cord injured athletes (SCI) represent an upper-body trained group whose response to exercise may be different to that of able-bodied subjects (Glaser, 1985). Spinal cord injury results in an interruption to the central nervous system and paralysis of musculature stimulated by neurones which synapse below the level of the spinal cord lesion. Disruption also occurs to the autonomic nervous system and sympathetic outflow may be impaired. Spinal cord injured athletes, therefore, have a smaller active musculature and, with higher lesions, the absence of an abdomino-thoracic pump to facilitate venous return (Davis et al., 1981). As a consequence of these factors and with the absence of a sympathetically driven redistribution of blood, venous pooling occurs below the level of the spinal cord lesion (Glaser, 1985). To complicate the haemodynamics, SCI perform upper-body isotonic exercise which elicits higher blood pressures compared to lower-body exercise (Pendergast, 1989).

Whether the training-specific patterns of cardiac adaptation observed in able-bodied athletes occur in SCI athletes has yet to be determined. It was the purpose of this study to report initial findings from M-mode echocardiograms obtained from male SCI involved in endurance and resistance/power training.

2 Methods

2.1 Subjects
Seven highly trained SCI endurance athletes (mean age and body mass ($\pm$SE) = 33.7$\pm$0.5 years and 72.7$\pm$1.1 kg) and six highly trained SCI resistance/power athletes (24.8$\pm$0.6 years and 71.4$\pm$1.2 kg) participated in the study. A questionnaire regarding training, medication and medical history, and level of spinal cord injury were completed by each subject. Lesions in the endurance (END) group ranged from C6-T12 with one subject having spina bifida. In the resistance (RES) group lesions ranged from T1-T5 with one lesion being incomplete and one subject having spina bifida.

2.2 Data collection
An echocardiographic examination was undertaken using a Hewlett Packard (Andover, Massachusetts) HP Sonos 100 ultrasound imaging system. Subjects lay supine and were prepared with three electrodes to allow a concurrent single lead ECG waveform to be monitored. A 2.5 MHz transducer was placed in the 3rd/4th intercostal space and a 2-D sector scan obtained in the left parasternal long axis view. An M-mode recording was taken across the tips of the mitral valve and perpendicular to the left ventricle. Recordings of M-modes were made on video tape and analysed using a digitisation method. Measurements of left ventricular septal thickness (ST), posterior wall thickness (PWT), and left ventricular internal dimension at end diastole (LVIDd) were taken across four cardiac cycles and followed the guidelines of the American Society of Echocardiography (Sahn et al., 1978). Left ventricular mass (LVM) was determined using the previously validated cube formula of Devereux and Reichek (1977). Coefficient of variation, calibration error and resolution error were calculated according to Dainty and Norman (1987) and a maximal error of 4.2% was established for the digitisation technique.

To assess global left ventricular function the ejection fraction (EF), fractional shortening (FS), and stroke volume (SV) were calculated from M-mode data. A 2-D apical four chamber view was obtained for accurate placement of a Doppler sample gate in the left ventricular inflow and outflow tracts. Recordings were analysed for peak early passive (Evel) and late atrial active (Avel) diastolic filling velocity and for peak systolic velocity (Svel).

A resting 12-lead electrocardiograph (ECG) was obtained using a Schiller Cardiovit C6/12 (Baar, Switzerland) system. Recordings were analysed for rhythm and conduction abnormalities and for the determination of resting heart rate. Blood pressure was taken by auscultation at rest and body mass determined using Seca seated beam balance scales.

2.3 Statistical Analysis
Statistical analysis was performed using Statsoft Statistica software. All absolute data were analysed with one way analysis of variance (ANOVA). Previously, M-mode echocardiographic data had been scaled to body mass, fat free mass and body surface area. Methods of calculating body surface area and fat free mass in able-bodied subjects may not be appropriate for SCI subjects. Absolute data were therefore scaled for body mass only, using one-way analysis of co-variance (ANCOVA). Functional data were co-varied with heart rate.

3 Results

All subjects presented with absolute wall thicknesses, chamber dimensions and wall thickness/chamber dimension ratios within normal limits (Table 1.). All absolute functional data were within normal limits (Table 2.).

Table 1. Mean (±SE) absolute values and ranges of M-mode echocardiographic measurements in endurance and resistance trained SCI athletes

	ST (cm)		PWT (cm)		LVIDd (cm)		LVM (g)	
	mean (±SE)	range	mean (±SE)	range	mean (±SE)	range	mean (±SE)	range
END	0.98 (0.02)	0.78-1.12	0.92 (0.02)	0.71-1.15	4.96 (0.05)	4.47-5.49	198 (6.93)	125-249
RES	0.88 (0.02)	0.74-1.02	0.90 (0.01)	0.78-1.07	5.06 (0.10)	4.05-5.74	187 (9.40)	136-288

Absolute wall thicknesses, LVIDd, and LVM were not significantly different between groups. No significant differences were found between groups for any of the M-mode variables when scaled to body mass.

Table 2. Mean (±SE) absolute data for left ventricular functional indices

	FS %	EF %	SV (ml)	Evel (cm. s^{-1})	Avel (cm. s^{-1})	Evel:Avel	Svel (cm. s^{-1})
	mean (±SE)	mean (±SE)	mean (±SE)	mean (±SE)	mean (±SE)	mean (±SE)	mean (±SE)
END	25.4 (0.86)	58.1 (1.43)	71.6 (2.42)	68.9 (1.76)	37.8 (0.60)	1.83 (0.05)	80.5 (2.08)
RES	25.8 (0.93)	58.5 (1.46)	84.8 (1.98)	83.7 (3.05)	41.6 (1.33)	2.02 (0.05)	81.2 (3.75)

No significant differences were found in functional indices between groups when absolute values were analysed with ANOVA or when co-varied with heart rate. Resting systolic and diastolic blood pressure was not significantly different between END (mean ±SE = 131/76 ±1/1 mmHg) and RES (mean ±SE = 121/75 ±2/1 mmHg) groups.

Mean resting heart rates were lower but not significantly different in END (mean ±SE = 52 ±1.2 beats min^{-1}) compared to RES (mean ±SE = 61 ±1.4 beats min^{-1}). Resting ECG revealed that eight athletes (5 END and 3 RES) had a resting sinus bradycardia. Analysis of ECG recordings revealed evidence of right bundle branch block in two athletes (both RES) and one athlete had a left posterior fascicular block (END). One athlete (END) had voltage criteria for left ventricular hypertrophy (S in V_1 + R in V_5 = 4.2 mV) and two athletes (1 END and 1 RES) had evidence of intra-ventricular delay (R duration of 72 m s^{-1} in lead III in one case and 57 m s^{-1} in lead II in the other). Four athletes (3 END and 1 RES) had T-wave abnormalities.

4 Discussion

The main finding of the present study was that there appeared to be no training-specific structural adaptation of the left ventricle in the SCI athletes. The mean values for both groups of athletes were greater than those reported for trained SCI athletes by Huonker et al. (1994). This may represent differences in athletes' training status in the two studies or may be an artefact of the relatively small sample sizes of both studies. The similarity in cardiac structural characteristics between END and RES groups is in contrast to findings in lower-body trained athletes (Morganroth et al., 1975). Because of greater elicited blood pressures upper-body endurance training may therefore evoke haemodynamic overload patterns that are similar to the overload patterns of resistance training. The similar haemodynamic stress may explain the similarity in cardiac structure between the groups. The larger venous returns which generate the volume overload of lower body endurance training may not occur when using the smaller active musculature involved in upper-body endurance training.

Perrault and Turcotte (1994) have suggested that the large chamber dimensions reported in able-bodied endurance athletes may be a result of increased pre-load due to hypervolaemia enhancing venous return. Increases in total blood volume due to endurance training in SCI athletes have not been documented and may be much smaller relative to able-bodied athletes. Even if this does occur it is possible that blood may pool below the level of the lesion and may not result in a greater venous return. If echocardiographically determined chamber dimension is influenced by an endurance training-induced hypervolaemia this may not influence values obtained from SCI athletes.

Morgan and Baker (1991) have suggested that neural and hormonal factors may also influence the development of cardiac enlargement. Whether central and autonomic nervous system disruption affects neural and hormonal factors that subsequently affect myocardial structure has not been determined. Furthermore, the influence of factors such as excessive myocardial noradrenaline release (Cowell et al., 1986) and autonomic hyperreflexia also warrant investigation.

Pulsed-wave Doppler assessment of resting diastolic and systolic function revealed comparable values to those reported for able-bodied populations (Feigenbaum, 1994). Findings in able-bodied athletes have been equivocal. Finkelhor et al. (1986) and MacFarlane et al. (1991) reported larger E:A values and suggested that diastolic flow may be enhanced in trained athletes and DeMaria et al. (1978) reported improved systolic function in athletes compared to controls. However, Douglas (1989) found normal cardiac function in ultra-endurance triathletes and Colan et al.(1985) and Pearson et al. (1986) found no difference between resistance trained athletes and controls. To determine whether training has an effect on cardiac function in SCI athletes requires the inclusion of an appropriatly matched control group in future studies.

The prevalence of ECG abnormalities observed in both groups is consistent with findings in able-bodied athletes. Conduction blockages have been associated with bradycardia induced by enhanced vagal tone and/or reduced intrinsic heart rate (Smith et al., 1989). The ECG abnormalities present in the athletes in this study may be a result of a similar response to exercise training or due to a disruption to autonomic balance resulting from spinal cord injury.

A number of confounding factors may have contributed to the data reported. Age has been shown influences cardiac dimensions in able-bodied individuals (Gerstenblith et al., 1977). The END group were significantly older (P<0.01) than the RES group. Age related changes in cardiac dimensions are thought to be associated with age related changes in blood pressure and cardiac function (Fifer et al., 1985). Whilst there were inter-individual differences in blood pressure, this was not significantly different between groups. Resting blood pressure has been shown to exert a significant influence on cardiac structure in able-bodied subjects (Drayer et al., 1983, Ren et al., 1984). The range of blood pressures found in the athletes studied may have a more potent chronic haemodynamic influence on cardiac structure than the acute haemodynamic loads of exercise training.

The range of lesion levels (C6-T12) amongst the athletes may also have had an effect on haemodynamics at rest and during exercise due to the innervation of different amounts of skeletal musculature and different degrees of autonomic system disruption. Lesion level may also affect anthropometric variables such as body mass, fat free mass and body surface area. In this study only body mass was accounted for in the statistical analysis and the influence of other anthropometric variables was not established.

These initial findings suggest that no training-specific differences occurred between the two groups studied. Due to the small sample size further research should address the question of whether exercise training has any effect on cardiac dimensions and function in SCI subjects. To develop this study further requires the inclusion of a sedentary control group. The present study highlights a number of confounding and interesting issues relating to cardiovascular responses to training that warrant further investigation.

5 References

Colan, S.D. Sanders, S.P. MacPhereson, D. and Borrow, K.M. (1985) Left ventricular diastolic function in elite athletes with physiologic cardiac hypertrophy. **Journal of the American College of Cardiology**, 6, 545-549.

Cowell, L.L. Squires, W.G. and Raven, P.B. (1986) Benefits of exercise for the paraplegic: a brief review. **Medicine and Science in Sports and Exercise**, 18, 501-508.

Dainty, D.A. and Norman, R.W. (eds) (1987) **Standardizing Biomechanical Testing in Sport.** Human Kinetics, Champaign, Illinois.

DeMaria, A.N. Neumann, A. Lee, G. Fowler, W. and Mason, D.T. (1978) Alterations in ventricular mass and performance induced by exercise training in man evaluated by echocardiography. **Circulation**, 57, 237-243.

Davis G.M. Shepherd, R.J. Jackson, R.W. (1981) Cardio-respiratory fitness and muscular strength in the lower limb disabled. **Canadian Journal of Sport Science**, 6, 159-165.

Devereux, R.B. and Reichek, N. (1977) Echocardiographic determination of left ventricular mass in man. Anatomic validation of this technique. **Circulation**, 58, 613-618.

Douglas, P.S. (1989) Cardiac considerations in the triathlete. **Medicine and Science in Sports and Exercise**, 21 (Supplement), S214-S218.

Drayer, J.I.M. Weber, M.A. and Deyoung, J.L. (1983) BP as a determinant of cardiac left ventricular muscle mass. **Archives of Internal Medicine**, 143, 90-94.

Ehsani, A.A. Hagberg, J.M. and Hickson, R.C. (1978) Changes in left ventricular dimensions and mass in response to physical conditioning and deconditioning. **American Journal of Cardiology**, 42, 52-56.

Feigenbaum, H.(1994) **Echocardiography**. Lea and Febiger, Philadelphia.

Fifer, M.A. Borrow, K.M. Colan, S.D. and Lorrell, B.H. (1985) Early diastolic left ventricular function in children and adults with aortic stenosis. **Journal of the American College of Cardiology**, 5, 1147-1148.

Finkelhor, R.S. Hanak, L.J. and Bahler, R.C. (1986) Left ventricular filling in endurance trained subjects. **Journal of the American College of Cardiology**, 8, 289-293.

Gerstenblith, G. Frederiksen, J. Yin, C.P. Fortuin, N.J. Lakatta, E.G. and Weisfeld, M.L. (1977) Echocardiographic assessment of a normal adult ageing population. **Circulation**, 56, 273-278.

Glaser, R.M. (1985) Exercise and locomotion for the spinal cord injured. **Exercise and Sport Science Reviews**, 13,263-303.

Grossmann, W. Jones, D. McLauren, L.P. (1975) Wall stress and patterns of hypertrophy in the human left ventricle. **Journal of Clinical Investigations**, 56, 56-64.

Huonkar, M Schumaker, O. Schmid, A. and Keul, J. (1994) Effects of dynamic training on the dimensions and functions of the heart and extremity arteries in paraplegics. **European Journal of Applied Physiology and Occupational Physiology** (abstract), 69 (Supplement).

MacFarlane, N. Northridge, D.B. Wright, A.R. Grant, S. and Dargie, H.J. (1991) A comparative study of left ventricular structure and function in elite athletes. **British Journal of Sports Medicine**, 25, 45-48.

Menapace, F.J. Hammer, W.J. Ritzer, T.F. Kessler, K.M. Warner, H.F. Spann, J.F. and Bove, A.F. (1982) Left ventricular size in competitive weight-lifters. **Medicine and Science in Sports and Exercise**, 14, 72-75.

Morgan, H.E. and Baker, K.M. (1991) Cardiac hypertrophy. Mechanical, neural and endocrine dependence. **Circulation**, 83, 13-24.

Morganroth, J. Maron, B.J. and Henry, W.L. (1975) Comparative left ventricular dimensions in trained athletes. **Annals of Internal Medicine**, 82, 521-524.

Pearson, A.C. Schiff, M. Mrosek, D. Labovitz, A.J. and Williams, G.A. (1986) Left ventricular diastolic function in weight lifters. **American Journal of Cardiology**, 58, 1254-1259.

Pendergast, D.R. (1989) Cardiovascular, respiratory, and metabolic responses to upper body exercise. **Medicine and Science in Sports and Exercise**, 21 (Supplement), S121.

Perrault, H. and Turcotte, R. (1994) Exercise induced cardiac hypertrophy: fact or fallacy. **Sports Medicine**, 17, 288-308.

Ren, J.F. Hakki, A-H. Kotler, M.N. Iskandrian, A.S. (1984) Exercise systolic blood pressure. A powerful determinant of increased left ventricular mass in patients with hypertension. **Journal of the American College of Cardiology**, 5, 1224-1228.

Sahn, D.J. DeMaria, A. Kisslo, J. and Weyman, A. (1978) The committee on M-mode standardization of the American Society of Echocardiography. Recommendations regarding quantitation in M-mode echocardiography: results of a survey of echocardiographic measurements. **Circulation**, 58, 1072-1082.

Smith, M.L. Hudson, D.L. Graitzer, H.M. and Raven, P.B. (1989) Exercise training bradycardia: the role of autonomic balance. **Medicine and Science in Sports and Exercise**, 21, 40-44.

7 The potential of 3-d woven composite components incorporated within ankle-foot orthoses for improving disabled gait

E.S. Wallace and R. McIlhagger

1 Introduction

Ankle-foot orthoses (AFOs) continue to be widely used in the management and correction of the pathological ankle. The stiffness properties of these devices should provide for control or management of unwanted movements, while permitting for existing normal movements to occur. Polypropylene is a material commonly and successfully used in the production of AFOs which are matched to the clinically determined needs of the patient. The adjustment of the stiffness of custom-made polypropylene AFOs is achieved by the systematic removal of material at the lower section of the calf shell where bending principally occurs, which often results in a device which cannot endure the subsequent bending stresses when the device is routinely worn.

Carbon fibre has been considered as perhaps the most valuable composite to orthopaedic appliances. Its impressive properties include its lightness, durability, and the ability to be stiff and reinforced in any required area. Carbon fibre has been associated with composite orthotic devices, although the disadvantages of time and expense in their production have also been noted (Berry, 1987). It has been shown (Balmaseda et al., 1988) that the structural and mechanical properties of orthoses alter the stability and kinetic performance of gait, as reflected in the foot-floor force characteristics.

The integration of a carbon fibre component within a polypropylene AFO at the lower calf shell section where bending principally occurs may help to reduce the costs compared to a complete carbon fibre orthosis. In addition, the carbon fibre component may provide superior flexural modulus properties compared to polypropylene. Furthermore, the stiffness of the orthosis could be readily adjusted if interchangeable components, each with a different stiffness, were integrated within the AFO. The aim of the study was to determine experimentally the effects of such a prototype AFO on the gait of a patient suffering from paralytic drop foot, and to compare these findings with a conventional polypropylene AFO. The prototype produced for analysis allowed for the attachment of two interchangeable carbon fibre plaques, each with different flexural modulus properties.

2 Method

One adult male with paralytic drop-foot and seven matched
normal adult males participated in the study. The subjects
had previously given their written informed consent. The
analysis of data pertaining to the normal subjects, for
whom AFOs would not ordinarily be prescribed, has been
recommended previously (Balmaseda et al., 1988), since it
permits the determination of the minimum gait alterations
due to the devices when the normal neuromuscular
compensatory mechanisms are active. The subjects walked at
a freely chosen speed along a 15 m walkway which
incorporated a surface-mounted Kistler forceplate, and on a
separate occasion along a 10 m walkway which incorporated a
surface mounted Musgrave^R Footprint pressure plate (W M
Automation, Belfast). Further particulars and details of
methods used have been presented previously (Wallace,
1992).

The walking conditions examined were those of barefoot
gait (BF), shod with normal shoes only (SH), shod while
wearing a flexible polypropylene AFO (FAFO), and shod while
wearing each of two versions of the carbon fibre AFO (VAFO1
and VAFO2). The VAFOs used in the study were obtained from
a modified polypropylene device, which had the lower calf
shell portion removed and replaced with one of two
interchangeable carbon fibre plaques by means of a
mechanical attachment. The relative stiffness of the
patient's AFOs were previously determined, with the
stiffness of VAFO1 and VAFO2 being approximately 12% and
50% respectively that of the polypropylene AFO (FAFO). A
total of ten acceptable trials was recorded for each
subject for each condition.

The mean walking speed for each condition was
determined. Selected force data obtained from the Kistler
forceplate were subsequently analyzed to give mean values
for initial peak vertical force (F1), the second peak
vertical force (F2), medio-lateral impulse (I_{M-L}), the ratio
between the positive and negative antero-posterior impulses
($+I:-I_{A-P}$), and the vertical impulse expressed in relation
to body weight (I_v). Data obtained from the pressure plate
system were analyzed to give the foot abduction angle
during ground contact (θ), the path of the centre of
pressure (COP), and the relative times (% of total time of
contact) for initial contact (t_{CON}), midstance (t_{MS}), and
acceleration phase (t_{ACC}).

A one-way repeated measures analysis of variance was
used to indicate significant difference for given variables
between conditions, with Scheffe post hoc F-tests used to
identify significant difference at the 0.05 level. Plots
of the locus and path of the centre of pressure (COP) were
plotted based on a method proposed by Motriuk and Nigg
(1990). This technique normalises for different foot
abduction angles and foot dimensions, and thereby
facilitates comparisons between conditions and between
subjects. Mean plots of the ten trials for each condition
were obtained and analyzed to indicate initial foot
contact, path of the COP, and COP location in the forefoot.

3 Results

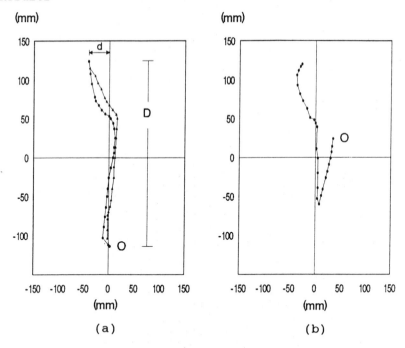

Figure 1. Paths of the centre of pressure for the
normals (a), and the patient (b), during barefoot walking.

The initial forefoot ground contact for the affected limb
of the patient while walking barefoot is typical of this
pathological condition ("O" in Fig 1b), and is in stark
contrast to that obtained for the normals ("O" in Fig 1a).
It is noted that subsequent to the point in time when the
path of the COP starts to move in the direction of
progression, the COP path for the patient resembles that of
the normal subjects. The locus of the COP in the region of
the metatarsal heads is given as "d" in Fig 1, and by
expressing this value in relation to the standardised foot
length (D/d), it is also possible to compare within and
between subject conditions.   The trace of the COP for the
patient during shod walking with and without the use of the
AFOs resembled that of the normals as given in Figure 1a.
Other mean data obtained from the Musgrave Footprint
pressure plate are given in Table 1.   One-way ANOVA
(repeated measures) for pairs of conditions are given in
Table 1.   Superscript numerals indicate significant
differences ($P<0.05$) for associated conditions for a given
variable. There was no significant difference between
conditions for foot abduction angle (θ), although these
values were approximately twice the magnitude of those for
the normal subjects who were unaffected by the application
of the orthoses for this parameter.   The location of the
COP in the region of the metatarsal heads (D/d) was
significantly different ($P<0.05$) for the barefoot condition

Table 1. Pressure plate parameters for the patient

	CONDITION				
	BF	SH	FAFO	VAFO1	VAFO2
θ *(deg)*	25.3	23.0	23.5	23.8	24.7
D/d	6.9	9.1	10.1	10.7	13.5
$t_{CON\,(\%)}$	-	4.1[1]	5.2[1,2]	7.7[2]	8.0[2]
$t_{MS\,(\%)}$	53.4	59.1	66.0	59.8	60.2
$t_{ACC\,(\%)}$	42.8	37.1	28.8	32.5	30.8

(superscript numerals indicate significant difference (P<0.05) for associated conditions for a given variable)

compared to all the other conditions for the patient. This was attributed to the confining effects of the shoe on the patient's foot. No contact time was recorded for barefoot walking, since heel strike was not observed for this condition. While heel strike did occur for the shod only (SH) condition, its duration was significantly less than the equivalent durations for all the AFOs. Furthermore, the two carbon fibre versions of the AFO had significantly longer initial contact durations compared to the polypropylene AFO. Although not indicated in the above table, similar significant trends were also observed for each of the other two contact phases (MS and ACC). Walking speeds and force plate data (means) for the patient are given in Table 2.

There was a significant increase in walking speed when shoes were worn by the patient compared to barefoot gait, with a further significant increase noted for the two versions of the prototype AFO (VAFO1 and VAFO2). The magnitude of the load acceptance (F1) was minimally, though significantly, higher for shod (SH) and VAFO2 compared to the barefoot condition. A similar finding was observed for the propulsive component of the vertical GRF (F2), for the barefoot and the shod condition, but not for VAFO2.

Table 2. Speed of gait and force parameters for the patient

	CONDITION				
	BF	SH	FAFO	VAFO1	VAFO2
Speed $(m.s^{-1})$	1.11[1]	1.22[1,2]	1.23[3]	1.27[2,3]	1.30[2,3]
F1 *(xBW)*	0.97[1]	1.02[1]	1.00	1.01	1.03[1]
F2 *(xBW)*	0.97[1]	1.02[1]	0.99	1.02[1]	0.99
I_{M-L} *(N s.kg^{-1})*	0.44[1]	0.33[1]	0.30[1,2]	0.25[1,2]	0.26[1,2]
+I: $-I_{A-P}$	0.77	0.98[1]	0.63[1,2]	0.72[1,2]	0.70[1,2]
I_V *(%BW)*	72.5	76.1	74.8	75.0	75.8

(superscript numerals indicate significant difference (P<0.05) for associated conditions for a given variable)

The more flexible version, VAFO1 also demonstrated a
significantly higher value for this parameter.Medio-
lateral impulse (I_{M-L}) decreased significantly for the FAFO
condition and decreased further for the VAFO conditions.
All AFOs reduced the ratio of the positive to negative
antero-posterior impulse ratio ($+I:-I_{A-P}$), with the more
pronounced effect associated with the FAFO condition. None
of the AFOs had any significant effect on the vertical
impulse (I_V). The devices had little demonstrable effect on
any of these parameters for the normal subjects.

4 Discussion

Drop-foot gait is characterised by the absence or reduction
in functional ability of the pre-tibial musculature,
resulting in the inability of the patient to control the
lowering of the forefoot to the ground subsequent to heel
contact during walking. The application of plastic AFOs is
an effective means of reducing this effect, but the
necessary rigidity of the orthosis may also reduce the
normal propulsive abilities of the walker. Before an
analysis of the effects of orthoses is carried out, it is
first necessary to establish the characteristics of
barefoot gait.
    The forefoot contact of the patient during barefoot
walking reflects the absence of dorsiflexion ability. That
is, during normal gait the dorsiflexors contract
concentrically during early swing resulting in a heel
contact for the next contact phase, and then the same
muscle group contracts eccentrically subsequent to heel
contact in a controlled lowering of the forefoot to the
ground. Clearly the patient in the present study cannot
perform this controlled movement, and therefore the
application of an AFO is justified. However, the patient
possesses normal abilities subsequent to initial contact;
therefore effective matching of this patient to an AFO
should not inhibit this natural and normal ability.
    The application of normal footwear alone produced an
effect on the stance phase of gait, in that heel strike was
observed. The duration of this phase was significantly
less than the equivalent times for the AFO conditions, with
foot slap still occurring. The fact that heel strike did
occur is accounted for by the elastic nature of the shoe.
The sole of the shoe was bent during normal toe-off and
subsequently straightened due to its stored elastic energy
during the swing phase, resulting in the presentation of
the heel to the ground at the next contact phase. This was
not observed for barefoot gait since in swing the bare foot
of the swing limb is a non-rigid body with no such
elasticity. Therefore, in the absence of the dorsiflexor
musculature, the foot remains in the plantarflexed position
which resulted from the active plantarflexion of the ankle
joint during terminal stance. This plantarflexed position
of the ankle joint is thus maintained until the next ground
contact phase, resulting in forefoot ground contact.

All of the AFOs increased the contact time (t_{CON}), but despite being more flexible than the polypropylene AFO the best control of foot lowering was achieved by the carbon fibre versions. This suggests the superior function of the carbon fibre versions of the prototype in this important phase of initial ground contact. The relatively high values for the midstance and acceleration phases of contact during barefoot gait are largely accounted for by the absence of heel-strike contact (t_{CON}) - given that values for the respective phases are expressed as percentages of total contact time. However, the polypropylene AFO (FAFO) had a more pronounced and significant lowering effect on the acceleration phase compared to the carbon fibre versions. Thus the FAFO would appear to be too stiff and restrictive of normal plantarflexion action associated with this phase of contact. Furthermore, the less stiff carbon fibre orthosis (VAFO1) was slightly superior to the stiffer carbon fibre version in this phase of contact. This is further evidenced in the antero-posterior impulse ratios.

The forceplate data indicated load acceptance (F1) during initial ground contact was slightly superior for the stiffer carbon fibre orthosis, while the less stiff carbon fibre version was somewhat superior during the propulsive phase (F2). However, total vertical impulse did not discriminate between AFO types. None of the AFOs contributed to a reduction in the excessive angle of foot abduction (A), although the carbon fibre versions had a superior desirable effect on the control of unwanted medio-lateral deviation of the foot during contact. Finally and significantly, the increase in freely chosen speed of gait for the carbon fibre versions of the orthosis verifies their overall superiority. This finding, along with the findings given above, suggests the potential of carbon fibre as a suitable component material which may be incorporated within plastic ankle-foot orthoses.

5 References

Balmaseda, M.T. Koozekanani, S.H. Fatehi, M.T. Gordon, C. Dreyfus, P.H. and Tanbonliong, E.C. (1988) Ground reaction forces, centre of pressure, and duration of stance with and without an ankle-foot orthosis. **Archives of Physical and Medical Rehabilitation**, 69, 1009-1012.

Berry, D.A. (1987) Composite materials for orthotics and prosthetics. **Orthotics and Prosthetics**, 40, 35-43.

Motriuk, H.U. and Nigg, B.M. (1990) A technique for normalising centre of pressure paths. **Journal of Biomechanics**, 23, 927-932.

Wallace, E.S.(1992) The development and evaluation of a variable stiffness ankle-foot orthosis. **University of Ulster**, Unpublished Doctorate thesis.

8 Activity, body composition and lipoprotein concentrations in growth hormone deficient adults
W. Bell, J.S. Davies, W.D. Evans and M.F. Scanlon

1 Introduction

Growth hormone deficiency (GHD) in adults is associated with marked alterations to body composition. In general, there is an increase in fat mass and a decrease in fat-free mass (FFM) (Jorgensen et al., 1994). The extent to which an increase in fat mass modifies fat patterning still remains uncertain.

A variety of physiological consequences arise as a result of GHD. These include cardiac dysfunction (Cuneo et al., 1991a), diminished basal metabolic rate (Jorgensen et al., 1993) and reductions in aerobic power (Cuneo et al., 1991b) and strength (Cuneo et al., 1991c). Loss of strength is thought to be due to a reduced muscle mass rather than a changed muscle fibre function (Cuneo et al., 1992). In addition, abnormal lipid profiles are known to coexist with GHD (Keller and Miles, 1991).

It seems likely that some of the above complications will be implicated in the premature cardiovascular mortality observed in hypopituitary patients (Rosen and Bengsson, 1990). The long-term effect of treatment with GH on cardiovascular mortality has not yet been fully assessed.

The psychosocial development of GHD patients is also compromised. There are, for example, significant differences between GHD patients and normal individuals in the degree of social isolation, physical mobility, sleep patterns, and emotional status. Reduced energy and vitality are two of the major reasons why GHD patients participate in fewer leisure time activities (Bjork et al., 1989).

The purpose of the present report, therefore, was to identify the extent to which an active lifestyle, during untreated GHD, affected the components of body composition and the concentration of lipoproteins in GHD adults.

2 Methods

2.1 Patients
Twenty-seven male and 24 female GHD patients between the ages of 21 and 60 years were investigated. Growth hormone deficiency was confirmed by a peak plasma GH response of <5μg/l following insulin-induced hypoglycaemia (nadir response <2.0 mmol/l) or growth hormone releasing hormone at a dose of 1 μg/kg body mass iv. Growth hormone deficiency was isolated in 5 cases and was part of a spectrum of hypopituitarism due to a variety of causes in 46 cases. The mean period of GHD was 6.9 ± 4.6 years. All patients were on stable replacement therapy, where appropriate, with varying combinations of sex steroids, thyroxine, corticosteroids and desmopressin. Informed consent was obtained from patients and all procedures were approved by the University of Wales' College of Medicine ethics committee.

2.2 Physical activity
Individual leisure time activity was recorded on a social anamnes case record form using a 5-point rating scale. This information was used to classify patients into two groups; those engaged in sports (active) and others whose main leisure time pursuits involved only sitting or taking walks (less-active).

2.3 Anthropometry and body composition
Stature was measured on a Harpenden stadiometer to the nearest 0.1 cm and body mass to the closest 0.1 kg using a digital scale. Dual energy x-ray absorptiometry (DXA) measurements of whole-body fat, lean and bone mineral mass were made with a QDR 1000/W whole body scanner using software version 5.47P (Hologic Inc., Waltham, Mass. USA). Each patient was aligned with the long axis of the DXA couch and remained motionless during the scan. The analysis is based on the differential attenuation of radiation at two photon energies (70 and 140 kVp) as it passes through bone and soft tissue. The attenuation data are displayed as a digital image whose picture elements (pixels) correspond to individual measurement points through the patient. Pixels containing bone are decomposed into bone mineral and soft tissue masses. Those pixels not containing bone are further decomposed into lean and fat components using a soft tissue calibration phantom which is scanned simultaneously with the patient. The total masses of bone mineral, fat and lean compartments are summed to obtain an estimate of total body mass. The effective radiation dose of 5 μSv is very low and the short term precision of the technique is better than 1%.

2.4 Biochemical analyses
Prior to anthropometric and body composition measurements being taken a 20 ml sample of blood was venesected from each

patient following a 12 hour fast. Serum was removed from coagulated samples and aliquots frozen at -70°C for high density lipoprotein (HDL) and at -20°C for all other variables. Apolipoprotein (a) [Lp(a)], total cholesterol (TC), triglycerides (Tg), HDL and low density lipoprotein (LDL) cholesterol were determined using standard procedures (Morgan et al., 1992).

3 Results

Descriptive data for males and females are given in Table 1. Active males (n=5) were signficantly (P<0.05) taller (181.4 ± 6.1 vs 173.8 ± 8.4 cm) and heavier (103.2 ± 13.5 vs 87.9 ± 16.6 kg) than less-active males (n=22). On the other hand differences in height (163.5 ± 7.3 vs 163.5 ± 11.8 cm) and body mass (66.2 ± 12.6 vs 71.3 ± 13.8 kg) were not evident between active (n=5) and less-active (n=19) females.

Table 1. Descriptive data (mean ± SD) for male and female patients * = P<0.05

	Males		Females	
	Active	Less-active	Active	Less-active
Age (yr)	48.2±10.6	44.3±10.5	45.0±13.8	44.7±8.6
Height (cm)	181.4±6.1	173.8±8.4*	163.5±7.3	163.5±11.8
Mass (kg)	103.2±13.5	87.9±16.6*	66.2±12.6	71.3±13.8
BMI (kg/m^2)	31.6±5.5	29.0±4.7	24.6±2.9	26.6±4.5

Body composition is expressed in both absolute and relative terms (Table 2). There were obvious differences in absolute values between sexes. In males the contrast between active and less-active groups yielded significant differences in bone mineral mass (3.5 ± 0.2 vs 2.8 ± 0.6 kg, P<0.001), lean tissue mass (72.9 ± 7.3 vs 60.3 ± 9.2 kg, P<0.01) and FFM (76.4 ± 7.3 vs 63.1 ± 9.7 kg, P<0.01). This was not the position in females, however, and differences between active and less-active groups in these variables were not significant.

In relative terms differences between active and less-active groups in the components of body composition were not significant in either males or females (P>0.05). As might be expected, fat mass was smaller and FFM greater in active than less-active patients. The average fat mass in males was about 26% and in females 34%.

Table 2. Absolute and relative values (mean ± SD) for body composition ** = P<0.01   *** = P<0.001

		Males		Females	
		Active	Less-active	Active	Less-active
Bone	(kg)	3.5+0.2	2.8+0.6***	2.1+0.5	2.4+0.5
FM	(kg)	26.0+6.5	24.2+8.5	22.1+8.4	25.3+8.4
Lean	(kg)	72.9+7.3	60.3+9.2**	41.0+6.5	42.6+7.2
FFM	(kg)	76.4+7.3	63.1+9.7**	43.1+6.8	45.0+7.6
Bone	(%)	3.4+0.5	3.2+0.4	3.2+0.4	3.4+0.4
FM	(%)	25.1+3.4	27.1+5.6	33.2+7.6	35.3+6.7
Lean	(%)	71.5+3.1	69.7+5.5	63.6+7.6	61.3+6.5
FFM	(%)	74.9+3.4	72.9+5.6	66.8+7.6	64.7+6.7

Table 3 presents the results of the biochemical analyses. Lp(a) and Tg were found to be non-Gaussian and corrected using a log10 transformation. All results, however, are reported in standard units. There were no significant differences in any of the lipoprotein concentrations between active and less-active patients in either males or females (P>0.05).

Table 3. Lipoprotein concentrations (mean ± SD) in active and less-active patients. All differences P>0.05

		Males		Females	
		Active	Less-active	Active	Less-active
TC	(mmol/l)	5.3+0.8	6.1+1.4	6.7+1.7	6.0+0.6
Tg	(mmol/l)	2.0+0.6	2.1+1.1	1.8+1.2	1.3+0.5
HDL	(mmol/l)	0.8+0.3	1.0+0.3	1.1+0.3	1.2+0.5
LDL	(mmol/l)	3.6+0.7	4.2+1.2	4.8+1.8	4.2+0.9
Lp(a)	(mg/dl)	141+98	200+213	291+355	183+189

4 Discussion

In the group as a whole (n=51) 27% of patients spent most of their leisure time sitting, 53% took frequent walks and 20% were actively engaged in sports. About a third (37%) felt their level of physical activity was satisfactory but the majority (63%) thought it insufficient (P>0.05). Just less than one-half (41%) considered their illness had interfered with participation in leisure time pursuits (P>0.05).

There were clear differences in height and body mass between active and less-active males, active males being taller and heavier. These size differences were reflected in the significantly larger absolute amounts of bone mineral mass, lean mass and FFM of active males, but were removed when standardised for size. Thus contrasts in body composition between active and less-active males are accounted for by dissimilarities in size and not variations in the level of physical activity. In females, size and body composition was similar in both groups.

Growth hormone deficiency is known to be associated with hypercholesterolaemia. Patients deficient in GH show mild increases in TC and LDL (Libber et al., 1990) as well as reduced HDL (Eden et al., 1993). Exercise has a positive effect on lipoprotein concentrations, as it does on body composition, but its effect is strongly influenced by the level of energy expenditure (Durstine and Haskell, 1994). It may be that the level of energy expenditure in active GHD patients is insufficient to produce changes large enough to be significant although Chong et al. (1994) have shown that GHD adults do not have a reduced total energy expenditure compared to controls.

Physical activity is an important contributory factor to individual health and well-being and provides psychological as well as physical benefits. Despite the many problems encountered in GHD, an active lifestyle should be encouraged.

Acknowledgements
We are very grateful for the assistance of Mr J.H. Pearce and Mr D.Coleman in performing the DXA measurements and to Dr R. Morgan for the biochemical analyses.

5 References

Bjork, S. Jonsson, B. Westphal, O. and Levin, J-E. (1989) Quality of life of adults with growth hormone deficiency: a controlled study. **Acta Paediactrica Scandinavica**, 356, 55-59.

Chong, P.K.K. Jung, R.T. Scrimgeour, C.M. Rennie, M.J. Paterson, C.R. (1994) Energy expenditure and body composition in growth hormone deficient adults on exogenous growth hormone. **Clinical Endocrinology**, 40, 103-110.

Cuneo, R.C. Salomon, F. Wilmshurst, P. Byrne, C. Wiles, C.M. Hesp, R. and Sonksen, P.H. (1991a) Cardiovascular effects of growth hormone treatment in growth-hormone-deficient adults: stimulation of the renin-aldosterone system. **Clinical Science**, 81, 587-592.

Cuneo, R.C. Salomon, F. Wiles, C.M. Hesp, R. and Sonksen, P.H. (1991b) Growth hormone treatment in growth hormone-deficient adults. II. Effects on exercise performance. **Journal of Applied Physiology**, 70, 695-700.

Cuneo, R.C. Salomon, F. Wiles, C.M. Hesp, R. and Sonksen, P.H. (1991c) Growth hormone treatment in growth hormone-deficient adults. 1. Effects on muscle mass and strength. **Journal of Applied Physiology**, 70, 688-694.

Cuneo, R.C. Salomon, F. Wiles, C.M. Round, J.M. Jones, D. Hesp, R. Sonksen, P.H. (1992) Histology of skeletal muscle in adults with GH deficiency: comparison with normal muscle and response to GH treatment. **Hormone Research**, 37, 23-28.

Durstine, J.L. and Haskell, W.L. (1994) Effects of exercise training on plasma lipids and lipoproteins, in **Exercise and Sport Sciences Reviews** (ed J.O. Holloszy), Williams and Wilkins, London, Vol 22, pp. 477-521.

Eden, S. Wiklund, O. Oscarsson, J. Rosen, T. and Bengtsson, B-A. (1993) Growth hormone treatment of growth hormone deficient adults results in a marked increase in Lp(a) and HDL cholesterol concentrations. **Arteriosclerosis and Thrombosis**, 13, 296-301.

Jorgensen, J.O.L. Moller, J. Alberti, K.G.M.M. Schmitz, O. Christiansen, J.S. and Moller, N. (1993) Marked effects of sustained low growth hormone (GH) levels on day-to-day fuel metabolism: studies in GH deficient patients and healthy untreated subjects. **Journal of Clinical and Endocrinological Metabolism**, 77, 1589-1596.

Jorgensen, J.O.L. Muller, J. Moller, J. Wolthers, T. Vahl, N. Juul, A. Skakkeboek, N.E. and Christiansen, J.S. (1994) Adult growth hormone deficiency. **Hormone Research**, 42, 235-241.

Keller, U. and Miles, J.M. (1991) Growth hormone and lipids. **Hormone Research**, 36 (Suppl 1), 36-40.

Libber, S.M. Plotnick, L.P. Johanson, A.J. Blizzard, R.M. Kwiterovich, P.O. and Migeon, C.J. (1990) Long-term follow up of hypopituitary patients treated with human growth hormone. **Medicine**, 69, 46-55.

Morgan, R. Bishop, A.J. Young, W.T. Matthews, S.B. and Rees, A. (1992) The relationship between apolipoprotein (a), lipid and lipoprotein levels and the risk of coronary artery disease. **Cardiovascular Risk Factors**, 2, 105-111.

Rosen, T. and Bengtsson, B-A (1990) Premature mortality due to cardiovascular disease in hypopituitarism. **The Lancet**, 336, 285-288.

9 Seating comfort of the disabled during leisure and light sporting activities

P. Dabnichki and A.D. Crocombe

1 Introduction

Many studies have been devoted to the formation and prevention of pressure sores and different ways of pressure relief have been studied and tested. These studies (Engel, 1991) deal with severely disabled people. No results are reported on the seating comfort of patients taking part in light sporting activities or rehabilitation exercise. The movement of the body during such exercise can cause very unfavourable load distributions, which are exacerbated when we take into account the lack of sensitivity of immobilised people and the difficulties they experience in readjusting to their original position. This problem can be quickly resolved by a proper choice of material and depth of cushion. To do this the local pressure distribution should be known. The more comfortable seating provides a better opportunity for the disabled to keep a proper body posture and favourable pressure distribution helps to avoid unwanted complications as ischaemia, oedema and so on. Additionally it is well known that correct posture is of a crucial importance for the health and fitness level of these people.

The paper presented is a development of some earlier studies by the same authors (Dabnichki et al., 1994a, Dabnichki and Crocombe, 1994b). A non-linear finite element model was developed and applied to the case of severely immobilised people endangered by the formation of pressure sores. In that paper a novel computational method was applied and a hyperelastic model was used for the tissue. Under the static conditions considered, the resultant pressure distribution was a function solely of the tissue properties, patient weight and cushion stiffness. Full symmetry was enforced and it was assumed that there was no inclination of the sagittal plane of the body to the seat. Under these conditions the shear and compressive stresses in the buttock tissue are summarised in Table 1 for various cushion characteristics.

It can be seen that the cushion material causes a considerable variation in the peak shear and compressive stresses in the soft tissue. It must be added that an even bigger reduction is possible as the compliant cushion used in those calculations was relatively stiff. If one takes into consideration the fact that the disabled are exposed to these levels of pressure for very long periods of time it becomes clear how important this issue is. A huge variety of cushions are currently available on the market but no clear advice can be given to the user as how to select a cushion according to their anthropometric data and needs. Measuring devices are not widely available and the accuracy of their data is questionable. So computer models could provide a useful alternative. However their results should be rigorously checked and validated.

Table 1. Cushion type and peak stresses

Cushion characteristic	Compressive stress (kPa)	Shear stress (kPa)
Smooth and rigid	51	8.1
Rough and rigid	48	7.3
Rough and compliant	42	5.5

2 Methods

2.1 The finite element model

Stress analysis of the buttock region has been carried out numerically using the finite element analysis ANSYS 5.0A (1992). In this method the region of interest is subdivided into a mesh of much smaller, regular regions known as elements. These can be processed to provide the displacements and stresses at nodes (which lie at the element vertices in this study). The finite element mesh used in this work is shown in Fig. 1. This represents the body at zero inclination to the cushion. It consists of 4-noded quadrilateral hyperelastic elements, specified as HYPER56 in ANSYS 5.0A. These are elements that allow the stiffness of a material to increase with strain, a behaviour that is exhibited by soft tissue. In the earlier study Dabnichki and Crocombe (1994b) used a different type of hyperelastic element and that caused much slower convergence. This element is used in the meshing of both cushion and tissue, the only difference is in the material model assigned to these elements. The soft tissue part is divided into 520 elements which use a Mooney-Rivlin material model while the cushion consists of 132 elements which use a compressible Blatz-Ko foam-type material model. The ishial tuberosity and the upper boundary of the mesh are modelled as a rigid body which can move only vertically. This model results in a high level of pressure under the ishial tuberosity and simulates the experimental setting of Reddy et al. (1982). The justification for this model is that the scale of bone deformation is in the range of microns which is negligible compared to the displacement of the tissue. The interface between the tissue and the cushion was modelled using node to surface type contact elements (CONTACT48 in ANSYS 5.0A). These elements have a big advantage over the standard node to node contact elements in the case of large deflection analysis as they ensure compatibility in x- and y-direction displacements on the interface. So, unlike our earlier work, proper contact without penetration can be obtained. The algorithm for contact solution is computationally expensive as a symmetrical contact model was used, both surfaces were modelled as master and slave simultaneously. Contact elements were also placed between the two halves of the buttock to prevent mutual penetration. Overcoming this problem is difficult because the topology of this contact is complicated.

More questionable is the assumption of a rigid upper boundary, despite the fact that existing studies (Reddy et al., 1982) take this for granted. This was checked by the authors in a specially designed experiment described later. No vertical or horizontal displacements of the tissue were detected at this position and thus it was concluded that these boundary conditions were sufficiently realistic.

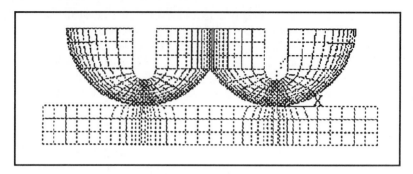

Fig.2. Finite element mesh of the buttock tissue under the ishial tuberosity by zero angle of inclination of the body.

2.2 Material properties, computational methods and experimental tests

The nature of the problem requires the use of advanced computational techniques. This is due mainly to the nonlinearity of the tissue behaviour (particularly large deflections and strains). Added to this the inherent non-linear nature of the contact problem makes the solution very complicated. It is extremely difficult to find suitable computational tools to achieve convergence of the solution. In our case the main problems arose from the compressibility of the cushion material, typically a foam rubber material. Rigorous mathematical proof of the existence of solution of this type of problem has not yet been found. Further the speed of convergence and the effect of different computational parameters and techniques cannot be easily established. The only possible way of tackling these problems was through trial and error which showed that the best convergence occurred when we optimised the load step and used full Newton-Raphson iterations with adaptive descent. Sometimes during the solution it was necessary to change some options and to include a predictor or line search option. The standard wave front solver with a convergence limit of 1% of the applied load was used. As the load was applied in very small load steps the global value of the out of balance forces was less than 0.001 N. Further details of these techniques can be found in the ANSYS user manual (1992).

The other major problem was the choice of constitutive equations describing the material response of the tissue. Some of the published data (Reger et al., 1990) proved to be unreliable. Earlier studies used a non-linear hyperelastic model for the tissue behaviour (Dabnichki et al, 1994a and Dabnichki and Crocombe, 1992). We still believe this to be a reasonable model and thus its use has been continued in this study. Additional arguments supporting this model include the results of experiments studying the level of deflection of the buttock tissue conducted by the authors. They broadly confirmed the results obtained using these data. Briefly we present a description of the experiment.

Ten subjects were asked to sit on a transparent seat. The reaction force under their feet was measured as well as their weight. Three synchronised video cameras were used to collect data. The seat had a grid which enabled the size of the contact zone to be measured. Markers fixed on the body enabled measurement of the tissue deflection to be made. As already mentioned these data correlated well with our numerical results confirming the material model used. The size of the contact zone was obtained with an accuracy of 5 mm. An additional advantage of using the same material data is that we were able to compare the results with our previous studies.

The data from the experiment described above are for static loading conditions. In the case of leisure and light sports activities the dynamic effects of body motion can be neglected as its role is not dominant. As the cushion properties are almost identical under static and dynamic conditions, it is sufficient to model any dynamic inertia forces as static loads. To the load caused by the body weight were added a) loads caused by additional weights like barbells or b) moments generated by the movement of the upper body. However, the symmetry assumption is no longer valid and this led to a significant rise in computational time. Additional complications arose when an inclined body was studied. The moment around the point of initial contact generates a tangential force and this causes sliding of the buttock with respect to the cushion. Contact problems involving sliding are very difficult even in the case of small deflections.

The strong nonlinearity of the problem requires the application of the load in small steps. As flexible load stepping was implemented the number of steps varied from analysis to analysis but was in the range of 450-1100 load steps. Each load step required between 3 and 9 equilibrium iterations, each of which is equivalent to a complete linear analysis of the problem.

3 Results and Discussion

Previous studies of pressure distribution have always been devoted to the formation and prevention of pressure sores. No existing work has gone beyond this point and no attempt has been made to develop a more general computational approach to the seating comfort problem. The reason for this is clear; the studies of Ferguson-Pell (1990) were conducted in a hospital environment and the patients have limited sensation in the buttock region. This means it is difficult to obtain an objective response about seating comfort. We suggest that the calculated stress level could be used as an estimation of the level of comfort of a given cushion. However for an accurate assessment one needs to model conditions that are very close to reality. So we have tried to simulate, as realistically as possible, the resulting loads over the buttock caused by leisure and light sporting activities.

Taking into consideration the rationale for the modelling described above it was concluded that the following effects should be studied in order to investigate the magnitude of the change in the pressure distribution they induce in the soft tissue:

a) Inclination of the sagittal plane of the body from the vertical and its influence on the pressure distribution.

b) Modification of the cushion and the effect on the peak tissue stresses.

c) Sliding normal to the sagittal plane.

d) Placement of additional weight over the body (barbells, ball catching and so on).

Preliminary studies showed that the most important factor affecting the stress distribution is the angle of inclination of the body. This inclination leads to a higher concentration of compressive stress caused by the asymmetric load distribution and a higher shear stress around the tissue-cushion interface.

A summary of the main results of the study are presented in Table 2 below. This is the first study devoted to the influence of body posture and light movements on pressure distribution and seating comfort. A similar experimental study was conducted by Candadai and Reddy (1994), where a buttock model filled with gel was studied under different angles of inclination.

Table 2. Maximum tissue shear and compressive stress for various body inclinations

Inclination to the vertical axis (^{0})	Compressive stress (kPa)	Shear stress (kPa)
10	43	6.1
20	46	6.8
30	54	7.9

As can be seen from Table 2 the body posture has an important influence on the stress distribution and its effect should be considered when choosing cushion material. Some of the stress levels are higher than the case of normal contact on a rigid surface and this may be considered to be unacceptably high. Adding weight to the natural body weight proved not to be hazardous providing that the person keeps his/her proper posture. In this case the overall level of stress intensity increases but the peak stress stays almost unchanged. However, the model showed that proper choice of cushion material can keep the peak stresses almost constant despite the out of sagittal plane movement and inclination. Since recently very good methods have been introduced for designing sandwich foams (Gibson and Ashby , 1988), it is important to predict maximum loads and stress concentration in order to produce an appropriate seat. To design such a seat it is necessary to consider not only the anthropometric data of the user (Graber and Krouskop, 1982), but also his or her level of physical activity. Such a seat has different demands than standard hospital seats. This includes the need for higher stiffness in order to maintain uniform pressure distribution during physical activities. Such a choice is not straightforward considering the non-linear nature of the problem. The model developed allows an assessment to be made of different cushion characteristics on the pressure distribution. The main difficulty is that material data provided by industrial sources are not in an appropriate form to be used in stress analyses without further calculations. However, an additional module was developed allowing the stress-strain curve to be derived from the load-displacement curve obtained from existing standard tests.

The influence of cut-outs on the cushion surface on the stress distribution was studied numerically. These cut-outs are commonly used to provide better ventilation for the seat. Preliminary studies show that this modification has an adverse effect as it causes a stress concentration in the tissue. The reason for this is the significant sliding which occurs between the buttock and the cushion caused by the change of the body angle. The increase of the shear stress is up to 20% around the contact with the cut-out. As many authors regard shear stresses as the main cause of skin sores and ulcers, such a risk should be analysed carefully.

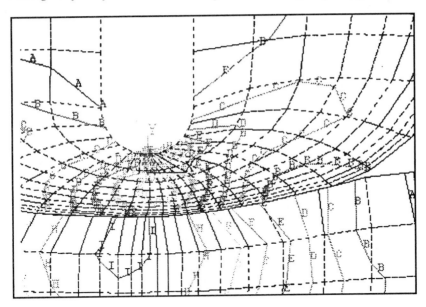

Fig.2. Stress intensity contours in the deformeg shape of the tissue under the ishial tuberosity.

4 Conclusion

This study was conducted with a clear understanding that the problem of the general ergonomics of non-hospitalised disabled people is underestimated and has not received sufficient attention. The manufacturers are concerned with many other issues such as flammability, chemical content, weight, price and so on. Their tests are conducted in the framework of the existing standards and their results cannot be directly related to seating comfort. The direct measurements are affected by difficulties in the calibration of the devices used, complicated geometrical shape of the interface and mostly by the large displacement encountered. As the capability of the manufacturers for producing almost any material with desired characteristics increases, it is an exciting option to provide sufficient insight into the problem using computer models. The results of this study show that such a model can be validated by means of comparatively simple experimental tests. The results from the computer models give a more comprehensive picture than the results from the tests. The model developed allows an estimation of the pressure distribution in the buttock region caused by different loading conditions and cushion materials. It provides important data for designing appropriate seats for the disabled.

5 Acknowledgement

The cushion material properties are courtesy of Vitafoam Ltd.

6 References

ANSYS Users Manual for revision 5, (1992), Swanson Analysis Systems Inc., DN-R300:50-1

Reger, S.I. McGovern, T.F. and Chung, K.C. (1990), Biomechanics of tissue distortion and stiffness by magnetic resonance imaging, in **Pressure Sores - Clinical Practice and Scientific Approach, (ed D. L. Bader, Dan),** Macmillan Press Ltd, London, pp177-190

Candadai, R.S. and Reddy, N. P. (1994), Stress distribution in a physical model of buttock: effect of simulated bone geometry, **Journal of Biomechanics**, 25, 1403-1411.

Dabnichki, P.D. and Crocombe, A.D. (1992), Finite element model of the buttock - cushion interaction**, in Proceedings of the XXVIII World Congress of Theoretical and Applied Mechanics**, Haifa, Israel.

Dabnichki, P.A. Crocombe, A.D. and Hughes, S.C. (1994a), Deformation and stress analysis of supported buttock contact, **Proc. Instn of Mech. Eng., Part H: Jounal of Engineering in Medicine**, 208, 9-17.

Dabnichki, P.D. and Crocombe, A.D. (1994b), The non-linear contact of seating and the resultant tissue stress analysis**, Proceedings of the Second World Congress of Biomechanics**, Amsterdam, Netherlands.

Engel, P. (1991), Aspects of wheelchair seating comfort, **, Preliminary proceedings of an International Workshop, Ergonomics of Manual Wheelchair Propulsion: State of the Art**. Amsterdam, Netherlands.

Ferguson-Pell M.W. (1990), Seat cushion selection, choosing a wheelchair system, **Journal of Rehabilitation Research and Development, Clinical Supplement No 2**.

Gibson, L.J. and Ashby, M.F. (1988), **Cellular Solids, Structure & Properties**, Pergmon Press, Oxford, pp. 241-276.

Graber, S.L. and Krouskop, T.A. (1982), Body build and its relation to the pressure distribution in the seated wheelchair, **Archives of Physical Medicine and Rehabilitation**, 63, 17-20.

Reddy, N.P. Himanshu, P. and Cochran G.V.B. (1982), Model experiment of study the stress distribution in a seated buttock, **Journal of Biomechanics**, 15-7, 493-504.

10 Pre-competition anxiety and self-confidence in elite and non-elite wheelchair sports participants

E. Campbell and G. Jones

1 Introduction

Over the last ten years there has been a dramatic increase in the number of opportunities for disabled athletes to compete at an elite level (Campbell & Jones, 1994). The result is that top level disabled sport is becoming more competitive and the rewards for success, and the disappointments associated with failure, are often great. These factors can cause intense situations in which the ability to cope with the accompanying stress is crucial in determining performance success. Knowledge of how disabled athletes respond in these situations is of importance if sport psychologists are to provide effective services. However, it is not possible merely to apply current sport psychology theories and psychological techniques as the majority have not been developed or investigated using disabled sport populations (Crocker, 1993). The authors are aware of only one study which has considered how disabled athletes respond in highly stressful sporting situations (Campbell & Jones, in press).

Campbell & Jones (in press) examined the normal pre-competition temporal patterning of anxiety and self-confidence responses of 103 wheelchair sport participants. A modified format of the trait version of the competitive state anxiety inventory (CSAI-2) (Albrecht & Feltz, 1987; Jones & Swain, in press) (i.e., Competitive Trait Anxiety Inventory-2; CTAI-2) was used to measure three dimensions of the subjects' normal competitive anxiety responses: 'intensity' of cognitive anxiety, somatic anxiety and self-confidence symptoms; 'frequency' of the symptoms; and 'direction' of cognitive and somatic anxiety symptoms (i.e., interpretation of symptoms as either debilitative or facilitative for performance). The dimensions of 'frequency' and 'direction' were considered due to Jones' (in press) suggestion that the intensity-alone approach to the assessment of competitive anxiety is limited. The subjects' responses were measured at three time periods preceding an important competition; 1 week, 2 hours, and 30 minutes before competition. The findings suggested that wheelchair sport participants experience similar pre-competition anxiety and self-confidence responses to non-disabled sport participants. Previous literature has suggested, however, that pre-competition anxiety patterning may vary as a function of individual difference variables such as skill level (Martens et al., 1990). The major purposes, therefore, of the study reported here were to extend Campbell & Jones' (in press) study and examine whether the individual difference variable of skill level influences the normal pre-competition anxiety response of wheelchair sport participants.

Early studies of non-disabled sport participants have generally shown that less experienced and non-elite performers experience a steady increase in anxiety right up to and even during performance; experienced and elite performers demonstrate a similar pre-event increase, but then a reduction just prior to and even during competition (Highlen & Bennett, 1979; Mahoney & Avener, 1977). These early studies have tended to be limited due to either; considering anxiety as a unidimensional construct, or conceptualising anxiety as multidimensional but then using the recently criticised intensity-alone approach. Research which has used a multidimensional approach has shown elite performers to experience lower cognitive and somatic anxiety, and higher levels of self-confidence immediately prior to competition (Martens et al., 1990). Recent studies have considered multidimensional anxiety and modified the CSAI-2 to measure both 'intensity' and 'direction' of symptoms in elite and non-elite athletes just prior to competition (Jones, Hanton & Swain, 1994; Jones & Swain, in press). Generally, the findings have indicated no differences between elite and non-elite athletes on the intensity of anxiety symptoms, but that elite performers interpret their anxiety states as being more facilitative to performance than non-elite performers. Jones & Swain's (in press) study is of particular relevance to the present study as it considered the 'normal' pre-competition anxiety responses of elite and non-elite cricketers using the CTAI-2 (Albrecht & Feltz, 1987). They modified the CTAI-2 to measure both intensity and direction of competitive anxiety symptoms and their results supported previous findings using the CSAI-2. Jones & Swain, however, only investigated pre-competition anxiety responses immediately prior to competition and did not consider the temporal patterning of responses.

As previously stated, little research has considered how disabled athletes respond in stressful situations. The purpose of the present study was to examine the normal pre-competition temporal patterning of anxiety and self-confidence in elite and non-elite wheelchair sport participants. Theoretical predictions regarding the temporal patterning of the intensity of cognitive anxiety and self-confidence are that both should remain stable during the pre-competition period; somatic anxiety on the other hand, is predicted to increase just prior to the onset of competition (Martens et al., 1990). No previous research has examined temporal changes in the direction and frequency of anxiety as a function of skill level. Thus, this aspect of the study was largely exploratory in nature.

2 Method

The subjects comprised 103 male (n=87) and female (n=16) wheelchair sport participants from a variety of sports whose ages ranged from 19 to 46 years (mean=31.01; SD=7.54). The sample was drawn from a range of sports to enable an adequate sample size to be obtained: athletics (track and field); basketball; and swimming. The elite (n=39) wheelchair sport participants competed at international level and the non-elite (n=64) at national level. The subjects possessed a range of impairments from lower limb amputation to tetraplegia. All subjects volunteered to participate in the study.

Previous researchers (e.g., Albrecht & Feltz, 1987; Jones & Swain, in press) have adapted the CSAI-2 to measure competitive trait anxiety (CTAI-2) by altering the test instructions so that the subjects can complete it based on how they 'normally' feel. Developers of other state-trait measures (e.g. NcNair, Lorr, & Droppleman, 1971) have used similar procedures. The CTAI-2 comprises 27 items with nine items in each of the three subscales; cognitive anxiety, somatic anxiety and self-confidence. Examples of cognitive anxiety items include "I am concerned about this competition" and "I am concerned about performing poorly", while somatic anxiety items include "I feel nervous" and "my body feels tense". Self-confidence items include "I feel at ease" and "I am confident about performing well".

The CTAI-2 was modified to measure intensity, frequency, and direction. The direction subscale had previously been developed by Jones & Swain (1992) and the frequency subscale by Swain & Jones (1993).

Intensity: each subject was asked to rate the intensity with which each symptom was normally experienced on a scale from 1 ("not at all") to 4 ("very much so"). The possible intensity scores on each subscale ranged from 9 (low) to 36 (high).

Frequency: each subject was asked "How frequently do you experience this thought or feeling at this stage ?". This was measured on a 7-point Likert-type scale ranging from 1 ("not at all") to 7 ("all of the time"). The possible frequency scores on each subscale ranged from 9 (low) to 63 (high).

Direction: the direction subscale was included for the cognitive and somatic anxiety items. Subjects were asked to rate the degree to which the intensity of each symptom they normally experienced was facilitative or debilitative to their subsequent performance. This was assessed on a scale from -3 ("very debilitative") to +3 ("very facilitative"), so that possible direction subscale scores ranged from -27 to +27.

All wheelchair sport participants were asked to complete the CTAI-2 based on how they normally felt at three time points prior to an important competition; 1 week before, 2 hours before, and 30 minutes before. These time points were selected based on previous research with non-disabled sport participants (Jones, Swain & Cale, 1991). Subjects were presented with trait-oriented instructions modified from the recommendations of Martens et al. (1990). Subjects were asked to complete the CTAI-2 away from the competition environment and assured of confidentiality of their responses.

Separate two-way repeated measures multivariate analyses of variance (MANOVA) (skill level by time to competition) were conducted on each of the three response dimensions (i.e., intensity, frequency and direction) of the modified CTAI-2. Where MANOVAs were significant, univariate two-way repeated measures analyses were carried out; significant differences between means were investigated by follow-up Scheffe tests.

3 Results

The MANOVA for **intensity** was significant (Wilks Lambda = 0.87, $F_{6,96}$ = 2.38, P<0.05). Means, standard deviations and F ratios for the follow-up univariate analyses are shown in Table 1. These analyses revealed a significant interaction only for cognitive anxiety intensity ($F_{2,202}$ = 4.17, P<0.05). Follow-up Sheffe tests showed that cognitive anxiety intensity of elite wheelchair sport participants did not increase pre-competition. However, the non-elite wheelchair sport participants increased from 1 week to 2 hours before competition.

Table 1. Means, standard deviations and F ratios for intensity subscales

	1 week		2 hours		30 minutes			
	Elite	Non-elite	Elite	Non-elite	Elite	Non-elite	df	F
	Mean (SD)	Mean (SD)	Mean (SD)	Mean (SD)	Mean (SD)	Mean (SD)		
Cog. Anx.	19.39 (4.84)	19.05 (5.56)	19.36 (5.55)	21.48 (5.90)	20.36 (6.49)	22.44 (7.05)	2,202	4.17
Som. Anx.	13.46 (3.76)	13.75 (4.87)	17.69 (5.79)	17.53 (4.71)	27.26 (10.76)	28.0 (14.27)	2,202	0.09
Self-Conf.	25.80 (5.35)	24.20 (5.67)	28.97 (8.40)	25.56 (8.68)	24.95 (5.69)	22.34 (7.18)	2,202	0.79

The MANOVA for **frequency** was significant (Wilks Lambda = 0.87, $F_{6,96}$ = 2.48, P<0.05). Means, standard deviations and F ratios for the univariate analyses are shown in Table 2. These analyses revealed a significant interaction only for cognitive anxiety frequency ($F_{2,202}$ = 4.75, P<0.01). Follow-up Scheffe tests showed that elite wheelchair sport participants reported an increase in cognitive intrusions from 1 week to 2 hours before competition, whereas the non-elite sport participants reported an increase at each time point i.e., from 1 week, to 2 hours, to 30 minutes before competition. In addition, the non-elite wheelchair sport participants had a higher frequency of cognitive intrusions 30 minutes before competition than the elite wheelchair sport participants.

Table 2. Means, standard deviations and F ratios for frequency subscale

| | 1 week | | 2 hours | | 30 minutes | | df | F |
| | Elite | Non-elite | Elite | Non-elite | Elite | Non-elite | | |
	Mean (SD)	Mean (SD)	Mean (SD)	Mean (SD)	Mean (SD)	Mean (SD)		
Cog. Anx.	26.08 (9.55)	24.63 (9.07)	30.23 (11.18)	32.42 (10.50)	30.59 (12.80)	35.98 (15.57)	2,202	4.74
Som. Anx.	18.54 (5.02)	21.31 (9.31)	26.36 (10.50)	26.88 (9.97)	31.59 (11.97)	32.67 (11.62)	2,202	0.59
Self-Conf.	38.31 (10.36)	35.72 (10.65)	39.41 (11.54)	38.62 (9.74)	41.56 (10.79)	40.70 (10.64)	2,202	0.53

The MANOVA for **direction** showed no difference in temporal patterning of interpretation of anxiety symptoms as a function of skill level (Wilks Lambda = 0.92, $F_{4,98} = 2.10$, P>0.05). Means and standard deviations for the cognitive and somatic anxiety direction scores at the three time points are shown in Table 3.

Table 3. Means and standard deviations for direction subscales

| | 1 week | | 2 hours | | 30 minutes | |
| | Elite | Non-elite | Elite | Non-elite | Elite | Non-elite |
	Mean (SD)	Mean (SD)	Mean (SD)	Mean (SD)	Mean (SD)	Mean (SD)
Cog. Anx.	4.46 (8.35)	2.36 (8.51)	2.80 (10.10)	0.39 (10.35)	4.64 (9.82)	0.5 (12.07)
Som. Anx.	3.49 (7.68)	4.05 (7.29)	4.0 (8.94)	1.63 (7.16)	7.31 (9.14)	2.03 (10.61)

4 Discussion

This study considered the normal temporal patterning of pre-competition anxiety and self-confidence as a function of skill level in wheelchair sport participants. This type of research design was advocated by Crocker (1993) who proposed that the study of individuals with a disability could both extend our current understanding of sport psychology theories, and help us to understand more about disability.

The findings for elite wheelchair sport participants' cognitive anxiety intensity supported previous theoretical predictions that cognitive anxiety intensity would remain stable during the pre-competition period (Martens et al., 1990). The non-elite wheelchair sport participants, however, did not follow the predicted temporal patterning with increases in cognitive anxiety intensity occurring from 1 week to 2 hours before competition. This is useful information for sport psychologists working with elite and non-elite wheelchair sport participants as it can help them prescribe appropriate pre-competition intervention strategies.

The present study showed no differences in the temporal patterning of somatic anxiety and self-confidence intensity as a function of skill level. However, inspection of the mean somatic anxiety intensity scores suggests that both elite and non-elite wheelchair sport participants normally experience an increase in somatic anxiety intensity as competition approaches. This supports previous theoretical predictions made for able-bodied sport participants (Martens et al., 1990). Inspection of the mean self-confidence scores suggests that both elite and non-elite wheelchair sport participants experience an increase in self-confidence from 1 week to 2 hours before competition, and then a decrease from 2 hours to 30 minutes before competition. These results do not support previous theoretical predictions of self-confidence remaining stable during pre-competition. These findings might be explained by Campbell and Jones' (in press) suggestion that individuals with a disability may not be taught a competitive orientation to life and as a consequence do not develop the personal dispositions and skills, such as competitiveness and coping strategies, to maintain self-confidence in a competitive situation. Future research should identify possible factors which may influence a disabled sport participant's ability to maintain self-confidence in a competitive situation; for example cause of disability i.e., whether an individual was born with, or acquired a disability later in life.

The results for the frequency subscale showed a difference between elite and non-elite performers' temporal patterning of cognitive anxiety frequency; no differences were found for somatic anxiety and self-confidence frequency. The elite wheelchair sport participants reported an increase in cognitive intrusions from 1 week to 2 hours before competition, whereas, the non-elite sport participants reported an increase at each time period i.e., from 1 week, to 2 hours, to 30 minutes before competition. In addition, the non-elite sport performers experienced a greater frequency of cognitive intrusions 30 minutes prior to competition, than the elite sport performers. These findings suggest that elite wheelchair sport performers are more able to control the frequency of their thoughts immediately prior to competition. The present study also shows that cognitive anxiety intensity and frequency have different pre-competition temporal patterning. This provides further evidence, with a disabled sport population, for Jones' (in press) proposal that the intensity-alone approach to competition anxiety is limited.

Finally, the results from the present study showed no difference between elite and non-elite wheelchair sport participants' temporal patterning of directional perceptions of somatic and cognitive anxiety. From inspecting the mean scores it would appear that elite performers generally perceive their cognitive and somatic anxiety symptoms to be more facilitative to performance, than the non-elite performers. However, both groups showed large within-group variation. Several recent empirical investigations (e.g., Jones et al., 1994; Jones & Swain, in press) have shown that a higher proportion of elite performers, compared to non-elite performers, view their anxiety symptoms immediately prior to competition as facilitating their forthcoming performance. Similar investigations should be carried out with wheelchair sport participants.

In summary, findings from the present study suggest that elite and non-elite wheelchair sport participants show similar pre-competition temporal patterning of somatic anxiety and self-confidence responses. However, the temporal patterning of wheelchair sport participants' cognitive anxiety intensity and frequency responses appears to be influenced by the individual's skill level. Finally, the present study suggests that future research is needed to identify and understand factors that may influence the maintenance of wheelchair sport participant's self-confidence during pre-competition.

5 References

Albrecht, R.R., & Feltz, D.L. (1987) Generality and specificity of attention to competitive anxiety and sport performance. **Journal of Sport Psychology,** 9, 231-248.

Campbell, E., & Jones, G. (1994) Psychological well-being in whelchair sport participants and nonparticipants. **Adapted Physical Activity Quarterly,** 11, 404-415.

Campbell, E. & Jones, G. (in press) Pre-competition anxiety and self-confidence in wheelchair sport participants. **Adapted Physical Activity Quarterly.**

Crocker, P.R.E. (1993) Sport and exercise psychology and research with individuals with physical   disabilities: Using theory to advance knowledge. **Adapted Physical Activity Quarterly,** 10, 324-335.

Highlen, P.S. & Bennett, B. (1979) Psychological characteristics of successful elite wrestlers: An exploratory study. **Journal of Sport Psychology,** 1, 123-137.

Jones, G. (in press) More than just a game: research developments and issues in competitive anxiety in sport. **British Journal of Psychology.**

Jones, G., & Swain, A.B.J. (1992) Intensity and direction dimensions of competitive state anxiety and relationships with competitiveness. **Perceptual and Motor Skills,** 74, 467-472.

Jones, G., & Swain, A.B.J. (in press) Predispositions to experience facilitative and debilitative anxiety in elite and non-elite performers. **The Sport Psychologist.**

Jones, G., Hanton, S., & Swain, A.B.J. (1994) Intensity and interpretations of anxiety symptoms in elite and non-elite sports performers. **Personality and Individual Differences,** 17, 657-663.

Jones, G., Swain, A.B.J., & Cale, A. (1991) Gender differences in precompetition temporal patterning and antecedents of anxiety and self-confidence. **Journal of Sport and Exercise Psychology,** 13, 1-15.

Mahoney, M.J. & Avener, M. (1977) Psychology of the elite athlete: An exploratory study. **Cognitive Therapy and Research,** 1, 135-141.

Martens, R. Burton, D., Vealey, R.S., Bump, L.A. & Smith, D.E. (1990) **Development and validation of the competitive state anxiety inventory-2 (CSAI-2).** In R. Martens, R.S. Vealey, & D. Burton (Eds.), **Competitive Anxiety in Sport.** Champaign, Illinois: Human Kinetics. pp. 117-213.

McNair, D.M., Lorr, M., & Dropplemann, L.F. (1971) **Manual for the Profile of Mood States.** San Diego: Educational and Industrial Testing Service.

Swain, A.B.J., & Jones, G. (1993) Intensity and frequency dimensions of competitive state anxiety. **Journal of Sports Sciences,** 11, 533-542.

Part Two

Environmental Factors, Ergogenic Aids and Exercise Performance

11 The travelling athlete
T. Reilly

1 Introduction

Travel is nowadays a necessary part of the habitual activity of athletes. It may entail travel overseas for purposes of competition or travel across country for domestic contests. Besides, many athletes may not reside close to good quality training facilities and may regularly have to travel by car or public transport for the purpose of training. The stresses associated with habitual travelling have been studied in 'commuters' to work but little is known about the existence of 'travel fatigue' in athletes. It is likely that any detrimental effects are compounded by subjective feelings of tiredness associated with training and by boredom.

Travel fatigue linked with long distance air-flights pose a different range of problems for athletes and team management. In general these travel stresses apply to all visitors to overseas countries. They include the procedures associated with obtaining and presenting the necessary travel documents, enough money and so on, checking in and getting through security, passport and customs screening. These stresses are common irrespective of direction or distance of travel. They can be accentuated by delay in boarding at take-off. They call for a positive psychological approach to facing these routines and overriding any negative feelings.

Travel fatigue in long-haul flights may be associated with a gradual dehydration due to ambient conditions on board. This is due to the water vapour content of the cabin air which is low in comparison with fresh air. Headaches may also be linked to a combination of low air pressure and loss of body water in the dry air within the aeroplane (de Looy et al., 1988). Diuretics such as caffeine and alcohol may compound the effect and are unsuitable for rehydration purposes. Stiffness due to spending a long time in a cramped posture can be relieved by simple stretching or isometric contractions of the muscles affected. These should help to eliminate residual stiffness at the end of the journey.

After-effects attributable to the flight itself wear off quickly once the destination is reached. Flights eastward or westward that entail travel across time-zones lead to a disturbance or the circadian body clock. This desynchronisation of biological rhythms is the cause of 'jet-lag' and one of the problems that arises may be a difficulty in sleeping.

2 Jet-Lag

Jet-lag is the name given to a group of symptoms that affect travellers in different ways and to different extents. The symptoms include: fatigue, inability to sleep at an appropriate time, loss of appetite, constipation, loss of concentration and drive, and headache. In other words they represent a general malaise. In such circumstances nobody is likely to perform at his or her best. Physical exertion will be that much more difficult, and fine skills are likely to be accomplished less well.

Jet-lag affects individuals differently, but in general:

- It is more pronounced (that is, it is more severe and lasts longer) after a flight to the east than one to the west through the same number of time-zones.
- It is more pronounced the more time-zones you cross.
- Younger and fitter people tend to suffer less than do older members of the population.

On average it will take about 1 day for every time-zone crossed to recover completely from the effects of jet-lag (Reilly and Mellor, 1988). Experience at the 1994 British Olympic Association's training camps in Tallahassee was that it took 5 days for the majority of athletes to be completely clear of jet-lag symptoms, although a few had recovered by the third day in the U.S.A. (Reilly, 1994a). The journey had entailed a 5 hour time-zone transition. It should be noted that the effects are periodic and can be more intense at particular times of the day. The athlete may be totally unaware of any adverse effects, unless he/she has to do something quickly, take decisions or perform sports skills.

Jet-lag is due to the disruption of the body's 'circadian rhythm'. This rhythm is a function of the body-clock which controls a whole host of physiological functions. It determines the cyclical rise in body temperature during the day to an evening peak and a subsequent drop to a trough in the middle of the night's sleep. It also determines the sleep-wakefulness cycle. There is a lot of research evidence to show that the body-clock also affects physiological measures that themselves influence sports performance (Reilly, 1994b). They include leg strength (Taylor et al., 1994), back strength (Coldwells et al., 1994), metabolism (Reilly and Brooks, 1982) power output (Reilly and Marshall, 1994) and self- paced exercise intensity (Atkinson et al., 1994).

Normally the body clock is in harmony with the 24 hour changes between daylight and darkness. Since the earth spins on its axis, the sun is at its maximum height above the horizon at any point on the earth's surface once in every 24-hour period. This time is called *local noon*. In order to standardise all these times, the world has been divided into 24 time-zones. The time-zone that all others are related to passes through England i.e. *Greenwich Mean Time* (GMT). Countries to the east of the U.K. have clocks that are ahead of this, because the sun rises earlier, whereas time to the west appears delayed with respect to this reference. This idea of having a local time that reflects the position of the sun in the sky is simple - but adjusting to a new local time when we fly to a new time-zone causes difficulties for our internal clock (de Looy et al., 1988).

3 Adjusting to a different time-zone

The body-clock is slow to adjust to the change in schedule that is required on travelling to a new country with its own local time. This means that, before adjustment has taken place, the athlete might be training or competing at a time when the body's signal denotes a preference to be asleep, and attempting sleep when the body-clock is directing wakefulness. It is during this period - before adjustment has taken place - that jet-lag is experienced. Once the body-clock has adjusted, jet-lag does not return - until the next journey across time-zones (usually on the return trip home).

Full adjustment of the body-clock takes several days, as already explained. The aim must be to speed up this process of adjustment as much and as safely as possible. Only when fully adjusted to the new time-zone can performance be at its peak. This applies to training as well as to competition. Until that time, it will be more difficult for an individual to produce maximal effort. While adjustment is taking place, the shape of the normal rhythm is changed. It becomes flatter (has a lower amplitude, a lower peak value and a lower average value (Reilly et al., 1995).

The body-clock is a poor time-keeper. Left to itself, it would run slow, with a period of 25 to 27 hours rather than the 24-hour day which is required in order to stay in time with the alternation of light and dark. (Minors and Waterhouse, 1981). Under normal circumstances, the body-clock is adjusted in the same way as a watch that keeps poor time - by external signals. There are several signals that adjust the circadian rhythms, and making use of them helps the body to adjust to time-zone transitions. **The main ones are:**

- The pattern of sleep and activity (including exercise).
- The timing and type of meals.
- Exposure to social influences and the alternation of natural daylight and darkness in the environment.
- Exposure to ultraviolet light, generally by receiving direct sunlight out of doors.

One manoeuvre frequently adopted by athletes prior to flying overseas in a westward direction is to go to bed 1-2 hours later than normal each night and get up 1-2 hours later each morning. This might not always be possible, but its main benefit is to promote thinking ahead about times in the country of destination. It is not useful to try to adjust fully to the time-zone transition before the journey, since this will interrupt training schedules and lifestyle too much and will not adjust the body-clock very much (Reilly and Maskell, 1989). This applies to both a phase delay (getting to sleep later) or a phase advance (getting to bed earlier). Where there is a choice of flight times and airports, the athlete should select a schedule that makes planning to adjust all the easier. This would consist of a flight that gets the traveller to the U.S.A. destination in the evening, for example. Of course, the ideal travel schedule is seldom available but at least alternatives that are on offer can be consulted.

4 The use of drugs to offset jet-lag and sleep-loss

Travellers often read about pills and other treatments that are purported to promote adjustment to a new time-zone or to reduce the effects of jet-lag. In addition, some travellers make considerable use of sleeping pills (particularly some short-acting benzodiazepines). Apart from any rules that might govern their use by athletes, these drugs have not been tested extensively for any side-effects they might have upon maximum performance in top-class athletes, sportsmen or sportswomen (Reilly et al., 1995).

Although there might be a role for drugs known as hypnotics in promoting sleep during the nights immediately after a flight, their use is more appropriate for non-athletes. Besides they should only be used in exceptional cases and under prescription of the sports medicine advisor to the squad. It is suggested they should not be used for at least four days prior to the competition.

It is unlikely that sleep loss itself will have a major deleterious effect on exercise and performance. In normal conditions the effects of substantial sleep disturbances are more pronounced on complex tasks than on gross measures such as muscle strength (Reilly and Piercy, 1994). Indeed the circadian variation in performances such as all-out swims is greater than that induced by partial deprivation over sleep three consecutive nights (Sinnerton and Reilly, 1991). Difficulties in sleeping after crossing multiple time-zones are self-correcting after a few nights but disturbances may last longer than this following eastward flights.

It is thought that the manipulation of sleep substances may help to accelerate the adjustment to a new time-zone. Tryptophan, for example, is a precursor of sleep hormones but there is no convincing evidence that it ensures quality sleep. Administration of melatonin (a pineal gland hormone) has also been advocated (Arendt et al., 1987) but there are still potential problems with recommending its use by athletes.

Diuretics (caffeine, alcohol) should be avoided in the evening since they may disrupt sleep. Caffeine would have a role to play in elevating arousal levels early in the day. The timing and type of meals are also influential in resynchronising the body clock and it is important for the individual to fit into the pattern of meal times according to the new locality as quickly as possible.

5 Overview

It is essential that circadian rhythms are taken into account when travelling across multiple time-zones to compete in sports. Performance can be adversely affected even when flights are within one country, coast to coast in U.S.A. and Australia for example. In such instances it can be beneficial to adapt normal training times in advance of the trip to suit the time scheduled for competition (Jehue et al., 1993). It seems that exercise itself provides a strong signal to the body clock to aid the process of resynchronisation to the new time zone. Whilst jet-lag symptoms persist, even if only periodically during the day, it is recommended that exercise training is light in intensity and low in possibilities of physical contact where accidents and injuries might occur.

6 References

Arendt, J, Aldhous, M., English, J, Marks, J, Arendt, J.H., Marks, M and Folkard, S. (1987) Some effects of jet-lag and their amelioration by melatonin. **Ergonomics**, 30, 1375-1354

Atkinson, G. Coldwells, A, Reilly, T and Waterhouse, J, (1994) The influence of age on diurnal variations in competitive cycling performance **Journal of Sports Sciences**, 12, 127-128.

Coldwells, A, Atkinson, G., and Reilly, T. (1994) Sources of variation is back and leg dynamometry. **Ergonomics**, 37, 79-86.

de Looy, A., Minors, D.S., Waterhouse, J. Reilly, T, and Tunstall-Pedoe, D. (1988). **A Coach's Guide to Competing Abroad.** National Coaching Foundation, Leeds.

Jehue, R., Street, D, and Huizenga, R. (1993). Effects of time-zone and game time changes on team performance; National Football League. **Medicine and Science in Sports and Exercise**, 25, 127-131.

Minors, D.S. and Waterhouse, J. (1981) **Circadian Rhythms and the Human.** John Wright, Bristol.

Reilly, T. (1994a) Body clock and lifestyle disturbances, **in Proceedings. British Olympic Association International Conference The Travelling Athlete's Environment,** British Olympic Association, London, pp 40-48.

Reilly, T. (1994b) Circadian rhythms, in **Oxford Textbook of Sports Medicine** (eds, M. Harries, C. Williams, W.D. Stanish and L.J. Micheli,) Oxford University Press, Oxford, pp. 238-254.

Reilly, T. and Brooks, G.A. (1982) Investigation of circadian rhythms in metabolic responses to exercise. **Ergonomics**, 25, 1093-1107.

Reilly, T. and Maskell, P, (1989) Effects of altering the sleep-wake cycle on human circadian rhythms and motor performance in **Proceedings First 1OC Congress on Sports Sciences** (Colorado Springs), pp. 106-107.

Reilly, T. and Mellor, S. (1988) Jet lag studies on Rugby League players following a near-maximal time-zone, in **Science and Football** (eds T.Reilly, A.Lees, K. Davids, W. Murphy). E and F.N. Spon, London, pp. 249-256.

Reilly, T and Piercy, M. (1994) The effect of partial sleep deprivation on weight-lifting performance. **Ergonomics**, 37, 107,-115.

Reilly, T., Atkinson, G. and Waterhouse, J. (1995) **Biological Rhythms and Exercise**. Oxford University Press, Oxford.

Sinnerton, S and Reilly, T (1992) Effects of sleep loss and time of day in swimmers, in **Biomechanics and Medicine in Swimming: Swimming Science VI**. (eds, D. McLaren, T. Reilly, and A.Lees) E and F.N. Spon, London, pp.399-405.

12 Training and exercise at high altitudes
B.D. Levine

1 Introduction

High altitude presents a unique challenge to athletic
competiton. Athletes must cope with hypoxia, cold, and
dehydration, yet still maintain maximal performance. The
timing of altitude exposure and the degree of
acclimatization are also critical to a successful outcome.
This physiological adaptation to high altitude may in fact
be beneficial, and altitude training is frequently used by
elite athletes to improve sea level performance. However
the objective benefits of altitude training and the optimal
strategy of how high to live or train are controversial
(Levine 1992). On one hand, acclimatization to high
altitude results in central and peripheral adaptations
which improve oxygen delivery and utilization. Moreover,
hypoxic exercise may increase the training stimulus thus
magnifying the effects of endurance training. Conversely,
hypoxia at altitude limits training intensity, which in
elite athletes may result in relative deconditioning. The
added stress of training under hypoxic conditions may also
increase the risk of overtraining. We have therefore
proposed that **living at altitude but training near sea
level** will result in acclimatization without detraining,
thereby improving sea level performance (Levine 1991).

2 Physical Features of a High Altitude Environment

At high altitude, barometric pressure is reduced, with a
parallel decrease in the inspired partial pressure of
oxygen (PIO_2); by 5,500m (18,000 ft.), the atmospheric
pressure is reduced to one-half its sea level value and the
PIO_2 is only 75mmHg (figure 1). **Hypobaric hypoxia is thus
the most prominent physiological manifestation of high
altitude** (Hackett 1989). Temperature also decreases with
altitude at a rate of approximately $6.5^{\circ}C/1,000m$. Other
features include dry air (increasing the risk of
dehydration), a decrease in air density and therefore air

resistance, and an increase in the amount of ultraviolet light (4%/300 m) which increases the risk of sunburn.

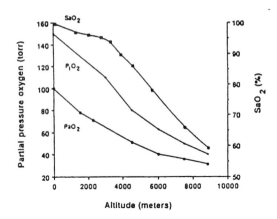

Altitude (meters)

Figure 1: The relationship between altitude, inspired partial pressure of oxygen (PIO$_2$) and its associated effect on arterial partial pressure of oxygen (PaO$_2$) and oxyhaemoglobin saturation (SaO$_2$). Note progressive fall in inspired-arterial gradient for oxygen with increasing altitude, presumably due to hyperventilation and decreases in the atmospheric-alveolar gradient for oxygen. Saturation is well maintained at rest up to 3,000 m, but falls acutely during exercise because of diffusion limitation in the lung (not shown). Adapted from Hackett et al, (1989) with permission.

3 The Effect of High Altitude On Exercise at Altitude

Altitude induced hypoxia reduces the amount of oxygen available to do physical work. Maximal aerobic power ($\dot{V}O_2$ max) is reduced by approximately 1% for every 100 m above 1500 m in normal individuals (Buskirk, 1966). For well-trained athletes, this effect is even greater, and reductions in VO$_2$max and performance can be identified at altitudes as low as 500 m (Terrados, 1985, Squires, 1982). Moreover, during exercise at high altitude, ventilation is greater for any given submaximal workrate, as is blood lactate concentration, which increase the sensation of dyspnea and fatigue. However **peak** blood lactate concentration is **lower** in individuals acclimatized to high altitude, a condition which has been termed "the lactate paradox" (Reeves, 1992)

In order to help understand the effect of altitude on exercise performance, it is useful to consider the "oxygen cascade," which describes the steps through which oxygen must pass (Sutton, 1988): from the **environment** (determined by altitude achieved), into the **alveoli** (a function of ventilation and therefore the hypoxic ventilatory response), across the **pulmonary capillary** (limited by diffusion), to be transported by the **cardiovascular system** (a function of cardiac output and haemoglobin concentration) and eventually diffused into **skeletal muscle** (dependent on muscle capillarity and biochemical state) to be used by muscle **mitochondria** (influenced by oxidative enzyme activity) for aerobic respiration and ATP production (Figure 2).

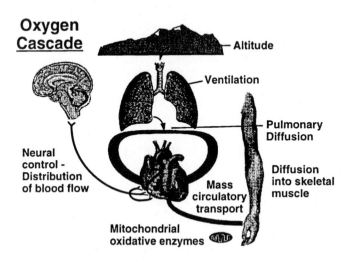

Figure 2: The "Oxygen Cascade" depicting the pathway of oxygen transfer from the environment to skeletal muscle mitochondria.

The reduction in $\dot{V}O_2$max at altitude likely occurs because of diffusion limitation in both the lung and skeletal muscle during exercise (Torre-Bueno, 1985, Wagner, 1993), both of which are exacerbated by the high pulmonary and systemic blood flow (cardiac output) of endurance athletes (Figure 3).

Altitude affects endurance athletes and sprinters in different ways (Peronnet, 1991). For endurance events lasting longer than about 1-2 minutes, performance is significantly impaired at altitude because of the hypoxia induced reduction in aerobic power. However for short, sprint events (400 m or less), most of the ATP required for muscular contraction of fast twitch fibers comes from glycolytic metabolism which is not dependent on oxygen transport. The reduced air resistance at altitude thus actually improves sprint performance. That is why, for example, all the times in events shorter than 400 m in the Mexico City Olympics (altitude 2,100 m) in, 1968 were very fast, and many world records were set. However all events longer than 1,500 m were substantially slower than sea level times.

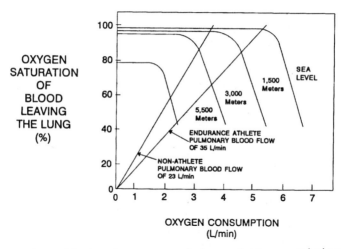

Figure 3: The effect of oxygen uptake and the requisite pulmonary blood flow (cardiac output) on oxygen saturation of blood leaving the lungs at different altitudes. For an untrained individual with a V̇O₂max of 3.5 l/min and a peak pulmonary blood flow of 23 l/min, blood is well saturated at sea level and altitudes up to 5,000 ft (1,500 m) at peak exercise; but becomes progressively less saturated with exercise at increasing altitude. For an endurance athlete however, who may have a VO₂max of 5 l/min and a peak pulmonary blood flow of 35 l/min, diffusing capacity is closely matched to oxygen uptake and there is diffusion limitation even at altitudes between sea level and 5,000 ft. This phenomenon likely occurs because there is much more plasticity in the capacity of the cardiovascular system to respond to training, compared to the lung where diffusing capacity is relatively constant. Adapted and modified from RL Johnson, Pulmonary diffusion as a limiting factor in exercise, Circ Res (Suppl 1) 20:I154-I160,, 1967.

4 The Acclimatization Process

Chronic exposure to altitude stimulates the process of acclimatization, which includes a number of physiological adaptations that improve **submaximal** work performance at altitude (Maher, 1974). These adaptations may affect oxygen transport along each step of the oxygen cascade. Increases in alveolar ventilation and reductions in mixed venous oxygen content are critical adaptations for maximizing exercise capacity at altitude (Sutton, 1988). During exercise at extreme altitude (i.e., Himalayan mountaineers), chemoreceptor sensitivity, manifested as the hypoxic ventilatory response may be one of the most important characteristics allowing work under conditions of severe hypoxia (Schoene, 1984). Oxygen carrying capacity of the blood also increases due to an increase in haemoglobin and hematocrit (Hansen, 1967, Hannon, 1969) thereby

improving aerobic power (Buick, 1980, Kanstrup, 1984).
Moreover, peripheral uptake of oxygen by skeletal muscle
may be facilitated by increased capillary density (Tenney,
1970, Banchero, 1975), mitochondrial number (Ou, 1970),
and tissue myoglobin concentration (Reynafarje, 1975,
Terrados, 1990), as well as by increased concentrations of
2,3-DPG (Mairburl, 1986). Buffer capacity of skeletal
muscle is also increased which may improve anaerobic
capacity and endurance Mizuno, 1991). Finally, substrate
utilization is enhanced by increasing mobilization of free
fatty acids and increasing utilization of blood glucose
thus sparing muscle glycogen (Young, 1982, Brooks, 1991).
This results in decreased metabolite accumulation such as
lactate (Young, 1982) or ammonia (Young, 1987) during
submaximal exercise. Although submaximal exercise capacity
increases markedly with acclimatization, this effect is
less dramatic with maximal exercise. At higher altitudes
(4,000 m and above) $\dot{V}O_2$ max never returns to sea level
values despite prolonged acclimatization (Saltin, 1968).
However at altitudes below 2,500 m maximal oxygen uptake
may approach sea level values after 1-2 weeks of
acclimatization, at least in non-athletic populations
(Mairburl, 1986).

The ventilatory changes begin immediately upon
exposure to the hypoxic environment and continue to
increase over the first few days at altitude. This
hyperventilation causes a respiratory alkalosis which
stimulates renal excretion of bicarbonate over the first
week to normalize acid-base balance. The sympathetic
nervous system is activated acutely with increases in
sympathetic nerve activity (Saito, 1988) and arterial
concentrations of adrenaline (Mazzeo, 1991). This results
in an increase in heart rate and cardiac output so that
tissue oxygen delivery remains nearly constant with sea
level values (Vogel, 1974, Woelfel, 1993). By 2-3 weeks,
systemic and regional blood flow have returned towards sea
level values as oxygenation improves (Bender, 1988).

Haematocrit and haemoglobin concentration increase
within 24-48 hours, because of a reduction in plasma volume
rather than an increase in red cell mass. Erythropoietin
begins to increase within the first few hours of hypoxia,
and peaks by approximately 48 hours (Berglund, 1992).
Erythropoietin levels remain elevated only for 7-8 days at
altitude despite continued exposure, and red cell mass
increases slowly in a time dependent fashion (Berglund,
1992). It may take as long as 1-2 years of continued
altitude exposure for sea level natives to acquire the same
red blood cell mass as high altitude natives at the same
altitude. Most of the metabolic changes appear to be
complete by 2-3 weeks of altitude exposure. The
ultrastructural changes in capillary density, mitochondrial
number and muscle fibre size probably take a number of
weeks to become complete.

There is abundant evidence that for competitions at altitude this acclimatization process is critical and clearly improves performance **at altitude.** Therefore if possible, adequate time for acclimatization should be allowed to maximize performance at altitude. Most of the short-term benefits of acclimatization are obtained after 2-3 weeks which for a competition at altitude, should allow maximal acclimatization while at the same time minimizing the detraining that may occur during training at altitude. Some athletes and coaches believe that if adequate time for acclimatization is not possible, then competing immediately upon arrival at altitude may be best. However this hypothesis has not been rigorously tested.

Recreational athletes who hike, climb, or mountain bike but aren't interested in athletic competition are also affected by the hypoxia of altitude. For non-endurance trained individuals who plan to perform exercise at altitude, exercise training at sea level provides important advantages. In fact, endurance and maximal aerobic power at altitude will improve to the same extent as endurance and maximal aerobic power at sea level from a training programme at sea level in untrained subjects (Levine, 1990).

5 Failure of Acclimatization - High Altitude Illness and Overtraining

With higher altitudes (> 2,500 m) and rapid ascent rates (> 300 m sleeping altitude/day above 3,000 m), a maladaptive state may develop called acute mountain sickness (AMS), characterized by headache, nausea, anorexia, fatigue, and difficulty sleeping (Hackett, 1989). Fortunately, this process is usually mild and self-limited; in such cases, rest and analgesics are sufficient treatment. There is no evidence that competitive athletes are at any greater risk of developing AMS than non-athletes, though exercise may exacerbate the development of AMS and should be reduced appropriately in symptomatic individuals. For patients who do not improve with rest, the addition of supplemental oxygen or descent to a lower altitude virtually always results in prompt symptom relief. Other effective treatments include acetazolamide, dexamethasone, and simulated descent using a portable hyperbaric bag. The problem is best prevented by limiting the rate of ascent, allowing for rest or acclimatization days, maintaining adequate hydration, avoiding alcohol or sedatives during the early acclimatization phase, and particularly limiting training volume and intensity during the first few days at altitude. The use of drugs to prevent AMS is discouraged in endurance athletes who are going to moderate altitude (below 3,000 m) unless a clear history of recurrent AMS is obtained.

In some indivuduals, AMS may progress to a more severe and life-threatening form, including high altitude pulmonary (HAPE) or cerebral (HACE) oedema. The characteristics of are dyspnoea at rest, cyanosis, severe hypoxaemia, and noncardiogenic pulmonary oedema. The signs and symptoms of HACE include vomiting, ataxia, a reduction in the level of consciousness, and in some cases, frank coma. Both of these syndromes can quickly result in death unless immediate descent occurs. Fortunately, both HAPE and HACE are very rare at the relatively low altitudes to which most athletes are exposed.

Another potential serious problem with training at altitude is the apparent increased risk of overtraining (Marinelli, 1994). It is helpful to make the analogy between exercise training and the pharmacological administration of a medication (Figure 4). Any medication has a specific dose-response relationship, accompanied by a toxic/therapeutic range. These parameters define the optimal dose and frequency of administration to maximize benefit but minimize side-effects and toxicity. Exercise can be considered as a "medication," with a training response that is proportional to volume and intensity, but a clear toxic effect of too much exercise characterized by musculoskeletal injury and the systemic effects of overtraining.

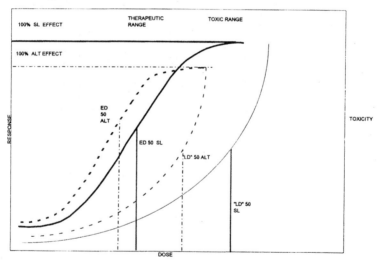

Figure 4: The "dose-response" (bold lines) and "toxic-therapeutic range" (thin lines) of exercise training at sea level (solid lines) and altitude (broken lines). With altitude training, there is a reduction in the maximal response possible due to the reduction in training volume and intensity. There is likely to be an increase in the response for any absolute dose due to the increase in metabolic stress at any given workrate. However there is also an increase in the risk of overtraining, thus narrowing the toxic-therapeutic range.

Although the **mechanical** stress of exercise is likely to be less at altitude due to the reduction in training speed (Table 1), the **metabolic** stress may well be greater, at least with regard to the effect of hypoxia and the central nervous system. The magnitude of systemic hypoxemia during usual exercise training at moderate altitude has recently been shown to be much more severe than previously expected with arterial oxyhaemoglobin saturations of less than 80% during base training at 2,700 m (Harper, 1995). Thus exercise training at altitude may narrow the toxic/thereputic range of exercise, **possibly** enhancing the training effect (discussed below) but also increasing the risk of toxicity. Becuase the aetiology of overtraining is as yet poorly defined, this hypothesis is difficult to test, but it is a universal caution of athletes, coaches and scientists experienced with altitude traing (personal communication, United States Olympic Committee High Performance Summit, October, 1994), that overtraining may be increased at altitude.

Table 1 Training Workloads and Intensity Associated with Base and Interval Training at Altitudes of 2,700 and 1,200 m*

	Base Training		Interval Training	
	2,700 m	1,200 m	2,700 m	1,200 m
Percent of sea level 5 km speed	70.2 ± 2.0	80.9 ± 1.6†	98.1 ± 2.3	103.1 ± 1.1‡
Percent of sea level $\dot{V}O_2$max	62.5 ± 2.5	70.7 ± 2.4	82.5 ± 1.8	88.5 ± 0.8†
Heart rate (beats/min)	160 ± 4	163 ± 2	171 ± 2	181 ± 2†
Lactate (mmol/L)	4.1 ± 0.5	2.0 ± 0.3†	9.3 ± 0.8	11.9 ± 0.8†

*$\dot{V}O_2$max was measured in the laboratory at sea level (SL, 150 m) in 19 competitive distance runners. Average sea level velocity over a 5 km distance was derived from a time trial on the track. In the field at high altitude (2,700 m, n = 9) or near sea level (1,200 m, n = 10), a lightweight (800 g) device was used that contains a turbine flow meter and polarographic electrode to measure $\dot{V} O_2$, and that does not impede running performance (Cosmed K2). Heart rate (telemetry), capillary blood lactate concentration (membrane diffusion), and running speed were also measured during base and interval training; means ± SE.

†p < 0.05 compared to 2,700 m.
‡p < 0.06 compared to 2,800 m.
Data from Levine and Stray-Gundersen (1992)

6 The Effect of High Altitude on Exercise Performance at Sea Level

The physiological benefits of altitude training for endurance exercise at sea level must derive either from the development of acclimatization, an enhancement of the training effect by hypoxic exercise or both (Levine, 1992). These beneficial effects must be compared with the detrimental effects of altitude training, including a reduction in training intensity, and an increased risk of "overtraining." The ultimate outcome of training at altitude is a balance between these positive and negative factors which may be different in individual athletes at different stages of their training programme.

The positive advantages of acclimatization have been well described above. Whether hypoxic exercise per se also provides an enhancement of the training effect during altitude training is controversial, and probably depends on both the mode and the intensity of training. When a small enough muscle mass is used (i.e., one leg) so that the same absolute workrates can be performed under hypoxic and normoxic conditions, hypobaric hypoxic exercise results in greater increases in endurance, accompanied by greater increases in oxidative enzyme capacity than normoxic exercise training (Terrados, 1990). Although one animal study using swimming rats suggested that the same synergistic effect between exercise and hypoxia can be observed in whole-body exercise (Bigard, 1992), this has been difficult to prove in humans (Roskamm, 1969, Bannister, 1978, Terrados, 1988, Levine, 1990, Levine, 1993). This response may be due to a greater metabolic stimulus under hypoxic conditions, as long as the mechanical stimulus to synthesis of contractile proteins is maintained. It is intriguing to note that at least from the perspective of skeletal muscle, in certain models of prolonged and sustained stimulation (chronic electrical stimulation) there can be dramatic increases in muscle mitochondria, capillary density and oxidative enzyme capacity. In some studies, 3 weeks of electrical stimulation can transform skeletal muscle into a infatiguable state nearly equivalent to cardiac muscle (Michael, 1994). Such observations argue for the concept that there may be a continuous linear increase in muscle adaptation with increased metabolic stress. In general, controlled studies employing trained athletes have not been able to confirm a benefit of hypoxic exercise without concomittant acclimatization.

Many scientists, athletes and coaches have been intrigued by the similarities between altitude acclimatization and endurance training (Grover, 1986). Numerous reports since the 1940's have suggested that endurance athletes may achieve some benefit from altitude training for sea level performance (Balke, 1964, Balke,

1965, Dill, 1971, Daniels, 1975). The ultimate result has depended on the type of athlete studied, the altitude achieved, and the methods of testing and training, with runners improving more than swimmers, and athletes training at lower altitudes improving more than higher altitudes (over 4,000 m) (Faulkner, 1967,, 1968, Buskirk, 1967). Moreover studies that examine only maximal oxygen uptake as an index of performance may miss important adaptations such as changes in substrate utilization (Young, 1982, Brooks, 1991) or buffering capacity of skeletal muscle (Mizuno, 1990) that may improve anaerobic capacity and athletic performance after altitude training. When appropriate control groups have been included, living and training at altitude has not been proven to be superior to similar training at sea level (Adams, 1975, Levine, 1991).

7 Alternative Strategies - "Living High-Training Low"

Over the last 5 years, the Dallas group has been intensively involved in an effort to define the optimal utilization of altitude training (Levine, 1991, 1992, 1993, 1995), Stray-Gundersen, 1992, 1993, 1994, 1995, Stine, 1992; Schultz, 1994; Harper, 1995). With support from the United States Olympic Committee, we have studied 60 collegiate and post-collegiate runners (44 males, 16 females) using the following paradigms: living at altitude (2,500 m) - training at altitude (2,500-2,800 m), n=15; living at altitude (2,500 m) - training **near** sea level (1,250 m), n=23; living **near** sea level (1,250 m) - training **near** sea level (1,250 m), n=10; living **at** sea level (150 m) - training **at** sea level (150 m), n=6; and living **at** sea level (150 m) - training at altitude (2,500 m in a hypobaric chamber), n=6. This experience has led us to 4 primary interim conclusions:

(a) **Athletes train faster, and at greater aerobic power near sea level than at altitude** (Stine, 1992, Levine, 1992). Our studies represent the first time that actual training intensities for base and interval work have been quantified in the field at altitude. During high intensity, interval type workouts, running speed, oxygen uptake, heart rate and lactate are all lower at altitude, suggesting that **interval workouts are best performed as close to sea level as possible.** During base training, running speed and oxygen uptake are lower at altitude, but heart rate is the same as at sea level, and submaximal lactate is slightly higher. The best altitude for base training is thus still unclear

(b) **Supervised training, regardless of at what altitude the athlete lives or trains (between sea level and 2,800 m), results in an increase in VO$_2$max, an improvement in 5,000 m time, and a reduction in submaximal heart rate

and lactate.   A training camp has the advantage of carefully supervising training and nutrition, treating injuries quickly and appropriately, and removing the athlete from the stresses of every day life that may distract from training.   Even in world class, elite athletes, supervised training may result in significant improvements in performance (Telford, 1994, personal communication). This factor may be very important in the improvement seen in uncontrolled studies, and must therefore be controlled in any study of altitude training. A recent small pilot study demonstrated that most of the effect of supervised training can be identified within 2 weeks of sea level training (Stray-Gundersen, 1993).

(c) **Nutritional factors, particularly iron stores, play a critical role in the ability to respond to altitude training** (Stray-Gundersen, 1993,1995, Schultz, 1994).   In our early studies, 12 of 41 (7 females, 5 males) were found to have reduced iron stores based on a low serum ferritin level.   The athletes with low ferritin levels prior to altitude exposure (male and female) were unable to increase the volume of red cell mass (blood volume minus plasma volume) and did not increase $\dot{V}O_{2max}$.   Since iron is also a critical moiety in myoglobin, as well as mitochondrial cytochromes, iron deficiency may not only compromise oxygen carrying capacity, but may also inhibit oxygen extraction (a-v O_2 difference) and reduce O_2 flux, thereby limiting $\dot{V}O_2max$ and performance, even in non-anemic athletes.   Thus iron stores must be normalized before undertaking a period of altitude training.   We have recently demonstrated that high doses of oral iron (200-600 mg elemental iron/day in divided doses),which is usually best tolerated in liquid, paediatric preparation (Feosol, 1 tbsp, 1-3x/day), can successfully support erythropoiesis during altitude training (Schultz, 1994, Stray-Gundersen, 1995).

(d) **Living at altitude but training near sea level is the only modality we studied that increased total blood volume, without the usual plasma volume contraction seen during altitude acclimatization.**   This observation may be due to changes in aldosterone, ADH, and the renin-angiotensin system at altitude that appear to be normalized by intermittent periods of normoxia (Withey, 1983, Milledge, 1983).   It also may include a component of heat acclimatization that can be maintained when training is performed in a warm environment.

8 Practical Strategies for Implementing Altitude Training

From a practical perspective, the critical question to answer for athletes and coaches is what is the appropriate "dose" of altitude and training? Specific issues include: 1) how high to live and how long to reside at altitude; 2)

how high to train, and what kind of training is best; and
3) when to compete upon return to sea level? Adaptation to
altitude depends on oxygen delivery to peripheral tissues
which decreases linearly with oxyhaemoglobin saturation.
Thus red cell mass does not appear to increase in men until
PaO_2 decreases below approximately 65 mmHg, when saturation
begins to fall (Weil, 1968). Similar data are not
available for women. For most individuals, this "threshold
altitude" is approximately 2,200 - 2,500 m, though some
small changes have been reported in endurance athletes at
altitudes as low as 1,250 m (Stray-Gundersen, 1993). Above
2,500 m such adaptations are likely to be greater with
increasing altitude unless acute mountain sickness
intervenes or marked hypoxia (above 4,000 m) results in a
catabolic state characterized by weight loss with reduction
in muscle mass. An altitude of 2,500-2,800 m thus appears
optimal to maximize acclimatization and minimize
complications. At least 2 weeks, and preferably 4 weeks
are necessary to obtain a significant acclimatization
response.

As far as training is concerned, high intensity,
interval workouts should be conducted as close to sea level
as possible, preferably below 1500 m, to maximize running
speed and training intensity. The appropriate altitude at
which to conduct base training is less clear. Base
training near sea level will allow relatively normal
training intensity and may prevent the loss of plasma
volume that often accompanies altitude acclimatization. In
contrast, base training at altitude, as long as it occurs
at a low enough altitude to maintain similar running speeds
and absolute workrates as at sea level, may facilitate an
increase in mitochondrial oxidative enzyme activities and
maximize peripheral oxygen utilization. This strategy
however carries a significant risk of precipitating
overtraining. It is important to emphasize that altitude
training is not a substitute for a focused, well designed
training programme with appropriate rest and nutrition. A
sample altitude training schedule based on a 4 week
mesocycle, emphasizing low intensity, base work during the
first week with progressive increases in volume and
intensity is provided in (table 2). Many other strategies
are employed by athletes and coaches based on experience
(Dick, 1992).

Table 2   Sample Schedule of Altitude Training
Based on 4 week "Mesocycle"*

Week 2 (Medium Week)	Week 1 (Acclimatization Week 2,200 m - 2,500 m)
Mon. Base training	
Tues. 8 x 600 m 105% 5 K race pace PM recovery run	Mon. Base training Tues. Base training PM base training
Wed. Base training	Wed. Base training
Thurs. Base training	Thurs. Base training
Fri. Easy run	Fri. Base training
Sat. 5 K road race PM recovery run	Sat. Base training (or off)
Sun. Base training	Sun. Long run
2/0/9	0/1/8 (#hard/#long/ #total workouts)
Week 4 (Easy Week)	**Week 3 (Hard Week)**
Mon. Easy run	Mon. Long run PM recovery run
Tues. 8 x 600 m 105% 5 K race pace PM recovery run	Tues. Base training Wed. 5 x 1,000 m 105% 5 K race pace PM recovery run diet log
Wed. Base training	
Thurs. Base training	Thurs. Base training PM base training
Fri. Base training	Fri. Base training PM 10 x 200 m 110% 5 K race pace
Sat. Off	Sat. Base training
Sun. Long run	Sun. Long run
1/1/7	2/2/11

*This schedule presumes that athletes begin a period of
altitude training with substantial base training that
includes regular interval workouts. They must also have
normal iron stores. Many other strategies for altitude
training exist that include shorter but repetitive cycles
(see Dick, 1992).

A final critical question is what is the appropriate
timing for competition after a period of altitude training?
Many athletes and coaches believe that the best
performances are delivered 2-3 weeks after returning from
altitude (Dick, 1992), though this belief is not universal.
This observation may be related to alterations in skeletal
muscle acid-base balance that are changing rapidly after
return from altitude. Alternatively, it may be necessary
to have a period of normoxic training to maximize
neuromotor coordination, particularly if all interval
workouts have been performed under the slower training

conditions of high altitude. When living and training occur at altitude, this empirical observation may well be true. However, when sufficient high intensity workouts are performed at low altitude to maintain foot speed and therefore neuromuscular coordination, the best time for a competition may well be immediately upon return from altitude, when the acclimatization is maximal. In fact we have observed that for athletes who "live-high and train-low", 5,000 m time, and maximal aerobic power are greatest in the first few days after return to sea level (Stray-Gundersen, 1994,, 1995).

9 Acknowledgements

Virtually all the work on altitude training by the Dallas group presented in this paper and conference was performed in collaboration with James Stray-Gundersen, M.D., Director of the Baylor/UT Southwestern Sports Science Research Center, and has been a joint intellectual and logistical effort. This paper was adapted (with permission) to a large extent from Levine BD and Stray-Gundersen (1995).

References

Adams, W.C., Bernauer, E.M., Dill, D.B., Bomar, J.B. (1975) Effects of equivalent sea-level and altitude training on VO$_2$max and running performance. Journal of Applied Physiology 39(2):262-265.

Balke, B. (1964) Work capacity and its limiting factors at high altitude. *in* **Physiological Effects at High Altitude**, WH Weihe, ed, New York, NY, MacMillan; p. 233-240.

Balke B, Nagle FJ, Daniels JT (1965) Altitude and maximum performance in work and sports activity. Journal of the American Medical Association 194(6):176-179.

Banchero N (1975) Capillary density of skeletal muscle in dogs exposed to simulated altitude. Proceedings of the Society of Experimental Biology and Medicine 148:435-439.

Bannister EW, W Woo (1978) Effects of simulated altitude training on aerobic and anaerobic power. European Journal of Applied Physiology 38:55-69.

Berglund B (1992) High-altitude training, aspects of haematological adaptation. Sports Medicine, 14:289-303.

Bigard AX, A Brunet, CY Guezennec, H Monod (1991) Skeletal muscle changes after endurance training at high altitude. Journal of Applied Physiology 71:2114-2121.

Brooks GA, GA Butterfield, RR Wolfe, BM Groves, RS Mazzeo, JR Sutton, EE Wolfel, JT Reeves (1991) Increased dependence on blood glucose after acclimatization to 4,300 m. Journal of Applied Physiology 70:919-927.

Buick FJ, Gledhill N, Froese AB, Spriet L, Meyers EC (1980)
Effect of induced erythrocythemia on aerobic work
capacity. Journal of Applied Physiology 48(4):636-642.

Buskirk ER (1966) Physiology and performance of track
athletes at various altitudes in the United States and
Peru. *in* **The Effects of Altitude on Physical
Performance**, RF Goddard, ed.   Chicago, IL: Athletic
Inst; pp 65-72.

Buskirk ER, Kollias J, Akers RF, Prokop EK, Reategui EP
(1967) Maximal performance at altitude and return from
altitude in conditioned runners. Journal of Applied
Physiology 23(2):259-266.

Daniels J, N Oldridge (1975) The effects of alternate
exposure to altitude and sea level on world-class
middle distance runners. Medicine and Science in Sports
and Exercise 2:107-112.

Dick FW (1992) Training at altitude in practice.
International Journal of Sports Medicine 13 (Suppl
1):S203-206.

Dill DB, Adams WC (1971) Maximal oxygen uptake at sea
level and at 3,090-m altitude in high school champion
runners. Journal of Applied Physiology 30(6):854-859.

Ekblom B, Goldbarg AN, Gullbring B (1972) Response to
exercise after blood loss and reinfusion. Journal of
Applied Physiology 33(2):175-180.

Faulkner JA, Daniels JT, Balke B (1967) Effects of
training at moderate altitude on physical performance
capacity. Journal of Applied Physiology 23(1):85-89.

Faulkner JA, Kollias J, Favour CB, Buskirk ER, Balke B
(1968) Maximum aerobic capacity and running
performance at altitude. Journal of Applied Physiology
24(5):685-691.

Green HJ, JR Sutton, A Cymerman, PM Young, CS Houston
(1989) Operation Everest II: adaptations in human
skeletal muscle. J Appl Physiol 66:2454-2461.

Grover RF, JV Weil, JT Reeves (1986) Cardiovascular
adaptation to exercise at high altitude. Exercise and
Sport Science Reviews 14:269-302.

Hackett PH, RC Roach, JR Sutton (1989) High altitude
medicine, *in* **Management of Wilderness and Environmental
Emergencies**, PS Auerbach and EC Gehr, eds, CV Mosby,
St. Louis, p. 1-34.

Hannon JP, JL Shields, CW Harris (1969) Effects of
altitude acclimatization on blood composition of women.
Journal of Neurophysioly 26:540-547.

Hansen JR, JA Vogel, GP Stelter, CF Consolazio (1967)
Oxygen uptake in man during exhaustive work at sea
level and high altitude. Journal of Applied Physiology
26:511-522.

Harper KM, J Stray-Gundersen, MB Schecter, BD Levine (1995)
Training at moderate altitude causes profound hypoxemia
during exercise in competitive runners, Medicine and
Science in Sports and Exercise 27:S00, *in press.*

Kanstrup IL, B Ekblom (1984) Blood volume and haemoglobin concentration as determinants of maximal aerobic power. Medicine and Science in Sports and Exercise 16:256-262.

Levine BD, K Engfred, DB Friedman, M Kjaer, B Saltin, P Clifford, NH Secher (1990) High altitude endurance training: effect on aerobic capacity and work performance. Medicine and Science in Sports and Exercise 22:S35.

Levine, B.D., J. Stray-Gundersen, G. Duhaime, P.G. Snell, D.B. Friedman (1991) Living high - training low: the effect of altitude acclimatization/normoxic training in trained runners. Medicine and Science in Sports and Exercise 23:S25.

Levine BD, J Stray-Gundersen (1992) A practical approach to altitude training: where to live and train for optimal performance enhancement. International Journal of Sports Medicine 13(Suppl1):S209-S212.

Levine BD, J Stray-Gundersen (1992) Altitude training does not improve running performance more than equivalent training near sea level in trained runners. Medicine and Science in Sports and Exercise 24:S95.

Levine BD, Engfred K, Friedman DB, Kjaer M, Secher NH, Saltin B (1992) Altitude training without acclimatization: effect on sea level work performance, substrate utilization and muscle oxidative capacity. Physiologist 35:179.

Levine BD, RC Roach, CS Houston (1992) Work and training at altitude, *in* **Hypoxia: Mountain Medicine**, JR Sutton, G Coates, CS Houston, eds., Queen City Publishers, Burlington, Vermont, p. 192-201.

Levine BD, D Verstraete, B Murchison, J Stray-Gundersen (1993) Altitude training without acclimatization does not improve sea level performance more than sea level training. Medicine and Science in Sports and Exercise , 25:S105.

Levine, B.D., J.Stray-Gundersen (1995) Training at moderate altitude increases blood oxygen content, maximal oxygen uptake and running performance. **Hypoxia and the Brain**, *in press.*

Maher JT, LG Jones, LH Hartley. Effects of high altititude exposure on submaximal endurance capacity of men. Journal of Applied Physiology 37:895-898, 1974.

Mariburl H, W Schobersberger, E Humpeler, W Hasibeder, W Fischer, E Raas (1986) Beneficial effects of exercising at moderate altitude on red cell oxygen transport and on exercise performance. Pflugers Archives 406:594-599.

Marinelli M, GS Roi, M Giacometti, P Bonini, G Banfi (1994) Cortisol, testosterone, and free testosterone in athletes performing a marathon at 4,000 m altitude, Hormone Research 41:225-229.

Mazzeo RS, PR Bender, GA Brooks, GE Butterfield, BM Groves, JR Sutton, EE Wolfel, JT Reeves (1991) Arterial catecholamine responses during exercise with acute and chronic high-altitude exposure. American Journal of Physiology 261:E419-E424.

Michel JB, GA Ordway, JA Richardson, RS Williams (1994) Biphbasic induction of imediate early gene expression accompanies activity-dependent angiogenesis and myofiber remodeling of rabbit skeletal muscle. Journal of Clinical Investigations 94:277-285.

Milledge JS, DM Catley, ES Williams, WR Withey, BD Minty (1983) Effect of prolonged exercise at altitude on the renin-angiotensin system. Journal of Applied Physiology 55:413-418.

Mizuno M, C Juel, T Bro-Rasmussen, E Mygind, B Schibye, B Rasmussen, B Saltin (1990) Limb skeletal muscle adaptation in athletes after training at altitude. Journal of Applied Physiology 68(2):496-502.

Ou LC, SM Tenney (1970) Properties of mitochondria from hearts of cattle acclimatized to high altitude. Respiratory Physiology 8:151-159.

Peronnet F, G Thibault, DL Cousineau (1991) A theoretical analysis of the effect of altitude on running performance. Journal of Applied Physiology 70:399-404.

Reeves JT, EE Wolfel, HJ Green, RS Mazzeo, AJ Young, JR Sutton, GA Brooks (1992) Oxygen transport during exercise at altitude and the lactate paradox: lessons from Operation Everest II and Pikes Peak. Exercise and Sports Science Reviews 20: 275-296.

Reynafarje C, J Faura, D Villavicencio (1975) Oxygen transport of haemoglobin in high altitude animals. Journal of Applied Physiology 38:806-810.

Saito M, T Mano, I Iwase, K Koga, H Abe, Y Yamazaki (1988) Responses in muscle sympathetic activity to acute hypoxia in humans. Journal of Applied Physiology 65:1548-542.

Saltin B (1970) Aerobic and anaerobic work capacity at 2300 meters. Med Thorac 2:107-112.

Saltin B, RF Grover, CG Blomqvist, LH Hartley, RL Johnson (1968) Maximal oxygen uptake and cardiac output after 2 weeks at 4,300 m. Journal of Applied Physiology 25:400-409.

Schoene RB, S Lahiri, PH Hackett, RM Peters Jr, JS Milledge, CJ Pizzo, FH Sarnquist, SJ Boyer, DJ Graber, KH Maret. Relationship of hypoxic ventilatory response to exercise performance on Mount Everest (1984) Journal of Applied Physiology 56:1478-83.

Schultz WW, Stray-Gundersen J, Schecter M, Levine BD (1994) Vigorous oral iron supplementation can maintain iron stores during altitude training. Medicine and Science in Sports and Exercise 26:S181.

Squires RW, ER Buskirk (1982) Aerobic capacity during acute exposure to simulated altitude, 914-2286 meters. Medicine and Science in Sports and Exercise 14:36-40.

Stray-Gundersen J, C Alexander, A Hochstein, D deLemos, BD Levine (1992) Failure of red cell volume to increase to altitude exposure in iron deficient runners. Medicine and Science in Sports and Exercise 24:S90.

Stray-Gundersen J, A Hochstein, BD Levine (1993) Effect of 4 weeks altitude exposure and training on red cell mass in trained runners. Medicine and Science in Sports and Exercise 25:S171.

Stray-Gundersen J, Levine BD (1994) Altitude acclimatization/normoxic training (high/low) improves sea-level endurance performance immediately on descent from altitude. Medicine and Science in Sports and Exercise 26:S64.

Stray-Gundersen J, N Mordecai, BD Levine (1995) O_2 transport response to altitude training in runners. Medicine and Science in Sports and Exercise 27:S00, *in press.*

Stine TA, BD Levine, S Taylor, W Schultz, J Stray-Gundersen (1992) Quantification of altitude training in the field. Medicine and Science in Sports and Exercise 24:S103.

Sutton JR, JT Reeves, PD Wagner, BM Groves, A Cymerman, MK Malconian, PB Rock, PM Young, SD Walter, CS Houston (1988) Operation Everest II: oxygen transport during exercise at extreme simulated altitude. Journal of Applied Physiology 64:1309-1321.

Terrados N, M Mizuno, H Andersen (1985) Reduction in maximal oxygen uptake at low altitudes; role of training status and lung function. Clinical Physiology 5(Suppl. 3):75-79.

Terrados N, J Melichna, C Sylven, E Jansson, L Kaijser (1988) Effects of training at simulated altitude on performance and muscle metabolic capacity in competitive road cyclists. European Journal of Applied Physiology 57:203-209.

Terrados N, E Jansson, C Sylven, L Kaijser (1990) Is hypoxia a stimulus for synthesis of oxidative enzymes and myoglobin? Journal of Applied Physiology 68(6):2369-2372.

Torre-Bueno JR, PD Wagner, HA Saltzman, GE Gale, RE Moon (1985) Diffusion limitation in normal humans during exercise at sea level and simulated altitude. Journal of Applied Physiology 58:989-995.

Vogel JA, LH Hartley, JC Cruz, RP Hogan (1974) Cardiac output during exercise in sea-level residents at sea level and high altitude. Journal of Applied Physiology 36:169-172.

Wagner PD (1993) Algebraic analysis of determinants of VO_2max. Respiratory Physiology 93:221-237.

Weil JV, G Jamieson, DW Brown, RF Grover (1968) The red cell mass - arterial oxygen relationship in normal man. Journal of Clinical Investigations 47:1627-1639.

Withey WR, JS Milledge, ES Williams, BD Minty, EI Bryson
(1983)   Fluid and electrolyte homeostasis during
prolonged exercise at altitude. Journal of Applied
Physiology 55:409-412.
Wolfel EE (1993)   Sympatho-adrenal and cardiovascular
adaptation to hypoxia. *in* Hypoxia and Molecular
Medicine, JR Sutton, CS Houston, G Coates ed, Queen
City Printers, Inc., Burlington   p. 62-80.
Young AJ, WJ Evans, A Cymerman, KB Pandolf, JJ Knapik, JT
Maher (1982)   Sparing effect of chronic high-altitude
exposure on muscle glycogen utilization. Journal of
Applied Physiology 52:857-862.
Young PM, PB Rock, CS Fulco (1987)   Altitude
acclimatization attenuates plasma ammonia accumulation
during submaximal exercise. Journal of Applied
Physiology 63:758-764.

13 Nutritional optimisation of exercise performance
C. Williams

1 Introduction

The links between food and performance have always held the interest of sportsmen and sportswomen (collectively called athletes). All too frequently, it is the influence of supplements on performance, rather than commonly available foods, which have attracted the attention of sportsmen and women. Many sports have a 'food culture' of their own and pass on perceived wisdom from generation to generation almost untouched by the advances in nutritional sciences. The tenacity with which strength athletes cling to their belief that training is only effective when it is accompanied by a high protein diet is one such example.

Before considering those nutritional strategies which help optimise sports performance, a number of assumptions must be made and some concerns aired. The first assumption is that athletes follow the recommendations to eat a wide range of foods in sufficient quantity to cover their daily energy expenditures. Furthermore, the carbohydrate content of their diets accounts for between 50 and 60% of their daily energy intake, protein contributes between 12 and 15 % and fat makes up the remainder (Williams and Devlin, 1992). There is, at present, no evidence to recommend that athletes who consume well balanced diets will improve their performance if they consume additional vitamins and minerals. However, the potential for inadequate intakes of these micronutrients does exist in those athletes who eat too little in relation to their energy expenditures. This negative energy balance is often the result of athletes trying to reduce their body weights in order to compete in weight categories far below their normal body weights. Improvements in running performance as a result of reducing body weight is a common experience but continuing to lose weight will not produce proportional improvements in performance times. Before athletes can train hard and recover quickly they must eat a well balanced diet and there are no legal short-cuts to optimum performance for those who do not pay attention to their nutritional needs. Many athletes are unable to implement these recommendations because they have not been taught some of the basic principles of nutrition. For example, not being able to select high carbohydrate, low fat foods prevents athletes from benefiting from nutritional strategies designed to achieve optimum performances.

Many athletes regard an increase in protein intake as the first step in the nutritional support of their training. However, there is no need for an increase in protein intake because a well balanced diet contains between 1.2 and 1.7 g/ kg (body weight) of protein a day (Grandjean and Rudd, 1994; Williams, 1994). This amount of protein is greater than the WHO recommendations of 0.8 g/kg and sufficient to maintain nitrogen balance even during heavy training (Lemon, 1991). Adequate amounts of protein intake can also be achieved by vegetarians with no lesser capacity for heavy exercise than meat-eating athletes (Kiens, 1993).

In order to optimise their performance, athletes have to achieve the right balance between training and diet. Every training programme is built on the permutation of three elements namely, intensity, duration and frequency. The capacity of athletes to cope with training depends to a large extent on their ability to cover their energy expenditure during heavy exercise. Furthermore, a training programme which includes prolonged heavy exercise assumes that the athlete can recover between training sessions. Nutritional preparation for heavy training or frequent competition can improve performance and help rapid recovery. Athletes must, therefore, have the motivation not only to carry out the training programme agreed with the coach but also to be able to follow dietary prescriptions designed to optimise their preparation for and recovery from heavy exercise.

There are well founded nutritional guidelines to help prepare for heavy exercise, to extend exercise capacity and to recover from exercise. These strategies are based on delaying fatigue by providing fluid and fuel in the most effective ways. Fatigue during prolonged heavy exercise occurs when the rate of energy expenditure, by active muscles, cannot be covered by their energy production. This is largely the result of a reduction in the carbohydrate stores of skeletal muscles to critically low levels (Bergstrom and Hultman, 1967). Carbohydrate is stored in the liver and in skeletal muscles as glycogen granules, which are coiled chains of glucose molecules (Williams, 1982). During training and competition there is always a reduction in muscle glycogen, even if the activity involves sprinting over relatively short distances repeatedly, as in the multiple sprint sports such as hockey, soccer, rugby and tennis (Williams, 1987). Therefore, the rationale for high carbohydrate diets is obvious when seen in the light of the exercise demands on the limited glycogen stores in skeletal muscles (Costill and Hargreaves, 1992). The nutritional preparation for optimum performance, whether in training or in competition, is based on delaying the depletion of muscle and liver glycogen stores in order to ensure the continued provision of this fuel for muscle metabolism. Dehydration is equally as effective in accelerating the onset of fatigue, as is muscle glycogen depletion, but potentially more of a health threat (Maughan, 1991). Therefore, optimum fluid intake is part of the nutritional strategies used to improve exercise tolerance. Thus, delaying the onset of fatigue is the main contribution of nutrition to improved sports performance and so nutritional preparation and training work in concert to improve the fitness of the athlete for competition.

The nutritional contribution to improved performance can be usefully considered in three phases, namely preparation for, participation in and recovery from training or competition.

2 Preparation

An increase in muscle glycogen before prolonged heavy exercise increases endurance capacity during cycling (Bergstrom, Hermansen, Hultman and Saltin, 1967) and improves running performance in long distance races (Karlsson and Saltin, 1971).

Muscle glycogen concentration can be increased by reducing (tapering) the amount of training during the week before competition and increasing the carbohydrate content of the diet, to about 70% of the daily energy intake, during the three days before the event (Sherman, Costill, Fink and Miller, 1981). Although high muscle glycogen stores are a necessary preparation for endurance competitions they are only pre-conditions and not predeterminants of success because there are other factors, not least of which is training status, that influence performance. Nevertheless, all other things being equal, entering a competition with well stocked carbohydrate stores is essential for successful performance.

In attempting to ensure carbohydrate stores are well stocked before competition or a period of heavy training, such as team training week-ends, a high carbohydrate meal, about three hours before exercise is alsorecommended. However, consuming carbohydrate within the hour before exercise was shown to cause an early onset of fatigue (Foster, Costill and Fink, 1979). On the basis of this one study, athletes were strongly recommended not to consume any carbohydrate just before exercise. More recent studies have established that drinking even concentrated glucose solutions 30 minutes before prolonged exercise does not impair performance (Chryssanthopoulos, Hennessy and Williams, 1994a). However, concentrated carbohydrate solutions are not the best way of providing fluid or fuel before or during exercise, mainly because they empty slowly from the stomach and, under some circumstances, may cause abdominal discomfort (Maughan and Noakes, 1991). Furthermore, the 'insulin rebound' phenomenon which is the result of the large rise in blood glucose following the ingestion of a concentrated glucose solution before exercise is short lived and the oscillations in blood glucose concentrations go unnoticed by the athlete (Chryssanthopoulos et al., 1994a).

Many athletes, especially women, have abdominal discomfort after eating light meals before exercise and so train or compete after an overnight fast of 10 to 12 hours. The disadvantage of missing breakfast before training or competition can be overcome by drinking a carbohydrate-electrolyte solution (5 to 7%), in small quantities, frequently throughout exercise (Chryssanthopoulos, Williams, Wilson, Asher and Hearne, 1994b)

This strategy may also be recommended for athletes competing in events, such as marathon races, which begin early in the day. A nutritional strategy which requires athletes to eat breakfast at 04.00 or 05.00 hours in order to prepare for a 07□:00 or 08:00 hours race will not be widely accepted. Therefore, alternative methods of ensuring good nutritional preparation are needed and hence the recommendation to drink carbohydrate-electrolyte solutions during a race or training (Chryssanthopoulos et al., 1994b).

3 Participation

During prolonged continuous or discontinuous exercise ingestion of fluid helps delay the onset of severe dehydration. Drinking small volumes of a carbohydrate-electrolyte solution throughout exercise is a means of obtaining fluid and fuel. Insulin secretion is depressed during exercise and so consuming even concentrated carbohydrate solutions does not lead to large changes in plasma insulin concentrations and subsequent decreases in blood glucose concentrations. Endurance running capacity (Wilber and Moffatt, 1992) as well as endurance racing performance (Tsintzas et. al., 1993) is improved to a greater extent when a sports drink is consumed during exercise than when runners consumed water. A well formulated carbohydrate-electrolyte solution is more effective than water in providing fluid and fuel during prolonged exercise. Individual preferences, in terms of frequency and volume of solution consumed, should be worked out during training and not left to the day of the competition.

4 Recovery

Even during a training session on a Winter's evening in Northern Europe, athletes will routinely lose 2 to 3 % of their body weight in sweat. Therefore, post-exercise rehydration is one of the nutritional priorities after training or competition. When rapid rehydration is necessary, in order to prepare for exercise within a few hours, then water is not the best rehydration fluid (Gonzalez-Alonso, Heaps and Coyle, 1992). Drinking water alone leads to disinclination to continue drinking well before rehydration is complete, whereas a carbohydrate-electrolyte solution is more effective in restoring fluid balance.

Athletes who undertake a period of daily heavy training or competition for several days must replace their glycogen stores between training sessions. This can be achieved by increasing the daily carbohydrate intake to about 10 g/kg body weight (Sherman, 1992). Athletes who fail to increase their carbohydrate intake between daily training sessions will be unable to complete subsequent periods of heavy exercise. For example, when a group of runners were asked to repeat a 90 minute treadmill run after a 24 hour recovery period when, on one occasion, they ate their normal amount of carbohydrate and on another occasion they increased their carbohydrate intake to 10 g/kg body weight, only after the high carbohydrate diet were they able to match their previous day's performance (Fallowfield and Williams, 1993). In a similar study university soccer players consumed either their normal diet during a 24-hour recovery period or a high carbohydrate diet. After the recovery, they attempted to repeat a 90 minute training session which involved a mixture of shuttle running, sprinting and walking (Nicholas et al., 1994). Only after the high carbohydrate diet were the soccer players able to reproduce their performance during the 90 minutes of intermittent shuttle running. Therefore, the evidence is quite clear that a high carbohydrate diet is essential for recovery of fitness between daily training sessions involving prolonged heavy exercise.

Immediately after exercise, muscle glycogen resynthesis is at its most rapid (Ivy, 1991) and so drinking a carbohydrate-electrolyte solution during the first few hours of recovery and then eating high carbohydrate meals is the current recommendation for a rapid recovery of fitness (Sherman, 1992). Athletes who can recover quickly can train frequently and so derive the most from their investment of time and energy in training.

In summary, athletes who consume a wide range of foods in sufficient quantities to cover their daily energy expenditures will ensure that they are healthy enough to undertake heavy training. Optimisation of training can be helped by employing nutritional strategies to ensure that the athlete's limited carbohydrate stores are well stocked before exercise and restored rapidly after exercise.

5 References

Bergstrom, J. Hermansen, L. Hultman, E. and Saltin, B. (1967) Diet, Muscle Glycogen and Physical Performance. **Acta Physiologica Scandinavica**, 71, 140-150.

Bergstrom, J. and Hultman, E. (1967) A study of the glycogen metabolism during exercise in man. **Scandinavian Journal of Clininical and Laboratory Investigations**, 19, 218-228.

Chryssanthopoulos, C. Hennessy, L. and Williams, C. (1994a) The influence of pre-exercise glucose ingestion on endurance running capacity. **British Journal of Sports Medicine**, 28, 105-119.

Chryssanthopoulos, C. Williams, C. Wilson, W. Asher, L. and Hearne, L. (1994b) Comparison between carbohydrate feedings before and during exercise on running performance during a 30 km treadmill time trial. **International Journal of Sport Nutrition**, 4, 374-386.

Costill, D. and Hargreaves, M. (1992) Carbohydrate Nutrition and Fatigue. Sports Medicine, 13, 86-92.

Fallowfield, J. and Williams, C. (1993) Carbohydrate intake and recovery from prolonged exercise. **International Journal of Sport Nutrition**, 3, 150-164.

Foster, C. Costill, D. and Fink, W. (1979) Effects of preexercise feedings on endurance performance. **Medicine Science in Sports and Exercise**, 11, 1-5.

Gonzalez-Alonso, J. Heaps, C. L. and Coyle, E. F. (1992) Rehydration after exercise with common beveridges and water. **International Journal of Sports Medicine**, 13, 399-406.

Grandjean, A. and Rudd, J. S. (1994) Energy intake of athletes. In M. Harries, C. Williams, W. D. Stanish, & L. J. Micheli (Eds.), **Oxford Textbook of Sports Medicine** Oxford University Press, Oxford, pp. 53-65.Ivy, J. L. (1991) Muscle glycogen synthesis before and after exercise. Sports Medicine, 11, 6-19.

Karlsson, J. and Saltin, B. (1971) Diet, muscle glycogen and endurance performance. **Journal of Applied Physiology**, 31, 203-206.

Kiens, B. (1993) Translating nutrition into diet:diet for training and competition. In D. Macleod A,D. R. Maughan J. C. Williams, C. Madeley R. J. Sharp C,M. and R. Nutton W., (Ed.), **Intermittent High Intensity Exercise: Preparation, stresses and damage limitation**, E &FN Spon, London, pp. 175-182.

Lemon, P.W.R. (1991) Effect of exercise on protein requirements. **Journal of Sports Sciences**, 9, 53 - 70.

Maughan, R. (1991) Fluid and electrolyte loss and replacement in exercise. **Journal of Sports Sciences**, 9, 117-142.

Maughan, R. J. and Noakes, T. D. (1991) Fluid replacement and exercise stress: a brief review of studies on fluid replacement and some guidelines for the athlete. **Sports Medicine**, 12, 16 - 31.

Nicholas, C. Nuttall, F. Hawkins, R. Green, P. and Williams, C. (1994) Influence of diet on recovery from intermittent high intensity exercise. **Journal of Sports Sciences**, 12, 147.

Sherman, M. (1992) Recovery from endurance exercise. **Medicine and Science in Sports and Exercise**, 24 (Suppl), S366-S339.

Sherman, W. Costill, D. Fink, W. and Miller, J. (1981) Effect of exercise-diet manipulation on muscle glycogen and its subsequent utilization during performance. **International Journal of Sports Medicine**, 114, 114-118.

Tsintzas, K. Liu, R. Wililiams, C. Campbell, I. and Gaitanos, G. (1993) The effect of carbohydrate ingestion on performance during a 30-km race. **International Journal of Sport Nutrition**, 3, 127-139.

Wilber, R. and Moffatt, R. (1992) Influence of carbohydrate ingestion on blood glucose and performance in runners. **International Journal of Sport Nutrition**, 2, 317-327.

Williams, C. (1982) Dietary manipulation and athletic performance. (B. Davies and G. Thomas) in **Science and Sporting Performance: Management or Manipulation**, Claredon Press, Oxford, pp. 1-22.

Williams, C. (1987) Short term activity. (eds.) D. Macleod, R. Maughan, M. Nimmo, T. Reilly, C. Williams (Eds.), **Exercise: Benefits, Limits and Adaptations** E. & F.N. Spon, London, pp. 59- 60.

Williams, C. (1994) Nutritional aspects of soccer: training and competition, in **IOC Book of Soccer** (ed B. Ekblom, Blackwell Scientific Publications, Oxford, pp.74-110

Williams, C. and Devlin, J. (1992) **Foods, Nutrition and Sports Performance.** (Ed.)E & FN Spon., London.

14 The effect of caffeine and Temazepam on performance during exercise in two mental performance tasks

A. Miles, D. MacLaren and T. Reilly

1 Introduction

Mental performance during exercise depends on the balance between the level of fatigue and the level of arousal (Tomporowski and Ellis, 1986). To determine the role of arousal in the exercise-mental performance relationship, observations of mental performance under differing conditions of arousal need to be made. Such manipulation can be achieved through the administration of pharmacological agents that either stimulate or depress the central nervous system (CNS).

Caffeine is a widely used stimulant which has direct effects on the CNS. It has been reported to have stimulant effects on the cardiovascular system, the respiratory system, the muscle contractile processes and fat metabolism as well as direct CNS stimulation (Powers and Dodd, 1985). The central nervous stimulatory effects of caffeine at rest include enhanced performance in a variety of mental tasks such as vigilance and reaction time (Lieberman, 1992).

Depressant drugs such as the benzodiazepines which are used therapeutically as mild tranquilisers. One of the non-addictive benzodiazepines is temazepam which has a short-lived CNS depressant effect. Temazepam is used therapeutically to lower arousal levels and to induce sleep, and the exact physiological effects are largely dose-dependent. Hartley (1992) reported that the benzodiazepines have detrimental effects on a variety of mental tasks including choice reaction time and digit-substitution tasks. Previously Wesnes and Warburton (1983) reported that accuracy and reaction time in a rapid information-processing task was impaired the morning after the administration of temazepam as a result of a 'hangover' effect.

The provision of caffeine prior to exercise has widely been reported to extend the duration of exercise (Powers and Dodd 1985). Conversely, no data exist concerning the effect of temazepam ingestion on exercise performance. It is likely that temazepam impairs physical performance and thus reduce the duration of exercise.

Whilst there is evidence to suggest that mental performance under resting conditions is affected by chemical manipulation of arousal, no previous data exist concerning manipulation of arousal and mental performance during exercise. The aim of this experiment is therefore to identify whether pharmacological manipulation of arousal levels affects performance in two mental tasks during prolonged moderate exercise.

2 Methods

Five male subjects (Mean age = 21.4 $\pm$ 2.7 years; body mass = 79.4 $\pm$ 8.4 kg;) took part in this study. The study was approved by the Ethics Committee of the Liverpool John Moores University. In accordance with their requirements each subject completed a short questionnaire concerning any previous use of temazepam or known depressive conditions before signing an informed volunteer consent form. Subjects were escorted home after the temazepam trials.

Each subject visited the laboratory on seven separate occasions. On the first visit, subjects performed an incremental exercise test on a Monark (Sweden) cycle ergometer to determine a value for their maximum oxygen uptake (Mean VO_2max = 51.6 $\pm$ 5.4 ml kg^{-1} min^{-1}). After a short rest, subjects then performed a familiarisation trial of a choice reaction time (CRT) task and a mental addition (MA) task whilst cycling against no resistance.

The six subsequent trials were performed according to a single blind Latin-square type design. On the morning (between 08:00 h and 09:00 h) of each trial subjects visited the laboratory and performed the appropriate mental performance task (Morn.Before) whilst cycling against no resistance. Later in the day (between 14:00 h and 17:00 h) subjects arrived at the laboratory 60 min prior to the scheduled exercise start time and completed a mental performance task (Ingestion) before consuming the test drug. The caffeine (5 mg kg body weight^{-1}) and placebo doses were consumed 60 min before exercise and the temazepam dose (total of 20 mg) was consumed 30 min prior to exercise. This was to ensure that peak plasma levels occurred close to the beginning of exercise.

Before commencing exercise the subjects again performed the mental performance task (PreEx) whilst cycling against no resistance. Subjects then began exercising at an exercise intensity corresponding to 65% of their pre-determined VO_2max and were encouraged to maintain the desired exercise intensity for as long as possible.

Mental performance was monitored after 25 min, 45 min, 65 min and 85 min of exercise and 10 min after the cessation of exercise (10 min Post). After each test session, subjects visited the laboratory the following morning (between 08:00 h and 09:00 h) and completed a further mental performance task (MornAfter).

The Choice Reaction Time task used in this study took the form of a BBC BASIC computer program. On commencement of the test a small white box appeared in one of four boxes on the centre of the screen. Subjects responded by pressing one of the corresponding keys operated by the forefinger and the index finger of each hand. No feedback was given and subjects were presented continuously with 640 trials, consisting of four randomised blocks of 160 trials. Performance of the task lasted between 4 and 5 min. In order that the task could be performed during exercise, the keyboard was mounted on the handlebars of the cycle ergometer and the monitor positioned on a stand such that the screen was directly in front of the subject's line of view. On completion of the task the computer program produced data for the mean Choice Reaction Time (CRT) and Percentage Error over all 640 trials and for each block of 160 trials.

The Mental Addition task involved the presentation of a series of 35 mm slides each consisting of five columns of two-digit numbers. The slides were projected on to a wall approximately 2 m in front of the subject at head height. Subjects were asked to add the columns of numbers as quickly and as accurately as possible and to give the answer orally. On completion of the fifth column, the next slide was presented immediately. The presentation of slides was continuous for 10 min and the number of calculations made, the number of correct responses and the Percentage Error were recorded.

3 Results

Analysis of the CRT data for each test showed no significant differences between the four blocks (P>0.05). All data from each test were therefore treated as mean data for the 640 trials. Analysis of the speed of response at each test point for each of the three trials (Figure 1) showed no significant differences either between trials ($F_{2,8}=1.09$) or within trials ($F_{7,28}=1.70$). The percentage improvement in the speed of response between the 'PreEx' test and the '25 min' test for each trial (Figure 2) showed no significant between trials differences. Analysis of the Percentage Errors revealed no significant differences between trials ($F_{2,8}=1.35$) or within trials ($F_{7,28}=2.12$) (Mean error = $7.9 \pm 2.0\%$).

The number of sums answered at each test point for each of the three trials (Figure 3) showed significant differences within trials ($F_{7,28}=3.8$; P<0.01) but no differences between trials. Post-hoc analysis revealed that the number of sums answered in the 'MornAfter' tests was greater (P<0.01) than in the 'MornBefore' tests and also greater than the number of sums answered in the 'PreEx' tests. The percentage improvement between the number of sums answered in the 'PreEx' test and the '25 min' test (Figure 2) showed a significant between trials difference ($F_{2,8}=9.01$; P<0.01).

The improvement in the temazepam trial (-1.4 ± 3.0) being less than in both the other two trials (Caffeine 10.9 $\pm$ 2.8; Control 10.9 $\pm$ 5.7). Analysis of the Percentage Error showed significant within trial differences ($F_{7,28}=4.33$; P<0.01). Post-hoc analysis revealed that the percentage of errors made in the 'MornAfter' test for each trial was less than in the corresponding 'MornBefore' trial (p<0.01).

No significant differences in the duration of exercise ($F_{2,12}=0.31$) were evident (**CRT:** Control = 95.6 ± 9.6 min; Caffeine = 105.2 ± 12.4 min; Temazepam = 93.4 ± 11.5 min. **MA:**Control = 113.0 ± 11.8 min; Caffeine = 110.2 ± 9.9 min; Temazepam = 99.6 ± 8.8 min).

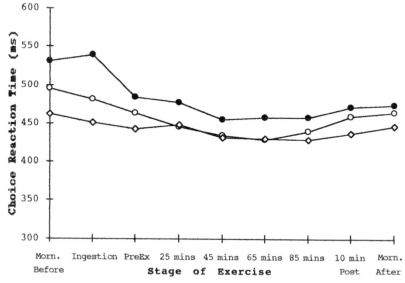

Figure 1. Choice Reaction time data before, during and after exercise under three different conditions of arousal; Control -O-; Caffeine -O-; Temazepam -<>-; (n=5).

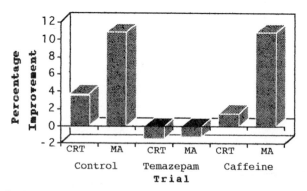

Figure 2. Percentage Improvements in mental performance between PreEx and 25min of exercise for each of the three different conditions of arousal.

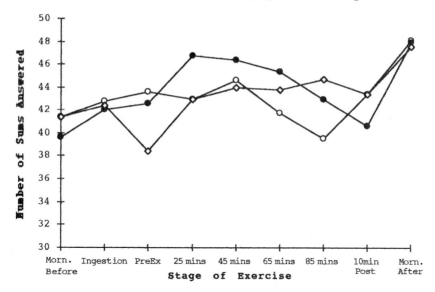

Figure 3. Number of Sums Answered before, during and after exercise under three different conditions of arousal; Control -O-; Caffeine -O-; Temazepam -<>- (n=5).

4 Discussion

The data from the control trial revealed no within trial differences in mental performance. This suggests that performance in the two mental tasks was unaffected by both the repeated performance of the tasks and the stimulus of exercise. There was no evidence that the two tasks show a familiarisation effect with repeated performance or a facilitation effect with the onset of exercise. In the caffeine and temazepam trials the speed of response and the number of sums answered showed a similar pattern of performance with levels remaining constant throughout. Since mental performance did not differ significantly between trials there is no evidence that caffeine enhances mental performance or that temazepam impairs mental performance under prolonged exercise conditions.

Further examination of the changes in mental performance between the PreEx and 25 min tests (Figure 2) do however highlight between trial differences. The percentage change in mental performance with the onset of exercise in the control and caffeine trials showed improvements in performance whilst the temazepam trials showed impaired performance. It is possible that any facilitation is related to levels of arousal with temazepam serving to lower arousal and thus reduce performance levels. Wesnes and Warburton (1983) suggested that the benzodiazepines decelerate the turnover of noradrenaline which could cause impairment in mental performance. Further observations of mental performance under conditions of temazepam ingestion and exercise are needed to explore this area.

The exercise time in the caffeine trials was no longer than in the control trial, suggesting that the provision of caffeine (5mg kg body weight[-1]) failed to extend the duration of exercise. This disagrees with previous observations which have reported extensions in performance after the ingestion of caffeine (Powers and Dodd 1985). The failure to observe an extension in performance in this study may be due to the fact that only five subjects completed the study and the between-subject range of exercise times was large (control: 77.0 min to 116.5 min; caffeine:79.5 min to 150.5 min). The exercise times achieved in the temazepam trial were not significantly shorter than in the control trial. No previous data exist concerning exercise duration after temazepam ingestion but the data from this study suggest either that a 20 mg dose of temazepam 30 min prior to exercise is insufficient to impair exercise performance or that the stress of exercise overrides the depressant effects of the drug.

No differences existed between mental performance on the morning before and the morning after exercise, suggesting that no 'hangover' effect was evident. The stress of prolonged exercise may override the depressant effect of temazepam and thus leave no such 'hangover effect'.

Administration of caffeine or temazepam prior to submaximal exercise did not affect mental performance in this study. The magnitude of the exercise-induced response may however, be affected by central nervous stimulation or depression. There was no evidence that performance in mental performance tasks the morning after ingestion of temazepam was adversely affected.

5 References

Hartley, L.R.(1992) Prescribed psychotropic drugs: the major and minor tranquilisers, in **Handbook of Human Performance**, Vol.2. Academic Press, London. pp279-318.

Lieberman, H.R. (1992) Caffeine, in **Handbook of Human Performance**, Vol.2. Academic Press, London. pp75-98.

Powers, S.K. and Dodd S. (1985) Caffeine and endurance performance. **Sports Medicine**, 2, 165-174.

Tomporowski, and Ellis, (1986) Effect of exercise on cognitive processes: a review. **Psychological Bulletin** 99, 338-346.

Wesnes, K and Warburton, D.M. (1983) Stress and drugs, in **Stress and Fatigue in Human Performance**, (ed. R. Hockey), John Wiley, Chichester. pp203-43.

15 An investigation into the combined effects of creatine and sodium bicarbonate supplementation on repeated bouts of high intensity exercise in elite cyclists

D. Maclaren and G. Adamson

1 Introduction

Muscular contraction and relaxation are fuelled exclusively by the free energy liberated during the dephosphorylation of adenosine triphosphate (ATP). Adenosine triphosphate is the only direct fuel that can power muscular contraction. The store of skeletal muscle ATP is limited, and so must be rapidly resynthesised from its breakdown products to avoid muscular fatigue (Hultman, 1987). During maximal exercise of short duration, this replenishment comes from the creatine phosphate (CP) stores, the myokinase reaction, and anaerobic glycolysis (Meyer et al., 1985).

Studies have shown that CP levels in muscle become severely depleted as a result of intense dynamic exercise (Cheetham et al., 1986). The consequences are reduced force generation by muscle. Recent studies have shown that creatine supplementation can increase the CP levels in muscle (Harris et al., 1992) and that this in turn leads to an enhanced performance by delaying fatigue during repeated bouts of maximal exercise (Balsom, 1993; Greenhaff et al., 1993).

Following exhaustive high intensity exercise, the production of lactic acid leads to an increase in hydrogen ions (H^+) and a concomitant decrease in pH levels in both muscle and blood (Hermansen and Osnes, 1972). Accumulation of H^+ may lead to impairment of contractile processes in muscle, whilst a reduction in pH may inhibit the activity of key glycogenolytic enzymes (MacLaren et al., 1989). Acidosis may, to some extent, be buffered by intra- and extracellular buffering mechanisms. The bicarbonate ion (HCO_3) is a major buffer in the human, and so many investigations have used bicarbonate ingestion to boost buffering and subsequently examine the effects on performance (MacLaren, 1986). To date, no investigation has been undertaken to determine the combined effects of creatine and sodium bicarbonate supplementation on repeated bouts of high intensity exercise. This study investigated whether sodium bicarbonate ingestion and creatine supplementation have combined or singularly beneficial effects during such exercise bouts.

2 Methods

Eight male subjects (mean age = 24.6 ± 3.5 years and body mass = 70.3 ± 8.6 kg), who were all competitive cyclists, took part in this study which was approved by the Ethics Committee of Liverpool John Moores University. Subjects were given oral and written information on the experimental design before completing a volunteer's consent form. The investigation involved the cyclists being tested in the laboratory on four separate occasions, and on each occasion they performed the tests under the following conditions:-

  (i)   Exercise following creatine and placebo ingestion (Cr).
 (ii) Exercise following double placebo ingestion (Pl).
(iii) Exercise following sodium bicarbonate and placebo ingestion (SB).
 (iv) Exercise following creatine and sodium bicarbonate ingestion (Cr + SB).

     The creatine, sodium bicarbonate and placebo (maltodextrin) were distributed to the cyclists according to a double blind, counterbalanced design. The subjects were required to ingest these substances at different time periods prior to each ride. Twenty grams of creatine or placebo were ingested daily by the cyclists in four 5 g doses taken over 5 consecutive days; a total of 100 g per subject was thereby administered. Sodium bicarbonate (0.3 g/kg body mass) or a placebo, were adminstered in capsule form two hours prior to testing following guidelines by George and MacLaren (1988). A four week period elapsed between the second and third sessions of testing. This acted as a wash-out period to accommodate for excess creatine levels returning to normal.
     Subjects arrived in the laboratory no later than 20 minutes prior to testing, so that the Monark 814E cycle ergometer could be adjusted and a heart rate monitor (Polar, Kempell, Finland) fitted to record heart rate every 5 seconds. The protocol consisted of 3 repeated 1 minute sprints on the Monark ergometer with resistance in the form of weights applied at 8.72% body weight, under guidelines of the British Association of Sport and Exercise Sciences (BASES). Each 1 min sprint was interspersed with 10 min recovery (1 minute active to avoid blood pooling, 9 minutes static).
     A 2 min warm-up was completed by subjects prior to testing, with the resistance applied equal to that of the test. This was followed by 3 minutes of static rest seated on the ergometer. Prior to each of the sprints, subjects were required to reach a cadence of 100 rev min^{-1}, at which point the experimentor gave a 5 s count down, before lowering the weights and starting to record the information. Verbal encouragement was given throughout the tests. Peak power, mean power, and fatigue index (final 5 s power value expressed as a percentage of the peak power) were determined.
     Fingerprick blood samples were taken using a Mannheim Autoclix, at rest and following the 1 minute active recovery of the third sprint. Duplicate blood samples were analysed for lactic acid using an Analox microstat GM-7 analyser (London, England).
     Data were subjected to analysis of variance (ANOVA) and where significant differences were apparent a post-hoc test was employed. Significance was accepted at $P < 0.05$.

3 Results

Means and standard deviations ($\pm$S.D.) were calculated for each variable of each sprint under each treatment condition. They are displayed in Tables 1 to 3.
     Analysis of variance were used to investigate intra-treatment differences between the four sprints. Results showed no significant differences between any of the measured variables and the four treatment conditions in any of the repeated sprints. No significant differences were observed when the means of the sprints for each variable were combined ($P > 0.05$).

Table 1.   Variable means ($\pm$ SD) for the four treatment conditions of SPRINT 1

	Resting HR (beats/min)	Max.HR (beats/min)	Peak Power (watts)	Mean Power (watts)	Fatigue Index
Pl	87 $\pm$ 15	179 $\pm$ 10	1111 $\pm$ 186	859 $\pm$ 184	63.2 $\pm$ 9.8
Cr	86 $\pm$ 14	175 $\pm$ 9	1124 $\pm$ 201	898 $\pm$ 159	66.6 $\pm$ 5.4
SB	88 $\pm$ 15	179 $\pm$ 14	1121 $\pm$ 219	886 $\pm$ 197	65.7 $\pm$ 11
Cr+SB	86 $\pm$ 16	177 $\pm$ 9	1110 $\pm$ 243	899 $\pm$ 212	65.7 $\pm$ 7.3

Table 2.   Variable means ($\pm$SD) for the four treatment conditions of SPRINT 2

	Resting HR (beats/min)	Maximum HR (beats/min)	Peak Power (watts)	Mean Power (watts)	Fatigue Index
Pl	105 $\pm$ 9	179 $\pm$ 9	1105 $\pm$ 189	855 $\pm$ 170	63.3 $\pm$ 6.7
Cr	109 $\pm$ 6	179 $\pm$ 7	1139 $\pm$ 219	904 $\pm$ 198	65.9 $\pm$ 5.3
SB	103 $\pm$ 4	180 $\pm$ 9	1084 $\pm$ 225	876 $\pm$ 189	67.4 $\pm$ 8.0
Cr+SB	109 $\pm$ 6	179 $\pm$ 7	1083 $\pm$ 278	892 $\pm$ 210	71.7 $\pm$ 8.8

Table 3.   Variable means ($\pm$SD) for the four treatment conditions of SPRINT 3

	Resting HR (beats/min)	Max. HR (beats/min)	Peak Power (watts)	Mean Power (watts)	Fatigue Index
Pl	111 $\pm$ 9	178 $\pm$ 8	1071 $\pm$ 156	836 $\pm$ 172	65.4 $\pm$ 9.0
Cr	116 $\pm$ 7	178 $\pm$ 6	1081 $\pm$ 175	858 $\pm$ 169	65.1 $\pm$ 6.9
SB	110 $\pm$ 6	177 $\pm$ 7	1048 $\pm$ 224	850 $\pm$ 201	69.2 $\pm$ 8.2
Cr+SB	115 $\pm$ 8	176 $\pm$ 7	1060 $\pm$ 255	854 $\pm$ 225	69.7 $\pm$ 4.8

Analysis of variance showed that there were no significant differences in lactate levels at rest and following the third sprint as a result of the four treatments (Table 4).

Table 4.   Mean lactate values ($\pm$SD) as a result of sprinting after different treatments.

TREATMENT							
Pl		Cr		SB		Cr + SB	
Rest	Sprint 3	Rest	Sprint 3	Rest	Sprint 3	Rest	Sprint 3
1.9	12.2	2.1	13.3	2.1	12.3	2.0	14.0
$\pm$0.2	$\pm$2.8	$\pm$0.7	$\pm$2.3	$\pm$0.5	$\pm$2.7	$\pm$0.7	$\pm$3.8

4 Discussion

Creatine supplementation has been shown to elevate muscle creatine phosphate levels significantly (Harris et al., 1992), and thereby improve high-intensity exercise (Balsom et al., 1993; Greenhaff et al., 1993). The non-significant increase in power and distance attained for subjects during creatine trials in each of the sprints compared with placebo in this study is in contrast to recent investigations involving creatine supplementation and intense exercise (Balsom et al., 1993; Greenhaff et al., 1993; Harris et al., 1993). This may have been due to the fact that 60 s sprints were used in this investigation compared with sprints lasting less than 30 seconds in the studies by Balsom et al.(1993) and Harris et al.(1993). The choice of 60 s repeated bouts of intense activity was related to two factors. Firstly, it was expected that an elevated CP store would lead to an enhanced mean power output due to more prolonged use of the CP stores before the glycolytic processes took over, and secondly that breakdown of CP liberates inorganic phosphate (P_i), a stimulatory metabolite of phosphofructokinase activity. The consequences of the latter would be enhanced glycolysis, a greater mean power, and a higher lactate level. Patently, although there were 2.6 to 5.7% increases in mean power and a 9% higher post-sprint lactate concentration between Cr and Pl, these findings were not significant.

A further complication could be attributed to the counterbalanced design of this study whereby half of the subjects ingested creatine in the first series of tests followed by placebo in the second series of tests. The four weeks allowed for the 'wash-out' period may have proved too short for restoration of 'normal' muscle CP concentrations prior to the placebo ingestion for half the subjects in the second series of tests. It is possible that muscle CP stores were elevated, although no biopsy samples were taken to determine whether this had in fact occurred.

The use of sodium bicarbonate to enhance high-intensity exercise has been substantiated in a number of studies when exercise is of 1 to 30 minutes duration, and a dose of at least 0.2 g/kg body mass is used (George & MacLaren, 1988; MacLaren,1986; McNaughton, 1992). During this type of exercise blood pH is regulated by buffering systems such as the bicarbonate (HCO_3) ion. Increasing the buffering capacity by sodium bicarbonate ingestion prior to intense exercise should allow a greater accumulation of lactic acid, with its associated H^+ ions, and therefore result in a greater energy production from anaerobic glycolysis (Parry-Billings & MacLaren, 1986). The sodium bicarbonate treatment produced findings similar to creatine; non-significant improvements in mean power of 1.5 to 3.5% compared with placebo. Surprisingly, the lactate concentrations post-exercise were almost identical with placebo. Other investigations have shown bicarbonate ingestion to promote lactate efflux from exercising muscle (MacLaren & Mellor, 1985).

It was originally hypothesized that the combination of two potential performance enhancing substances (Cr+SB) would significantly improve power output during the repeated sprints, by increasing high energy phosphagen stores and increasing the rate of lactate efflux from muscle. Statistical analysis of the data showed improvements were non-significant. The Cr+SB trials did produce non-significant improvements in all three of the 1 min sprints compared with Pl; a 2.2 to 4.7% increase in mean power was not as great as creatine alone, but the 4.7% increase which occurred during the first sprint was greater than for Cr.   The results from this study highlight that the ingestion of creatine or sodium bicarbonate either singly or in combination do not significantly affect power output in repeated 60 s cycle sprints. Positive, but not significant, trends in mean power output were discernible with creatine and creatine in combination with sodium bicarbonate, and with elite performers these small percentage improvements may be significant in competition. It may be that a counterbalanced design is not appropriate when investigating creatine supplementation due to the length of time for 'wash-out'. Other investigations need to consider a matched-group approach or unidirectional study whereby placebo is given first, followed by creatine.

5 Acknowledgements

The authors wish to acknowledge "Science in Sport" (Preston, UK) for the supply of creatine and the placebo.

6 References

Balsom, P.D., Ekblom, B., Soderlund, K., Sjodin, B. and Hultman, E. (1993) Creatine supplementation and dynamic high intensity intermittent exercise. **Scandinavian Journal of Medicine and Science in Sport,** 3, 143-149.

Cheetham, M.E., Boobis, L.H., Brooks, S. and Williams, C. (1986) Human muscle metabolism during sprint running. **Journal of Applied Physiology,** 61, 54-60.

George, K.P and MacLaren, D.P.M (1988) The effect of induced alkalosis and acidosis on endurance running at an intensity corresponding to 4mM blood lactate. **Ergonomics,** 31, 1639-1645.

Greenhaff, P.L., Casey, A., Short, A.H., Harris, R.C., Soderlund, K., and Hultman, E. (1993) The influence of oral creatine supplementation on muscle torque during repeated bouts of maximal voluntary exercise in man. **Clinical Science,** 84, 565-571.

Harris, R.C., Soderlund, K., and Hultman, E. (1992) Elevation of creatine in resting and exercised muscle of normal subjects by creatine supplementation. **Clinical Science,** 83, 367-374.

Harris,R.C, Viru, M., Hultman, E. and Greenhaff,P.L, (1993) The effect of oral creatine supplementation on running performance during maximal short term exercise in man. **Journal of Physiology,** 467, 74P.

Hermansen, L. and Osnes, J.B. (1972) Blood and muscle pH after maximal exercise in man. **Journal of Applied Physiology,** 32, 304-308.

Hultman, E, Soderlund,K, Spriet, L.L. (1987) Energy metabolism and fatigue in working muscles, in **Exercise, Benefits, Limits, and Adaptions** (eds D.Macleod, T. Reilly, C. Williams, and R. Maughan), London , E&FN Spon, pp63-85.

MacLaren, D.P. (1986) Alkalinisers, hydrogen ion accumulation and muscle fatigue: A brief review, in **Sports Science: Proceedings of the VIII Commonwealth and International Conference on Sport, Physical Education, Recreation, and Dance** (eds J.Watkins, T.Reilly, and L.Burwitz),E&FN Spon, London, pp.104-109.

MacLaren, D.P., Gibson,H., Parry-Billings, M., and Edwards,R.H.T. (1989) A review of metabolic and physiological factors in fatigue. **Exercise and Sports Science Reviews,** 17, 29-66.

MacLaren, D.P., and Mellor, S. (1985) The effect of induced alkalosis and acidosis on the lactate threshold and performance at 95% $\dot{V}O_2$ max. **British Journal of Sports Medicine,** 19, 237.

Mcnaughton,L.R. (1992) Bicarbonate ingestion; Effect of dosage on 60 s cycle ergometry. **Journal of Sports Sciences,** 10, 415-423.

Meyer,R.A, Sweeney,H.L, Kushmerick,M.J. (1985) A simple analysis of the phosphocreatine shuttle. **American Journal of Physiology,** 246, C365-C377.

Parry-Billings M. and MacLaren, D.P.M (1986) The effect of sodium bicarbonate and sodium citrate ingestion on anaerobic power during intermittent exercise.**European Journal of Applied Physiology,** 55, 524-529.

Part Three

Equipment Design and Technique Analysis

16 The effect of wearing foot orthotics on selected physiological, psychological and biomechanical parameters during submaximal running

C. Burton and T. Reilly

1 Introduction

The incidence of lower extremity trauma sustained by runners has escalated with the growing popularity of running (Gross and Napoli, 1993). Many of these problems may be related to foot structure and function during the support phase of running (Bates, James and Osternig, 1978; Drez, 1980) with excessive foot pronation being thought to be a major cause. Foot orthotic devices are frequently prescribed with the aim of holding and supporting the foot in a biomechanically optimal position. The position of the foot where it functions most efficiently with the least amount of stress on the joints, ligaments and tendons is referred to as the "neutral position of the subtalar joint." Orthotic devices have been found to diminish or eradicate compensatory motion at the subtalar joint (McKenzie, Clement and Taunton, 1985; Subotnick, 1983).

In distance running, it is important to minimise the rate of energy expenditure for a given speed. Changes in the patterns of movement and muscle activity brought about by a modification in the mechanical work performed might, in turn, affect the economy of movement. However, many previous studies into the effect of orthotics on the oxygen cost of running have concluded that if orthotics do improve running economy by enhancing running mechanics, the additional mass of the orthotics negates any mechanical improvement (Burkett et al., 1985; Hayes et al., 1983). In the present study, the possibility of improving running economy with the use of orthotics was examined by comparing the oxygen demands, ventilation, heart rate and blood lactate levels while running barefoot, in shoes and in shoes plus orthotics.

Stride rate and stride length, may be altered by adding weight to the feet. Martin (1985) showed that 1 kg added to the feet produced small but significant increases in stride length (1.4 cm). Well trained subjects run most economically when predetermined stride length remains close to one adopted by the subjects (Cavanagh and Williams, 1982). Stride frequency can be measured to detect any mechanical alterations between conditions.

Many physically stressful situations evoke a response in individuals which can differ in many ways. How an individual perceives these stresses may be reflected in his/her performance. Thus, perceived exertion and discomfort ratings may be used to establish any differences in psychological states between experimental conditions.

Little literature is available as to whether light-weight functional orthotics (<100 g per pair) affect the economy of movement. The existance of such an influence was examined by comparing selected physiological, psychological and biomechanical parameters of running in barefeet, in shoes and in shoes plus orthotics.

2 Method

Seven experienced male runners who had been fitted with orthotics to correct or reduce the amount of pronation volunteered as subjects for this investigation. Mean age (± SD) and mass (± SD) for the group were 31.7 (± 12.3) years and 62.6 (± 6.1) kg, respectively. The mean distance run by subjects was 68.58 (± 17.81) km per week and all were familiar with treadmill running. Subjects were asked to minimise the intensity and duration of their training the day prior to testing. Subjects were also instructed not to run on the day of testing. All required orthotics in order to run without pain. Orthotics had been worn from 6 months to 3 years at the time of testing. An attempt was made to restrict the study to persons who were using similar orthotics (mean mass of 90 g per pair). All devices prescribed were biomechanical functional orthotic appliances and had been moulded using a non-weightbearing, neutral position casting technique. Informed consent was obtained from all subjects prior to their participation in the study.

Heart rate was monitored during the treadmill runs using a short range radio telemetry system (Sports Tester PE 3,000, Kempele). A transmitter was worn at the base of the sternum at the xiphisternal joint and signals were transmitted to a receiver in a wrist-worn microcomputer. The $\dot{V}O_2$ and $\dot{V}E$ values were determined using a Sensor Medics 2900Z Gas Analysis system (driven by an IBM compatible microcomputer). Fingertip blood samples were drawn directly preceding and immediately following the cessation of exercise, for the later analysis of blood lactate levels. Samples were taken using an autoclix lancet, collected in a 20 ml capillary tube containing anti-coagulants. Lactate analysis was performed by means of an Analox Instruments Ltd. (London) GM7 Analyser.

Immediately after each run, assessments of perceived exertion and discomfort were made. Borg's (1986) category ratio scale was used to rate the effort of each run in general and the RPE scale was used to rate the perceived exertion of the legs, arms and breathing. Corlett and Bishop's (1976) numbered diagram of the body was used in conjunction with an 11-point scale to evaluate the perceived discomfort (RPD) of eight body segments (neck, shoulders, upper arms, lower arms, upper back, lower back, upper legs, lower legs). Stride frequency was used to establish any variation in running mechanics between the three experimental conditions. A Sony video 8 camera with 10x zoom lens was used to film the subjects from the start of the second minute to the end of the ninth minute. Stride frequency was determined by totalling the number of strides within this time period and expressing it in foot strikes.min^{-1}.

The selection of a running protocol was based upon previous research on running economy (Burkett, Kohrt and Buchbinder, 1985). Each subject ran on the treadmill under three conditions: (1) barefoot, (2) shoes, and (3) shoes plus orthotics. The order of the test conditions was counterbalanced in order to eliminate sequence bias as a potential confounding variable. Warm-up consisted of walking at 1.33 m.s^{-1} for 3 min and then jogging at 2.66 m.s^{-1} for 2 min. Each subject then performed three 10 min bouts of running on a motorised treadmill at 3.83 m.s^{-1}. The subject was fitted with a mouthpiece connected to a two-way, non-rebreathing valve and a hose directing the expired air to a mixing chamber for open circuit gas analysis. When subjects were breathing into this apparatus a nose-clip was worn at all times to ensure all expired air was collected through the two-way non-rebreathing valve. The carbon dioxide and oxygen gas analysers were calibrated prior to the arrival of the subject, using mixed gas of known concentration. Recovery between runs consisted of resting until mean heart rate had returned to within 10 beats of the pre-exercise resting level. Except for the pre- and post-run blood lactate levels, the physiological variables were measured throughout the tests.

The average value per minute over minutes 4-9 were used in statistical analysis to reflect steady state values. Using the observations for each subject, the differences between all conditions were investigated by the use of two-way analyses of variance (ANOVA). A follow-up test of least significant differences was performed on all ANOVA results which differentiated between the effects of the foot conditions.

3 Results

The mean (±SD) physiological measures ($\dot{V}O_2$, $\dot{V}E$, blood lactate levels and heart rate) of the subjects for each of the experimental conditions are summarised in Table 1. Blood lactate levels are expressed as pre- and post- exercise differences. The $\dot{V}O_2$ expressed in relative terms (ml.kg^{-1}.min^{-1}) shows that the shoes plus orthotics condition was the most economical (shoes plus orthotics < barefoot < shoes). With economy expressed in absolute terms (l.min^{-1}), the barefoot condition is the most efficient (barefoot < shoes plus orthotics < shoes) although no significant difference was found for either $\dot{V}O_2$ readings (P>0.05).

Although there was a tendency for the physiological variables of heart rate and absolute O_2 consumption to be least for the barefoot condition and highest for the shoes condition, the means were not significantly different according to ANOVA ($F_{2,14} = 1.91$; $P = 0.19$). The Friedman non-parametric test supported the observations that barefoot < shoes plus orthotics < shoes. A significant difference (P<0.05) occurred for oxygen consumption expressed in absolute terms between the three experimental conditions.

Table 1. Mean physiological and biomechanical responses to running under the three conditions

Condition	Barefoot	Shoes	orthotics	F Value
$\dot{V}O_2$ (l.min^{-1})	2.765 ± 0.493	2.887 ± 0.538	2.768 ± 0.536	1.91
$\dot{V}O_2$ (ml.kg^{-1}.min^{-1})	44.11 ± 5.68	45.48 ± 6.05	43.42 ± 5.08	1.51
$\dot{V}E$ (l.min^{-1})	76.1 ± 17.7	82.7 ± 21.04	77.47 ± 19.39	3.5
Blood lactate (mmol.l^{-1})	1.51 ± 0.96	2.11 ± 0.91	1.83 ± 0.81	3.42
Heart rate (beats.min^{-1})	151 ± 16	155 ± 15	153 ± 17	3.24
Foot strikes (min^{-1})	187 ± 20	179 ± 12	175 ± 19	4.3*

* significant at P<0.05, no asterisk = not significant (P>0.05)

Table 2. Mean psychological responses to running under the three experimental conditions

Condition	Barefoot	Shoes	orthotics	F Value
RPE Legs	10.4 ± 2.1	10.1 ± 2.0	7 ± 1.7	32.57**
RPE Arms	9.4 ± 1.1	9.4 ± 1.1	9.4 ± 1.6	0
RPE Breathing	9.6 ± 2.3	9.4 ± 2.4	10.7 ± 3	1.0
RPE Run in General	2.6 ± 0.5	3 ± 0	1 ± 1	20.91**
RPD Upper Legs	1.9 ± 1.9	2.3 ± 1.7	1 ± 1.4	9.35*
RPD Lower Legs	4.4 ± 2.6	3.9 ± 1.7	1.1 ± 1.1	14.23**

* significant at $P<0.01$, ** significant at $P<0.001$, no asterisk = not significant ($P>0.05$)

It can be seen from Table 1 that the difference in stride frequency was highly significant ($P<0.001$) between the three running conditions. The shoes condition produced a greater stride frequency than the shoes plus orthotics condition ($P<0.05$) while the barefoot condition produced the greatest stride frequency of all three conditions ($P<0.001$).
Out of the subjective responses data, there were only two body regions which caused discomfort over the experimental conditions, these being the upper legs and lower legs. Table 2 represents the mean values of all perceived exertion parameters and ratings of above zero for subjective discomfort. Running in shoes plus orthotics was rated significantly lower in exertion ($P<0.01$) than was running barefoot or in shoes. The perceived exertion of the legs followed the same trend as that of the RPE for the run in general ($P<0.001$). No differences for perceived exertion of the arms and breathing were recorded between any of the three running conditions. Perceived discomfort of the upper legs was significantly less when wearing shoes plus orthotics compared to the barefoot condition ($P<0.05$) or the shoes condition ($P<0.01$). Perceived discomfort of the lower legs was significantly greater for the barefoot ($P<0.001$) and shoes ($P<0.01$) conditions compared to the shoes plus orthotics condition.

4 Discussion

The results for stride frequency indicate that an alteration in the running mechanics occurred between all three conditions. This was reflected also in changes in the metabolic cost of running. In terms of the different responses to $\dot{V}O_2$ between conditions, cases of significant difference between shoes and shoes plus orthotics were pertinent to this research. Burkett, Kohrt and Buchbinder (1985) noted wearing orthotics weighing 160 g caused an increase in both absolute and relative $\dot{V}O_2$.

In the present study, light-weight orthotics were employed (mean = 90 g per pair). Although absolute and relative oxygen consumption values were not highly sensitive to the different foot conditions, the small changes observed provide evidence of the metabolic adjustments produced by loading of the lower extremity, the oxygen cost of running in shoes being greater than the shoes plus orthotics condition. Thus, in the present study, it appears that changes in $\dot{V}O_2$ may be attributed to the additional mass associated with the shoes rather than to the alterations in pronation due to wearing orthotics. The use of orthotics may reduce unnecessary muscular movement and therefore improve running economy. The fact that significant differences in $\dot{V}O_2$ were not observed in this study suggests that the enhanced mechanical alterations were reduced by the additional mass of the orthotics.

A possible explanation for the increase in stride frequency seen during barefoot running focuses on the modification of stride parameters made during barefoot runs to reduce the initial shock of impact. It has been shown that decreasing stride length (thus increasing stride frequency) at a given speed reduces the amount of shock which must be absorbed by the musculoskeletal system (Clarke, Frederick and Cooper, 1982). Stride frequency was higher when running in shoes than in shoes plus orthotics thus implying an alteration in the biomechanics of running while wearing orthotics. Clarke et al. (1983) have shown that longer strides cause greater shock to the legs following foot strike. However, the decreased stride frequency, hence increased stride length seen during the shoes plus orthotic condition showed no higher ratings of RPE or RPD than the shoes condition. This might be explained by the fact that orthotics reduce the amount of pronation and therefore the amount of stress being placed on the lower extremities, reducing in turn the perceived discomfort level.

The perceived exertion was perceived to be decreased significantly for the shoes plus orthotics condition but no significant difference was apparent between the barefoot or shoes condition. The RPE for the arms displayed uniform mean values for each shoe condition. Thus, it may be assumed that the wearing of shoes and orthotics does not affect the activity of the arms. A significantly lower rating in RPE for the run in general was found while running in shoes plus orthotics compared to the barefoot or shoes conditions. This finding shows parallel trends with the RPE for the legs. The subjective ratings of exertion were reduced whilst wearing shoes plus orthotics compared to running in shoes which supports the physiological observations of this study. However, the improvement in economy found during barefoot running compared to running in shoes plus orthotics was not reflected in the RPE. Thus, it can be concluded that wearing orthotics provides a psychological benefit to runners who need these devices.

From the eight body segments displayed to the runners for perceived discomfort, only the upper and lower legs experienced any perceived discomfort. Perceived discomfort of the upper and lower legs while wearing shoes plus orthotics produced significantly lower ratings of discomfort than the barefoot or shoes conditions. Since excessive pronation is characterised by the ankle collapsing medially, many overuse injuries caused by a variation of normal foot anatomy occur from the knee down, hence the greater ratings of discomfort when not wearing orthotics for the lower legs than upper legs (Table 2). Thus, apart from the RPE for the arms and breathing, all other subjective responses showed a reduction in perceived exertion/discomfort while wearing shoes plus orthotics. This corresponds to the reduction in physiological strain for the shoes plus orthotics condition, verifying the correspondence between subjective feelings and physiological responses. These findings support the view that orthotics improve running economy by reducing the amount of compensatory motion about the lower leg and foot, therefore decreasing the risk of injury.

Orthotics may serve to improve running economy to a greater extent during longer runs than used in the present study. Since many subjects indicated that they were able to run approximately 1-3 miles (1.6 - 4.8 km) without orthotics before experiencing pain or discomfort, 10 min was the restricted running time under each experimental condition. It is thought that a longer exercise period (i.e. > 30 min) would produce significant results for all parameters investigated in the present study because over-pronation would occur over a longer time period, placing a greater stress on the body. In addition to the physiological parameters used in the present study, electromyography could be used to examine further the effects that foot orthotics have on muscle activity. This could lead to an improved understanding of the importance of orthotics in the treatment of muscular overuse injuries in the leg.

If the light-weight orthotics used in this study do improve running mechanics, the amount of improvement is attenuated due to the additional cost of running associated with the mass of the orthotics. For runners with mechanical abnormalities, orthotics play a major role in the prevention of lower extremity injuries and are essential when running greater distances than examined in the present study. Nevertheless the present study demonstrates these benefits, particularly in perceived exertion and subjective discomfort.

5 References

Bates, B.T., James, L.R. and Osternig, L.R. (1978). Foot function during the support phase of running. **Running,** 3, 24-31.

Borg, G. and Ottoson, D. (1986). **The Perception of Exertion in Physical Work.** Macmillan Press, Ltd., London.

Burkett, L.N.; Kohrt, W.M. and Buchbinder, R. (1985). Effects of shoes and foot orthotics on $\dot{V}O_2$ and selected frontal plane knee kinematics. **Medicine and Science in Sports and Exercise,** 17, 158-163.

Cavanagh, P.R. and Williams, K. (1982). The effect of stride length variation on oxygen uptake during distance running. **Medicine and Science in Sports and Exercise,** 14, 30-35.

Clarke, T., Frederick, E.C. and Cooper, L.B. (1982). The effects of shoe cushioning upon selected force and temporal parameters in running (Abstract). **Medicine and Science in Sports and Exercise,** 14, 144.

Clarke, T., Cooper, L.B. Clark, D.E. and Hamill, C.L. (1983). The effect of varied stride rate upon shank deceleration in running. **Journal of Sports Sciences,** 3, 41-49.

Corlett, E.N. and Bishop, R.P. (1976). A technique for assessing postural discomfort. **Ergonomics,** 19, 175-182..

Gross, M.L. and Napoli, R.C. (1993). Treatment of lower extremity injuries with orthotic shoe inserts: An overview. **Sports Medicine,** 15, 66-70.

Hayes, J., Smith, L. and Santopietro, F. (1983). The effects of orthotics on the aerobic demands of running (Abstract). **Medicine and Science in Sports and Exercise,** 15, 169.

Martin, P.E. (1985). Mechanical and physiological responses to lower extremity loading during running. **Medicine and Science in Sports and Exercise,** 17, 427-433.

McKenzie, D.C., Clement, D.B. and Taunton, J.E. (1985). Running shoes, orthotics and injuries. **Sports Medicine,** 2, 334-347.

Subotnick, S.I. (1983). Foot orthoses: An update. **Physician and Sportsmedicine,** 11 (8), 103-109.

17 A comparison of impact forces in running shoes and military boots

A. Lees and K. Craig

1 Introduction

When the foot strikes the ground during walking or running a large impact force is generated. This impact force, characterised by its magnitude and rate of loading, is thought to be a contributory factor in overuse injuries resulting from locomotor activity. Attempts to reduce it have resulted in several generations of running footwear with increased protective capability and a whole host of features designed to promote impact absorption. Typical examples are thick wedges of closed cell foam in the midsole of the shoe, shock absorbent pads or gel placed under the heel, and gas compartments underneath the foot.

Military boots, though, have remained largely traditional in design. They offer very little cushioning and the effects of this are often seen as injury at an early stage of training. Giladi et al. (1985) reported a 31% incidence of stress fractures in new recruits after a 14 week training period. Their study was concerned with identifying anthropometric characteristics of the lower limb which were related to the incidence of stress fractures and they identified foot arch height as a factor. In a similar study, Simkin et al. (1989) reported that limb alignment was also a factor. They attempted to modify this by using orthotic devices with some shock absorbing properties and found that these helped to prevent stress fractures. Box (1989) has suggested that the incidence of injuries in new recruits when wearing military boots is over four times that expected when wearing running shoes.

It appears from these studies that shock absorbing footwear can be effective in reducing the effects of overuse injury. Although these epidemiological studies suggest the positive benefit of shock absorbing footwear, none of them has measured the forces produced by military boots and compared them with alternative, more shock absorbing footwear. Therefore, the aim of this study was to investigate the relative impact forces between running shoes and military boots during walking and running.

2 Method

Eight healthy young athletic adults (mean age 20.9 ± 0.6 yrs; mass 89.9 ± 10.5 kg, height 1.80 ± 0.07 m), all of whom had experience of running in military boots, acted as subjects. They completed an informed consent form which included details of the procedures involved and the goals of the study.

They were asked to walk or run over a Kistler force platform located in an indoor runway, firstly at a natural walking pace, and then secondly at a slow jog of 2.7 m.s^{-1} (± 5%). This speed was used as it corresponded to the accepted pace of 'speed marching' used in the British Army. The speed of progression was recorded by three light gates connected to a digital timer. Subjects were asked to complete the experiment in three footwear conditions (a supplied running shoe, a standard military issue boot, and barefoot). Each condition was repeated six times but subjects were given as much practice time as they required to ensure they could judge the required speed and hit the platform with the right foot on each occasion without interrupting their gait pattern.

The magnitude of the impact force and the load rate of the force, both divided by body weight were computed from the ground reaction force data. The data were analysed using a two-way ANOVA (locomotor style, footwear condition). A significance level of $P<0.05$ was used.

3 Results

A typical vertical ground reaction force for walking and running are given in Figures 1 and 2 respectively. In these curves, the impact peak (I) associated with heel strike can be clearly seen at the beginning of the trace. The impact peak was chosen for analysis, as it has been shown (Nigg, 1986; Frederick and Hagy, 1986) that the impact peak is more sensitive to locomotor variations (for example speed changes) and that the loading (L) and drive off (D) peaks vary little with these locomotor variations and are a function of body mass. Therefore this study concerned itself only with the impact characteristics of the vertical ground reaction force. In both barefoot and boot conditions the impact peak was an identifiable feature of the force curve.

When some subjects wore running shoes, the peak was absent. Under these circumstances there was always a clear change in gradient where the peak was expected, and this point was used to represent the impact peak numerically .

For walking, there was little difference between any of the footwear conditions in relation to maximum impact force when (Table 1), and none of these differences was significant. With regard to the impact force load rate, the running shoes produced a lower load rate than the barefoot or boots conditions and was significantly different ($P<0.05$).

WALK

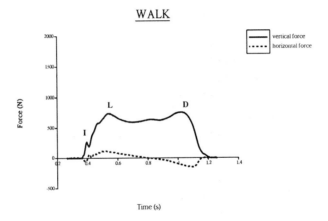

Figure 1. Vertical and horizontal ground reaction force in walking.

JOG

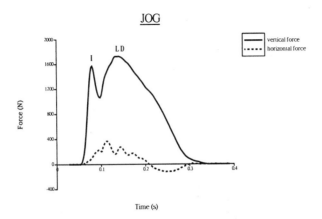

Figure 2. Vertical and horizontal ground reaction forces in jogging.

When running, the running shoes produced a noticeable reduction in magnitude of the impact force compared to the barefoot and boots condition (Table 2). There was a significant difference ($P<0.05$) between the running shoes and the boots condition, but not between the running shoes and barefoot condition, nor between the boots and barefoot conditions. For the impact force load rate, the running shoes produced a significantly lower ($P<0.05$) load rate than the barefoot or boots conditions. In addition, during running, there was a significant difference ($P<0.05$) between the barefoot and boots, with the boots producing lower a load rate than the barefoot.

Table 1. Impact force and load rate (mean and standard deviation) for walking in the three footwear conditions

			walking		
		barefoot	shoes	boots	P
impact force	mean	0.746	0.618	0.678	NS
(N.kg^{-1})	SD	0.202	0.252	0.228	
load rate	mean	41.1	12.1	32.6	<0.05
(kN.s^{-1}.kg^{-1})	SD	13.3	2.6	15.8	

Table 2. Impact force and load rate (mean and standard deviation) for running for the three footwear conditions

			running		
		barefoot	shoes	boots	P
impact force	mean	1.541	1.204	1.597	<0.05
(N.kg^{-1})	SD	0.353	0.241	0.280	
load rate	mean	73.5	35.0	54.5	<0.05
(kN.s^{-1}.kg^{-1})	SD	20.3	11.9	21.5	

4 Discussion

The data reported on impact force peak and impact force load rate are similar to normative data presented by Munro et al. (1987). Neither the impact peak nor the load rate correlated with body mass, which agrees with the suggestions of Nigg (1986) and Frederick and Hagy (1986) that body mass does not determine the impact force characteristics. The factors affecting impact force peak and load rate are therefore expected to be related to individual locomotor characteristics and to footwear conditions.

There was only a small reduction in the magnitude of the impact force peak when walking in running shoes compared to barefoot and boots, and this was not significant. This finding implies that the subjects were able to modify their gait characteristics in response to the force load they were experiencing despite the large difference in footwear conditions. In particular, the impact force in barefoot conditions, normally expected to be high, was not significantly higher than that for the other conditions. The ability for the musculo-skeletal system to adapt to the conditions it meets has been suggested by Frederick (1986) who found that the knee flexion velocity of the touch-down leg increased as running speed increased, enabling faster running to be undertaken without a proportional increase in applied force. It may be that in walking, these 'kinematically mediated' responses are also operational. This is suggested from the load rate data for walking. There are quite noticeable differences in load rate between running shoes and the two other conditions. The load rates are greater for these conditions but the force peaks are similar. The musculo-skeletal system must be able to recognise a level of force it is willing to sustain, and introduce shock absorbing mechanisms in a reactive manner to control the force experienced by the system. Subjects were allowed practice before completing each series of tests, and so there would have been ample opportunity for this adaptation to take place. Further evidence for this adaptation is the fact that two of the eight subjects produced load rates in boots greater than the load rate produced in barefeet. These subjects may not have been very used to walking in barefeet and may have modified their gait style to accommodate the unusual sensory experiences of barefoot walking.

The impact force for running does show a significant reduction for the running shoe condition. This suggests that the subjects do not have sufficient capability to mediate the higher forces found in the barefoot and boots conditions. That subjects appear to be modifying their gait in some way under the higher force conditions (barefoot and boots) is suggested by the fact that five out of the eight subjects produce higher impact forces with the boots condition than the barefoot condition. The variability in the data for the running shoe condition (demonstrated by the standard deviation in Tables 1 and 2) is similar to walking, but it is higher for the boots condition and highest for the barefoot condition. Subjects are clearly having more difficulty coping with the higher impact, and more unusual barefoot condition. The load rate during running is higher in barefoot than in the boots condition even though the peak forces do not differ. This might be taken as evidence that the musculo-skeletal system is still able to control the limit of force acting on it even though it is unable to reduce it below a certain level.

The higher forces and load rates found for military boots compared to running shoes constitutes clear evidence of the potential hazard they impose. This hazard appears to be less when walking, due to the ability of the user to control the level of force they experience. Nevertheless, the greater load rates imposed by the boots still may mean that the biological structures are more susceptible to mechanical damage and so lead to overuse injuries. When running in boots, even at low speeds, the forces and load rates are significantly elevated. Under these conditions the boots impose a clear hazard to the user. Although not tested at higher speeds, the disadvantageous conditions that the boot generates would be expected to become worse as a function of speed.

The link between selected biomechanical variables (in this case impact force and load rate) and overuse injury has not been directly made, except in the most general sense. A notion introduced in this study in order to interpret the data has been to suggest an adaptability of the musculo-skeletal system's response to load in order to limit the level of force it experiences. If this is the case, then the process of functional adaptation would itself be a factor in overuse injuries, as elements of the biological system would be less well developed to tolerate these newly applied stresses. Therefore, the process of adaptation and an individual's adaptability to a novel locomotor task may be worthy of more detailed study in the future as a basis for investigating the causality of overuse injuries.

5 Conclusions

It is concluded from these data that selected types of footwear have the ability to reduce impact force loading on the body when compared to the unshod foot. The military boot applies a greater stress on the body than the conventional running shoe and this is apparent mainly during jogging and running actions. That the military boot produces almost 50% higher load rates than running shoes is seen as a cause for concern for new recruits. Sudden changes in the stress imposed on the body is a classic 'training error' and predictably will lead to higher incidence of injury, confirming the epidemiological evidence from military studies.

6 References

Box,C. J. (1989) A survey of overuse lower limb injuries in army training - phase 2. Army Personnel Research Establishment, Farnborough

Frederick, E. C. and Hagy, J. L. (1986). Factors affecting peak vertical ground reaction forces in running. International Journal of Sports Biomechanics, 2, 41-49.

Frederick, E. C (1986) Kinematically mediated effecys of sport shoe design: a review. Journal of Sports Sciences, 4,1 69-184.

Giladi, M., Milgrom, C., Stein, M., Kashtan, H., Margulies, J., Chisin, R., Stienberg, R. and Aharonson, Z. (1985) The low arch, a protective factor in stress fractures. A prospective study of 295 military recruits. Orthopaedic Review,14, 81-84.

Munro, C. F., Miller, D. I. and Fuglevand, A. J. (1987) Ground reaction force in running: a re-examination. Journal of Biomechanics, 20, 147-155.

Nigg, B. M. (1986) The Biomechanics of Running Shoes. Human Kinetics: Champaign, Illinois

Simkin, A., Leicter, I., Giladi, M., Stein, M. and Milgrom, C. (1989) Combined effect of foot arch structure and an orthotic device on stress fractures. Foot & Ankle, 10, 25-29.

18 An investigation of selected methods for the assessment of insole materials used within the shoe

G. Barton and A. Lees

1 Introduction

During the development phase of shoe manufacture, insole materials are tested mechanically, without the use of human subjects (Pratt et al., 1986). This does not provide any information about the behaviour of those materials within their target environment, which is inside the shoe. An insole material which performs well only in the mechanical laboratory tests is of limited practical use. Insole materials must be evaluated within the shoe (SanFilippo et al., 1992) during the activity for which they are designed.

The optimal properties of insoles may vary with a given use. Insoles designed for walking shoes, sports shoes or orthopaedic shoes may possess quite different properties. Insoles already commercially available can form a standard series, and a new insole material could be evaluated by finding the element of the series to which it best corresponds.

The basis of this comparison could be pressure related information under the foot within the shoe, measured by the MICRO-EMED system (Novel München, Germany). Naturally the behaviour of an insole during such a dynamic activity as walking can be described only by several variables, which raises the question of whether these several variables should be handled individually or contextually (Ripley, 1987). Repeated measures analysis of variance (ANOVA) can be used to compare single variables, while the contextual analysis of multiple variables requires capabilities of neural networks (NN) or linear discriminant analysis (LDA).

Therefore the aim of the study was to find out which of these methods can differentiate between two insole materials (a standard and a developmental) in their ability to decrease vertical pressure and related variables.

2 Materials and methods

A group of seven healthy male subjects (mean ± SD age:
30 ± 8.7 years, mean±SD body mass: 75.5 ± 5.5 kg) walked on
a treadmill (1.11 m/s, 1.73/s cadence) in the same shoe
under three conditions. Two were insoles (ASTRON) of
different density but the same thickness, and one was
without an insole. Pressure data below the foot were
recorded by the MICRO-EMED system (Novel München, Germany).
Seven variables (total area of contact, total force,
maximal pressure and x and y coordinates of both the
maximal pressure and those of the centre of pressure) of
ten successive steps were averaged. Total force and maximal
pressure were normalised to body weight. The resultant
twenty-one sets of data are listed in Figure 1. The three
methods used to evaluate differences in experimental
conditions were:
  - An ANOVA and Newman-Keuls test, which were used to
evaluate differences sequentially in the seven variables
among the three conditions (two insoles and no insole);
  - A neural network, which can learn from examples, and
because the learnt information is stored in an abstract
form across the network's structure, it can generalise.
This means that appropriate classifications will be made
even for inputs not actually included in the training set
(Miller et al., 1992). The back-propagation algorithm was
employed, introduced by Rumelhart et al. (1986). A three-
layered, feedforward NN was constructed with seven input,
five hidden and three output neurons. After dividing the
twenty-one sets of data into two groups, the NN was trained
with the seven variables of the first group and tested with
the data of the second group. Subsequently this was
repeated with the two groups swapped around.
  - LDA which can separate two or more conditions given
measurements for these conditions on several variables
(Manly, 1986). It finds the combination of coefficients
that maximises the separation between the conditions. An
LDA was used to classify the patterns of the first group
based on the second group as predictors. Subsequently the
two groups were swapped around.
  Figure 1 illustrates the data and the two different
approaches to the data handling. The way data were
considered is illustrated by the frames surrounding the
data.

(a)

#	Subj.#	Cond.	Area (cm²)	Force (N)	Pmax (N/cm²)	Pmx (cm²)	Pmy (cm²)	SwpX (cm²)	Swpy (cm²)
1	Subj1	A	134.8	15.17	0.53	8.05	22.25	4.43	13.28
2	Subj1	D	142.1	15.40	0.40	7.75	21.95	4.26	13.35
3	Subj1	N	132.8	15.50	0.57	8.15	22.25	4.34	13.23
4	Subj2	A	122.2	15.89	0.38	6.40	21.95	3.98	13.38
5	Subj2	D	121.7	15.25	0.39	6.75	22.40	4.13	13.80
6	Subj2	N	111.3	15.98	0.42	4.60	19.70	3.83	13.13
7	Subj3	A	140.2	14.55	0.31	7.05	22.85	3.89	14.08
8	Subj3	D	134.4	13.66	0.27	6.40	21.95	3.98	14.19
9	Subj3	N	122.4	11.56	0.41	9.48	22.15	6.02	13.16
10	Subj4	A	132.5	14.24	0.33	6.65	16.55	4.02	13.11
11	Subj4	D	131.0	14.39	0.32	8.15	22.50	3.92	13.47
12	Subj4	N	123.6	14.14	0.36	7.65	23.15	3.99	13.17
13	Subj5	A	134.8	14.11	0.32	4.15	14.15	3.61	12.55
14	Subj5	D	129.5	14.91	0.31	5.75	15.45	3.87	12.51
15	Subj5	N	123.2	14.27	0.37	7.05	18.60	4.16	12.75
16	Subj6	A	108.6	15.55	0.33	6.35	19.25	4.45	13.87
17	Subj6	D	113.0	15.62	0.33	5.65	19.05	4.23	13.74
18	Subj6	N	102.0	15.39	0.33	5.60	19.25	4.28	13.65
19	Subj7	A	146.1	15.90	0.46	8.25	22.25	4.10	13.23
20	Subj7	D	149.6	15.85	0.43	8.25	22.25	4.08	13.66
21	Subj7	N	140.9	14.98	0.47	7.80	21.95	3.97	13.37

(b)

#	Subj.#	Cond.	Area (cm²)	Force (N)	Pmax (N/cm²)	Pmx (cm)	Pmy (cm)	SwpX (cm)	Swpy (cm)
1	Subj1	A	134.8	15.17	0.53	8.05	22.25	4.43	13.28
2	Subj1	D	142.1	15.40	0.40	7.75	21.95	4.26	13.35
3	Subj1	N	132.8	15.50	0.57	8.15	22.25	4.34	13.23
4	Subj2	A	122.2	15.89	0.38	6.40	21.95	3.98	13.38
5	Subj2	D	121.7	15.25	0.39	6.75	22.40	4.13	13.80
6	Subj2	N	111.3	15.98	0.42	4.60	19.70	3.83	13.13
7	Subj3	A	140.2	14.55	0.31	7.05	22.85	3.89	14.08
8	Subj3	D	134.4	13.66	0.27	6.40	21.95	3.98	14.19
9	Subj3	N	122.4	11.56	0.41	9.48	22.15	6.02	13.16
10	Subj4	A	132.5	14.24	0.33	6.65	16.55	4.02	13.11
11	Subj4	D	131.0	14.39	0.32	8.15	22.50	3.92	13.47
12	Subj4	N	123.6	14.14	0.36	7.65	23.15	3.99	13.17
13	Subj5	A	134.8	14.11	0.32	4.15	14.15	3.61	12.55
14	Subj5	D	129.5	14.91	0.31	5.75	15.45	3.87	12.51
15	Subj5	N	123.2	14.27	0.37	7.05	18.60	4.16	12.75
16	Subj6	A	108.6	15.55	0.33	6.35	19.25	4.45	13.87
17	Subj6	D	113.0	15.62	0.33	5.65	19.05	4.23	13.74
18	Subj6	N	102.0	15.39	0.33	5.60	19.25	4.28	13.65
19	Subj7	A	146.1	15.90	0.46	8.25	22.25	4.10	13.23
20	Subj7	D	149.6	15.85	0.43	8.25	22.25	4.08	13.66
21	Subj7	N	140.9	14.98	0.47	7.80	21.95	3.97	13.37

Figure 1. (a) ANOVA compared individual variables (i.e columns) among the three conditions (b) NN and LDA learned to associate a set of 7 variables with their conditions considering half of the data (training), and the second half was evaluated based on the results of training. Subsequently the two halves were swapped around and the same protocol was repeated.

3 Results

The results of the ANOVA are shown in Table 1. The Newman-Keuls test showed that total area of contact with no insole material was significantly less (P<0.01) than the area under all other conditions. No significant difference was found between the insoles (P>0.05). The maximal pressure for one of the insoles was significantly lower (P<0.01) than without an insole, but there was no significant difference between the insoles. The rest of the variables showed no significant result. These findings agree with those of SanFilippo et al. (1992). Note that all but one variables showed significant differences among subjects.

Table 1. Results of the ANOVA

Variables	F between subjects	F between groups
Area	49.01 (P<0.0001)*	21.33 (P=0.0001)*
Force	6.17 (P<0.005)*	1.38 (P>0.05)
Pmax	11.81 (P<0.0005)*	6.89 (P=0.01)*
Pmx	3.25 (P<0.05)*	0.38 (P>0.05)
Pmy	5.03 (P<0.05)*	0.79 (P>0.05)
SwpX	0.95 (P>0.05)	0.94 (P>0.05)
Swpy	7.79 (P<0.005)*	3.01 (P=0.08)

When trained with the first group (ten sets of seven variables), the NN recognised 4 sets of data correctly; the LDA recognised 6 sets of data correctly from the second group. When trained with the second group (eleven sets of seven variables), the NN recognised 3 sets of data correctly, the LDA recognised 5 sets of data correctly from the first group.

4 Conclusions

The repeated measures ANOVA could not identify a single variable which was different between the insoles. The simultaneous analysis of the variables (NN and LDA) could differentiate between the insoles, although it could not decide which was better (which is an inherent property of the latter two methods). This proved that the contextual data handling (NN and LDA) was superior to the isolated data analysis (ANOVA).

The advantage of the NN approach compared to LDA is that NN can generalise, provided that the training set covered a representative group of patterns (Miller et al., 1992). It can be stated that neural networks could be applied to fit an insole material to the member of a standard series it matches the most, because of their generalisation ability and contextual data handling.

In this study the low number of patterns could account for the relatively low performance of the NN. Holzreiter et al. (1992) have shown that the generalisation ability of a NN depends on the number of training patterns, and so future work should assess NN using a larger sample of subjects.

5 References

Holzreiter, S.H. and Köhle, M.E. (1993) Assessment of gait patterns using neural networks. **Journal of Biomechanics**, 126, 645-651.

Manly, B.F.J. (1986) **Multivariate Statistical Methods, A primer.** Chapman & Hall, London.

Miller, A.S. Blott D.H. and Hames T.K. (1992) Review of neural network applications in medical imaging and signal processing. **Medical and Biological Engineering & Computing**, 30, 449-464.

Pratt, D.J. Rees, P.H. and Rodgers, C. (1986) Assessment of some shock absorbing insoles. **Prosthetics and Orthotics International**, 10, 43-45.

Ripley, B.D. (1987) An introduction to statistical pattern recognition, in **Interactions in Artificial Intelligence and Statistical Methods** (ed B. Phelps), Gower Technical Press Ltd, Hampshire, pp. 176-187.

Rumelhart, D.E. Hinton, G.E. and Williams, R.J. (1986) Learning internal representations by error propagation, in **Parallel Distributed Processing** (eds D.E. Rumelhart and J.L. McClelland), MIT Press, Cambridge, MA. 318-362.

SanFilippo, P.B. Stess, R.M. and Moss, K.M. (1992) Dynamic plantar pressure analysis, Comparing common insole materials. **Journal of the American Podiatric Medical Association**, 82, 507-513.

19 The shock attenuation characteristics of soccer shin guards

A. Lees and S. Cooper

1 Introduction

Shinguards are used by soccer players to protect their shins and ankles from the effects of direct contact by an opponent's boot. Their primary function is to protect the skin, underlying soft tissues and bones of the lower leg from external impacts. They prevent injury by means of shock absorption, spreading the load, and by modifying the energy absorption characteristics of the system. Early forms of shinguard consisted of old newspapers placed between the sock and the leg. The earliest proprietary brands were made of material and leather with thin rods of wood placed longitudinally within the construction to give it form and to aid its function. More recently, with the advent of plastic and foam materials the contemporary shinguard is usually made of some form of plastic external shell with an inner foam cushioning material. The wearing of these shinguards has been mandatory in English soccer since 1990, and yet their effectiveness in reducing the severity of impact has not been evaluated, and no standard methods for their evaluation exist. Therefore the aim of this study was to develop an appropriate method for testing the effectiveness of a shinguard in terms of shock and energy absorption and to evaluate, by comparison, the effectiveness of different shinguard types and constructions.

2 Method

The method used to evaluate shock attenuation and energy absorption due to impact was similar to that used in the testing of cricket leg guards and followed the requirements of the British Standards Institution BS 6183 Part 1. The test equipment consisted of a weighted shaft (mass of 5.0 ± 0.1 kg) which terminated in a hemispherical striking face of diameter 73 ± 1 mm. It was instrumented with an accelerometer attached to its upper surface and dropped from a height of 400 ± 5 mm. The shinguard was placed around a wooden leg form, which was firmly attached to the base of the impact tester which was in turn attached to a solid floor. Data were sampled at 2000 Hz and on impact, a measure of deceleration was recorded. The shaft tended to bounce two or three times on the shinguard, and the recording of the subsequent bounces enabled the flight time of the striker to be calculated on the basis of projectile theory. This in turn enabled the energy return from the shinguard to be calculated.

Five shinguards of different materials and constructions were used. Two (A and B) were of a material construction within which a removable polyethelyn (hard plastic) shell was placed. Any padding which the shinguards had was very thin and light, and its hardness could not be measured using the Shore A scale. One (C) was of a ribbed construction in which six polyethelyn strips were placed in pockets longitudinally along the shinguard, and it had a thin polyester backing. These three shinguards also had ankle shells attached to them to provide ankle protection but these were not considered during this analysis.. Two (D and E) were of a simpler construction which was of a external polyethelyn shell with an EVA (ethylene vinyl acetate) backing designed to absorb impact. The hardness of each shinguard type together with the EVA backing for D and E was measured using a Shore A hardness meter. The shinguards were typical examples covering the price range and construction types available from a well stocked sports shop. Each shinguard was tested ten times and the mean and standard deviation (SD) of each series reported.

Data were analysed statistically using a one way ANOVA to establish differences. The level at which significance was established was set at $P < 0.05$.

3 Results

A typical recording from the accelerometer is given in Figure 1. Shaft release is the point at which the acceleration value becomes negative. It represents falling under gravity and provides a means for calibrating the accelerometer trace. The first and largest peak is the impact peak. This is followed by two further peaks representing the second and third bounce. The trace then settles down to a zero level as the system comes to rest. The time between the first and second peak enables the rebound height to be calculated, and the energy return is computed as a percentage of the drop height to the rebound height. A similar process is carried out for the second and third peaks. The dwell time is measured as the time the signal is positive during an impact.

Initially, ten impacts were made on the wooden leg form without any shinguard in place. This was done to establish the effect of the presence of a shinguard and to provide a comparative baseline for further measures. The wooden leg form produced a mean impact deceleration of 97.8 ± 3.4 g, a dwell (contact) time of 12.9 ± 2.4 ms and an energy return of 29.6 ± 1.8 %. The results from the shinguards are given in Table 1.

The ANOVA results showed that there were significant differences between shinguards with respect to peak deceleration ($F_{4,45} = 82.2$, P<0.001), dwell time ($F_{4,45} = 5.7$, P<0.01) and energy return ($F_{9,45} = 24.6$, P<0.001) . The location of the differences can be established from inspection of Table 1, but no further analysis of the data was deemed necessary.

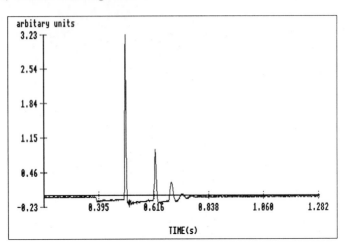

Figure 1. A typical impact acceleration recording.

Table 1. Values for measured parameters characterising shinguard shock attenuation (mean and standard deviation)

shinguard type	hardness price * category	(Shore A)	peak deceleration g	dwell time ms	energy return %
A	H	91	62.6	17.8	47.0
			5.5	2.5	2.1
B	H	85	53.8	16.3	40.7
			3.5	0.8	2.4
C	M	45	69.9	15.1	44.9
			4.5	1.2	3.9
D	M	97 + 14#	42.4	17.2	50.3
			1.9	3.5	2.0
E	L	98 + 27#	47.2	17.8	50.7
			2.7	3.6	2.1

* price category   H = high cost, M= medium cost, L = low cost
# represents the hardness of the outer shell followed by the inner foam padding

4 Discussion

The application of the British Standard's method for testing cricket pads to the testing of shinguards appears to be sound. The method has enabled results to be gained which can be interpreted in terms of the properties of the shinguards. The values for impact deceleration were found to be between 40 - 70 g while those required to meet BS 6183 Part 1 are from 225 to 275 g. Such a large discrepancy between the two values does not imply that soccer shinguards have extraordinary shock absorption properties. The material, thickness and construction of both cricket pads and shinguards are quite different, and a general considered that the cricket pads offer more protection to the leg than shinguards. Some other factor must affect the magnitude of the results. It may be that the wooden form used as a leg substitute for attaching the shinguards, responded differently compared to the aluminium form used for assessing cricket pads. It is not known how much difference these materials would make, or what other factors may be involved. The data collected in this study therefore are not thought to be comparable to that produced under BS 6183 Part 1.

The striking mass and drop height used were those required by the above standard. Although the striking mass will not replicate the velocity of impact of cricket ball with pad, it does attempt to replicate the energy of impact at about 120 J. In soccer, the effective mass of the foot would be about 2.5 kg (Plagenhoef, 1971) and a typical kicking velocity (Isokawa and Lees, 1987) would be about 18 m.s^{-1} giving an impact energy of 400 J. The striking conditions during testing are therefore an under-estimate of what might occur in a game. Nigg and Yeadon (1986) have demonstrated that the specific response of a material to an impact test is a function of the striking conditions, and that as striking mass increases the response of the material changes in an unexpected manner. It is apparent that impact testing is best performed in a comparative sense, which has been the case for the data reported in this study, and interpreted for the specific conditions used.

These results show that shinguards *per se* are effective in providing a substantial reduction in impact deceleration. They appear to do this by increasing the dwell time of the striker on the shinguard by 30 - 40 %. Thus the materials used allow the impact impulse to be dissipated over a larger period of time and as a result reduce the magnitude of the impact force by between 40 - 60%. The harder outer shell of the shinguards will also act as an area elastic surface (Nigg and Yeadon, 1986) and as such be effective in spreading the load. This in turn will reduce the pressure between the shinguard and the leg. Thus a combination of peak force reduction and an increase in impact area will substantially reduce the localised pressure, and therefore the likelihood for skin abrasion and penetration from boots or studs.

With regard to energy absorption, it should be noted that shinguards do not in themselves contain sufficient material to absorb a high proportion of the energy available during impact. This energy is either transmitted to the structure being hit or reflected back to the striking implement causing it to rebound. The extent that the energy will be reflected back to the striking implement is a function of the visco-elastic properties of impact mass and leg. More severe injuries, such as fractures, are the result of high energy rather than high force impacts. The leg form used in the testing encourages much of the impact energy to be absorbed. The energy return value of nearly 30% meant that over 70 % of the impact energy was absorbed. Whether this will cause a fracture or not would depend on the initial energy of impact, the site and direction of impact and the underlying strength of the leg on which it impacts. In general, the probability of fracture for any single impact cannot be established. However, with the shinguard in place the energy return to the striking mass increased, indicating that the energy absorbed by the leg form was reduced from 70 % to between 50 - 60 % of the total impact energy. This implies that the shinguards are effective in protecting the leg against impacts of this nature by encouraging more energy to be reflected. However, in the game situation, an impact may be made between foot and leg, for example, during a sliding tackle. In this situation the impact energy is determined by the energy of the whole striking object (the opponent's body), and due to its large mass will produce an impact energy likely to exceed that required to cause a fracture.

With regard to individual shinguards, it is apparent from the data that some perform better than others. Those (D and E) which have a low impact deceleration also have a high energy return, indicating less energy absorbed by leg. They perform well on both shock and energy absorption. This is attributable to their construction which is one of a hard outer shell and a shock absorbent backing. The hard shell spreads the load, and the backing helps absorb shock and return energy. It is likely that these shinguards operate in a similar manner to a running shoe which also is successful at absorbing shock and returning energy. The opposite is true for the shinguards A and B. This is because their construction offers the hard external outer shell but no shock absorbent backing to aid further in the absorption of shock and energy. Despite their higher cost, and superior cosmetic appearance, these performed less well. Shinguard C is characterised by poor impact absorption which is due to the ribbed construction. The ribs will be suitable for widely spread impacts but are not very effective against impacts which cover a small target area. The shock and energy absorbing properties of each do not appear to relate to the price of the product.

5 Conclusion

It is concluded that the shock and energy absorption characteristics of shinguards can be quantified by the methods used, although the data should only be used for a comparative evaluation. The shinguard does have a protective role, reducing the impact acceleration by up to 60% and by reducing the energy absorbed by the leg by up to 20%. The specific response of a shinguard to impact is determined by both the materials and methods of construction. There are differences in performance between shinguard types but these do not appear to relate to the price of the product.

6 References

British Standards Institution (1981). Protective equipment for cricketers. BS 6183: Part 1.

Isokawa, M. and Lees, A. (1987) A biomechanical analysis of the instep kick motion in soccer. In: T. Reilly et al. (eds) First World Congress of Science and Football. E & F.N. Spon:London

Nigg, B. M. and Yeadon, M. R. (1986) Biomechanical aspects of playing surfaces. J. Sports Sciences, 5, 117-145.

Plagenhoef , S. (1971). Patterns of Human Motion. Englewood Cliffs, N.J.: Prentice-Hall.

20 Effects of a weightlifting belt on spinal loading during performance of the dead-lift

T. Reilly and S. Davies

1 Introduction

Weightlifting is characterised by risk of back injury due to the high loads placed on the lumbar intervertebral discs. Weightlifters' belts are marketed with the expressed aim of preventing back injuries whilst lifting heavy loads. They may do so by supporting and stabilizing the spine and by raising intra-abdominal pressure which would help to reduce the spinal compression forces. This has been confirmed in studies of the effects of wearing a weightlifter's belt on performance of the dead-lift (Harman et al., 1989) and squat (Lander et al., 1990). Use of an abdominal belt by industrial workers has been reported to increase intra-abdominal pressure whilst lifting loads of 72.7 - 90.9 kg (McGill et al., 1990). It is unclear whether this potentially beneficial effect is maintained over multiple repetitions of lifting activities.

Measurement of spinal shrinkage has been employed to indicate compressive loading on the spine (Reilly et al., 1990). The technique has been used in both industrial and sport contexts. Tyrrell et al. (1985) showed that spinal shrinkage, measured using precision stadiometry, increased with the load lifted. Later, Garbutt et al. (1994) reported the amount of shrinkage occurring during circuit weight-training, the additional shrinkage reducing in magnitude from the first to the third circuit of exercises. This reflects the phenomenon of creep:- continuous deformation under a constant load at a decreasing rate (Kaigle et al., 1992). The outflow of tissue fluid from the intervertebral disc with compression loading is the primary mechanism involved in the creep response. A potential benefit of a weightlifter's belt is that the increased intra-abdominal pressure would contribute towards reduction of forces on the spine and so help maintain the shock-absorption characteristics of the intervertebral discs.

A standard weightlifter's belt was reported to reduce the discomfort associated with performing a circuit training regimen consisting of six common weight-training exercises. There was a tendency towards a decrease in shrinkage whilst the circuit was performed when a belt was worn compared to a trial without a belt (Bourne and Reilly, 1991). The change in exercises used in the circuit from station to station would have altered the forces on the spine and influenced the dynamic response characteristics of the discs. This would be avoided, if multiple repetitions of one exercise known to induce spinal loading were used. Consequently the aim of this study was to establish the efficacy of a weightlifter's belt in attenuating spinal shrinkage during multiple repetitions of the dead-lift. A further aim was to examine the relationships between shrinkage and estimated cross-sectional area of the lumbar discs.

2 Methods

Ten male subjects participated in the study, after giving written informed consent. Their mean (±S.D) age was 22·7 (±2·7) years, body mass 71·5 (±8·0) kg. All had experience of weightlifting and were without a history of back pain.

The subjects performed 8 sets of 20 repetitions of the dead-lift with 10 kg on an Olympic bar. This was done on two separate occasions, once whilst wearing a belt (Diversified Products, Swansea) and once without the belt. Subjects had prior familiarisation with the exercise regimen which took 21 minutes to perform. A recovery of 1 minute was allowed between sets.

The subjects had a further familiarisation visit to the laboratory for training on the stadiometer (Reilly et al., 1991). Each subject was deemed to be trained when 10 consecutive measures could be reproduced with SD less than 0 · 5 mm. Cross-sectional area of the L3-L4, L4-L5 and L5-S1 discs was estimated using the anthropometric procedure of Colombini et al. (1989).

The dead-lift was performed according to standard instructions. The subject stood close to the barbell, feet about 45 cm apart. The grip was about 'shoulder-width'; the knuckles of one hand were to the front of the bar, and the other to the rear. The back was kept straight, buttocks low and the shoulders forward of the barbell. On inhalation, the subject stood erect keeping the arms straight and exerting maximum force from the leg muscles against the floor until the barbell rested across the thighs with the shoulders taken back.

The trials were completed between 09:30 and 11:30 hours to control for circadian variation (Wilby et al., 1987). A 15 minute period in the Fowler posture was used to standardise for any effect of prior morning activity on spinal column length. A reference measurement of stature was taken before performing the dead-lifts: thus measurement was repeated immediately on cessation of exercise. This was completed within 2 minutes. The perception of effort was rated according to Borg (1982).

Comparisons of data for the two conditions were made using t-tests. A non-parametric sign test was employed to analyse the data for perceived exertion. Relationships between shrinkage, lumbar disc area and body mass were investigated using the Pearson - product moment correlation.

3 Results and Discussion

Mean shrinkage was greater when no belt was worn compared to when the belt was used ($P<0·05$). The magnitude of shrinkage incurred (Table 1) when no belt was worn exceeded the 3·6 (± 3·3) mm reported by Bourne and Reilly (1991) whose session lasted 31 (± 4) minutes. It was, however, close to the 5·5 mm reported by Leatt et al. (1986) after 25 min circuit weight-training.

Table 1. Shrinkage and perceived exertion (Mean ± SD) for the two experimental trials (with belt, no belt)

Effect	Condition	
	With belt	Without belt
Shrinkage (mm)	2.08±0.05	4.08±1.28
Perceived exertion	13.4±1.3	16.2±1.6

The wearing of the protective belt provided a 49% attenuation to the shrinkage in stature incurred during the performance of the exercise regimen under normal conditions. This was reflected also in a reduction in the perceived effect associated with the dead-lift regimen.

The shrinkage incurred under the normal condition (no belt) was influenced by anthropometric factors. This was manifest by the significant correlations between shrinkage and body mass ($r= 0.65$; $P<0.05$) and between spinal shrinkage and estimated mean lumbar disc area at L4-L5 ($r= 0.72$; $P<0.05$). These correlations were evident only in the trial when no belt was worn. This suggests that the protective effects of the weightlifting belt may vary between individuals. All subjects showed some reduction in shrinkage and perceived exertion on wearing the belt. The reduction in shrinkage due to wearing the belt was significantly correlated with body mass ($r=0.63$; $P<0.05$) but not with lumbar disc area ($P>0.05$). This suggests that the larger individuals benefitted more from the protective effects of wearing the belt.

The main observation of this study was that wearing a weightlifter's belt was effective in reducing the load on the spine during multiple repetitions of the dead-lift. Concomitant with this effect was a decrease in the perceived effort. The shrinkage incurred in weightlifting was related both to body mass and lumbar disc area. The decrease in shrinkage associated with wearing the belt was significantly related to body mass but not to estimated lumbar disc area.

4 References

Borg, G. (1982) Psychophysical bases of perceived exertion. Medicine and Science in Sports and Exercise, 14, 377-381.

Bourne, N.D. and Reilly, T. (1991) Effect of a weightlifting belt on spinal shrinkage. British Journal of Sports Medicine, 25, 209-212.

Colombini, D., Occhipinti, E., Grieco, A. and Faccini, M. (1989) Estimation of lumbar disc areas by means of anthropometric parameters. Spine, 14, 51-55.

Garbutt, G., Boocock, M.G., Reilly, T. and Troup, J.D.G. (1994) Physiological and spinal responses to circuit weightlifting. Ergonomics, 37, 117-125.

Harman, E.A., Rosenstein, R.M., Frykman, P.N. and Nigro, G.A. (1989) Effects of a belt on intra-abdominal pressure. Medicine and Science in Sports Exercise, 21, 186-190.

Kaigle, A.M., Magnusson, M., Pope, M.H., Broman, H and Hansson, T. (1992) Invivo measurement of intervetebral creep: a preliminary report. Clinical Bromechanics, 7, 59-62.

Lander, J.E., Simonton, R.L. and Giacobbe, J.K.F. (1990) The effectiveness of weight-belts during the squat exercise. Medicine and Science in Sports Exercise, 22, 117-126.

Leatt, P., Reilly, T. and Troup, J.D.G. (1986) Spinal loading during circuit weight training and running. British Journal of Sports Medicine, 20, 119-124.

McGill, S.M., Norman, R.W. and Sharratt, M.T. (1990) The effect of an abdominal belt on trunk muscle activity and intra-abdominal pressure during squat lifts. Ergonomics, 33, 147-160.

Reilly, T., Boocock, M.G., Garbutt, G., Troup, J.D.G. and Linge, K. (1991) Changes in stature during exercise and sports training. Applied Ergonomics, 22, 308-311.

Tyrrell, A.R., Reilly, T. and Troup, J.D.G. (1985) Circadian variation in stature and the effects of spinal loading. Spine, 10, 161-164.

Wilby, J., Linge, K., Reilly, T. and Troup, J.D.G. (1987) Spinal shrinkage in females: circadian variation and the effects of circuit weight-training. Ergonomics, 30, 47-54.

21 The effect of rear wheel hub design and chain alignment on cycle economy
R.J. Tong, T.D. Dobbins and S-M. Cooper

1 Introduction

Cycling economy has been defined as the oxygen consumption for a given submaximal work-rate during cycling (Hagberg et al., 1978). This physiological measure is useful during Ôsteady stateÕ exercise in which the oxygen consumed is directly related to the energy expended, and has been used extensively in research on cycling. At a given sub-maximal work-rate, an individual with a lower oxygen consumption is regarded as being more economical. This is more important in longer duration exercise, such as endurance cycling, where success largely depends upon both the aerobic capacity of the individual and the economy of the performance.

It is well established that factors such as pedal cadence, power output, crank length, seat height, body position, chain ring design, shoe-pedal interface, aerodynamics, and environmental conditions can affect cycling economy (Nordeen-Snyder 1977; Seabury et al., 1977; Hagberg et al., 1978; Hagberg et al., 1981; Faria et al., 1982; Coast et al.,1985; Hull et al., 1992). In physiological terms, factors which affect cycling economy, such as load and cadence, have been fully investigated by Hagberg et al., (1981), Faria et al., (1982), and Coast et al., (1985). Coast et al. (1985) reported that not only is there an optimum pedal rate, but that optimal cadence varies depending upon the power output and the skill level of the rider. Biomechanical and cycle design factors have also been investigated, but there appears to have been limited collaborative research between exercise physiologists and engineers (Gonzalez et al., 1989; Dal Monte et al., 1987).

Recent technological advances in rear wheel hub design allow for a more efficient transfer of energy from the rider to the cycle, and consequently, the interface between the rider and the cycle warrants further investigation. One such technological advance is the rear wheel hub designed by Goldtec Cycle Components Ltd, (Cardiff).

The purpose of this study was twofold: (1) to investigate the effects of a new rear hub on cycling economy and; (2) to establish whether chain alignment affects cycling economy. For the purpose of this study, cycling economy was defined as the oxygen consumption at a power output of 250 W.

2 Method

Eight riders, ranging from elite class 1 to recreational cyclists, volunteered to take part in this study. The physical characteristics of the subjects (mean ± SD) are shown in Table 1. Maximum oxygen uptake was directly determined using a standard Kingcycle ramp protocol (Keen et al., 1992).

The procedures and possible risk factors were explained to the riders who prior, to the assessment, were asked to give their informed consent. Each rider reported to the laboratory on two separate occasions, and all tests were completed with the riders using their own cycle on a standard Kingcycle rig (EDS Portaprompt Ltd. High Wycombe, Bucks). Prior to testing, each subject's stature and body mass were recorded. Stature was measured to the nearest 0.1 cm using a Holtain fixed stadiometer and body mass was recorded using an Avery Beam balance to the nearest 0.1 kg.

Each test was preceded by a warm-up stage where the rider cycled at between 150 and 250 W for 5 minutes. This was followed by a 3 min trial at the test work-rate of 250 W. During the first test session each subject completed 3 trials of 3 min duration at a work-rate of 250 W with 2 min recovery between each trial. The rear wheel was then changed and the rider completed a further 3 trials at 250 W with 2 min recovery. The rear wheel hubs tested were the standard Shimano Durace hub and the Goldtec hub which is coated in titanium nitride. Both rear wheel hubs were modified and fitted with seven identical 12 teeth sprockets.

Table 1.   Physical characteristics of the subjects

	Age (yrs)	Stature (m)	Body mass (kg)	$\dot{V}O2max$ (ml/kg/min)	Max. heart rate (beats/min)
Mean	19.9	1.82	78.1	66.7	193
SD	9.1	0.04	9.5	7.5	7

During the second session of testing, the subjects performed
two, 3 min trials at a work-rate of 250 W followed by 2 min
recovery, for each of the 3 chain alignment positions. The
three chain alignment positions tested were: nearest to the
chain stays (position 1); in line with the front chain ring
(position 2) and nearest to the hub centre (position 3).

Expired air was continuously monitored using a Medigraphics
CPX on-line gas analysis system (Cardiokinetics, Manchester).
Data were averaged for each minute, with the final minute of
each stage considered to reflect 'steady state'. Heart rate was
continuously monitored using short range telemetry (Sports
Tester, Polar, Finland). The order of the testing was counterbalanced design to remove any ordering effects, and the tyre
pressure, chain tension and rider position were standardised
for each rider. Before each testing session, the Kingcycle rig
and gas analysis system were calibrated. The pneumotachograph
was calibrated using a 3 litre syringe at various flow rates.
The oxygen and carbon dioxide analysers were automatically
calibrated using oxygen and carbon dioxide from room air as a
reference point (20.93% and 0.03% respectively), and a
calibration gas with oxygen and carbon dioxide concentrations
of 12% and 5% respectively.

The results are presented as mean ($\pm$ SD) values. Differences
between the trials were assessed using analysis of variance for
repeated measures(ANOVA). In an attempt to guard against
violations of the assumption of sphericity for the ANOVA, and
in the absence of an estimate of epsilon, the Greenhouse-
Geisser adjustment was applied to the relevant degrees of
freedom values. Significant F ratios were investigated using
post-hoc Tukey tests.

3 Results and Discussion

Although the mean physical characteristics of the sample
were similar to those reported by Swain and Wilcox (1992),
and Hagberg et al.(1978), the range was slightly wider,
indicating that the sample were more heterogeneous. The
results of the incremental ramp Kingcycle test confirmed the
relationship between work-rate and oxygen uptake. The
maximum oxygen uptake values were similar to those reported
for endurance trained athletes from other sports.

One-way analysis of variance for repeated measures
indicated that significant differences existed between the
trials for the Goldtec and Durace rear wheel hubs (P <0.05).
Post-hoc analyses established the significant differences
between Durace trial 1, versus Goldtec trial 1 (P < 0.05),
Goldtec trial 2 and Goldtec trial 3 (P < 0.01), between
Durace trial 2 versus Goldtec 2 (P < 0.10) and Goldtec trial
3 (P < 0.05) and for Durace trial 3 versus Goldtec 2
(P<0.10) and Goldtec trial 3 (P < 0.05). The mean ($\pm$ SD)
values for oxygen uptake and heart rate for the Goldtec and
Durace tests are shown in Table 2.

Table 2. Mean (± SD) oxygen consumption and heart rate
values recorded for the Goldtec and Durace rear wheel hubs

		Trial	1	2	3	Mean
Oxygen	Durace	Mean	3215	3186	3184	3195
Uptake		SD	198	204	231	209
(ml/min)						
	Goldtec	Mean	3110	3120	3089	3099
		SD	174	156	137	151
Heart	Durace	Mean	145	147	149	147
rate		SD	9	10	10	9
(beats/min)						
	Goldtec	Mean	146	147	148	147
		SD	12	11	12	11

The mean oxygen consumption for cycling using the Goldtec rear
wheel hub was 3099 ml/min compared to 3195 ml/min using the
Durace rear wheel hub. This suggests an overall reduction in
oxygen consumption of 2.99%. Previous work on cycle design has
tended to focus on aspects such as seat height and position,
crank length and chain-ring shape. This significant reduction
in oxygen uptake would seem to add the design of rear wheel
hubs to the factors which affect cycling economy. Analysis of
the heart rate data failed to indicate any significant
differences (P > 0.05) between the two rear wheel hub designs.
Nordeen-Snyder (1977) reported that saddle height significantly
altered the oxygen cost of cycling and indicated that the most
efficient seat height was 107% of symphysis pubis height. Work
by Hull et al.(1992) investigating the effects of circular and
non-circular chain-rings indicated that no advantage occurred
as a result of non-circular chain-rings over circular chain-
rings. Carmichael et al. (1982) reported variations due to
crank length, whereas the findings of Conrad and Thomas (1983)
suggested crank length has no effect on cycling economy.
    The repeated measures analyses showed that there were no
significant differences between the 3 Durace or between 3
Goldtec trials (P > 0.05) This suggests that the data obtained
from the Kingcycle were reliable. The intraclass correlations
resulting from these ANOVA's were R_{xx} = 0.983 for the 3 Durace
trials and R_{xx} = 0.965 for the 3 Goldtec trials (P < 0.001).
    The results of the analysis of variance for the three chain
alignment positions showed that no significant differences
existed between the position trials (P > 0.05). This suggests
that data collected using the Medigraphics CPX on-line
gasanalysis system, in combination with the Kingcycle as an
ergometer, is a reliable method for the measurement of oxygen

uptake during 'steady state' exercise. The results of the chain alignment study are shown in Table 3.

Table 3. Mean (± SD) oxygen consumption ($\dot{V}O2$) and heart rate values recorded for the 3 different chain alignment positions

Position		3	3	2	2	1	1
Trial		1	2	1	2	1	2
VO2	Mean	3167	3090	3133	3142	3121	3156
(ml/min)	SD	192	146	166	177	161	190
Heart rate.	Mean	144	144	143	145	143	144
(beats/min)	SD	15	15	14	15	13	14

There were no significant differences in cycling economy between the three different chain alignment positions in the study ($P > 0.05$) The mean oxygen uptake for position 3 was 3128 (± 158) ml/min, for position 2 it was 3138 (± 162) ml/min and for position 1 it was 3139 (± 168) ml/min. Likewise, there were no differences in heart rate for the three chain alignment positions ($P > 0.05$). Several riders did suggest that they had noticed a difference when cycling under the three test conditions, and stated a preference for position 2 when the front chain-ring and rear sprocket were directly in line.

In summary, the findings of this study suggest that cycling economy is affected by rear wheel hub design but not by chain alignment. The Goldtec rear wheel hub offered a saving of 3% in terms of oxygen cost, and although this reduction is small, it may make the difference between a good performance and a record breaking performance.

4   Acknowledgements

This project was supported by Goldtec Cycle Components Limited, Caerphilly Business, Park, Mid Glamorgan, Wales.

5. References

Carmichael, J.K.S. Loomis, J.L. and Hodgson, J.L. (1982) The effect of crank length on oxygen consumption and heart rate when cycling at a constant power output. **Medicine and Science in Sports and Exercise,** 14, 162

Coast, J.R. and Welch, H.G. (1985) Linear increase in optimal pedal rate with increased power output in cycle ergometry. **European Journal of Applied Physiology,** 53, 339-342

Conrad, D.P. and Thomas, T.R. (1983) Bicycle crank arm length and oxygen consumption in trained cyclists. **Medicine and Science in Sports and Exercise,** 15, 111

Coyle, E.F. Feltner, M.E. Kautz, S.A. Hamilton, M.T. and Montain S.J. (1991) Biomechanical factors associated with elite endurance cycling performance. **Medicine and Science in Sports and Exercise,** 23, 93-107

Dal Monte, A. Leoardini, L.M. Menchinelli, C and Marini, C. (1987) A new bicycle design based on biomechanics and advanced technology. **International Journal of Sports Biomechanics,** 3, 287-292

Faria, I. Sjojaard, G. and Bonde-Peterson, F. (1982) Oxygen cost during different pedalling speeds for constant power output. **Journal of Sports Medicine and Physical Fitness,** 22, 295-299.

Gonzalez, H.K. and Hull, M.L.(1989) Multivariate optimization of cycling biomechanics. **Journal of Biomechanics.** 22, 1151-1161

Hagberg, J.M. Mullin, J.P. and Nagle, F.J. (1978) Oxygen consumption during constant load exercise. **Journal of Applied Physiology,** 45, 381-384

Hagberg, J.M. Mullin J.P. Geise, M.D. and Spitznagel, E. (1981) Effect of Pedalling Rate on sub-maximal Exercise Responses of Competitive Cyclists. **Journal of Applied Physiology,** 51, 447-451

Hull, M.L. Williams, M. Williams, K and Kautz, S. (1992) Physiological response to cycling with both circular and noncircular chain-rings. **Medicine and Science in Sport and Exercise,** 24, 1114-1122

Keen, P. Passfield, L. and Hale, T.(1992) Indirect determination of VO2 max using a sports specific (cycling) ergometry system. **Journal of Sports Sciences,** 9, 420

Nordeen-Snyder K.S. (1977) The effect of bicycle height upon oxygen consumption and lower limb kinematic. **Medicine and Science in Sports,** 9, 113-117

Seabury, J.J.,Adams, W.C. and Ramsey, M.R. (1977) Influence of pedalling rate and power output on energy expenditure during bicycle ergometry. **Ergonomics,** 20, 491-498

Swain, D.P. and Wilcox J.P. (1992) Effect of cadence on the economy of uphill cycling. **Medicine and Science in Sport and Exercise,** 24, 1123-1127

22 The sculling-sweeping perspective versus the pull-push perspective in free style swimming
J.P. Clarys and A.H. Rouard

1 Introduction

Since electromyography (EMG) has become a tool to analyse the muscular activity and aspects of motion patterns in swimming, it has focused mostly on the frontcrawl (58 % of swimming research). Since Ikaï et al. (1964), the model of movement in which the EMG was incorporated has been observed from the side with the swimmer's arm in a continuum of input-pull-push-output-recovery phases. This two-dimensional model was used and described by many but the detail of time and pattern distribution within the total arm cycle movement was determined by Vaday and Nemessuri (1971)(Fig. 1). With Ikaï et al. (1964) and Lewillie (1967, 1968) as methodological founders of EMG research in aquatics, over 30 different authors investigated the myoelectrical signals of the classic swimming technique (Clarys and Cabri, 1993) and all were studied with a two-dimensional pattern or a phase distribution seen from the side.In other words the muscular participation in the frontcrawl is well known albeit from the pull-push perspective. Clearly this two-dimensional pull-push movement pattern seen from its side view and as a standard model gives little detail of the inward and outward sculling of the upper extremity complex.

In reality, the underwater phase is a full pull phase divided into a downsweep, an insweep and an outsweep. No EMG data support this.

This study is focused on the third sculling and sweeping dimension of the propulsive arm movement in the frontcrawl using kinesiological EMG.

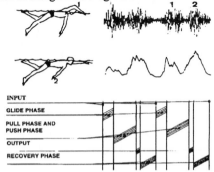

Figure 1. Arm motion phases and cycle timing in free style swimming based on the side view model.

2 Methods

2.1 Subjects
Nine healthy adult males were carefully selected amongst good French 100 m freestyle swimmers with an averaged personal best time of 58.62 ± 2.5 s (mean age : 17 years $\pm$ 2.6; height : 181 cm $\pm$ 9,0; body mass : 72.5 kg $\pm$ 11,5). All subjects swam 4 x 100 m. Beween each full out swim, 45 seconds rest were allowed.

2.2 Motion model
The quality of the repetitive and cyclic movement and the observation of the joint trajectories were controlled with two synchronized cameras (Sony EVO 9100, 30 Hz) perpendicular to each other. The movement was filmed over a distance of 8.40 m. The frontal views allowed for the fractionation of the upper limb movement into 4 phases (Fig. 2) : I) the initial press (A to B) : from the hand entry to the maximum external position of the hand also named as downsweep. II) The inward scull (B to C) : from the maximum external to the maximum internal position of the hand, also named as insweep. III) The outward scull (C to D) or outsweep : from the maximum internal position of the hand to the hand exit and finally the recovery : from the hand exit to the hand input, in other words returning the hand and arm forward through the air.

During the initial press (downsweep) the motion of the hand and arm is predominantly in a downward-sideward direction ; during the inward scull (insweep) the motion of the hand and arm is medial-caudal towards the body while the outward scull (outsweep) moves the hand and the arm predominantly parallel to the body and to the end slightly away from the midline of the body, backward and upward (Fig. 2 ; Hay, 1993).

At the completion of the underwater pull, the subject lifts the hand from the water and swings the arm forward. This recovery phase is a simple combination of a high flexed elbow, an opposite rotation of the trunk; an abduction of the shoulder swinging forward into nearly extension.

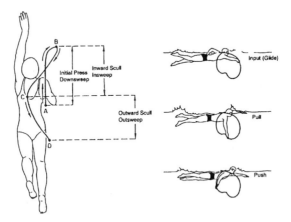

Figure 2. The sculling-sweeping versus the pull-push perspective (adapted according to Hay, 1993).

2.3 EMG data acquisition and analyses

The activity of the M. biceps brachii, the M. triceps brachii, the M. flexor carpi ulnaris (flex. car.), the M. brachioradialis (brachio.), the M. latissimus dorsi (lat.dor.) and the M. deltoideus anterior (delto. ant.) was recorded in all nine subjects and in the 4 maximal swims.

The EMG data were collected with a telemetric transmission method (Rouard et al., 1988 ; Billat et al., 1991). The electrical potentials were captured with Ag-AgCl Beeckman type electrodes (ø 11 mm) including pre-amplification (gain 1000). These sensors were fixed, after the classic cleaning procedures of the skin, at the midpoint of the contracted muscle belly with adhesive bandage. Realising the smaller size of the M. flexor carpi ulnaris, one can assume the potentials of other forearm flexors were captured too due to cross-talk. This was not considered as an obstacle. Each amplified EMG signal was connected to a voltage-frequency converter and coded with a sub-carrier frequency higher than the muscle frequency (15 to 500 Hz). Two kHz intervals between each sub-carrier frequency gave a better interband rejection. After summation, the resultant modulated a radio frequency transmitter that had a frequency of 72 MHz. Its power was 200 MW and its size minimized to 6 x 3 x 1.5 cm. This frequency permitted the use of a half metre flexible plastic antenna. The receiving device, which was on the side of the pool, was set at 72,455 MHZ. It had a sensitivity of 2 V, which could be decreased to minimize disturbances. It had a maximal range of 800 m.

To synchronize EMG's with the movement, the received signal was stored on the HiFi soundtrack of the underwater side videorecorder.

The raw EMG signals from each muscle of each 100 m swim were full-wave rectified, normalized to the highest peak (amplitude) and low pass filtered (cut off frequency 6 Hz) with a sample frequency of 1000 Hz. The MREMG (Mean Rectified-) was integrated for the cycles and for each phase. This integrated EMG (IEMG) was used as an indicator of muscular intensity (Clarys, 1985). The linear envelope of the MREMG was used to verify the pattern specificity over the 4 x 100 m swims (± 500 cycles/subject). This pattern quality control was analysed with the IDANCO system, a system based on three criteria of form similitude (IDentical, ANalogue, COnform). A simplified model of the IDANCO reasoning is shown in Figure 3.

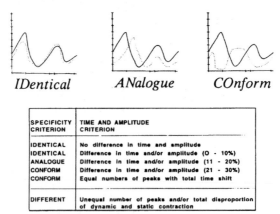

| *IDentical* | *ANalogue* | *COnform* |

SPECIFICITY CRITERION	TIME AND AMPLITUDE CRITERION
IDENTICAL	No difference in time and amplitude
IDENTICAL	Difference in time and/or amplitude (0 - 10%)
ANALOGUE	Difference in time and/or amplitude (11 - 20%)
CONFORM	Difference in time and/or amplitude (21 - 30%)
CONFORM	Equal numbers of peaks with total time shift
DIFFERENT	Unequal number of peaks and/or total disproportion of dynamic and static contraction

Figure 3. The IDANCO Pattern Quality Control System.

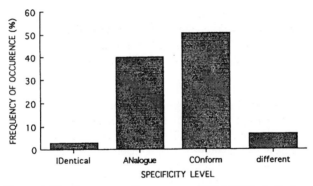

Figure 4. The frequency of occurence of IDANCO similarity.

Descriptive statistics were applied for each stroke and each phase for all the studied variables. The Wilcoxon test ($p< 0.05$) was used to compare the different tests and their different phases.

3 Results

Control of the arm cycle movement in both filmed dimensions and verification of its kinematics digitalisation indicated no or negligible pattern differences between cycles within each 100 m swim, nor between each swim, nor between subjects. By superimposing the MREMG (linear envelopes) in all these circumstances and applying the qualitative comparison IDANCO method, this specificity was observed in the muscular activity too, albeit in 93 % of the arm cycles. The 7 % of different patterns were not considered subsequently (Fig.4).

Due to the synchronisation between the video and the EMG we could study the muscle activity in each of the arm cycle phases separately and for the 4 x 100 m tests.

Figure 5 shows the means and standard deviations of the normalized IEMG of the six muscles investigated indicating the muscular involvement (= intensity) during the respective phases of the arm movement.

4 Discussion

We know from the earlier EMG work that the cyclic arm movement of a freestyle swimmer is controlled by a rhythmic, repetitive and undulating type of activity for most muscles active in the pull and push phase and observed from the side (Clarys, 1985). Viewing the motion in 3-D and decomposing it from the top in particular, it becomes a complex circular, motion including in- and out-sweeping changes of directions of hand and forearm and both adduction and abduction in the shoulder. All this occurs during the underwater pulling only. Such a motion can not be repeated properly if the subjects are not highly trained. The same arm motion needed to be repeated approximately 500 times in a 4 x 100 m swim, each at maximal effort until exhaustion. Both these conditions explain the importance of a population with a homogeneous performance.

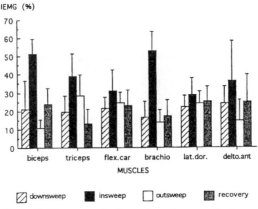

Figure 5. The muscular intensity of arm cycle phases.

Since this cycle is repeated many times we expected a combination of multiple functions such as agonist control with stabilizing co-activation and eccentric or antagonist work.

If one can accept the definition of antagonist work as the type of muscle loading that involves an external force application with resultant tension during physical lengthening of the musculotendinous unit and if pulling its own body through the water - creating hydrodynamic drag - is the muscle loading, one can assume different recruitment control strategies in this cyclic arm movement.

Interpretation of these control strategies over subjects and tests is possible only if the execution of all cyclic motions over all 4 tests remained similar. Since we have around 40 % of analogue specific and 50 % of conform specific patterns, with 3 % of identical patterns we confirm the similarity in EMG activity (Figure 4).

We did consider the IEMG of each muscle separately in each of the 4 phases, averaged for all cycles over all tests. It occurs clearly that the insweep movement is consistently demanding the highest muscular intensities (Fig. 5). The prime movers during this phase are the M. biceps brachii and the M. brachioradialis.

This insweep flexion and supination is supported by the M. flexor carpi ulnaris (and forearm flexors) to stabilize the hand. It is interesting to see the activity of the three antagonists, the M. triceps brachii, the latissimus dorsi and the anterior part of the M. deltoideus. According to Solomonow et al. (1988), this co-activation pattern of elbow (and shoulder) antagonists during maximal effort is nearly inversely related to the muscle's moment arm variation over the joint's range of movement and is estimated to generate a constant opposing torque. The purpose of this antagonist activity is most likely to maintain joint stability but also to supplement the prime movers' action by equalizing the pressure distribution in the joints.

Since we know that under the same loading conditions, eccentric work creates higher forces than concentric actions, but with significantly lower EMG (Albert, 1991), the muscular intensity of the triceps, latissimus dorsi and deltoideus may be considered as invariably high. For this matter, it may be noted that Matsui et al. (1970) found that the EMG activity for concentric actions exceeded that for eccentric actionsby a two to threefold factor.

5 Conclusions

The elite swimmers were selected on the bases of their similar athletic performance. In combination they produced a high level of repetitive and specific (simular) arm cycles, although this motion must be considered as very complex.

The M.biceps brachii and the M. brachioradialis were the propulsive prime movers but important co-activiation and eccentric work was observed.

The insweep part of the full-range pull movement was clearly dominant for all muscles studied.

In addition - and not part of the initial purpose - the EMG, the IDANCO quality control in particular, in this study has proven to be more selective than the kinematic analyses.

Finally these findings create new possibilities for remodelling the freestyle arm movement, e.g. by starting the insweep movement earlier!

6 References

Albert, M. (1991) **Eccentric Muscle Training in Sports and Orthopaedics**. New York, Churchill Livingstone.

Billat, R.P., Quezel, G.and Rouard, A.H. (1991) Transmission simultanéé par télémétrie de sic signaux EMG. **Innovation et Technologie en Biologie et Médecine**, 12,1,87-93.

Clarys, J.P.(1985) Hydrodynamics and electromyography : Ergonomics aspects in aquatics. **Applied Ergonomics**, 1, 6,11-24.

Clarys, J.P.and Cabri, J. (1993) Electromyography and the study of sports movements : A review. **Journal of Sports Sciences**, 11, 379-448.

Hay, J.G. (1993) **The Biomechanics of Sports Techniques.** 4th ed. Englewood Cliffs, NJ, Prentice-Hall, pp. 365-366.

Ikai, M., Ishii, K.and Miyashita, M. (1964) An electromyographic study of swimming. **Research Journal of Physical Education,** 7, 47-54.

Lewillie, L. (1967) Analyse télémétrique de l'electromyogramme du nageur. **Travaux de la Société Médicine Belge de l'Education Physique et du Sport**, 20, 174-177.

Lewillie, L. (1968) Telemetrical analysis of the electromyograph in **Biomechanics I.**(eds J. Wartenweiler, E.Jokl & M. Hebbelinck), Basel, S. Karger verlag, pp.147-149.

Matsui, H., Miyashita, M., Mochinoshi, M.and Hoskikava, T. (1970) The Electromyographic study of positive and negative work i **Copies of our Researches**, Nagoya, University Press, p. 36.

Rouard, A.H., Quezel-Ambrunaz, G.and Billat, R.P. (1988) A telemetric system for the analusis of six muscles activities in swimming in **Swimming Science V** (eds. B. Ungerechts, K. Wilke and K. Reischle) Champaign III : Human Kinetics, pp. 84-87.

Solomonow, M., Baratta, R., Zhou, B.H.and D'Ambrosia, R. (1988) Electromyogram co-activation patterns of the elbow antagonist muscles during slow isokinetic movement. **Experimental Neurology,**100, 470-477.

Vaday, M.and Nemessuri, N. (1971) Motor of free style swimming in **Swimming I** (eds. L. Lewillie and J.P. Clarys) Brussels, Université Libre de Bruxelles, pp. 161-167.

Part Four

Training and Fitness Assessment

23 Eurofit test Battery: a tool for measuring occupational motor fitness

E. Zinzen, D. Caboor, J. Borms, W. Duquet, P. Van Roy and J.P. Carys

1 Introduction

Certain professions require a high level of physical activity such as refuse collectors, fire-fighters or nursing personnel. The literature also indicates that these professions show a high risk of developing low back problems (LBP) (Magora, 1993; Battié et al., 1989; Burton et al., 1989). From the above, one could conclude that high physical demands can lead to low back problems. Conversely, physical activity has been promoted by back schools to prevent low-back problems (Knibbe, 1993). It is assumed that a well controlled training programme to build up physical fitness will provide more resistance against low-back problems for persons performing daily tasks with a high physical activity demand (Knibbe, 1993).

Therefore it seems to be of interest to measure the physical fitness of persons engaged in various occupational situations. The most popular tests to measure fitness are cardiovascular tests such as treadmill running or cycling on an ergometer. Another method of investigating physical fitness is the EUROFIT test battery (Council of Europe, 1988) which has been developed as a tool to measure and compare the motor fitness of young adults across the borders of Europe.

The purpose of this study was (1) to investigate the "motor" physical fitness of nursing personnel and (2) to investigate if there is a relationship between low motor fitness and the incidence of low-back problems (LBP), by using the EUROFIT test battery (with exception of the endurance test, due to the rather time-consuming aspect of this test).

2 Methodology

The EUROFIT test battery consists of two separate entities : a cardiovascular and a motor fitness part (Table 1). The motor fitness tests are simple, cheap and enjoyable for the subjects. The motor EUROFIT test battery is composed of the

Flamingo balance test (FLB), Plate tapping (PLT), Sit and Reach (SAR), Standing broad jump (SBJ), Hand grip strength (HGR), Sit-ups (SUP), Bent arm hang (BAH) and a 10x5 m Shuttle run (SHR). The equipment needed for these tests is simple and cheap : a metal or wooden beam (FLB); a table, adjustable in height, with two rubber disks (PLT); a sit and reach box (SAR); a long and a short gym mat (SBJ and SUP); a hand dynamometer with adjustable grip (HGR); a round horizontal bar at about 2 m height (BAH); a slip-proof floor of about 6 metres (SHR) and some stopwatches. All tests can be performed in a relatively small gym room in the form of a circuit. This way, a large number of people can be tested in a relatively short time.

Twenty five female nurses (mean age : 29.5 ± 6.5 years) and 12 male nurses (mean age : 29.9 ± 6.6 years) participated in the study. Four male and ten female nurses were defined as suffering from LBP on a life-time prevalence indication. The 37 nurses were selected on a voluntary basis from four different hospitals in Belgium. The EUROFIT tests were administered in the following standardized order : FLB, PLT, SAR, SBJ, HG, SUP, BAH and SHR. Rest periods between the tests were freely chosen and the subjects started when they felt ready for it. Each test had its own examiner giving standardized orders. The whole test circuit took about 15 minutes per subject. Following each test, the performer selected a rating of the perceived exertion (RPE) on Borg's scale (Borg, 1970).

Table 1. Composition of the EUROFIT test battery (Council of Europe, 1988)

Dimension	Factor	EUROFIT test
Cardio-respiratory endurance	Cardio-respiratory endurance	Endurance shuttle run (ESR) Bicycle ergometer test (PWC_{170})
Strength	Static strength	Hand grip (HGR)
	Explosive strength (power)	Standing broad jump (SBJ)
Muscular endurance	Functional strength	Bent arm hang (BAH)
	Trunk strength	Sit-ups (SUP)
Speed	Running speed - agility	Shuttle run : 10x5 m (SHR)
	Speed of limb movement	Plate tapping (PLT)
Flexibility	Flexibility	Sit and reach (SAR)
Balance	Total body balance	Flamingo balance (FLB)

Data were checked for normality and differences between means were tested for significance using a factorial ANOVA with factors gender and LBP, followed by a one-way ANOVA and the Scheffé-F as post-hoc test.

3 Results and Discussion

Figure 1 summarises the results of the different tests : male nurses performed significantly (P< 0.05) better than the female nurses on the SBJ, HGR, SUP, BAH and SHR tests. The better results of the males were considered due to normal sex differences.

On the other hand, no relationship between life-time prevalence LBP and the different EUROFIT tests was found (Figure 2). This could be due to the selection of the LBP-group based on a life-time prevalence, which may not be a strong enough indicator, and/or due to the rather small sample size. Another explanation could be that there is actually no relation or that the Eurofit tests are not able to demonstrate a possible relationship. The use of a stronger criterion such as point-prevalence LBP and a larger sample size could create more clarity.

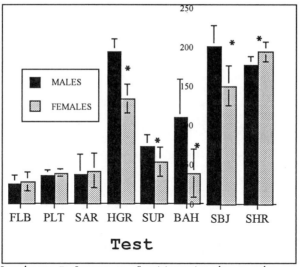

FLB: Flamingo Balance : # attempts in 1 min.
PLT : Plate tapping : plates tapped in 1 min.
SAR : Sit and reach : cm. │BAH : Bent arm hang : s.
HGR : Hand grip strength: N.   SBJ : Standing broad jump : cm.
SUP : Sit-up : # in 30 s. │SHR : Shuttle run : s.

Figure 1. Results of the EUROFIT test battery for Belgian male and female nurses. Significant differences between sexes are indicated with *.

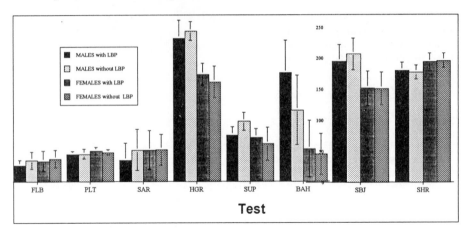

FLB: Flamingo Balance : # attempts in 1 min.
PLT : Plate tapping : plates tapped in 1 min.
SAR : Sit and reach : cm. |BAH : Bent arm hang : s.
HGR : Hand grip strength: N.   SBJ : Standing broad
jump : cm.
SUP : Sit-up : # in 30 s. |SHR : Shuttle run : s.

Figure 2. Comparison between nursing personnel with and
without life-time prevalence LBP.

Two subjects experienced LBP before and during the tests.
This number was not sufficient to analyse statistically with
the point-prevalence as a selection factor.
    In addition, subjects were asked to rate each EUROFIT
test on Borg's perceived exertion scale. No differences in
rating were found between the experimental groups
(male/female ; with LBP/without LBP). The PLT, SAR, SBJ and
HGR tests were considered to be light exercises, while FLB,
SUP, BAH and SHR were considered as moderately heavy. After
finishing the test session, all subjects declared having
enjoyed participating in the tests.
    Since no other EUROFIT data for nursing personnel or for
an adult population were found in the literature, the
results were compared with normative tables for 17-18 year
old school boys and girls (Lefèvre et al., 1993). The male
nurse population scored very low for the SAR, SBJ, PLT and
SUP tests; fair to good results were found for FLB and BAH
tests and very good results were found for HGR and SHR
tests(Table 2). In general, a poor level of physical fitness
was found for the male nurses in comparison with male
students. The scores of the female nurses, in comparison
with 17-18 year old female students, show approximately the
same results as do the scores of their male colleagues.

Table 2. EUROFIT percentile scores of male (m) and female (f) nursing personnel compared with a percentile table of 17-18 year old boys and girls (Lefèvre et al., 1993).

TEST	P10 Very low	P25 Low	P50 Mean	P75 Good	P90 Very good
FLB (n)	24.3	18.2	13.6	9.9 m	6.4
FLB (n)	25.2	18.1	13.5	10.3 f	6.7
PLT (n)	11.9	11.0 m	10.2	9.6	9.1
PLT (n)	12.6	f	11.0	10.3	9.7
SAR (cm)m	15.0	20.1	25.6	30.6	34.8
SAR (cm)f	18.6	23.5	28.3	32.4	35.5
SBJ (cm)	189.2m	204.6	219.6	233.8	247.0
SBJ (cm)	142.7f	156.1	170.4	184.7	197.7
HGR (N)	3.8	4.2	4.8	5.4 m	6.0
HGR (N)	2.4	2.7	3.0	3.3	3.6 f
SUP (n/30s)	21.5m	24.2	26.6	28.8	30.7
SUP (n/30sf)	16.4	18.8	21.1	23.5	26.3
BAH (s)	12.3	22.9 m	34.0	45.7	57.7
BAH (s)	0.3	2.8	7.2 f	14.0	22.8
SHR (s)	22.4	21.4	20.5	19.7	19.1 m
SHR (s)	23.9	23.0	22.1	21.2	20.5 f

Extrapolating these results to the daily work situation of the nurses, it is indicated that the static strength (HGR : taking patients, wash, wound care,...), running speed (SHR : hurrying from one patient room to another, emergencies,...), functional arm strength (BAH : lifting the patient, moving around with materials and papers,...) and the total body balance (holding patients, walking with patients,...) seem to be well trained. However flexibility (SAR : prevention of injuries,...), explosive leg power (SBJ : lifting patients with leg support, ...), speed of limb movement (PLT : fast material handling,...) and trunk strength (SUP : lifting patients,...) are weak in comparison with the students. The weak flexibility, trunk strength and explosive power can be an explanation for the high incidence of LBP in nursing personnel.

Back schools often focus on teaching lifting techniques with the use of leg strength and a straight trunk (Knibbe et al., 1993). Furthermore, it is known that a high level of flexibility can prevent injuries (Locke, 1983).

Therefore, and despite the fact that this study can not indicate a possible relationship between fitness and life-time prevalence of LBP, it is hypothesized that an increased level of flexibility, trunk and leg strength could be of help in preventing LBP in this population.

4 Conclusion

No relationship could be found between life-time prevalence of low back pain and EUROFIT physical fitness tests. In general, male nurses scored better than females in the fitness tests.

Compared to normative tables of 17-18 year old students, nursing personnel had a poor level of physical fitness. Trunk and leg strength together with flexibility scores, more especially, low in comparison with those of 17 - 18 year olds.

The tests were considered to be light or moderately heavy on Borg's perceived exertion scale. All subjects claimed to enjoy this test battery.

This experiment seems to indicate that the EUROFIT test battery can be used as a simple measuring tool in the evaluation of occupational motor fitness.

5 Acknowledgement

The authors like to acknowledge the "Belgian Federal Services for Scientific, Technical and Cultural Matters".

6 References

Battié, M.C.; Bigos, S.J.; Fischer, L.D.; Hansson, T.H.; Nachemson, A.L.; Spengler, D.M.; Wortley, M.D.and Zeh, J. (1989) A prospective study of the role of cardiovascular risk factors and fitness in industrial back pain complaints, **Spine**, 14, 141-147.

Borg,G (1970) Perceived exertion as an indicator of somatic stress, **Scandinavian Journal of Rehabilation Medicine**, 2-3, 92.

Burton, A.K.; Tillotson, K.M.and Troup, J.D.G. (1989) Predicting of low back trouble frequency in a working population, **Spine**, 14, 939-946.

Council of Europe, Committee for the development of sport (1988) **Handbook for the EUROFIT Tests of physical fitness**, Rome, p 72.

Knibbe, J.J.; Knibbe, N.E.; Elvers, J.H.W.; Oostendorp, R.A.B.and Wams H.W.A. (1993) **Inventarisatie van rugscholen in Nederland**, Stichting Wetenschap en Scholing Fysiotherapie,Amersfoort, NL, p 105.

Lefèvre, J.; Beunen, G.; Borms, J.; Renson, R.; Vrijens, J.; Claessens, A.l.and Van Der Aerschot H. (1993) **EUROFIT testbatterij**, BLOSO, Brussels, Belgium.

Locke. J.C. (1983) Stretching away from back pain injury, **Occupupational Health and Safety**, 52, 8-13

Magora A. (1993) Investigation of the relation between Low Back Pain and occupation, **Scandinavian Journal of Rehabilation Medicine**, 5, 186-190.

24 A simple assessment of cardiovascular fitness in children

V. Bunc

1 Introduction

Cardiovascular fitness is frequently considered the most important aspect of physical fitness. The generally accepted physiological criterion of cardiovascular fitness (maximal oxygen uptake - $\dot{V}O_{2max}$), is only a predisposition for physical performance. The practical inportance of oxygen consumption in the performance of exercise of moderate intensity (lasting 1-60 min) is supported by the significant correlation between physical performance and directly measured $\dot{V}O_{2max}$ (Astrand and Rodahl, 1986; Bunc et al., 1986, Bunc and Heller, 1990; Bunc, 1994; Cooper, 1968; Pugh, 1970). A high $\dot{V}O_{2max}$ does not guarantee good physical performance, since technique of motion and psychological factors may have an influence either positively or negatively. In work and exercise where the body is lifted (e.g., walking, running, cross-country skiing), oxygen uptake should be related to body mass. In this case, the individual's VO_{2max} provides a measure of the "motor effect". With this parameter the subject's ability to move his/her body can be evaluated. In practice this means that if we wish to characterize fitness level, we must evaluate $\dot{V}O_{2max}$ and physical performance at the same time.

When $\dot{V}O_{2max}$ is not directly measured, estimation can be made from performance tests. Although minimally a 10 % prediction error exists (Bunc 1994; Cooper, 1968), "motor" tests estimate cardiovascular fitness with less risk and are particulary useful for estimating large samples in a short time. The predicted group mean values of VO_{2max} are similar to the directly measured values, but individual estimates may be less precise (Astrand and Rodahl, 1986; Cooper, 1968).

The data for determination of $\dot{V}O_{2max}$ with a running test 1.5 miles (2.4 km) were first published by Balke (1963). An adaptation of the test was later published by Cooper (1968).

The purpose of this study was to determine norms for the estimation of cardiovascular fitness with regard to Czech and European standards and with regard to general relations between the mean velocity of movement and energy required for this activity. The basic element of evaluating physical performance and thus indirectly aerobic fitness, is the mean speed of movement on a 2000 m test.

2 Methods

For this study, 311 boys and 178 girls differing in age (age ranged from 6 to 18 years) and training state were tested in a laboratory on a treadmill. A graded exercise test to the point of voluntary exhaustion was used.

Subjects were taken from healthy unselected groups of probands without any systematic physical training. After two warm-up bouts at intensities ranging from 50 to 65% $\dot{V}O_{2max}$, each lasting 4 min, the initial intensity of exercise was about 60% $\dot{V}O_{2max}$ (this was determined retrospectively from real value of $\dot{V}O_2$ and $\dot{V}O_{2max}$). This was increased every minute by 1 km.h-1. The total duration of this graded exercise was between 6 and 8 min. The cardiorespiratory variables were assessed using an open system with a Jaeger apparatus (Dataspir I or Ergo-oxcyscreen, Jaeger).

Energy output for running, expressed indirectly by oxygen uptake per kg body mass ($\dot{V}O2.kg-1$) can be estimated from the intensity of exercise by means of various nomograms and/or equations (e.g., Astrand and Rodahl, 1986; Bunc and Heller, 1990; Pugh, 1970). The present author is in agreement with Astrand and Rodahl (1986) and Pugh (1970) in believing that the model relating energy cost of cyclical exercise should be as simple as possible. Therefore, only linear equations were used to relate intensity of physical activity to oxygen uptake. These relationships are linear in the submaximal range of 20-80% $\dot{V}O_{2max}$ (Astrand and Rodahl, 1986).

Over 95% of all leisure-time physical activities lie in the above mentioned submaximal range of intensities. If we extrapolate linear relationships to maximal exercise intensity, the inaccuracy of $\dot{V}O_{2max}$ resulting from the intensity of exercise increases by approximately 5% (Bunc et al., 1994). From this we can use the linear relationship for determining VO_{2max} from physical performance, or vice versa.

The VO_{2max} may be calculated from the values of maximal running speed according to general equations that are independent of training state, age, body mass, and speed. This general equation for women was established in the form (Bunc and Heller, 1990):

$$\dot{V}O2.kg-1(ml.kg-1.min-1) = 3.359*v(km.h-1) + 5.008$$

where v is running speed on flat terrain. The maximal error of VO2.kg-1 determination from the speed of running is about 10% in the range of speeds from 8-18 km.h-1.

A similar general equation for males has the form (Bunc et al., 1986):

$$\dot{V}O2.kg-1(ml.kg-1.min-1) = 3.749*v(km.h-1) - 2.133$$

where speed of running is expressed in the same units as for women. The maximal error of oxygen uptake determination in the range of speeds of 8-20 km.h-1 is about 12%.

To construct assessment Table we used the values from the laboratory and 2000 m track (for children of age less than 10 years 1500 m) set alongside values of $\dot{V}O_{2max}$ which were presented in the literature (Andersen et al., 1987; Asmussen, 1974; Astrand, 1960; Astrand and Rodahl, 1986; Knuttgen et al., 1973; Lange-Andersen et al., 1984; Macek et al., 1990; Seliger and Bartunek, 1977). The laboratory evaluation was conducted within one week of the track run. Values of $\dot{V}O_{2max}$, by age, which were not directly determined in the laboratory or presented in the literature, were calculated. For this calculation we assumed that $\dot{V}O_{2max}$ decreases linearly with increasing age (Astrand and Rodahl 1986). The missing data were calculated with linear interpolation.

For the cross-validation of the predictive linear models, two independent groups of boys and girls were studied. The non-trained men´s group included 31 8-15-year-old healthy boys and untrained group of women included 32 girls of the same age. The "active men" group consisted of 23 10-17-year old healthy boys exercising intensively at least four times a week. The "active women" group included 26 girls of the same age and training state. These groups performed the 2 km running test and both groups did the maximal treadmill test. Procedures and methods were the same as in the original study.

The relationship between the variables (predicted - according to prediction equations - and directly determined values of $\dot{V}O_{2max}$) was examined by Pearson´s product moment correlation coefficients. The statistical significance of differences in values of $\dot{V}O_{2max}$ was tested by a paired Student´s t-test.

3 Results

The subjects did not experience any serious symptoms that limited these running. Over 90 % of subjects reported no symptoms. The most frequently reported symptoms were those in the lower limbs.

The values of $\dot{V}O_{2max}$ determined from our measurements in different groups of untrained subjects, supplemented by data of other European authors, are presented in Table 1. The norms for cardiovascular fitness were divided into three groups. The "good" level of cardiovascular fitness was determined as the mean values from all data for each particular age. "Excellent" values were calculated as the mean plus one standard deviation, and "poor" values were constructed as the mean minus one standard deviation.

The same Table contains values for physical performance, that may be realized mainly from the above mentioned oxygen uptakes. The missing data for performance were calculated

Table 1. Norms of aerobic fitness and physical performance for boys and girls determined on a treadmill and during a 2000 m track run

Age (yrs)	Poor Speed (km/h)	Poor $\dot{V}O_{2max}$/kg (ml)	Good Speed (km/h)	Good $\dot{V}O_{2max}$/kg (ml)	Excellent Speed (km/h)	Excellent $\dot{V}O_{2max}$/kg (ml)
			Boys			
6	7.5	25.8	8.8	30.9	11.2	39.7
8	9.4	33.0	11.2	40.1	13.1	47.1
10	10.5	37.4	12.5	44.6	14.4	51.8
12	11.6	41.2	13.4	48.2	15.3	55.2
14	12.5	44.9	14.7	52.9	16.7	60.4
16	12.7	45.4	14.4	51.9	16.4	59.4
18	12.3	43.9	14.1	50.8	16.1	58.3
			Girls			
6	5.7	24.2	7.4	30.0	9.2	35.8
8	7.4	30.0	9.2	35.9	11.0	41.8
10	8.6	33.8	10.3	39.7	12.1	45.7
12	9.3	36.1	11.0	41.9	12.7	47.7
14	9.3	36.2	11.1	42.3	12.9	48.2
16	9.2	36.0	10.9	41.5	12.5	46.9
18	9.3	36.3	10.8	41.6	12.3	46.3

from oxygen uptake, assuming a general dependence between VO_2 and mean running speed over a distance of 2000 m and/or 1500 m.

The main results of the cross-validation are presented in Table 2. The estimated values of $\dot{V}O_{2max}.kg^{-1}$ for running were systematically smaller than the directly measured values in all the groups. The differences between the means were less than 2.2 ml.kg-1.min-1, i.e. 4.5% in all groups. The correlations coefficients between the measured and estimated values were highly significant ($P < 0.001$ in all cases).

4 Discussion

Physical fitness, and thus cardiovascular fitness, is not understood solely in terms of potential for tolerating physical stress. Often it is declared to be a dimension of health. The use of the Table 1 presented for assessment of cardiovascular fitness in practice is similar to the original system of Cooper (1968). The advantage of the present system of assessment is that this Table was constructed according to data for a European population. In practice this method is simpler than Cooper's original system because only one parameter (time) must be monitored.

Table 2 Measured (directly on the treadmill) and estimated maximal oxygen uptake from speed of running in flat terrain and the correlation coefficient between them in the cross-validation groups

		$\dot{V}O_{2max}.kg^{-1}$ $(ml.kg^{-1}.min^{-1})$	r
Running - non-trained	Boys (N=31)		
	Measured	48.6±4.2	0.896
	Estimated	46.4±4.4	
	Girls (N=32)		
	Measured	42.4±3.8	0.864
	Estimated	41.1±3.9	
- active	Boys (N=23)		
	Measured	57.4±5.1	0.882
	Estimated	55.8±5.6	
	Girls (N=26)		
	Measured	48.4±4.5	0.834
	Estimated	46.7±4.9	

The observed correlations between the measured and predicted $\dot{V}O_{2max}$ compared favourably with the best known predictive tests based on submaximal effort. In the original data of the Canadian Home Fitness Test, a correlation of r=0.91 was reported (Jette et al., 1976). For the Cooper 12 min walk/run test, the correlation coefficient was r=9o (Cooper, 1968). The Astrand-Rhyming nomogram (Astrand and Rodahl, 1986) showed a standard deviation of less than 6.7% for men and 9.6% for women for two-thirds of the subjects.

The mean speed during the 2000 m (1500 m) track trial can both characterize the level of physical performance, and be used for indirect determination of cardiovascular fitness in field conditions. The reliability of assessing $\dot{V}O_{2max}$ from the mean speed of motion varies around 15%.

These differences may seem to be large, but one should note that the errors of cardiorespiratory measurements during normal exercise are about 5 %. From this point of view it is legitimate to assume that the Table presented for the assessment of aerobic fitness in field conditions is valid. Motivation has a similar influence on results in this test as in other methods which use the maximal parameters.

5 References

Andersen, L.B., Henckel, O. and Saltin, B. (1987) Maximal oxygen uptake in Danish adolescents 16-19 years of age. **European Journal of Applied Physiology,** 56, 74-82.

Asmussen, E. (1974) Development patterns in physical performance capacity. **International Standards for Assessment,** McMillan, New York, pp. 435-448.

Åstrand, I. (1960) Aerobic capacity in men and women with special reference to age. **Acta Physiologica Scandinavica,**   49, suppl.169, 1-92.

Åstrand, P.O. and Rodahl, K. (1986) **Textbook of Work Physiology.** McGraw Hill, New York.

Balke, B. (1963) **A simple test for assessment of physical fitness.** Publ No 63-6, Civil Aeromed Res Inst, Oklahoma

Bunc, V., Heller, J. and Leso, J. (1986) Energy requirements of running on a treadmill and in the field. **Casopis lekaru ceskych,** 125, 1391-1394. (in Czech)

Bunc, V. and Heller, J. (1990) Energy demands in women's running on the treadmill and cross-country running. **Casopis lekaru ceskych,** 129, 650-653. (in Czech)

Bunc, V. (1994) A simple method for estimation aerobic fitness. **Ergonomics,** 37, 159-165.

Cooper, K.H. (1968) **Aerobics.** Evans and Co, New York.

Jette, M., Campbell, J., Mongeon, J. and Routhier, R. (1976) Canadian Home Fitness Test as a predictor of aerobic capacity. **Canadian Medical Association Journal,** 114, 680-682.

Knuttgen, H.G., Nordesjo, L.O., Ollander, B. and Saltin, B. (1973) Physical conditioning through interval training with young male adults. **Medicine and Science in Sports and Exercise,** 5, 220-226.

Lange-Andersen, K., Ilmarinen, J., Rutenfranz, J., Ottmann, W., Berndt, I., Kylian, H. and Ruppel, M. (1984) Leisure time sport activities and maximal aerobic power during late adolescence. **European Journal of Applied Physiology,**   52, 431-436.

Macek, M., Rutenfranz, J., Vavra, J., Mackova, J., Radvansky, J. and Danek, K. (1990) Comparison of the physical fitness of our population with similar data from some European countries. **Ceskoslovenska Pediatrie,** 45, 257-260.

Pugh, L.G.C.E. (1970) Oxygen intake in track and treadmill with observation on the effect of air resistance. **Journal   of Physiology (London),** 207, 823-835.

Seliger, V. and Bartunek, Z. (1977) **Mean values of various indices of physical fitness in the investigation of Czechoslovak population aged 12-55 years.** Czechoslovak Union of Physical Culture, Prague.

25 The effects of an 8 week skipping programme on the aerobic fitness and body fatness of 8-9 year old schoolchildren

G. Stratton and R. Waggett

1 Introduction

A recent meta-analysis of 28 investigating the effect of exercise programmes on children's cardiorespiratory fitness, indicated that aerobic training may only induce a small to moderate increase in cardiorespiratory fitness (Payne and Morrow, 1993). Few if any of these studies have objectively reported the intensity of the training programme. To increase cardiorespiratory fitness, Morrow and Freedson (1994) have recommended an intensity of 75% of maximum heart rate reserve, for twenty minutes, three times a week. A dearth of data on cardiorespiratory training in children makes a definitive prediction of a dose-response for increasing fitness impossible.

When attempting to measure cardiorespiratory fitness of children, the majority of physiological tests have been laboratory based and have employed $\dot{V}O_2$ max or $\dot{V}O_2$ peak using indirect calorimetry. Some investigators (Massicote and McNab, 1974) have used submaximal heart rate to detect changes in cardiorespiratory fitness following training programmes, although these have mainly been laboratory based. On the other hand, few studies have used field tests to measure aerobic fitness in children combined with a physiological measure such as heart rate. From the early 1990's, a "jump rope" (skipping) for heart health campaign, sponsored by the Health Education Authority has been in operation across primary and secondary schools in England and Wales. Jump rope has long been accepted as an appropriate activity for promoting cardiorespiratory fitness in children especially at primary school age. Investigations into the impact of jump rope programmes on the cardiorespiratory fitness of children are not well documented. Benedict, Vaccaro and Hatfield (1985) found that a daily skipping programme did not significantly increase maximal oxygen uptake or decrease body fat. Unfortunately this study did not assess the physiological intensity of the jump rope programme, and it is not known whether the exercise was of appropriate duration or intensity to have stimulated an increase in cardiorespiratory fitness.

Given the dearth of available literature in this area, a number of aims were generated for the present study. The first aim was to measure the typical cardiorespiratory load of jump rope exercise. The second aim was to investigate the effect of an 8 week jump rope programme on the cardiorespiratory fitness and skinfolds of 8 to 9 year old school children.

2 Method

2.1 Subjects

Forty three, 8 to 9 year old children from a school in the North-West of England agreed to take part in the study. Children were split by school class into a control group (8 girls: 11 boys) and an experimental group (10 girls; 14 boys). The experimental group followed a 4 day per week, 15 minute skipping programme for 8 consecutive weeks. The same instructor took all skipping sessions. The control subjects did not participate in the skipping sessions and maintained their normal physical activities.

2.2   Instruments

Body mass was measured to the nearest 0.1 kg. using portable scales (Seca). The sum of 5 skinfolds was computed after calf, triceps, biceps, suprailiac and subscapular skinfolds were measured to the nearest mm using a skinfold caliper (Holtain, UK). All anthropometric measurements were taken according to the techniques outlined by Lohman, Roche and Matorell (1988). Aerobic fitness was measured by recording heart rate (Sportstester, Polar: Kempele, Finland) at the end of the fourth minute of the 20 metre multi-stage shuttle run test (Ramsbottom et.al., NCF 1988). The intensity of the skipping programme was assessed using heart rate telemeters (Sportstester, Polar: Kempele, Finland). Telemeters were fitted to 4 children at the start of each 15 minute jump rope session. Children were chosen sequentially to wear the heart rate telemeters. Each child wore a telemeter an average of 5 times during the 8 week programme.

2.3   Procedure

The first visit to school involved measuring children's body mass, skinfolds and shuttle run performance in both experimental and control groups. During the shuttle run, 4 children wore heart rate telemeters which were set to record heart rate once every 5 s. The test of cardiorespiratory fitness was undertaken on 6 children at a time. Children ran in perfect time with the sound signal, back and forth on a 20 metre shuttle until the fourth minute, at which point the test was terminated. Telemeters were then removed and data downloaded onto a laptop computer (Polar, Apple Mac telemeter interface) for subsequent analysis. This test was repeated before and after the eight week "jump rope" programme. During the jump rope programme, 4 children from the experimental group were fitted with heart rate telemeters set to record heart rate once every 5 seconds for the session. Data were downloaded in the same manner as previously mentioned. Heart rate telemeters were set to record the time spent in heart rates greater than or equal to 150 beats min^{-1} during the jump rope session.

2.4   Data analysis

Data were analysed using a 2 x 2 x 2 x 2 MANOVA (groups x test sessions x submaximal fitness test heart rate x body mass and skinfolds) (Super ANOVA; Abacus concepts Inc. Berkely. USA). The analysis was undertaken on 20 sets of full data. (13 {before skipping programme}, experimental, 7 {before skipping programme} control; 12 {after skipping programme} experimental, 6 {after skipping programme} control). The significant alpha level was set at 0.01. The intensity of the jump rope programme was reported descriptively by summing all files using the Polar software interface.

3   Results

Table 1. Descriptive data for both experimental and control groups before and after the jump rope programme

Variables	Experimental Group				Control Group			
	Pre (n=13)		Post (n=12)		Pre (n=7)		Post (n=6)	
	Mean	SD	Mean	SD	Mean	SD	Mean	SD
Body mass (kg)	28.3	4.1	27.6	3.8	25.8	3.5	25.8	2.2
Sum of 5 skinfolds (mm)	32.8	5.8	31.7	4.6	34.4	3.1	36.5	2.2
Heart rate (beats min^{-1})	180	23.6	186	17.3	194	7.4	196	18.8

Children spent an average of 69.2 (± 5.6) percent of the 15 minutes skipping with heart rates exceeding 150 beats min-1. This was equivalent to 10.4 minutes per session which amounted to over 40 minutes per week in moderate to vigorous physical activity.

An overview of descriptive results for body mass, skinfolds, and heart rate at the end of the 4 minute shuttle run are presented in Table 1. There was no significant reduction in average skinfolds 32.8 (±5.8) mm before, compared to 31.7 (±4.6) mm after the skipping programme (F = 1.65: P>0.01). Significant changes were not observed in the experimental group for shuttle run heart rates, 180.0 (±23.6) beats min^{-1} and 185.5 (±17.3) beats min^{-1} (F = 1.45: P>0.01), or body mass 28.3 (±4.1) kg. and 27.6 (±3.8) kg. (F = 1.11:

P>0.01), before and after the skipping programme respectively. Control group results were not significantly different before and after the skipping programme for all dependent variables. Skinfold measures did decrease slightly over the 8 weeks for the experimental group, whereas the control group increased their skinfold measures. Body mass followed the trend set by skinfolds in the experimental group, whereas body mass stayed the same in the control group. Heart rate 4 minutes into the 20 MST increased by 5 beats min^{-1} in the experimental group before and after the skipping programme. However, the control group's heart rates increased slightly, and were almost 14 and 11 beats min^{-1} higher than the experimental group on comparison of before and after the skipping programme respectively. The analyses indicated that the overall effect of the programme was not significant (F = 1.19: P>0.01).

4   Discussion

Jump rope is clearly an appropriate activity for elevating heart rate in primary age children. The data from this study indicate that children spent the majority of the skipping session at heart rates thought to be intense enough to promote cardiorespiratory health (Morrow and Freedson, 1988). In terms of duration however, these sessions only included 10 minutes of activity per day, only half that recommended by Sallis and Patrick (1994). Nevertheless, this amounted to children experiencing 320 minutes with heart rates in excess of 150 beats min^{-1} over an 8 week period. Such a jump rope programme would significantly increase British children's habitual levels of physical activity when compared to data reported by Armstrong et al. (1991).

In agreement with Benedict, Vaccaro and Hatfield (1985), there were non significant changes in children's body mass, sum of skinfolds or submaximal heart rate following the 4 minute, 20 metre shuttle run. Nevertheless, there was a small reduction in skinfolds and body mass in the experimental group, compared to a small increase in skinfolds and a maintenance of body mass in the control group. It therefore seems that a jump rope programme of this type does initiate a reduction in adiposity, which may account for the parallel change in body mass.

Submaximal heart rates at the end of the 4 minute shuttle run increased after the training programme in the experimental group more than in the control group. This contradicted the hypothesis that submaximal heart rate should decrease after an appropriate cardiorespiratory training programme. Such an increase in heart rate could be due to the poor pace judgement of the children between tests. However, the children did practice their pace judgement prior to the study. In addition, during testing all children were paced during the test runs by an adult, and pace judgement was generally good. The problem with this type of test is that it may be affected by a number of extraneous variables such as environment, body temperature, and surface underfoot. These were kept as constant as possible through the test. In addition, even though children's heart rates reach a steady state more quickly than adults, perhaps one minute at each level of the 20 metre shuttle run test did not allow sufficient time for the children's heart rates to reach steady state. This is quite likely as heart rates were near predicted maximal values at the end of the tests. This was especially evident in the control group. Overall the results of this study agree with Payne and Morrow's meta analysis (1993), in that gains in cardiorespiratory fitness prior to puberty are difficult to achieve. Much of this poor response to training is probably due to the immaturity of the neuro-endocrine system in stimulating functional adaptation in the cardiorespiratory system in children of this age (Katch, 1983).

5   Conclusions

The main conclusions are as follows. First, jump rope exercise in children can be of sufficient intensity for the maintenance of cardiorespiratory fitness. Second, jump rope exercise programmes seem to stimulate a small reduction in adiposity and body mass. Third, this jump rope programme did not reduce submaximal heart rate, neither did it have an overall effect on cardiorespiratory fitness. Further studies should combine criterion laboratory measures of cardiorespiratory fitness such as VO2peak and PWC170 with field measures such as the one used in this study.

6   References

Armstrong, N., Williams, J., Balding, J., Gentle, P., and Kirby, B. (1991) Cardiopulmonary fitness, physical activity patterns and selected coronary risk factor variables in 11-16 year olds. **Pediatric Exercise Science,** 3, 319-328.

Benedict, G., Vaccaro, P., and Hatfield, B., D. (1985) Physiological effects of an eight week precision jump rope program in children. **American Corrective Therapy Journal,** 39,108-111.

Katch, V.L. (1983) Physical conditioning of children. **Journal of Adolescent Health Care,** 3, 241-246.

Lohman, T., Roche, A.F., and Marorell, R. (Eds.) (1988) **Anthropometric Standardisation Manual.** Human Kinetics, Champaign, IL.

Massicote, D. R., and McNab, R. B. J. (1974) Cardiorespiratory adaptations to training at specified intensities in children. **Medicine and Science in Sports,** 6, 242-246.

Morrow, J. R. and Freedson, P.S. (1994) The Relationship between Habitual Physical Activity and Physical Fitness in Adolescents. **Pediatric Exercise Science,** 6, 315-329.

Payne, V.G., and Morrow, J. R. (1993) Exercise and VO2max in Children: A Meta Analysis. **Research Quarterly for Exercise and Sport,** 64, 305-313.

Ramsbottom, R., Williams, C., Brewer, J., and Hazeldine, R. (1988) **The 20 metre Multi stage fitness test.** National Coaching Foundation, Leeds. UK.

Sallis, J. F., and Patrick, K. (1994) Physical Activity Guidelines for Adolescents: Consensus Statement. **Pediatric Exercise Science,** 6, 302-314.

26 Variations in the physiological profile of the England senior netball squad over a 12 month period

A. Borrie, I. Campbell, N. Mullan and C. Plamer

1 Introduction

Netball is a court-invasive sport primarily played by females. The game is characterised by brief periods of high intensity activity such as sprinting, jumping and defending, interspersed with periods of less intense activity and recovery. Consequently the sport demands both aerobic and anaerobic fitness (Steele and Chad, 1992; Woolford and Angove, 1991).

The England Senior Netball squad has been physiologically monitored since 1987 as part of an on-going Sports Science Support Programme aimed at enhancing performance. The support programme involves the assessment of the physiological changes that occur during the stages of a netball season and preparation for international netball tournaments. In addition to the monitoring function the support programme attempts to enhance performance through the preparation of appropriate training programmes. In this paper data are presented from four monitoring sessions over a single year. Key issues relating to the physical development of the England netball squad during that period are identified.

2. Method

2.1 Monitoring sessions and training

Data were collected over a period from April 1993 to June 1994. Scheduling of assessment dates, international competion and planned training peaks are schematically represented in Figure 1. Data collection took place on four occasions of which the final data collection only included measures of standing vertical jump. During the study period, and prior to April 1993, training advice was given to players on the basis of periodised training plans. The 12 month period between April 1993 and April 1994 incorporated three different training peaks occuring in April and July 1993 and in April 1994. The monitoring sessions in April 1993 and April 1994 occurred during the same month as a training peak whereas the monitoring session in September 1993 occured at the start of the domestic season following an eight week period of active recovery. The monitoring session in June 1994 was conducted after a specific 10 week speed and plyometric training programme.

2.2 Subjects and Assessments

Nine females (aged 24.6 ± 3.1 years) participated in the monitoring programme. All players had a minimum of 12 months experience of playing international netball at either senior or under-21 level. In the monitoring programme both physiological and anthropometric variables were assessed. The anthropometric variables measured were height, body mass and skinfold thicknesses. Skinfolds were measured at seven sites; biceps, triceps, subscapula, iliac crest, abdomen, thigh and calf (as described by MacDougall et al., 1991). Performance variables included standing vertical jump (SVJ), sprint ability and $\dot{V}O_2$ max was estimated. Standing vertical jump was measured using a switch mat connected to a laptop PC (Amstrad NB386SX) with jump height being calculated from time in the air according to the formula $h=(g.t^2)/2$, where t is half the flight time. Subjects started each jump with hands on hips and then reached up with one hand only when jumping. Jumping ability was therefore assessed separately for dominant (Dom) and non-dominant (Non) hands. Sprint ability was assessed using a 3 x 7 metre multiple sprint test (Mullan et al., 1994). Aerobic power ($\dot{V}O_2$ max) was estimated using a multi-stage shuttle run (Brewer et al., 1988). Data were compared using a one-way ANOVA with post-hoc analysis by the Bonferroni technique.

During the period April 1993 -April 1994 self-report training diaries were completed by squad members detailing the frequency, volume and intensity of training sessions. The diaries were assessed at regular intervals and the data collated to allow for the calculation of mean frequency of training sessions, matches and squad practices on a weekly basis. Actual training frequencies were then compared to the frequency suggested in the training programme in order to assess the balance of the training undertaken and the level of adherence to the programme.

Year	1993									1994					
Month	Ap	My	Ju	Jul	Au	Se	Oc	No	De	Ja	Fe	Ma	Ap	My	Ju
Assessment	A					A							A		A
Training Peak (TP)	TP			TP									TP		
International Tournaments															

Figure 1. Schematic representation of the relationship between between assessment sessions, training peaks and international tournaments during the study period.

3 Results

When comparing the three full monitoring sessions were compared   only skinfold measures showed significant change over the period covered (Table 1). The post-hoc analysis showed the Sept'93 values to be significantly lower than either April'93 (t=2.59, P<0.01) or April'94 (t=2.62, P<0.01). There was also a clear trend (P=0.09) in the $\dot{V}O_2$ max data with the mean for Sept'93 (46.5 ml.kg.min⁻¹) being 3.9 and 2.1 ml.kg.min⁻¹ lower than in April 1993 and April 1994 respectively. The variation in SVJ, both dominant and non-dominant, did not follow the same pattern as the variation in $\dot{V}O_2$ max. with values declining from April 1993 to April 1994. When the first three sessions are assessed independently of the results from June 1994 there is no difference in the mean values (Dom $F_{(2,33)}$= 0.52, P=0.59; Non $F_{(2,33)}$= 0.94, P=0.42).

Table 1. Anthropometric and physiological characteristics of the England netball squad during a 12 month period (April 1993 to April 1994)

Variable	April '93 Mean	SD	Sept. '93 Mean	SD	April '94 Mean	SD	June '94 Mean	SD	F	p
Height (cm)	174.5	6.7	172.8	4.9	174.5	3.3	--		0.02	0.98
Weight (kg)	69.0	7.9	65.0	6.6	71.3	9.2	--		0.91	0.41
Sum of Skinfolds (mm)	77	15	95	14	83	12	--		4.24	.02*
SVJ (Dom) (cm)	38.5	5.4	37.5	6.2	36.5	4.6	42.4	4.9	2.65	0.06
SVJ (Non) (cm)	38.7	4.5	36.6	5.5	36.6	4.8	41.1	4.7	2.27	0.09
Sprint (s)	4.48	0.18	4.48	0.11	4.42	0.11	--		1.61	0.41
VO$_2$ max (ml.kg^{-1}.min^{-1})	50.4	4.4	46.5	3.2	48.6	4.11	--		2.6	0.09

Table 2. Suggested and actual training frequency of aerobic and speed/plyometric training during two training periods, May-June 1993 and Feb-April 1994.

	May-June 1993 Aerobic	Spd/Plyo.	Total	Feb-April1994 Aerobic	Speed/Plyo	Total
Actual	2	3	5	2	3	5
Suggested	2.3	1.5	3.8	2.1	0.9	3

4 Discussion

4.1 Comparative data

The values obtained throughout the study for height are comparable to mean values for elite English netball players (172 cm) (Bale and Hunt, 1986) and Australian state players (175cm) (Withers and Roberts, 1981). The current values are also generally higher than the range of values reported for the Welsh U-21 squad (163.9-174.5 cm) (Bell et al., 1994). In terms of body mass the values from the three assessments in this study are higher than the mean of 65.5 kg previously reported for elite English players (Bale et al., 1986) but lower than the mean of 74.4 kg for Australian players (Withers and Roberts, 1981). All the VO$_2$ max values from this study (46.5-50.4 ml.kg.$^{-1}$min^{-1}) are higher than the mean reported by Withers et al (1981) for the Australian players (45 ml.kg.$^{-1}$min^{-1}). Surprisingly the current values are also markedly lower than the results reported for the Welsh U-21 squad (53 ml.kg.$^{-1}$min^{-1}). It should however be noted that in both the Australian and Welsh studies VO$_2$ max was measured directly and not estimated.

4.2 Variation in physiological and anthropometric variables during the study period.

Comparison of the data obtained at the training peaks in April 1993 and 1994 shows a trend towards the squad having had a stronger profile in 1993, with higher values for VO$_2$ max and SVJ and lower skinfold measures. However, the training programme had been designed with the intention that players should achieve the same physiological peak in both April 1993 and 1994. Whilst recognising that the differences were not statistically significant and could be due to biological variation, the training frequency data (Table 2.) suggests that the international competition in April 1993 may have had a beneficial effect upon training during the weeks preceeding the monitoring session. Comparison of the training frequency data from July 1993 and April 1994 shows that a greater amount of training was being undertaken in May-July 1993 (3.8 sessions per week), prior to international competition (World Games), than in Feb.-April 1994 (3.1 sessions per week), prior to domestic competition (County and Regional tournaments). This suggests that the external stimulus of international competition has a beneficial effect on training adherence for this squad.

The variation in $\dot{V}O_2$ max during the study was expected as the players moved from a period of relatively intense training (prior to April 1993), through a transitional phase of active recovery (prior to Sept. 1993) to an increased training load building up to April 1994. In contrast, the lack of variation in speed and SVJ throughout this 12 month cycle was not expected. The training plan was designed to allow for a cyclical development of aerobic fitness, sprint ability and SVJ performance. The values for these variables were expected to be lower in Sept.1993 than at either of the April monitoring sessions.

The reason for the lack of variation in speed and SVJ can be seen in Table 2. The training frequency data show that the squad was not achieving the prescribed levels of speed and plyometric training at the crucial stages during the training year. The frequency of speed and plyometric training was lower than frequencies recommended in the training literature of 2-3 sessions per week (Bompa, 1987; Young, 1991). In contrast the level of aerobic training was maintained at a level above that suggested by the training guidelines thereby drawing training time away from speed and plyometric sessions. The data indicate that the minimal changes in standing vertical jump and sprint times during the period April 1993-1994 can be attributed to the overemphasis on aerobic training at the expense of speed and plyometric training.

A specific speed and plyometric programme was implemented during April-June 1994 as a direct response to the imbalance in training frequency. An intensive player education programme was conducted alongside a specific 10 week training period with the emphasis mainly on plyometrics. The training guidelines specified three plyometric training sessions per week as a target frequency with each session consisting of 90-120 ground contacts. The focus on this element of fitness was sucessful with improvements in SVJ of 9% (Dom) and 7% (Non) from the April monitoring session. A separate ANOVA on the SVJ data from April and June 1994 confirmed that the increase was significant for both dominant ($F_{(1,20)}=8.9$, $P<0.01$) and non-dominant hands ($F_{(1,20)}= 6.08$, $P<0.01$). This indicated that the players had always had the potential to achieve higher levels of performance in SVJ and that the previously identified lack of improvement was partly due to the specificity of the training being done. The causes underlying the lack of adherence to the speed and plyometric aspects of the training programme, and the subsequent unbalanced development of fitness, are currently being investigated through a qualitative research programme.

In summary the data show the expected variation in $\dot{V}O_2$ max and skinfold measures over the duration of the study although the differences between monitoring sessions were not statistically significant. In contrast there was minimal variation in sprint speed and vertical jump measures during the period April 1993 to April 1994. Data on training frequency identified a lack of sprint and plyometric training, together with an overemphasis on aerobic training, as contributing to the lack of variation in measures of sprint speed and standing vertical jump. A specific focus on plyometric training over a 10 week period realised substantial gains in vertical jump ability indicating that previous measures didn't reflect the potential of the group.

5 Acknowledgements

The authors would like to acknowledge the support of the United Kingdom Sports Council in funding the All England Netball Association Sports Science Support Programme.

6 References

Bale,P. and Hunt, S. (1986) The physique, body composition and training variables of elite and good netball players in relation to playing position. **Australian Journal of Science and Medicine in Sport**, 18 (4), 16-19

Bell,W., Cooper,S.-M., Cobner,D. and Longville,J. (1994) Physiological changes arising from a training programme in under-21 international netball players. **Ergonomics**, 37, 149-158

Bompa, T.O. (1987) Periodisation as a key element of planning. **Sports Coach**, 11 (1), 20-23

Brewer,J. Ramsbottom,R. and Williams,C. (1988) **Multi-stage Fitness Test**. Leeds: National Coaching Foundation

MacDougall,J.D., Wenger,H.A. and Green,H.J., (1991**) Physiological Assessment of the High-Performance Athlete**. Champaign, Illinois: Human Kinetics

Mullan, N.F, Campbell,I. and Taylor,A. (1994) A study to investigate the reliability and construct validity of current netball sprint tests (777 and 505). **Journal of Sports Sciences**, 12, 146

Steele,J. and Chad,K. (1992) An analysis of the movement patterns of netball players during matchplay. **Sports Coach**, 15 (1), 21-28

Withers,R.T. and Roberts,R.T.G. (1981) Physiological profiles of representative women softball, hockey and netball players, **Ergonomics**, 24, 583-591

Woolford, S.M. and Angove, M. (1992) A comparison of training and game intensities for national level netball players. **Sports Coach**, 15 (2), 28-32

Young,W. (1991) Plyometrics for Netball. **Sports Coach**, 14 (4), 26-28

27 An ergonomic evaluation of the physiological stress of three dance styles on student dance teachers

L. Doggart, N.T. Cable and A. Lees

1 Introduction

In the U.K., dance is enjoying increasing popularity both as an exercise activity and in schools as part of a cultural education experience. This has led to the development of degree courses specialising in the teaching and health aspects of dance including various styles. Teachers of dance need to be skilled not only in each dance style in terms of technical awareness but also in the health and exercise benefits particular to the activity.

In order for an exercise actvitiy to elicit a cardiovascular training response, mean heart rate values must rise above 140 beats/min for a 15-20 minute period as specified by the American College of Sports Medicine (1991). Several research teams have investigated the physiological responses of elite level performers in various dance styles (Bell and Bassey, 1994; Blanksby and Reidy, 1988; Rimmer et al., 1994; Schantz and Astrand, 1984), Only Chemlar et al., (1988) attempted to quantify the physiological difference between the styles and level of participant. These authors dealt with certain profiling parameters, most notably muscular strength and oxygen consumption aspects, but did not relate the intensity of the activity, in terms of heart rate responses, to the standard of participation or dance style.

The aims of this study were to quantify the intensity of three dance styles and compare the heart rate responses of the participating student dance teachers.

2 Method

Fifteen student dance teachers (12 female, 3 male: age = 22.07 years, SD = 4.17) participated in the study. All the subjects had been participating in dance on a regular basis (experience = 7.47 years, SD = 4.58) and were currently participating in the three styles which included jazz, contemporary and African Caribbean.

The subjects were asked to wear a heart-rate short-range radio telemeter (Polar Sports Tester, Oy, Finland) during the dance class and heart rates were recorded every 15 seconds. Resting heart rate was recorded for twenty minutes prior to the start of each class. Prior to the commencement of testing,

all subjects were familiarised with the use of the heart rate
monitor. The female subjects were offered the option of
wearing the transmitter on a chest strap or fitted to a
specially designed sports bra for comfort.

After each class the heart rates were downloaded onto a
computer for analysis (including heart rate profile and heart
rate distribution). The class duration was also recorded.

The results were analysed descriptively to establish mean,
peak and range of heart rates. Differences in intensity of
each style of dance were investigated using a one-way analysis
of variance. Post-hoc analysis using Newman Keuls test was
used to highlight any differences between the styles.

3 Results

The mean and standard deviation for the duration of each dance
class was 94 (SD = 6) min; 85 (SD = 4) min; 118 (SD = 9) min,
for jazz, contenporary and African Caribbean respectively. The
average resting heart rate for the subjects was 54 (SD = 3)
beats/min. The mean heart rates were averaged over each style
for the fifteen subjects. An example of the heart rate
profiles for the three styles, on one subject, is displayed in
Figure 1a, 1b and 1c. Mean heart rate values were 134 (SD =
13) beats/min; 119 (SD = 9) beats/min; 131 (SD = 10)
beats/min, for jazz, contemporary and African Caribbean,
respectively. The mean heart rates were equivalent to 67%;
60%; and 66%, of the age-predicted maximum (220-age) for the
subjects for the three styles.

The peak heart rate and range between minimum and maximum
heart rate across the three styles were 193 (range = 118)
beats/min; 164 (range = 82) beats/min; 197 (range = 130)
beats/min, for the styles of jazz, contemporary and African
Caribbean. When the peak heart rates were analysed with
respect to a percentage of age-predicted maximum they equated
to 97.5%; 82.9%; and 99.5% of the age predicted maximum for
the three styles. The African Caribbean dance style produced
the largest peak heart rate (197 beats/min) and was also found
to have the greater range (130). This style produced the
lowest average recorded heart rate of 67 beats/min.

A significant difference ($F_{3,14}$27.65: $P<0.001$) was found
between the heart rate responses of the subjects across the
three styles. Post-hoc analysis using Newman Keuls test
revealed significant differences between jazz and contemporary
($P<0.001$) and between African Caribbean and contemporary
($P<0.005$). No significant difference was noted between the
styles of jazz and African Caribbean.

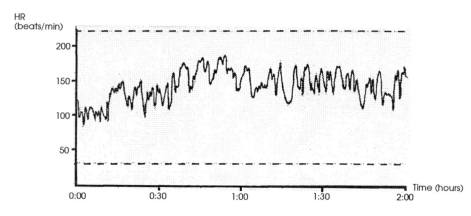

1a. African Caribbean

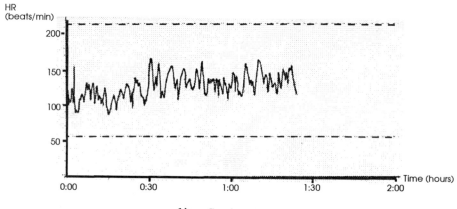

1b. Contemporary

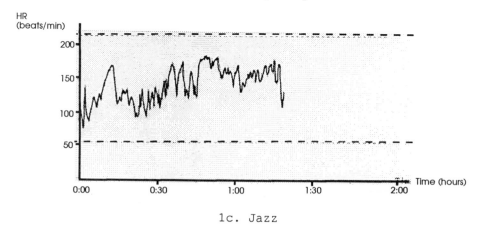

1c. Jazz

Figure 1. Heart rate profiles, from one subject,
for the three dance styles.

Table 1. Mean Heart rate (HR) responses to the dance styles for the subject group (n=15)

	Jazz	Contemporary	African Caribbean
Resting HR (SD)	62 (4)	62 (4)	62 (4)
Mean HR (SD)	134 (13)	119 (9)	131 (10)
Mean peak HR	193	164	197
Mean HR range	118	82	130

4 Discussion

One method of estimating training intensity is the monitoring of heart rate (Thomson and Ballor, 1991; Bell and Bassey, 1994)). This method is routinely used to monitor training intensity during dance activity (Koltyn and Morgan, 1992; Scharff-Olson et al., 1992)). A slow resting heart rate is indicative of a high level of physical fitness in trained subjects (Peterson et al., 1986). The average resting heart rate of the subjects in the present study was found to be 62 beats/min (SD = 4). This is comparable to other previous studies of dancers; 63 beats/min (SD = 8), (Peterson et al., 1986); 68 beats/min (SD = 6), (Mostardi et al., 1983); 63 beats/min (SD = 4), (Blanksby and Reidy, 1988).
As a general rule, aerobic capacity will improve if exercise is of sufficient intensity to increase heart rate to about 60-70% of maximum. The highest heart rates measured at any time during the classes equated to 97.5%; 82.9%; 99.5% of age-predicted maximum for jazz, conmtemporary and African Caribbean respectively. Kirkendall and Calabrese (1983) recorded percentage maximum heart rates of 73% and 77% for females and males respectively in ballet classes. They concluded that the intensity and duration were inadequate to bring about desired changes in cardiorespiratory fitness. A similar finding was also reported by Schantz and Astrand (1984). However, during composite dance performance they recorded percentage maximum heart rates of 46% of the subjects' maximum.
Exercise which results in sustained heart rates in excess of 150 beats/min has been classified as extremely heavy (Astrand and Rodahl, 1977). In this study the subjects recorded an overall mean heart rate of 134 beats/min for jazz; 119 beats/min for contemporary and 131 beats/min for African Caribbean. According to the above definition, therefore, the three styles of dance are of a moderate activity level requiring the cardiovascular system to function at levels which require medium energy expenditures to match this

physiological stress.

The intermittent nature of all the dance classes is reflected in the heart rate profiles (Figure 1a, b, c). Although the peak heart rates recorded range from 82.9% to 99.5% of the age-predicted maximum, these values were only recorded for short periods of time (2-3 minutes). This heavy work intensity level would then be interspersed with similar rest periods allowing sufficient time for the body to recover. This sprint or burst-like quality of dance activity, because of its brief duration, would only moderately stimulate improvements in aerobic activity (Cohen et al., 1982).

The difference in the intensity of the dance styles was highlighted from the post-hoc analysis. Significant differences were found between contemporary and the other two styles. This may well have been a reflection on the nature of the dance activity. The musical timing, rhythm and pace of contemporary choreography is often left to individual interpretation. The relaxed and flowing body movements do not lead to a pronounced physiological response, but more to artistic impression. This is opposed to the vigorous and aggressive movements of tribal dance rituals, and the high tempo jazz rhythm.

Although the styles of dance monitored in the present study were of a moderate intensity, consideration must be given to the context in which the analysis was performed. The high intensity periods of activity were restricted due to the duration of the class. Previous research has suggested that the duration of the class was inadequate to elicit a cardiovascular training response. The longer time of the African Caribbean class, and hence the increase in the frequency of the high intensity activity periods, may stress physiological capacities more and increase the training response. It should also be noted the nature of the class depends on individual interpretation with respect to the choreographer and timetabling of the student dancers. Perhaps more emphasis was placed on the teaching aspect of the class and the aesthetic quality of the movement rather than the health and fitness response to the activity. The trade-off between these two important criteria for student dance teachers may prove to be an important factor when assessing dance activity.

5 Conclusion

It was concluded that jazz and African Caribbean dance styles were of significantly greater intensity than contemporary dance and would elicit a greater training effect. The physiological stress imposed by the three forms of dance exercise was of a moderate intensity (indicated by heart rate). This results in a lower cardiovascular response, as reflected in the mean heart rate values, which fell below the suggested heart rate (140 beats/min: 70% of the dance subjects' predicted maximum heart rate) for eliciting a cardiovascular training response as specified by the American College of Sports Medicine (1991).

6 References

American College of Sports Medicine (1991) **American College of Sports Medicine Guidelines for Exercise Testing and Prescription.** 4th edition. Lea and Febiger, Philadelphia.

Astrand, P.O. and Rodahl, K. (1990) **Textbook of Work Physiology.** McGraw-Hill Book Co., Sydney, Australia.

Bell, J.M. and Bassey, E.J. (1994) A comparison of the relation between oxygen uptake and heart rate during different styles of aerobic dance and a traditional step test in women. **European Journal of Applied Physiology,** 68, 20-24.

Blanksby, B.A. and Reidy, P.W. (1988) Heart rate and estimated energy expenditure during ballroom dancing. **British Journal of Sports Medicine,** 22, 57-60.

Chemlar, R.D., Schultz, B.B., Ruhling, R.O., Shepard, T.A., Zupan, M.F. and Fitt, S.S. (1988) A physiological profile comparing levels and styles of female dancers. **The Physician and Sportsmedicine,** 16, 87-96.

Cohen, J.L., Segal, K. R., Witriol, I. and McArdle W.D. (1982) Cardiorespiratory responses to ballet exercise and Vo2max of elite ballet dancers. **Medicine and Science in Sports and Exercise,** 14, 212-217.

Gordon, S. (1986) The demands of dance training, in **The Medical Aspects of Dance** (eds D. Peterson, G. Lapenskie and A. Taylor A), Sports Dynamics Press, Ontario, pp. 5-30.

Kirkendall, D.T. and Calabrese, L.H. (1983) Physiological aspects of dance. **Clinics in Sports Medicine,** 2, 525-537.

Koltyn, K.F. and Morgan, W.P. (1992) Efficacy of perceptual versus heart rate monitoring in the development of endurance. **British Journal of Sports Medicine,** 26, 132-134.

Mostardi, R.A., Porterfield, J.A., Greenberg, B., Goldberg, D. and Lea, M. (1983) Musculoskeletal and cardiopulmonary characteristics of the professional ballet dancer. **The Physician and Sportsmedicine,** 11, 53-61.

Rimmer, J.H., Jay, D. and Plowman, S.A. (1994) Physiological characteristics of trained dancers and intensity level of ballet class and rehearsal. **Impulse: The International Journal of Dance Science, Medicine and Education,** 2, 97-105.

Schantz, P.G. and Astrand, P.O. (1984) Physiological characteristics of classical ballet. **Medicine and Science in Sports and Exercise,** 16, 472-476.

Scharff-Olson, M., Williford, H. N. and Smith, F.H. (1992) The heart rate VO2 relationship of aerobic dance: A comparison of target heart rate methods. **Journal of Sports Medicine and Physical Fitness,** 33, 372-377.

Thomsen, D. and Ballor, D.L. (1991) Physiological responses during aerobic dance of individuals grouped by aerobic capacity and dance experience. **Research Quarterly for Exercise and Sport,** 62, 68-72.

Part Five

Methodology and Measurement Techniques

28 An examination of the validity and utility of selected methods for the assessment of habitual physical activity

J. Mitchell, T.H. Mercer and T. Springate

1 Introduction

Despite the well documented health benefits of habitual physical activity and exercise, the majority of people in post-industrial societies remain inactive (Health Education Authority & Sports Council, 1992; Stephens et al., 1985). Reliable information on population levels of physical activity is fundamental to the development, implementation and evaluation of public health policies to promote habitual physical activity, yet such information is sparse and of variable quality.

Survey techniques have traditionally been the preferred tool for activity assessment in epidemiological research. However, the validity and reliability of many survey techniques has not been established, or where it has (Ainsworth et al., 1993; Jacobs et al., 1993; Dishman & Steinhardt, 1988; Godin et al., 1986), there remains a need to establish the utility of such measures for large population-based research. Although exercise epidemiology research has indicated the existence of substantial gender differences in activity patterns (Stephens et al., 1985), there remains a few studies where female activity patterns have been examined. Therefore, the aim of this study was to investigate the inter-relationships of selected methods for the assessment of habitual physical activity in young adult women.

2 Method

Three separate studies were completed to determine the validity and utility of a range of assessment methods for estimating the habitual physical activity (HPA) of young adult women.

Study 1

Study 1 assessed HPA in 50 young adult women (age range 17-26 years) over a seven-day period by means of (i) daily diary (DD) (ii) Self-administered Physical Activity Questionnaire (SAQ) (Blair, 1984) and (iii) Interviewer-administered Physical Activity Questionnaire (IAQ) (Blair, 1984).

Subjects were required to complete the 7-day DD during, or at the end of, each day. The type and duration of all sustained activity ($\geq$5 minutes duration) were noted. Intensity levels of each activity recorded in the 7-day DD were analysed using the Energy Expenditure Index of McArdle et al. (1991). At the end of the study period, and without prior warning, subjects were required to complete both a Self-administered (SAQ) and Interviewer-administered (IAQ) Physical Activity Questionnaire (Blair, 1984). Energy expenditure was calculated for each activity reported via the self-report questionnaires, using the classification of activities and computations of Blair (1984).

Study 2

In Study 2, the relationship between heart rate (HR) estimates and DD estimates of HPA was examined in a group of 13 young adult women (age range 20-25 years) over a continuous five day period. Daily diary estimates were obtained using the method described in Study 1. Heart rate was monitored continuously for 12 hours each day via short range radio telemetry (SPORTTESTER PE 3000; Polar Electro: Finland). Heart rate was subsequently classified into "MODERATE" (100-124 beats.min^{-1}), "HARD" (125-149 beats.min^{-1}) and "VERY HARD" ($\geq$150 beats.min^{-1}) intensity bandwidths (Lange-Anderson et al., 1978). Combined total energy expenditure (kcal.min^{-1}) for "sleep", "work" and "leisure time" activities were also calculated.

Study 3

The relationship between HR and questionnaire estimates of HPA was examined in a group of 20 young adult women (20-25 years) over a period of seven days. Heart rate was monitored according to the method described in Study 2, while the interviewer-administered (IAQ) Physical Activity Questionnaire (Blair, 1984) described in Study 1 was used as the survey instrument.

3 Results

Study 1

Self-reported time spent at each intensity level for all methods of assessment is reported in Table 1. Pearson's product moment correlation coefficient calculations revealed significant (P$\leq$0.01) relationships between 7-day DD and IAQ estimated time spent in "MODERATE" (r = 0.668); "HARD" (r = 0.670) and "VERY HARD" (r = 0.883) activity. The SAQ and 7-day DD estimates of activity were also significantly (P$\leq$0.01) correlated for "MODERATE" (r = 0.316) and "HARD + VERY HARD" activity (r = 0.758). Only SAQ and IAQ estimates of "MODERATE" activity were not significantly related (P$\geq$0.05).

One-way ANOVA's revealed no significant difference (P$\geq$0.05) between the three self-report estimates for time spent in "MODERATE" ($F_{2,147}$ = 2.44), "HARD" ($F_{2,147}$=0.34) and "VERY HARD" ($F_{2,147}$=1.21) activity.

Study 2

Time spent in "MODERATE" activity, recorded by both methods, was higher than time spent in both "HARD" and "VERY HARD" activity (Table 2).

Table 1 Comparison of total time (min) spent in HPA, determined by self-report measures (IAQ; SAQ; 7-day DD)

	ACTIVITY TIME (min)	CORRELATION (r)	COEFFICIENT OF DETERMINATION (%)
MODERATE			
7-day DD	400.8 ± 228.1	0.316*	10
7-day SAQ	304.8 ± 299.9		
7-day DD	400.8 ± 228.1	0.669**	45
7-day IAQ	366.6 ± 196.5		
7-day SAQ	304.8 ± 299.9	0.246	6
7-day IAQ	366.6 ± 196.5		
HARD			
7-day DD	118.5 ± 130.4	0.670**	45
7-day IAQ	91.8 ± 109.5		
VERY HARD			
7-day DD	116.1 ± 139.3	0.883**	78
7-day IAQ	103.8 ± 123.2		
HARD + VERY HARD			
7-day SAQ	222.6 ± 255.3	0.758**	57
7-day DD	234.6 ± 208.6		
7-day SAQ	222.6 ± 255.3	0.830**	69
7-day IAQ	195.6 ± 182.9		
7-day DD	234.6 ± 208.6	0.835**	70
7-day IAQ	195.6 ± 182.9		

* $P \leq 0.05$ (r = 0.279)
** $P \leq 0.01$ (r = 0.361)

Five day DD estimates of time spent in "MODERATE" (514.1 ± 287.4 min.) and "HARD" (97.5 ± 43.3 min) activities were lower than HR estimates at the same intensities (575.4 ± 407.7 min and 49.6 ± 73.2 min, respectively). Despite the large difference in group mean values for "VERY HARD" activity, Pearson's product moment correlation coefficient calculations revealed a significant relationship between the 5-day DD and HR estimates of activity at this intensity (r = 0.566; P≤0.01). There were no significant relationships (P≥ 0.05) between the two activity assessment methods for any of the other intensity categories.

Table 2   Time (min) spent in HPA, determined by self-report (5-day DD) and heart rate telemetry.

	ACTIVITY TIME (min)	CORRELATION (r)	COEFFICIENT OF DETERMINATION (%)
MODERATE			
HR	575.4 ± 407.7	0.469	22
5-day DD	514.1 ± 287.4		
HARD			
HR	97.5 ± 43.3	0.157	2
5-day DD	49.6 ± 73.2		
VERY HARD			
HR	61.7 ± 28.2	0.566*	32
5-day DD	135 ± 106.8		
TOTAL			
HR	734.5 ± 441.2	0.374	14
5-day DD	698.7 ± 295.9		

*   P≤0.05 (r = 0.553)
**   P≤0.01 (r = 0.684)

Study 3

No significant relationship (P≥0.05) between 7 day IAQ and HR estimates of HPA were revealed, except for "VERY HARD" activity (r = 0.592; P≤0.05). See Table 3.

In both Study 2 and Study 3 subjects reported more time spent in "VERY HARD" activity, than recorded via the HR telemetry system. This pattern was reversed for "HARD" activity. Similarly, group means showed lower reported (IAQ) estimates of time spent in "HARD" activities compared with HR estimates recorded in this category. Conversely, higher "MODERATE" and "VERY HARD" activity was reported via IAQ than recorded via heart rate telemetry.

4 Discussion

Study 1

Total time spent in "MODERATE" to "VERY HARD" activity for all three estimates of HPA was approximately 14%. This supports the work of Lange-Anderson et al. (1978) who suggested that women spend approximately 11% of the day in "MODERATE" to "HEAVY" activity. The data from this study revealed high correspondence between all self-report measures at all intensity levels over the 7-day period, except SAQ and IAQ estimates of time spent in "MODERATE" activity, indicating that subjects are better able to recall activity of a higher intensity.

Table 3   Time (min) spent in HPA, determined by self-report (IAQ) and heart rate telemetry (HR)

	ACTIVITY TIME (min)	CORRELATION (r)	COEFFICIENT OF DETERMINATION (%)
MODERATE			
HR	793 ± 383.9	0.147	12
IAQ	297 ± 216.1		
HARD			
HR	181.6 ± 71.1	0.156	13
IAQ	73.5 ± 87.3		
VERY HARD			
HR	107.1 ± 63.9	0.592**	35
IAQ	163.5 ± 117.4		
TOTAL			
HR	1081.7 ± 447.6	0.258	19
IAQ	534 ± 248.7		

* $P \le 0.05$ (r = 0.444)
** $P \le 0.01$ (r = 0.561)

The high correlation between 7-day DD and SAQ (r = 0.758; $P \le 0.01$) for "HARD+VERY HARD" activity, revealed in this study partially support the findings of Sallis et al. (1985) who reported significant ($P \le 0.0001$) test-retest correlations for "MODERATE" and "VERY HARD" 7-day recall activity.

The modest correlations between SAQ and 7-day DD, compared to the moderate to high relationships revealed between DD and IAQ for "MODERATE" and "HARD + VERY HARD" activity support the notion that self-administered recall estimates of activity are less precise than interviewer-administered estimates (Montoye & Taylor, 1984), but may be more epidemiologically useful.

Study 2 and Study 3

Time spent in "MODERATE" to "VERY HARD" activity in these studies equates to approximately 20% of total HPA. The accumulated mean time spent with heart rate ≥ 125 beats.min^{-1} ("HARD" to "VERY HARD" activity) in Study 2 and Study 3 was 5.8% and 4.4%, respectively.

Significant correlations ($P \leq 0.01$) were revealed between 5-d DD and HR data, and SAQ and HR for "VERY HARD" activity only. These relationships explained only between 32% to 35% of the total variance. Discrepancies between the three activity assessment methods used in Study 2 and Study 3, may be due to the time period over which the activity was recorded. The 5-d DD asks subjects to record activity periods of ≥ 5 minutes; the SAQ records activity periods of ≥ 30 minutes, while HR monitoring data were analysed as total time spent in each of the activity categories.

The self-report (7-d DD and SAQ) estimates of HPA were significantly correlated at all intensities in Study 1, while the same relationships were not revealed in Study 2 or Study 3 for HR and self-report estimates of HPA, suggesting that HR data are not assessing the same behaviour as the self-report methods. The data from Study 2 and Study 3 revealed no significant correlations for both "MODERATE" and "HARD" activity between the estimates used. The high accuracy of recall of "VERY HARD" activity may be attributable to the planning and scheduling of activities which are more likely to be encoded into the memory than routine low intensity activity which may not be systematically attended to.

5 Conclusions

The results of these studies provide tentative support for the accuracy of recall estimates of HPA and support the utility of 7-day IAQ and SAQ for the assessment of HPA. Daily diary estimates of HPA patterns have previously been used as a criterion standard of HPA assessment. However, the value of prompting for increasing the accuracy of recall was confirmed and the results suggest that the IAQ may offer greater utility in epidemiological research. There appears to be little concordance between HR estimates and self-report estimates of HPA. These findings may reflect an inability of subjects to discriminate between selected intensity dimensions during self-report of habitual physical activity, memory decay over the recall period, or non-systematic attention to low intensity activity.

Although it was found that significant correlations only existed between the HR and self-report estimates of "VERY HARD" activity, both SAQ and IAQ provided an expedient method of assessing physical activity across all intensities, while maintaining an acceptable level of accuracy. It can be concluded that physical activity recall estimates are less intrusive and less time consuming than either the DD or HR monitoring, and therefore have greater potential utility in exercise epidemiology research.

6 References

Ainsworth, B.E., Jacobs, D.R. and Leon, A.S. (1993) Validity and reliability of self-reported physical activity status: the Lipid Research Clinics questionnaire. **Medicine and Science in Sports and Exercise,** 25, 92-98.

Blair, S.N. (1984) How to assess exercise habits and physical fitness, in **Behavioural Health: A Handbook of Health Enhancement and Disease Prevention** (eds J.D. Matarazzo, S.M. Weiss, J.A. Herd, N.E. Miller and S.E. Weiss). John Wiley, New York, pp. 424-447.

Dishman, R.K. and Steinhardt, M. (1988) Reliability and concurrent validity for a 7-d recall of physical activity in college students. **Medicine and Science in Sports and Exercise,** 20, 14-25.

Godin, G., Jobin, J. and Bouillon, J. (1986) Assessment of leisure time exercise behaviour by self-report: a concurrent validity study. **Canadian Journal of Public Health,** 77, 359-362

Health Education Authority and Sports Council. (1992) **Allied Dunbar National Fitness Survey.** Belmont Press, London.

Jacobs, D.R., Ainsworth, B.E., Hartman, T.J. and Leon, A.S. (1993) A simultaneous evaluation of 10 commonly used physical activity questionnaires. **Medicine and Science in Sports and Exercise,** 25, 81-91.

Lange-Anderson, K., Masironi, R., Rutenfranz, R. and Seliger, V. (1978) **Habitual Physical Activity and Health.** Copenhagen: W.H.O

McArdle, W.D., Katch, F.I. and Katch, V.L. (1991) **Exercise Physiology, Energy, Nutrition and Human Performance.** Lea & Febiger, London.

Montoye, H.J. and Taylor, H.L. (1984). Measurement of physical activity in population studies: A review. **Human Biology,** 56, 195-216.

Sallis, J.F., Haskell, W.L., Wood, P.D., Fortmann, S.P., Rogers, T., Blair, S.N. and Paffenbarger, R.S. (1985) Physical activity assessment methodology in the Five-City Project. **American Journal of Epidemiology,** 121, 91-106.

Stephens, T., Jacobs, D.R., and White, C.C. (1985) A descriptive epidemiology of leisure time physical activity. **Public Health Reports,** 100, 147-158.

29 The use of whole day (24 hour) heart rate monitoring in assessing physical activity patterns in primary school children

S. Atkins, L. Dugdill, R. Phillips, T. Reilly, and G. Stratton

1 Introduction

The relationship between physical activity and health has been established in adult populations (Blair et al, 1992; Powell et al. 1987).Less is known about the antecedents of physical activity in children. Sallis and Patrick (1994) produced guidelines for physical activity levels, in adolescents, from the limited data available. They suggested periods of moderate to vigorous physical activity, of 20 minutes or more, repeated three times weekly. These activity levels were chosen so as to promote cardiorespiratory health.

Heart rate monitoring (HRM) has been used during waking hours to evaluate levels of physical activity in adult and child populations (Freedson, 1989), and has been found to be a valid and reliable means of recording heart rate in children (Tsanakas et al., 1986).Heart rate monitoring provides a socially acceptable method of assessing physical activity without hindrance to normal daily activities (Saris, 1986). Transient factors such as climate, emotional state, specificity of exercising musculature, and training state may provide variation in results using HRM techniques.

Few studies have used HRM to determine resting heart rate to create a baseline for subsequent physical activity assessment. The primary aim of the current study is to provide 24 hour analysis of habitual physical activity during normal schooldays using heart rate as a criterion measure. Data analysis employed a heart rate threshold of >139 beats.min^{-1} as being reflective of appropriate physical activity (Armstrong et al, 1990a).

The use of 24 hour HRM provides information on resting heart rate, degree of deflection from resting heart rate during waking hours' activity, and the levels of activity of children during normal waking hours'. Resting heart rate is also used as an indicator of aerobic training threshold using the 75% of heart rate reserve recommended by Morrow and Freedson (1994).

2 Methodology

Fifteen boys aged 10.9 (S.D.± 1.9 years) and sixteen girls aged 10.3 (± 1.9) years gave informed consent to take part in this study. All children were resident in the South Liverpool area. Subjects were fitted with a short range radio telemeter (Polar, Kempele, Finland), to record heart rate minute by minute. The lightweight transmitter was attached to the chest using 40 mm diameter foam electrodes (Skintact, Bodycare Products, Kenilworth, Middlesex). Heart rate telemetry systems were fitted to subjects before attending school on three consecutive schooldays. Subjects were asked to record the time that they retired to sleep and their time of waking to provide a record of sleep periods.

Data were analysed each day using Polar HR Analysis Software 4.0 (Polar, Kempele, Finland) interfaced through a portable computer (Powerbook, Apple MacIntosh). Figure 1. illustrates a typical 24 hour heart rate time curve for a girl.

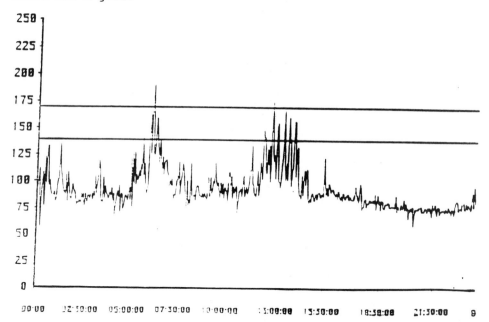

Figure 1. A typical female 24 hour heart rate curve.

Data were analysed for the following variables:- mean heart rate during sleeping hours, percentage time spent at individual heart rate ranges during waking hours, and sustained periods of 20 minutes with heart rate intensities >139 beats.min.$^{-1}$.

Estimation of 75% heart rate reserve was assessed using the following equation from Morrow and Freedson (1994),

$$RHR + .75 (MHR - RHR)$$

(RHR = resting heart rate and MHR = maximal heart rate).

Maximal heart rate is established using the formula;
$$220 - age.$$

3 Results

Complete 24 hour data for heart rate were collected from 7 boys and 16 girls during this study. The results showed that during the sleep period, (mean 9.4 ± 0.7 hours), boys and girls averaged 65 ($\pm$ 7.3) beats. min^{-1} and 72 ($\pm$ 5.7) beats. min^{-1} respectively.

Mean waking hours heart rate were 84 ($\pm$ 9.4) beats.min^{-1} for boys and 93 ($\pm$ 8.2) beats.min^{-1} for girls. Waking hour's heart rate monitoring showed periods of activity, with heart rate >139 beats.min^{-1}, of 4.4 ($\pm$ 4.7) % and 2.2 ($\pm$ 1.8) % for boys and girls respectively (Table 1). These values represent periods of 63.3 minutes and 31.7 minutes for boys and girls respectively. Three boys and three girls achieved heart rate >139 beats.min^{-1} for a sustained period of 20 minutes or more with no boy or girl achieving more than one 20 minutes period at this intensity.

Data analysis using the 75% of heart rate reserve equation showed values of 173 beats.min^{-1} and 175 beats.min^{-1} for boys and girls, respectively. Data from this study showed one boy and no girls achieved a sustained period of activity, above this threshold, in excess of 20 minutes duration. Data from several subjects did show heart rate intensity exceed 75% of heart rate reserve thresholds for very short periods, none of which where sustained for periods of five minutes or more.

Table 1. Summary of main findings for heart rate (beats.min^{-1}).

Variable	Boys (n = 15)		Girls (n = 16)	
	Mean	S.D.	Mean	S.D.
Age	10.9	1.9	10.3	1.9
Sleeping heart rate	65	7.3	73	5.7
Waking hours mean heart rate	84	9.4	93	8.2
Percentage of waking time where heart rate >139 beats.min^{-1}	4.4	4.7	2.2	1.8

4 Discussion

The present study was conducted to investigate the physical activity patterns of children aged 9-11 years, and to determine resting heart rate from recognised HRM techniques. In the current study activity levels above the 75% heart rate reserve threshold were estimated using the recommendations of Morrow and Freedson (1994).

Results indicate relatively small increases in heart rate, above values while sleeping, during physical activity in waking hours. Such small increases in heart rate above baseline values, and subsequent short periods of time above heart rate thresholds commonly associated with health and fitness related benefits, confirm low levels of physical activity in British schoolchildren (Armstrong et al., 1990a;1990b). Despite the small sample in this study evidently primary age schoolchildren fail to meet the recommended criteria for health related benefits resulting from physical activity. Data from this study indicated that levels of daily activity are similar to those reported by Armstrong et al. (1990a).

The incidence of sustained activity at intensities >139 beats.min^{-1} was very small among boys and girls, with three boys and three girls sustaining this intensity for twenty minutes or more. These results indicate a very low level of participation in activity levels recommended for providing health and fitness benefits. The greatest percentages of waking hours' time were spent with heart rates close to resting heart rate, measured by sleeping hours HRM.

These data show that boys achieved heart rates >139 beats.min^{-1} for 4.4($\pm$ 4.7) % of total waking hours time and girls achieving 2.2 ($\pm$ 1.8) % of total waking hours time, these percentages equating to 63.3 and 31.7 minutes respectively. Recommendations for time spent participating in physical activities are cited as between 20 and 60 minutes daily, at intensities recognised as giving health related benefits (Sallis and Patrick, 1994). Data from this study show boys and girls achieving periods of activity within these recommendations. However, boys achieved physical activity levels at recommended intensities for twice the period achieved by female subjects. The percentage of children achieving daily physical activity is consistently higher in males than females (Pate et al., 1994), and data from this study are similar to the findings of Armstrong et al (1990a) suggesting that British girls are less active than boys of the same age. In addition, only a very small proportion of subjects achieved these intensities for sustained periods of more than 20 minutes and no child achieved more than one period of sustained activity over three measurement days.

The use of sleeping heart rate to estimate the 75% mean heart rate reserve threshold (Morrow and Freedson, 1994) showed values of 173 beats.min^{-1} and 175 beats.min^{-1} for boys and girls respectively. One boy achieved a period of sustained activity above these thresholds. Data showed small heart rate "peaks", above reported thresholds for both boys and girls. The duration of these peaks was below

5 minutes and the aerobic fitness benefit gained from such
activity is likely to be negligible. In relation to the
reported thresholds, for 75% heart rate reserve, boys and
girls in this study exhibited very low levels of attainment
of those thresholds recommended for aerobic fitness
benefit. The current study was performed to assess habitual
activity levels and made no discrimination between habitual
activity and organised physical training programmes. Whilst
the reported thresholds appear to be difficult to attain
during the course of habitual physical activity, organised
physical activities may provide stimulus for a beneficial
aerobic fitness response.

The measurement of heart rate over 24 hours, using
recognised HRM techniques, provides the first reported
heart rate measurements of British schoolchildren whilst
sleeping. Reported baseline heart rates are similar to
basal heart rates reported by Malina and Roche (1983) for
children of similar age groups.

5 Conclusion

Despite the small sample size used, data from this study
re-affirm previous findings that British schoolchildren
have low levels of habitual physical activity. There is
little evidence that intensities and duration of physical
activities in this group of schoolchildren are sufficient
to provide positive health benefits through adequate
cardiovascular stress. Data confirm that boys spend greater
periods of time at intensities believed to have positive
health benefits than do girls. The measurement of sleeping
heart rate has provided an estimation of thresholds
recommended for aerobic fitness benefit using the 75% of
heart rate reserve method. The use of heart rate assessment
during sleep may be useful, therefore, in the direct
estimation of basal heart rate using socially acceptable
heart rate monitoring techniques.

6 References

Armstrong, N. Balding, J. Gentle, P. and Kirby, B. (1990a)
Patterns of physical activity among 11 to 16 year old
British children. British Medical Journal, **301**, 203-
205.
Armstrong N. Balding J. Gentle P. and Kirby,B. (1990b)
Estimation of coronary risk factors in British
children: a preliminary report. British Journal of
Sports Medicine, **24**, 61-65.
Blair, S. Kohl, H. Gordon, N. Pfaffenbarger, R.S. (1992)
How much physical activity is good for health? Annual
Review of Public Health, **13**, 99-126.
Freedson, P. (1989) Field monitoring of physical activity
in children. Paediatric Exercise Science, **1**, 8-18.
Malina, R.M. and Roche, A.F. (1983) Manual of physical
status and performance in childhood: Vol. 2. Physical
performance. New York: Plenum.

Morrow, J.R. and Freedson, P.S. (1994) Relationship between habitual physical activity and aerobic fitness in adolescents. Paediatric Exercise Science, **6**, 315-329.

Pate, R.R. Long, B.J. and Heath, G. (1994) Descriptive epidemiology of physical activity in adolescents. Paediatric Exercise Science, **6**, 434-447.

Powell, K.E. Thompson, P. Caspersen, C.J. and Kendrick, J.S.(1987) Physical activity and the incidence of coronary heart disease. Annual Review of Public Health, **8**, 253-287.

Sallis, J. F. and Patrick, K. (1994) Physical activity guidelines for adolescents: Consensus statement. Paediatric Exercise Science, **6**, 302-314.

Saris, W.H.M. (1986) Habitual physical activity in children: Methodology and findings. Medicine and Science in Sports and Exercise, **18**, 253-263.

Simons-Morton, B.G. Parcel, G.S. O'Hara, N.M. Blair, S.N.and Pate, R.R. (1988) Health related physical fitness inchildhood. Annual Review of Public Health, **9**, 403-425.

Tsanakas, J.N. Bannister, O.M. Boon, A.W. and Milner, R.D.G.(1986) The Sports Tester, a device for monitoring the free running test. Archives of Disease in Childhood, **61**, 912-914.

30 Reproducibility of indices of anterior tibio-femoral displacement in active and inactive men

N. Gleeson, S. Rakowski, D. Rees and T. Reilly

1 Introduction

The knee joint is one of the most complex and most frequently injured joints in the body (DeHaven and Lintner, 1986; Zarins and Adams, 1988). A model which defines the limits of normal knee movement comprises primary ligamentous restraints interacting with the other static stabilisers (osseous geometry, capsular structures, and menisci) and with the dynamic muscle stabilisers (Fu, 1993). The anterior cruciate ligament (ACL) is the principal ligamentous restraint to anterior tibio-femoral displacement (TFD) (Butler, Noyes and Grood, 1980).

An increasing orthopaedic interest has focussed on ACL insufficiency. This reflects in part, a general increase in the number of orthopaedically serious ACL injuries, and clinical interest in the relationship between injury, mode of surgical treatment intervention, and rehabilitation on short- and long-term knee joint function (Rees, 1994).

The assessment of pathological anterior laxity of the knee has focussed on tests such as 'anterior drawer', Lachman's and 'pivot shift' tests carried out clinically or under anaesthesia. While positive Lachman and 'pivot shift' tests show excellent qualitative correlation with ACL dysfunction by comparison to arthroscopic findings, such tests are subject to inter-clinician execution and perception biases. Consequently, instrumented knee testing, which uses mechanical devices attached to the leg to measure applied anterior force- TFD response curves indirectly via the change in relative position of bony landmarks about the knee, is becoming more frequently evaluated as an objective and quantitative method of assessing ACL insufficiency. The indices of anterior TFD at specific applied anterior tibial forces have become accepted as potential discriminators of ACL function (Daniel, et al., 1985).

A primary purpose of an index of ligamentous function is to provide a reliable estimate of performance capacity. The fundamental question of how many trials to establish a true measure of an individual's anterior TFD characteristics has been the subject of relatively few and methodologically diverse investigations. Markolf, Kochan and Amstutz (1984) investigated the reproducibility of anterior TFD using an instrumented research tool. Multiple intra-subject trials on separate occasions in two subjects revealed coefficient of variance scores of ±29% to ±33% for anterior TFD at 100N of applied anterior tibial force.

The aim of this study was to document the intra-subject variability and reproducibility associated with the day-to-day instrumented measurement of anterior TFD in active and inactive men with no previous history of knee injury.

2 Methods

Fourteen adult male professional soccer players ([mean ± SD] age 17.7 ± 0.6 years; height 1.80 ± 0.05 m; body mass 68.2 ± 6.2 kg) and seven inactive males (self-reported occasional recreational exercise) (age 18.8 ± 0.7 years; height 1.82 ± 0.05 m; body mass 69.1 ± 6.6 kg) gave their informed consent to participate in this study. Following familiarisation, each subject returned to the laboratory to complete a sequence of three test sessions each separated by a period of 7 days. All subjects were tested as near to the same time of day as possible (± 1 hour). The same test administrator performed all measurements.

Within each session the subjects completed a series of three assessments of the non-preferred and then preferred leg (defined as the leg chosen to kick a ball) using a laboratory instrument constructed to measure TFD. The apparatus and subject orientation during assessment are shown schematically in Figure 1. A commercial design (KLT: Smith & Nephew Donjoy Inc., Carlsbad, CA.) was modified to provide the base of the apparatus. This was constructed to provide an adjustable rigid chair-like framework and was designed to maintain the knee in a standardised position during the measurement of anterior TFD. The involved leg was secured by Velcro^{TM} straps and a clamping device at the distal femur and tibia, respectively. The knee joint was maintained at 0.44 rad of flexion (0 rad = full extension) and foot position at 0.26 rad of external rotation (Markolf, Kochan and Amstutz, 1984) and 0.35 rad of plantar flexion. The subject was seated in an upright position with a 0.26 rad angle between the back and seat supports.

Instrumentation to measure anterior TFD consisted of two linear inductive displacement transducers (DCT500C, RDP Electronics Ltd., Wolverhampton, U.K.: 0.025 m range). The latter incorporates spring-loaded plungers which were adjusted accurately in three planes to provide perpendicular attachment to the patella and tibial tubercle. During measurements, both transducers were secured to the skin surface using tape and able to move freely only in the anterior-posterior plane relative to the supporting framework. The instrument monitored only the relative motion between the patella and tibial sensors and so facilitated the exclusion of measurement artifacts caused by extraneous movements of the leg during the application of anterior displacement forces.

Anterior force was applied in the sagittal plane, at a rate of 67 ±7 N.s-1 [mean ± SD], and in a perpendicular direction relative to the tibia by an instrumented force-handle incorporating a load cell (Model 31E500N0, RDP Electronics Ltd., Wolverhampton, U.K.: range 500 N). This device was positioned behind the leg at a level 0.02 m distal to the tibial tubercle. The transducers were interfaced to an IBM compatible microcomputer via a 16 channel A/D 12 bit converter (Model PC-28A, Amplicon Liveline Ltd., Brighton, U.K.). Data from all transducers were sampled at 50 Hz.

Measurements on each knee were preceded by two practice trials. During each measurement, subjects were instructed to relax the musculature of the involved limb. Rapid but gentle manual anterior-posterior drawer oscillations were used to facilitate relaxation and to establish a neutral tibio-femoral position from which all measurements were initiated. Indices of anterior TFD were calculated as the mean of three intra-session replicates of the net displacement of the patella and tibial tubercle transducers at anterior tibial displacement forces of 40 N, 80 N, 120 N, 160 N and 200 N applied in the sagittal plane.

The displacement transducers were calibrated against known lengths throughout the range of linear operation specified by the manufacturer (0.025 m). The standard error of the estimate associated with the recording of displacement was ±1.6 x 10-5 m. The force transducer was calibrated against known masses through a biologically valid range (0 N -

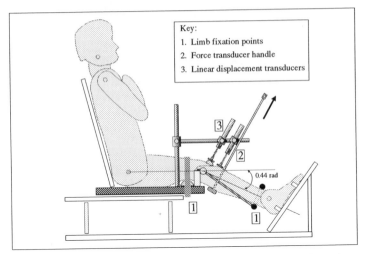

Fig. 1.   Subject and anterior TFD measurement apparatus orientation.

220 N) with correction for the mass of the apparatus and angle of force application. The standard error of the estimate associated with the application and recording of the applied force was ±0.003 N. Throughout the period of testing, the calibration of the force and displacement transducers was verified against objects of known mass and length, respectively.

The selected indices of anterior TFD were described using ordinary statistical procedures (mean ± SD). Coefficient of variation (V%) corrected for small sample bias was used to assess variability of indices across 3 trials. The latter index was calculated according to the expression (SD/mean).(1 + [1/4N]) where N is the number of trials. Intra-class correlation coefficients (R_I) were computed to describe single-measurement reliability (Winer, 1981). Standard error of a single measurement (SEM%) (95% confidence limits, computed as a percentage of the group mean score) was calculated for each index (Thomas and Nelson, 1990). Variability across 3 trials and absolute scores were compared using a 2 (leg [preferred and non-preferred]) x 5 (level of applied anterior force [40 N, 80 N, 120 N, 160 N, 200 N]) factorial repeated measures ANOVA with a between subjects factor of group [active and inactive]. An a priori alpha level of 0.05 was applied in all statistical procedures. All statistical analyses were programmed using SPSS/PC+ (V3.1) software (SPSS Inc., 1989).

3   Results

Table 1 shows group mean anterior TFD scores (±S.D.) in three inter-day trials under selected applied experimental conditions. Repeated measures ANOVA revealed no significant differences in absolute anterior TFD scores across inter-day trials under the experimental conditions. Table 2 shows group mean coefficient of variation (V%), intra-class correlation coefficient (R_I) and standard error of the measurement (SEM%) (95% confidence intervals, expressed as a percentage of the group mean score) for day-to-day assessments of indices of TFD for non-preferred and preferred knees.

Repeated measures ANOVA of V% scores revealed no significant differences in day-to-

Table 1. The mean (±SD) anterior TFD (mm) measured using selected applied forces of 40N, 120N, and 200N applied in the sagittal plane with a knee flexed to 0.44 rad (25°) in three inter-day trials for non-preferred (NP) and preferred (P) knees.

Applied force		Active		Inactive	
		NP	P	NP	P
40 N	Trial 1	0.52±0.38	0.58±0.43	0.59±0.38	0.61±0.43
	Trial 2	0.52±0.37	0.60±0.35	0.51±0.37	0.67±0.35
	Trial 3	0.54±0.31	0.70±0.51	0.54±0.31	0.74±0.51
120 N	Trial 1	1.35±0.64	1.52±0.51	1.25±0.64	1.58±0.58
	Trial 2	1.11±0.57	1.38±0.62	1.17±0.56	1.43±0.67
	Trial 3	1.10±0.47	1.63±0.70	1.06±0.43	1.72±0.75
200 N	Trial 1	1.81±0.77	2.00±0.80	1.87±0.75	2.12±0.89
	Trial 2	1.55±0.78	1.84±0.75	1.67±0.78	1.88±0.69
	Trial 3	1.58±0.66	2.15±0.91	1.55±0.76	2.19±1.01

day TFD variability between active and inactive groups, but a significant applied TFD force by knee interaction (Pillai's Trace = 0.87: $F_{[4,16]}$=27.4; P<0.0005). While the assessment of TFD demonstrated reduced measurement variability at increased applied force conditions in both legs, the preferred leg showed a greater reduction in this respect (range of mean V% across active and inactive groups, ±28% to ±20% and ±25% to ±12% for non-preferred and preferred legs, respectively). Consideration of R_1 scores suggests that active and inactive groups demonstrated similar levels of single measurement reliability across applied force and leg conditions, ranging between 0.73 and 0.94, and 0.67 and 0.91, respectively. SEM% scores (95% confidence intervals) for TFD ranged between ±13.3% (preferred leg, inactive, 120 N force) and ±73.6% (non-preferred leg, active, 40 N force).

4 Discussion

Results suggest that inter-day changes in indices of anterior TFD can be attributed to biological and technological error sources rather than to systematic learning effects. This finding suggests further that the assessment of the number trials to achieve appropriate anterior TFD measurement sensitivity can be made on reproducibility and reliability criteria alone. It seems that TFD may be assessed using protocols of similar measurement rigour in active and inactive groups.

The V% data suggest that the application of higher levels of applied force during the intra-leg estimation of anterior TFD will provide greater levels of measurement reproducibility and sensitivity. This effect is more pronounced in the assessment of the preferred leg. It may be that the latter observations are associated with a more consistent interaction of those factors limiting normal knee movement in the preferred leg under conditions of increased anterior force (Fu, 1993). Assessments of anterior TFD using low levels of applied force would appear to offer the greatest and criterion threat to the establishment of appropriate measurement sensitivity and utility.

Generally, R_1 for the indices of anterior TFD approaches or exceeds the clinically acceptable reliability coefficient threshold of greater than 0.80 (Currier, 1984). However, overall group mean V% and SEM% scores across the applied force and leg conditions for these indices, which range between ±56.0% (non-preferred leg, 40 N) and ±26.6%

Table 2. Group mean coefficient of variation (V%), intra-class correlation coefficient (R_I) and standard error of the measurement (SEM%) (95% confidence intervals, expressed as a percentage of the group mean score) for day-to-day assessments of indices of TFD for non-preferred (NP) and preferred (P) knees.

Applied force	V% [%]				R_I				SEM% [%]			
	Active		Inactive		Active		Inactive		Active		Inactive	
	NP	P	NP	P	NP	P	NP	P	NP	P	NP	P
40 N	36.6	25.1	19.5	25.8	0.75	0.93	0.91	0.77	73.6	39.8	37.5	40.3
80 N	24.6	19.9	19.7	23.5	0.73	0.92	0.85	0.60	54.8	27.4	43.1	21.1
120 N	23.9	14.1	21.8	17.5	0.76	0.93	0.83	0.75	46.2	23.6	44.9	13.3
160 N	22.5	12.0	23.2	14.9	0.79	0.94	0.81	0.75	40.0	19.2	44.7	14.7
200 N	20.0	12.7	21.0	13.9	0.83	0.93	0.82	0.67	35.4	21.8	38.5	24.0

(preferred leg, 200 N), and between ±55.6% (non-preferred leg, 40 N) and ±22.9% (preferred leg, 200 N) [95% confidence limits], respectively, indicate a limited capacity to discriminate physiological change in ACL functional capacity based on single-trial assessments for both intra- and inter-leg comparisons. Furthermore, they suggest that in many applications which require high levels of measurement sensitivity, it is imperative to use a mean score of multiple trials as the basis for estimating anterior TFD in order to reduce measurement error.

Estimated error of the mean score of multiple trials would be expected to vary inversely with the square root of the number of intra-leg replicates, assuming a normal distribution of the replicates (Winer, 1981). Using this criterion, the mean score of 25 intra-leg replicates would be needed to achieve an arbitrarily acceptable error of better than ±10% (95% confidence limits) for anterior TFD measurements. Similarly, the Spearman-Brown prophecy formula (Winer, 1981) used in conjunction with the calculation of SEM% suggests that at least 20 replicates would be needed to discriminate properly between scores from different legs with the same level of measurement sensitivity. These findings present a logistical threat to measurement utility. It should be noted that these estimates relate to the average group response which does not reflect fully the anterior TFD heterogeneity of some subjects within this sample.

The present study documents anterior TFD scores in a homogeneous asymptomatic young adult male population. The group mean scores (Table 1) demonstrate lower displacement compared to a group mean displacement of 3 mm exhibited by a heterogeneous group of 45 asymptomatic adults (mean age 27; range 17 - 49 years) during the application of a 100 N force (Markolf, Kochan and Amstutz, 1984) and compared to a group mean displacement score of 5.3 mm (range 2.5 - 8.2 mm) for men assessed using the protocol of the present study (mean age 28.7; range 23 - 39 years; 100 N) (Gleeson and Rakowski, unpublished observations). Similarly, following ACL reconstructive surgery, a subject may demonstrate substantial reductions in anterior TFD of the involved knee, from 11.2 mm (4 months post-surgery) to 4.3 mm (18 months post-surgery) during aggressive physiological rehabilitation (Gleeson and Rees, unpublished observations). Thus by comparison to these relatively large changes in capacity and large base-line scores, the present data may demand superior levels of measurement sensitivity in order to detect properly the small intra-leg changes in anterior TFD.

The mean differences in anterior TFD observed during inter-leg comparisons in the present study (0.35 mm) are consistent with those reported in the literature (Markolf, Kochan and Amstutz, 1984; Daniel, et al., 1985). Therefore, this study may present an authentic kinanthropometric challenge to meaningful comparisons between knees of the same individual.

The measurement sensitivity concerns which have been identified in this paper provide a basis from which to question the rationale for the application of instrumented knee testing for the indirect measurement of anterior TFD. The trade-off between measurement sensitivity and utility means that in applied clinical settings, the detection of potentially subtle and important differences in anterior TFD may not be possible. The data suggest strongly that the use of instrumented knee testing is justifiable in situations such as in adaptive recovery following injury or surgical interventions, where relatively large changes in capacity can be expected.

Acknowledgement: The authors acknowledge gratefully the contributions of Graham Barlow and Arthur Smallman, Senior Technicians Staffordshire University, who constructed the measurement apparatus, and thank Jane Kirkham and Sue Dugdale, Senior Physiotherapists M.C.H.T., for their assistance during preparatory work for this study.

5   References

Butler, D.L., Noyes, F.R. and Grood, E.S. (1980). Ligamentous restraints to anterior-posterior drawer in the human knee; A biomechanical study. **Journal of Bone and Joint Surgery**, 62A, 259-270.

Currier, D.P. (1984). **Elements of Research in Physical Therapy** (2nd ed.). Williams and Wilkins, Baltimore.

Daniel, D., Malcolm, L., Losse, G., Stone, M., Sachs, R. and Burs, R. (1985). Instrumented measurement of anterior laxity of the knee. **Journal of Bone and Joint Surgery**, 67A, 720-726.

DeHaven, K.E. and Lintner, D.M. (1986). Athletic injuries: Comparison by age, sport, and gender. **American Journal of Sports Medicine**, 14: 218-224.

Fu, F.H. (1993). Biomechanics of knee ligaments. **Journal of Bone and Joint Surgery**, 75A, 1716-1727.

Markolf, K., Kochan, A. and Amstutz, H. (1984). Measurement of knee stiffness and laxity in patients with documented absence of the anterior cruciate ligament. **Journal of Bone and Joint Surgery**, 66A: 242-253.

Rees, D. (1994). ACL reconstructions: Possible modes of failure. **Proceedings of the Royal College of Surgeons, Edinburgh - Football Association, Sixth Joint Conference on Sports injury**, Lilleshall, 2nd-3rd July.

Thomas, J.R. and Nelson, J.K. (1990). **Introduction to Research in Health, Physical Education, Recreation and Dance** (2nd ed.). Human Kinetics, Champaign, Illinois.

Winer, B.J. (1981). **Statistical Principles in Experimental Design** (2nd ed.). McGraw-Hill, New York.

Zarins, B. and Adams, M. (1988). Knee injuries in sports. **The New England Journal of Medicine**, 318, 950-961.

31 The characteristics of maximal dynamic lifting exertions on a hydrodynamometer

D.M. Fothergill, D.W. Grieve and A.D.J. Pinder

1 Introduction

There are well defined and long-standing methods of measuring muscular strength using maximal isometric exertions (Caldwell et al., 1974). However, with the introduction of computerized dynamometers, isokinetic and hydraulic resistive devices are now increasingly being used as both laboratory and diagnostic tools to assess dynamic strength (Hortobagyi et al., 1989).

The advantage of computerized dynamic strength tests is that they can provide information about performance over the entire range of motion more rapidly and efficiently than a series of isometric strength tests. Furthermore, since most human exertions require dynamic contraction of the musculature throughout a movement range, dynamic tests may provide more relevant measures than isometric ones.

In the present study maximal dynamic lifts were performed on a hydrodynamometer. In contrast to the widely used isokinetic devices, which operate at a preset velocity, the hydrodynamometer relies on a fluid to provide the resistance to motion making the speed of movement dependent on the effort. At present only a few studies have reported strength measures obtained using such devices (Grieve, 1984; Grieve & van der Linden, 1986; Hortobagyi et al., 1989). Furthermore, little is known about how maximal strength measured on hydraulic dynamometers compares with the more conventional laboratory tests of isometric strength. The objectives of this study were therefore 1) to describe and compare the characteristics of one and two-handed maximal lifting exertions in males and females at lift velocities up to 1 m/s using a hydraulic resistance dynamometer and 2) to compare dynamic forces obtained at specific heights with isometric measures of strength at the same heights.

2 Methods

2.1 Subjects
Nine males (Mean±SD, age= 29.1±11.7 years; height= 1785±98 mm; body mass= 74.4±8.7 kg) and nine females (Mean±SD, age= 29.1±7.4 years; height= 1669±55 mm; body mass= 58.4±5.3 kg) volunteered to participate in the experiments. Most of the subjects had no specific background or training in strength related sports or activities.

2.2 Apparatus
All dynamic lifting exertions were performed on the hydrodynamometer described by Grieve (1993), which was modified for the purposes of this study. The hydrodynamometer consisted of a 2 m high water-filled tube with an internal diameter of 200 mm. Inside this was located a close-fitting piston consisting of a 12 mm thick plate with a symmetrical array of holes. The plate was mounted on a central pillar and spider to stabilize the motion, and connected to a handle via a series of pulleys by stranded flexible stainless steel wire cable. When the handle was lifted. resistance to motion was provided by the viscous drag on the piston, and the inertia of the moving parts, which had an equivalent inertial mass of 6.8 kg. Theoretical and empirical considerations show that the viscous drag on the piston is a function of the square of the velocity. The amount of viscous resistance could be altered by opening or closing 48 17 mm diameter holes in the piston. Three resistances were selected and classified as low (28 holes), medium (20 holes), and high (12 holes).

During lifting exertions, linear displacement of the handle resulted in rotation of guide pulleys. The rotational motion of the guide pulleys was transmitted via a gearing mechanism to additional external pulleys connected to a velocity and a displacement transducer (JLT Group, Displacement transducer type PD1, Bushey Heath, Herts, UK). A force transducer (Ether Ltd., Dynamometer type UF2, Stevenage, Herts, UK) determined the applied lifting force by measuring the instantaneous tension in the cable connecting the handle to the piston.

The force transducer was calibrated by clamping the wire cable at the piston end and then hanging weights of known mass on the handle end. A calibration curve for the displacement transducer was determined from output recorded at 16 handle positions between 400 mm and 1855 mm from the floor. Both transducers gave linear signals over their full range to an accuracy of 1 N and 1 mm for force and displacement respectively.

The velocity transducer operated on the principle of magnetic induction and consisted of a closely wound wire coil located in a strong magnetic field. The rate at which this coil was drawn through the magnetic field induced a voltage in the coil that was proportional to the velocity of lift. During a calibration lift, output from the velocity transducer was integrated and then compared with the displacement output. The regression of integrated velocity on displacement was linear ($r^2 = 0.99$) and provided calibration constants with a coefficient of variation of 0.67%.

Outputs from the force, velocity and displacement transducers were amplified using a four-channel amplifier (Racal Instruments Ltd., London, UK) before being digitized to 12-bit resolution by an analogue-to-digital converter (ADC) (CED 1401 Intelligent Interface, Cambridge Electronic Design Ltd., Cambridge, UK) controlled by a BBC B microcomputer (Acorn Computers Ltd., Cambridge, UK). The CED 1401 sampled each transducer at 150 Hz. Force-time, velocity-time and displacement-time plots were displayed on a monitor and the data were stored for later analysis.

Isometric lifting strength was measured using a handle that was connected via a metal chain to a strain gauge transducer (Model 1269F, Takei Kiki Kogyo Co., Ltd., Tokyo) secured firmly to the floor. Output from the strain gauge transducer was passed to the ADC ports of a BBC B microcomputer for sampling, storage and analysis of the data.

2.3 Protocol

A practice lift was performed against each of the three resistances on the hydrodynamometer before recording the maximal efforts. Half the subjects completed the one-handed exertions first and the other half the two-handed exertions first. The order of presentation of the resistance levels was randomized for both the one and two-handed exertions. All one-handed exertions were performed with the dominant hand.

The instructions required the subject to lift as forcefully and as fast as possible from the starting position (400 mm from the floor) to just above head height. The initial starting posture required the subjects to adopt an over-arm grip on the hydrodynamometer handle and to place the feet together directly beneath the handle. Lifting technique was free style, with the constraints that foot position could not be altered during the lift. Exertions were performed at intervals not less than two minutes apart. Test-retest reliability coefficients for forces recorded throughout the lifting range during maximal lifts against the three levels of resistance were between $r=0.92$ and $r=0.99$ (Fothergill, 1992).

One and two-handed isometric lifting strengths at knee, knuckle, hip, shoulder and head height were assessed on a separate day. The protocol followed that described by Caldwell et al. (1974), in which strength measurements were determined from the average force recorded over the final three seconds of a five second maximal exertion. Foot placement with respect to handle position, and type of grip on the handle, were the same as for the dynamic experiments. The order of presentation of the one and two-handed exertions at the different heights was randomized similar to that described above.

2.4 Data analysis

To allow comparisons between subjects, force and velocity values were extracted from each subject's time derivative data at intervals of 0.25% of stature. Normalized strength was calculated for each subject by dividing the force data by body weight. The effects on force output of sex, hand height, number of hands, and resistance level were analyzed using split-plot repeated measures analysis of variance. The data used in this analysis were taken from that obtained at lift heights corresponding to knee, knuckle, hip, elbow and shoulder height. The same form of analysis was performed on the isometric lifting strength data.

Pearson product-moment correlations were used to examine the relationships between dynamic and static tests of lifting strength. The partial correlation technique was used to determine the net relationship between measures of strength without the confounding effect of body mass. Intercorrelations that exceeded $r = 0.71$ (i.e. $r^2 \times 100 = 50\%$) were judged to indicate more generality than specificity between the different strength tests (dynamic or static) and different task resistances. In order to remove the effects of error variance, the correction for attenuation was applied to the intercorrelations using reliability coefficients for the various strength measures (Ferguson, 1976). Significance was set at the 0.05 level for all statistical tests.

3. Results

3.1 Force-velocity-displacement characteristics of lifting exertions on the hydrodynamometer

The force-velocity-displacement characteristics for one and two-handed lifting exertions on the hydrodynamometer are illustrated in Figure 1. The data presented are mean values of force and velocity at 2% intervals of stature for the 9 male and 9 female subjects. The cross symbols represent the mean plus one standard error for force at head, shoulder, elbow, hip, knuckle and knee height. Analysis of variance on the position of peak force (expressed as a fraction of stature) revealed that subject gender ($F_{1,16} =1.17$; $P>0.05$) and the resistance level ($F_{2,32} = 2.747$; $P>0.05$) did not significantly affect the position (relative to stature) at which peak lifting force occurred. The position of peak force was, however, significantly lower for one-handed lifts (mean value over the three resistances = 35.9% of stature) than for two-handed lifts (mean value over the three resistances = 38.4% of stature) ($F_{1,16}=11.23$; $P<0.005$).

Normalized lifting strength (force (Newtons)/body weight) differed significantly between, (a) males and females ($F_{1,16}=9.0$; $P<0.01$), (b) the number of hands used (i.e. one or two-handed exertions, $F_{1,16}=253.3$; $P<0.0001$), (c) the task resistance ($F_{2,32}=61.7$; $P<0.0001$), and (d) the height of the hands above the ground ($F_{4,64}=49.8$; $P<0.0001$). When averaged over the three resistances, two hand conditions, and five heights, the female/male normalized dynamic lifting strength ratio was 0.68. This ratio decreased to 0.53 when dynamic lifting strength was expressed in absolute units of force (Newtons).

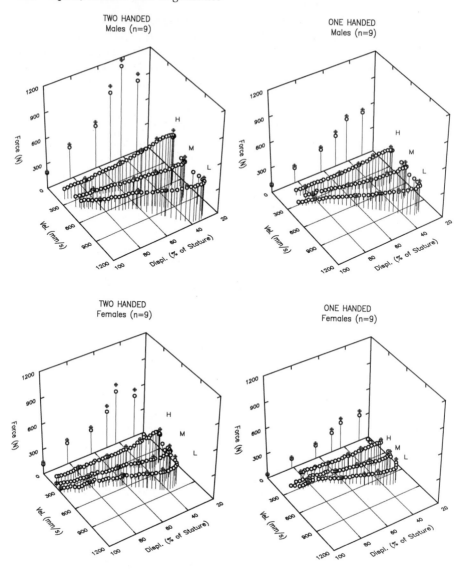

Figure 1. Male and female force-velocity-displacement characteristics for maximal one and two-handed lifting exertions against the low (L), medium (M) and high resistances (H). The + points represent the mean force plus one standard error at knee, knuckle, hip, elbow, shoulder and head height. Group means for maximal isometric lifting forces are shown on the force-displacement plane of each figure.

A significant interaction between sex and hand condition ($F_{1,16}=17.8$; $P<0.001$) indicated that strength differences between one and two-handed lifts were different for males and females. The mean one/two-handed strengthratios for the males and females were 0.63 and 0.67 respectively. On average, two-handed exertions were 1.55 times stronger than one-handed exertions ($P<0.0001$). However, strength differences between one and two-handed exertions changed significantly according to the height above the ground ($F_{4,64}=9.7$; $P<0.0001$). As lift height progressed from 30% to 70% of stature one/two-handed strength ratios decreased from approximately 0.75 to 0.50 in almost a linear fashion. Slight increases in the one-handed/two-handed strength ratios were observed against all dynamic resistances when the hands approached shoulder height (i.e., at approximately 80% of stature).

3.2 Static lifting strength and the interrelationship with dynamic lifting strength

An analysis of variance of the static forces divided by body weight revealed similar results to those found following analysis of the normalized dynamic forces. Isometric lifting strength changed significantly according to the number of hands used ($F_{1,16}=189.9$; $P<0.0001$) and hand height above the ground ($F_{5,80}= 104.8$; $P<0.0001$). In addition, significant two-way interactions were found between sex and one versus two-handed lifting (hands) ($F_{1,16}= 4.9$; $P<0.05$) and between hands and hand height ($F_{5,80}= 38.0$; $P<0.05$). The interaction between sex and hand height was not significant ($F_{5,80}= 2.2$; $P>0.05$). In contrast to the significant difference in normalized dynamic lifting strength between males and females, differences between males and females for normalized static lifting strength were not significant ($F_{1,16}= 3.4$; $P>0.05$).

The average ratio for female/male static strength per unit body weight was 0.76. When calculated using absolute values of force the f/m ratio decreased to 0.60. Differences in static lifting strength between one and two-handed exertions were found to be greater in females than in males ($P<0.05$). The average one/two-handed static lifting strength ratio was 0.49 for males and 0.46 for females. The largest difference between one and two-handed static exertions occurred at hip height for males (1/2 hand strength ratio = 0.45) and at head height for females (1/2 hand strength ratio = 0.39). If exertions at head height are omitted the mean one/two hand strength ratios change to 0.52 and 0.54 for the males and females respectively.

Although correlations between body weight and lifting strength were largely significant ($P<0.05$), body weight accounted for less than 50% the variance in dynamic and static lifting strength over most of the lifting range (mean r^2 x 100% = 32%; range 1% - 55%).

Intercorrelations among the different strength measures (i.e., between the different dynamic resistances and between dynamic and static lifting strength) were calculated using mean lifting scores derived from the average lifting force over knee, knuckle, hip, elbow and shoulder heights for each subject. The resulting single-order partial correlation coefficients (with body weight held constant) ranged from 0.74 to 0.93. The mean proportion of generality (r^2 x

100%) between static and dynamic lifting strength was 73% and 81% for one and two-handed exertions respectively.

4 Discussion

The present study affords a useful indication of the maximum lifting forces capable by males and females during one and two-handed lifting exertions at lift heights throughout the normal operating range. The wide range of task resistances investigated provide an insight into the force-velocity-displacement characteristics of whole-body lifting actions in an analogous way to that provided by early investigations of the mechano-physiological properties of isolated muscle fibres.

Contrasting results were observed for the difference between males and females in normalized dynamic and static lifting strength. This is likely, in part, to be due to the way in which dynamic and static strengths were measured. A dynamic lift requires the activation and deactivation of many individual muscles throughout the lift. Since dynamic lifting strength was obtained from instantaneous values at defined points in the force-displacement profile, differences between individuals in the rate of force development of the active muscles will likely have contributed a considerable amount of inter-subject variability in the strength measurements. In contrast, the static lifting strength data were unlikely to be affected by individual differences in the rate of force development. This was due to the fact that adequate time was provided for the subjects to coordinate and attain maximal activation of their musculature before their static lifting strength was measured. As a result, any differences in the rate of force development between males and females will likely have been masked under these latter test conditions. The potential for strength differences between males and females due to differences in the rate of force contraction has recently been shown by Bell and Jacobs (1986).

Despite the above differences, the results demonstrated high correlations between dynamic and static measures of lifting strength, and between dynamic lifting exertions against the different resistances on the hydrodynamometer. These findings suggest that, (1) these dynamic and static tests of lifting strength measure a common intrinsic ability to produce maximal lifting forces and, (2) individuals who do well (or poorly) on static tests of lifting strength attain the same relative level of performance on maximal dynamic lifting tests against a wide range of task resistances.

5 Acknowledgements

This work was carried out with the support of the U.K. Ministry of Defence under an extramural research agreement with the Army Personnel Research Establishment.

6 References

Bell, D.G. and Jacobs, I. (1986) Electro-mechanical response times and rate of force development in males and females. **Medicine and Science in Sports and Exercise**, 18, 31-36.

Caldwell, L.S., Chaffin, D.B., Dukes-Dobos, F.N., Kroemer, K.H.E., Laubach, L.L., Snook, S.N., and Wasserman, D.E. (1974) A proposed standard procedure for static muscle strength testing. **American Industrial Hygiene Association Journal**, 35, 201-206.

Ferguson, G.H. (1976) **Statistical Analysis in Psychology and Education**, 4th Ed., McGraw-Hill Book Company, New York, pp. 1-529.

Fothergill, D.M. (1992) **Dynamic and static strengths of the human in whole body exertions**, Ph.D. Thesis, University of London, England, pp. 209-282.

Grieve, D.W. (1984) The influence of posture on power output generated in single pulling movements. **Applied Ergonomics**, 15, 115-117.

Grieve D.W. (1993) Measuring power outputs of bi-manual dynamic lifts using a hydrodynamometer. **Proceedings of the XIVth Congress of the International Society of Biomechanics**, pp. 510-511.

Grieve, D.W. and van der Linden, J. (1986) Force, speed and power output of the human upper limb during horizontal pulls. **European Journal of Applied Physiology**, 55, 425-430.

Hortobagyi, T., Katch, F.I., and LaChance, P.F. (1989) Interrelationships among various measures of upper body strength assessed by different contraction modes. Evidence for a general strength component. **European Journal of Applied Physiology**, 58, 749-755.

32 The "Isotechnologies LiftStation" as a measuring technique for static forces

E. Zinzen, D.Caboor, P. Van Roy, A Grootaers and J.P. Clarys

1 Introduction

Work related low-back injuries are presently one of the greatest problems that the community faces. The economic costs in terms of medical expenses, lost production and compensation are enormous. Employees in heavy industry, particularly manual material handlers, have a high incidence of low-back problems and have received considerable attention in the literature (Aghazadeh and Ayoub, 1985; Garg et al., 1980; Jiang et al., 1986; Kamon et al., 1982; Mirka and Marras, 1990; Mital et al., 1986).

At present, a large amount of research has been conducted to increase understanding of lifting capacity. The early research utilised static strength testing as a tool for lifting evaluations. The results of this research support the theory that lifting capacity is a function of isometric back strength and that anthropometric measures are not good predictors of strength (Keyserling et al., 1978).

More recent research has shown that dynamic testing is a better predictor of lifting capabilities and can better determine a person's ability to perform lifting tasks (Aghazadeh and Ayoub, 1985; Garg et al., 1980; Jiang et al., 1986; Kamon et al., 1982; Mirka and Marras, 1990).

With this in mind Isotechnologies developed their "LiftStation®" (Isotechnologies, Hillsborough, USA). This is a three-dimensional lifting system which is developed to evaluate static and dynamic lifting tasks. In the dynamic mode the LiftStation measures displacements, velocity and acceleration in the three dimensions by one encoder at the base of the main column, one encoder inside the arm and one encoder inside the lateral sleeve about the main column (Fig.1). In the static mode the LiftStation measures force by means of two isometric handles with load cells. The software of the device proposed at the time of this study addressed five isometric exercises : leg lift, arm lift, push, pull and high-near lift.

The purpose of this study was to investigate the reliability, objectivity and validity of the static (isometric) force measurements of a prototype LiftStation.

2 Methodology

The results of this study were derived from two experiments: determination of the reliability and objectivity of the static force results and the determination of the LiftStation's validity.

2.1 Reliability and objectivity

To examine the reliability and objectivity, 18 volunteers (11 males, 7 females, mean age 21.9 ±1.4 years; mean body mass 68.8 ±13.1 kg, mean length 174.5 ±9.8 cm) performed the five isometric tests three times, twice with the same examiner and once with another examiner. Both examiners were highly trained before the tests were taken. Each subject was instructed as to proper position and lifting technique (Table 1). The positions and techniques were demonstrated. Each exercise was performed three times with a 30 seconds interval. The subjects were asked to exert maximal effort during the 5 s exercise. The maximal effort had to be reached gradually in the first 2 s and then held for the remainder of the test. The average force produced during the last 3 s was measured. One week rest was provided in-between each test.

The order of the tests for the examiners was set as follows : 6 subjects tested first by examiner 1 (X1), one week later again by examiner 1 (X2) and one week later by examiner 2 (Y). This was called X1 - X2 - Y. Six other subjects were tested in X1 - Y - X2 order and the last six were tested in the Y - X1 - X2 order and this to avoid learning errors.

Table 1. Postures during the isometric exercises

Isometric test	Posture	Horiz. dist.	Vert. dist.
1. Arm lift	elbows 90°	forearm length	elbow height
2. Leg lift	knees, hips shoulders flexed related to the hor. vert. dist. body is straight	0 cm	38 cm
3. High-Near lift	shoulders and elbows flexed related to the hor and vert.distance	25.5 cm	152 cm
4. Push	free	posture dep.	elbow height
5. Pull	free	posture dep.	elbow height

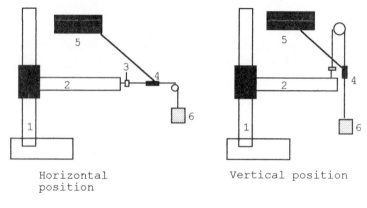

Horizontal
position   Vertical position

Legend :
1. Main column   2. Mechanical arm   3. Handle
4. Electric dynamometer   5. Pen writer (results o
dynamometer)   6. Weight (9 or 22 kg)

Figure 1. Set-up of the validation study.

2.2 Validity
To examine the validity of the LiftStation, results of the load cells of the handles were
compared with a calibrated electric dynamometer (VUB engineering dept.) which
measures force by means of strain gauges. A 22 kg and a 9 kg weight, weighed on a
SECA® (Germany) balance, were attached on the electric dynamometer and on the
handles in the different measuring positions (Fig.1). Each test was performed three
times.

3 Results and discussion

3.1 Reliability and objectivity
To examine the influence of the reliability and the objectivity, a two-way analysis of
variance was used. Differences were checked between the two examiners (X1,2 and Y)
and between the same examiner (X1 and X2). Objectivity and reliability coefficients
were calculated.The results (Table 2) indicate that there are no differences between the
different examiners (X1,2 and Y) meaning that the results of the test are objective. They
neither indicate differences between the same examiner (X1 and X2) meaning that the
results are reliable. However one exception is the arm lift. Probably this is due to a
difference in instruction given to the subjects. Examiner X allowed the subjects to get
on tiptoe while performing the test while examiner Y did not allow this position.

Table 2. Results of the objectivity and reliability study

Iso-metric test	P-value (Y-X1)	Object. coeff. (Y-X1)	P-value (Y-X2)	Object. coeff. (Y-X2)	P-value (X1-X2)	Reliab. Coeff (X1-X2)
leg lift	0.155	0.970	0.515	0.892	0.927	0.967
arm lift	0.0001*	0.889	0.223	0.945	0.0004*	0.838
push	0.526	0.825	0.728	0.882	0.827	0.850
pull	0.203	0.875	0.616	0.860	0.371	0.885
HN- lift	0.787	0.898	0.805	0.915	0.316	0.958

* significant (P<0.05)

This was already noticed during the first day of testing and the second time that examiner X took the tests he did not allow the subjects to get on tiptoe. This explains why no differences were found between X2 and Y.

The objectivity and reliability coefficients for all the test were found to be very high.

It is therefore concluded that the LiftStation is highly objective and reliable on the condition that always the same instructions are given to the subject.

3.2 Validity.
The results in Table 3 show that the electric dynamometer indeed is a valid device. In the horizontal position of the handles it indicates the exact values of the weights as measured on the SECA® balance. In the vertical position little deviations occurred possibly due to the technical set-up of the experiment (Fig.1). The chain was longer in this set-up and could cause more vibrations, noted by the pen-writer. The validity of the LiftStation was measured with an unpaired t-test between the measurements of the LiftStation and those of the electric dynamometer. The directions (horizontal and vertical) in which the measurements were taken and the handles (left and right) were taken into account. It is noticed that the direction of the handles slightly influences the measurements of force. For the 9 kg weight the vertical position measures 0.7 kg less than the horizontal position whilst for the 22 kg weight the vertical position measures 0.3 kg more than the horizontal position. These deviations are within the limits of the standard deviations which leads to the conclusion that the direction of the handles did not influence the measurements of the LiftStation.

On the other hand, rather large differences are noticed between the two handles (Table 3). For the 9 kg weight the left handle was measuring on average 2.3 kg less than the right handle and for the 22 kg weight the left handle measured on average even 2.5 kg less. These differences are much higher then their respective standard deviations (±0.58). Furthermore, for the 9 kg weight the left handle was underestimating and the right handle was randomly over- and underestimating. For the 22 kg weight both handles were inconsistently underestimating.

The p-values of the t-test between the electric dynamometer and the LiftStation indicate that the differences are significant (p<0.05) for the 9 kg weight and (p<0.01) for the 22 kg weight. By using the inter-class correlation we calculated the "validity coefficients" for the 9 kg and 22 kg weights which were respectively 0.437 and -0.518. These coefficients reflect the non-constant measurements which were seen in the raw data, although a constant weight was used.

Therefore it was concluded that the LiftStation was not a valid device. According to the manufacturer this was caused by a mechanical error in the load cells. The LiftStation now available on the market works with a new design of handles and load cells. Each load cell can now be calibrated by the standard software.

Table 3. Statistical comparison (unpaired t -test) and calculation of validity coefficient between the electric dynamometer (ED) and the LiftStation (LS).

SECA® balance	9 kg		22 kg		
	ED (kg)	LS (kg)	ED (kg)	LS (kg)	
H	9.0	5.9	22.0	14.5	left
O	9.0	7.3	22.0	14.1	handle
R.	9.0	7.3	22.0	13.6	
P	9.0	9.5	22.0	17.3	right
O	9.0	9.5	22.0	16.4	handle
S.	9.0	9.1	22.0	16.4	
mean	**9.0**	**8.1**	**22.0**	**15.4**	
SD	**0.00**	**1.49**	**0.00**	**1.51**	
V	8.5	6.4	22.5	14.5	left
E	9.5	6.4	22.5	14.5	handle
R	9.0	6.4	22.5	14.5	
T.					
	9.5	8.6	22.5	16.4	right
P	8.5	8.2	22.0	16.4	handle
O	9.0	8.2	21.0	17.7	
S.					
mean	**9.0**	**7.4**	**22.2**	**15.7**	
SD	**0.45**	**1.07**	**0.63**	**1.36**	
	P = 0.037		**P = 0.000**		
	r = 0.43		**r = -0.518**		

4 Conclusions

The prototype Isotechnologies LiftStation proved to be an objective and reliable measuring device for static forces, on condition that the examiners are well trained and giving the same instructions to the subjects.

The direction of the handles was not of influence on the measured force results.

The prototype LiftStation showed invalid measurements due to a mechanical error of the load cells. This problem was, according to the manufacturer, solved by a new design off load cells and calibration software.

The present observations emphasis that test equipment should be validated on human operators prim to its use for human strength assessment.

5. References

Keyserling, W.; Herrin, G. and Chaffin, D. (1978) An analysis of selected work muscle strength. **American Industrial Hygiene Association Journal**, 38, 662-675.

Aghazadeh, F. and Ayoub, M. (1985) A comparison for dynamic and static strength models for prediction of lifting capacity. **Ergonomics**, 28, 1409-1417.

Garg, A.; Mital, A. and Asfour, S. (1980) A comparison of isometric strength and dynamic lifting capability. **Ergonomics**, 23, 13-27.

Jiang, B.; Smith J. and Ayoub, M. (1986) Psychophysical modeling of manual materials handling capacities using isoinertial strength variables. **Human Factors**, 28, 691-702.

Kamon, E., Kiser, D. and Pytel, J. (1982) Dynamic and static lifting capacity and muscular strength of steelmill workers. **American Industrial Hygiene Association Journal**, 43, 853-857.

Mirka, G. and Marras, W. (1990) Lumbar motion response to a constant load velocity lift. **Human Factors**, 32, 493-501.

Mital, A.; Karwowski, W.; Mazouz, A. and Orsarh, E. (1986) Prediction of maximum acceptable weight of lift in the horizontal and vertical planes using simulated job dynamic strengths, **American Industrial Hygiene Association Journal**, 47, 288 292.

33 A comparison of statistical methods for assessing measurement repeatability in ergonomics research
G. Atkinson

1 Introduction

The importance of measurement repeatability in ergonomics and sports science research is often underestimated. Poor repeatability of measurements can influence the results of a study in which repeated measurements of a particular variable are recorded over time. In addition, a new measuring device will never be valid, compared to an established method, if it shows poor repeatability. The most important issue concerns measurement techniques that have been incorrectly deemed reliable through researchers employing the wrong statistical techniques. If an established "gold standard" has, in fact, poor reliability, highly reliable new methods will never agree with it and may, incorrectly, be deemed invalid.

In the ergonomics and sports science literature, measurement repeatability is often defined and calculated differently from the methods recommended in medical statistical texts. There seems disagreement on whether the component of aggregate systemic bias (e.g. human learning, training or fatigue influences across multiple trials) should be included in the assessment. Thomas and Nelson (1991) and Vincent (1994) thought this a major factor influencing the repeatability of human performance tests. Consequently, they recommended that repeatability be assessed over more than one retest using analysis of variance and intraclass correlation coefficients. Bland and Altman (1986) suggested that if any such trend is found in the retests, the particular method is not reliable and further analysis is irrelevant. Therefore, methods should be adapted until all human influences are removed from the data so that there are no significant differences between the means of a test and retest. After this has been established, **random** biological and mechanical variation can be assessed which is known as "agreement".

Although the correlation coefficient (r) is still recommended as a measurement of test-retest reliability in some texts (Coolican, 1994), Bland and Altman (1986) pointed out the inappropriateness of employing r, since it is a measure of relationship rather than agreement and is highly influenced by heterogeneity of subjects. Therefore, inclusion of male, female, fit, unfit, old and young subjects in the sample (a common situation in sports science research) will lead to an exaggeration of r. Bland and Altman (1986) also criticised the interpretation of r. They maintained that a piece of equipment should not be deemed reliable merely from an r-value being significant ($P<0.05$), since this gives no indication of agreement. They asserted that the comparison of equipment through r-values (e.g. Perrin, 1993) is meaningless given the multiple factors that affect the calculation of r, especially when the r-values are derived from different samples of subjects. The extent to which the, now, more popular intraclass correlation coefficient is affected by this subject heterogeneity has not yet been established with ergonomic data.

Coefficient of variation (CV) of repeated observations is a measure of agreement (Sale, 1991), but it assumes that the between-test variation increases as absolute values increase (Bland, 1987). In other words, with measurements of strength, it assumes that test-retest variability is greatest with the strongest subjects. Bland and Altman (1986) proposed more appropriate methods of calculating the 95% agreement limits between two trials and testing whether the above assumption is upheld before expressing agreement as CV.

The aim of the present paper was to examine how inter-subject variability influences the different statistical methods for assessing test-retest reliability.

2 Methods

2.1 Subjects
Ten young subjects, aged 18-28 years and ten old subjects, aged 47-65 participated in the study, after written informed consent was obtained. The mean (SD) height of the young and old subjects was 1.77 (0.07) and 1.72 (0.10) m, respectively. The mean (SD) body mass of the young and old group subjects was 72.0 (8.9) and 81.2 (10.3) kg, respectively.

2.2 Measurement protocol
The isometric strength of the leg extensors was measured on two occasions separated by 24-26 hours. A portable leg and back dynamometer (Takei, Tokyo) was used according to the methods outlined by Coldwells et al. (1994). In a session lasting 30 min, subjects familiarised themselves with the equipment and measurement protocols. During measurement, the knee extension angle and verbal motivation given by experimenters was controlled. The best of three trials was recorded in each test in kg. Each score was converted to force units (N).

2.3 Statistical analyses
The mean score from the test and retest was calculated for each subject. Differences between the groups in terms of the heterogeneity of scores was examined with an F-ratio test.

Test-retest repeatability was examined with (i) a Student's paired t-test, (ii) a Pearson's correlation coefficient, (iii) an intraclass correlation coefficient (Vincent, 1994), (iv) the 95% agreement limits (mean difference between test and retest ± the standard deviation of differences between test and retest scores multiplied by 1.96) (Altman, 1991) and (v) the coefficient of variation (the standard deviation of differences between test and retest divided by the overall mean score of the test and retest multiplied by one hundred). The relationship between subject mean scores and the difference between test and retest was examined by calculating the Pearson's correlation coefficient (this was termed the "error linearity test"). Coefficient of variation is an appropriate method of expressing agreement only if this correlation is not significant (Bland, 1987).

3 Results and Discussion

Table 1. Test-retest reliability using different statistical techniques. * The score in the first test was subtracted from that obtained in the retest.

Method	young athletic subjects	old subjects
Mean (SD) difference* in leg strength between test and retest (N)	1 (312)	48 (355)
t-test	t_9=0.01 (P=0.99)	t_9=0.43 (P=0.68)
Pearson's correlation	r=0.10 (P=0.78)	r=0.69 (P=0.03)
Intraclass correlation	R=0.26	R=0.83
95% agreement limits (N)	-610 to 613	-657 to 743
Error linearity check	r=0.17 (P=0.68)	r=0.26 (P=0.47)
Coefficient of variation	18.6%	21.1%

The mean (SD) leg strength, averaged over the test and retest, was 1676 (172) N and 1683 (410) N for the young and old subjects, respectively. The old group was significantly more heterogeneous than the young group in mean leg strength over the two trials ($F_{9,9}$=5.66, P=0.017). As an explanation for this, the young subjects were all Sport Science undergraduates who competed in sport regularly, whereas the older sample comprised sedentary individuals and veteran athletes.

The mean (SD) difference between test and retest for the young and older subjects, together with the various statistical techniques that were employed, are presented in Table 1. The non-significant t-test results indicated that there were no fatigue or learning influences between the two trials in either age-group. Although these results are useful, it is stressed that if there is great **random** variation between test and retest, the paired t-test is more likely to yield a non-significant difference. i.e. by only employing this approach, poor agreement **increases** the chance that the test and retest appear to agree (Altman, 1991).

According to the results of both Pearson's and intraclass correlation, the measurements showed poor repeatability in the homogeneous young group but "moderate" (Vincent, 1994) repeatability in the heterogeneous old group. This confirms the observations of Bland and Altman (1990) that intraclass correlation is associated with the same constraints that were indicated for Pearson's correlation. One possible solution to this problem is that whenever intraclass correlations are presented, the significance of the between-subjects F-value from the associated ANOVA should also be indicated.

Unfortunately, this indicator of heterogeneity has seldom been quoted in past repeatability studies.

In contrast to the correlation results, the 95% agreement limits were narrower in the young group compared to the old group suggesting better repeatability for measurements with the young subjects. To explain the significance of agreement limits, for any new young subject, it would be expected that two repeated measurements would differ by less than about 610 N, with any discrepancy being equally likely in either direction (Altman, 1991). The lack of a relation between mean strength scores and the test-retest difference for each subject suggests that agreement, in this case, should not be expressed as a coefficient of variation (i.e. the stronger subjects did not show greater test-retest variability). It should be noted that CV was calculated in the way suggested by Bland (1987) which differs to the method based on the standard deviation of **each** subjects repeated measurements (Sale, 1991). The application of the latter method to the present data would have meant a standard deviation being calculated from just two observations per subject.

According to Altman (1991), the problem of assessing repeatability should not be tackled through hypothesis testing. This is a difficult concept for an ergonomist to understand given the conventional method of deeming a piece of equipment repeatable from the significance of Intraclass or Pearson's correlation coefficients. The degree of measurement repeatability, should, alternatively, be related to both the sensitivity of other equipment designed to measure the same variable and the ergonomic significance of the variability (i.e. whether the variability associated with a piece of equipment hinders its use to measure differences between certain populations or conditions). Ideally, a database of information on repeatability and validity would exist for all ergonomic measuring equipment and a variety of different populations. Such data are just beginning to emerge in the assessments of body composition (Webber et al., 1994; Schaefer et al., 1994), rehabilitation (Ottenbacher and Stull, 1993) and energy expenditure (Li et al., 1993). In most cases, the widespread use of correlation methods mean that the reliability of new methods of measurement cannot, at present be compared to the repeatability of old methods. For example, Coldwells et al. (1994) found a very high correlation between leg strength measurements made in a test and a retest with the Takei dynamometer. However, the sample was heterogeneous, comprising male and female subjects. The present study found lower correlation coefficients but the agreement limits may still be narrow enough to render the equipment useful. Although the equipment is sensitive enough to detect relatively small circadian variations in leg strength (Coldwells et al., 1994), its degree of repeatability cannot be fully determined until it is compared with agreement limits derived with a different dynamometer or measurement protocol. The main aim of the present study was to assess statistical techniques rather than the Takei dynamometer. The reliability of this piece of equipment should be examined with a larger sample of subjects.

One disadvantage of the limits of agreement method is that it is not unit-free (Lee, 1992) so that methods that measure different quantities cannot be compared (e.g. isometric strength measured with a portable dynomometer and dynamic strength measured with an isokinetic dynomometer). In such cases, Lee (1992) recommended the use of intraclass correlation, although he stressed that the inter-subject variation should be quoted.

4 Conclusions

Similarly to when Pearson's correlation is used to assess measurement repeatability, intraclass correlation is compromised by a large inter-individual variation in scores. Agreement limits are not affected by sample heterogeneity and do not assume that an individual who scores highly on a performance test shows poorer agreement. Therefore, they might be adopted as the "universal" method of repeatability assessment in ergonomics and sport science research. It is also recommended that the ergonomic equipment that has been deemed repeatable in studies that have employed correlation coefficients should be re-examined with limits of agreement.

5 References

Altman, D.G. (1991) **Practical Statistics for Medical Research.** Chapman and Hall, London.

Bland, M. (1987) **An Introduction to Medical Statistics.** University Press, Oxford.

Bland, J.M. and Altman, D.G. (1986) Statistical methods for assessing agreement between two methods of clinical measurement. **Lancet** i, 307-310

Bland, J.M. and Altman, D.G. (1990) A note on the use of the intraclass correlation coefficient in the evaluation of agreement between two methods of measurement. **Computers in Biology and Medicine,** 20, 337-340

Coldwells, A., Atkinson, G., Reilly, T. and Waterhouse, J. (1994) Sources of variation in back and leg dynamometry. **Ergonomics,** 37, 79-86

Coolican, H. (1994) **Research Methods and Statistics in Psychology,** Hodder and Staughton, London.

Lee J. (1992) Evaluating agreement between two methods for measuring the same quantity: a response. **Computers in Biology and Medicine,** 22, 369-371.

Li, R.W., Deurenberg, P. and Hautvast, J.G.A.J. (1993) A critical-evaluation of heart rate monitoring to assess energy expenditure in individuals. **American Journal of Clinical Nutrition,** 58, 602-607.

Ottenbacher, K.J. and Stull, G.A. (1993) The analysis and interpretation of method comparison studies in rehabilitation research. **American Journal of Physical Medicine and Rehabilitation,** 72, 266-271.

Perrin, D.H. (1993) **Isokinetic Exercise and Assessment.** Human Kinetics Books, Champaign, Illinois.

Sale, D.G. (1991) Testing strength and power. In **Physiological Testing of the High-Performance Athlete** (eds J.D. MacDougall, H.A. Wenger and H.J. Green), Human Kinetics Books, Champaign, Illinois, pp. 21-106.

Schaefer, F., Georgi, M., Zieger, A. and Scharer, K. (1994) Usefulness of bioelectric impedance and skinfold measurements in predicting fat-free mass derived from total body potassium in children. **Pediatric Research,** 35, 617-624.

Thomas J.R. and Nelson J.K. (1990). **Research Methods in Physical Activity (2nd edition).** Human Kinetics Books, Champaign, Illinois.

Vincent, J. (1994) **Statistics in Kinesiology.** Human Kinetics Books, Champaign.

Webber, J., Donaldson, M., Allison, S.P. and MacDonald, I.A. (1994) Comparison of skinfold thickness, body mass index, bioelectrical-impedance analysis and dual-energy x-ray absorptiometry in assessing body composition in obese subjects. **Clinical Nutrition,** 13, 177-182.

34 Evaluation of the Cosmed K2 to measure maximum oxygen uptake

D.R. Jarvis, J.L. Allen, J.H. Chapman and M.L. Fysh

1 Introduction

The direct measurement of oxygen consumption ($\dot{V}O_2$) can provide information about the energy demands of physical activity. In turn, this information can be applied to the ergonomic evaluation of sport, leisure and recreation.

The use of Douglas bags has previously been shown to provide valid measurement of $\dot{V}O_2$ in a field setting (Lucia et al., 1993). This method can prove restrictive, time consuming and open to potential error in inexperienced hands. In addition, the measurement of respiratory responses during non-steady state exercise is not possible using Douglas Bags.

Advances in micro-technology have enabled the development of a computerised system which is capable of performing the role of a metabolic measurement cart outside the laboratory. The Cosmed K2 (Cosmed, Rome, Italy) is a portable telemetric system designed to measure a range of cardio-respiratory responses. It consists of a face mask, an optoelectronic flow meter and a polarographic O_2 electrode. The system is able to transmit respiratory flow signals over a distance of about one kilometre in a free field. Such a system provides a lightweight (850 g) and un-restrictive means of assessment.

There is, however, some question over the system's reliability. Lothian et al. (1993) and Kawakami et al. (1992) reported the system as unreliable. In contrast, investigations by both Lucia et al. (1993) and Crandall et al. (1994) could find no significant difference in comparisons of the K2 with other systems.

The purpose of this study was to assess the accuracy and reliability of the K2 to measure $\dot{V}O_2$. Subjects were assessed at both sub-maximal and maximal exercise levels. The K2 was compared against a respiratory mass spectrometer (Marquette Electronics Inc., Milwaukee, USA) which served as a reference system. The mass spectrometer (MS) has been shown to provide valid measurements of respiratory functions under differing conditions of exercise (Clausen, 1982; Jones, 1984).

2 Methodology

Thirteen physically active female subjects (age 21.8 ±1.9 years: mean ±SD) participated in the investigation. Each subject performed two graded maximal exercise tests on a cycle ergometer (Bosch Erg 550, Bosch, Berlin, Germany). Tests were performed at the same time of day, seven days apart. Subjects began exercising at an initial work-rate of 75 watts. The work-rate was then increased by 25 watts every 3 minutes until the subject reached exhaustion. A pedal frequency of 60 revolutions per minute was maintained throughout.

Oxygen consumption and minute ventilation ($\dot{V}E$) were measured using the MS and the K2. The order in which the equipment was used was randomised. Heart rates were monitored throughout using a standard electrocardiogram or the telemetry system of the K2. An appropriate warm-up time was allowed for the K2 in order to stabilise temperature at the oxygen electrode, and thus prevent any drift in recorded values (Crandall et al., 1994).

2.1 Data Analysis

In order to make comparisons at sub-maximal levels, differences in heart rate, $\dot{V}O_2$ and $\dot{V}E$ at four separate work-rates (75, 100, 125 and 150 watts) were analysed. Comparisons at work-rates above 150 watts were not carried out as several of the subjects were unable to continue exercising.

Differences in heart rate, $\dot{V}O_2$ and $\dot{V}E$ between the K2 and the mass spectrometer were analysed using the analysis of variance (ANOVA) technique. A post hoc Tukey test was performed to identify at which work-rates any differences occurred. Limits of agreement (Altman, 1991) were also calculated in order to assess how well the systems agreed.

To account for the potential differences in the speed of response of the two systems, only the data recorded in the final minute of each 3 minute stage was used for analysis (Crandall, 1994).

Comparison of recordings of maximum oxygen consumption ($VO_{2\ max}$) and VE at maximum were made using a paired t-test to identify any difference between the two systems.

3 Results

All subjects completed two graded maximal exercise tests. Subjects achieved the same maximum work-rate in each test. Mean values for heart rate, oxygen consumption and minute ventilation, recorded during the two tests, are shown in Table 1.

Table 1. Mean values for heart rate, oxygen consumption (VO_2) and minute ventilation ($\dot{V}E$): mean values (±SD)

Work-rate (w)	Heart rate (beats·min^{-1})		$\dot{V}O_2$ (ml·min^{-1})		$\dot{V}E$ (l·min^{-1})	
	K2	MS	K2	MS	K2	MS
75	124	124	1064	1228	27.8	28.0
	(±19)	(±11)	(±90)	(±83)	(±3.9)	(±2.6)
100	141	144	1323	1511	35.0	38.0
	(±18)	(±13)	(±81)	(±79)	(±4.0)	(±3.0)
125	156	159	1632	1742	43.8	46.4
	(±6)	(±13)	(±45)	(±81)	(±5.0)	(±5.1)
150	171	173	1970	2037	56.4	61.2
	(±15)	(±12)	(±140)	(±87)	(±7.9)	(±7.7)
VO_2max	183	183	2456	2033	70.9	77.2
	(±8)	(±3)	(±362)	(±256)	(±13.9)	(±15.2)

3.1 Heart rate
There was no significant difference between heart rates as measured by the two systems at any work-rate (Table 1).

3.2 Oxygen consumption
The mean ±SD for recorded values for $\dot{V}O_2$max were K2: 2456±362 ml·min^{-1} and mass spectrometer: 2333±256 ml·min^{-1}. The comparative mean values of $\dot{V}O_2$ at all levels are shown in Figure 1.

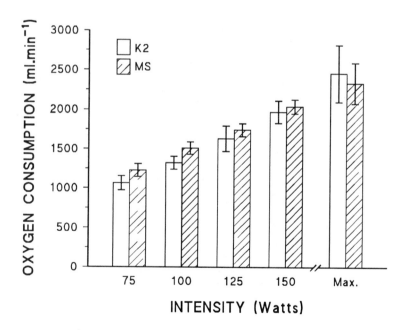

Figure 1. Oxygen consumption (ml·min^{-1}): comparison of mean values ±SD for K2 and mass spectrometer (MS).

Analysis of variance showed a significant difference between systems (P<0.05). Post hoc testing showed significant differences at the 75 and 100 watt work-rates (P<0.01). At these work-rates the K2 underestimated oxygen uptake in comparison to the MS. At $\dot{V}O_{2max}$, there was a tendency for the K2 to overestimate the MS, although this difference was not significant.

Further analysis of the data was undertaken by calculation of the limits of agreement (Table 2).

Table 2. 95% Limits of agreement for Cosmed K2 minus mass spectrometer: mean difference (±2SD)

Work-rate (w)	VO_2 Mean Difference: K2 minus MS ($ml \cdot min^{-1}$)	95% Limits of agreement ($ml \cdot min^{-1}$)
75	-163 (±235)	-399 to + 73
100	-188 (±179)	-367 to + 9
125	-110 (±349)	-459 to +239
150	- 67 (±337)	-404 to +270
VO_{2max}	123 (±449)	-326 to +572

The table illustrates the bias towards underestimation by the K2 at low intensities of exercise and a reversal of the trend at $\dot{V}O_{2max}$. Wide 95% limits of agreement were observed at all levels.

3.3 Minute ventilation

At $\dot{V}O_{2max}$, VE measured by the K2 was significantly lower than that of the MS (P<0.05). At sub-maximal work-rates, ANOVA identified a significant difference in VE between the two systems (P<0.05) although this was not significant at any specific work-rate (Table 1).

4 Discussion

The purpose of this investigation was to assess the accuracy and reliability of the K2. The ideal experimental design would be to collect data simultaneously with the two systems (Peel and Utsey 1993). Because this design is not possible, variability between tests may occur. As the statistical analysis revealed no significant difference in heart rates between the two comparative tests, this suggests that the work performed was of an equivalent nature. Therefore, any differences observed in $\dot{V}O_2$ between the tests was likely to be related to differences in the equipment and not in the work performed.

At sub-maximal work-rates, the K2 underestimated $\dot{V}O_2$. This agrees with the findings of both Crandall et al. (1994) and Dal Monte et al. (1989), who also found a tendency towards an overestimation at $\dot{V}O_{2max}$. Lothian et al. (1993) reported that the K2 similarly underestimated VO_2 for sub-maximal treadmill exercise in comparison with a

Quinton on-line oxygen analysing system. In contrast to other studies, peak $\dot{V}O_2$ was found to be underestimated by the K2 by 22.2%.

Previously, other workers have reported the K2 to underestimate $\dot{V}O_2$ at lower work-rates, but have not found it to be significant (Dal Monte et al., 1989; Lothian et al., 1993; Lucia et al., 1993). Work by Kawakami et al. (1992), on a single subject, did result in significant underestimations by the K2 compared to a Douglas Bag method at low work-rates and at rest. However, they found no significant difference between the two systems at $\dot{V}O_{2max}$. If there was a consistent difference it might be possible to convert K2 results to a reference standard. The wide limits of agreement preclude this option. The interpretation of these results depends on the ability to differentiate between biological variability resulting from independent trials and the measurement systems. According to Katch et al. (1982), the difference in $\dot{V}O_{2max}$ due to biological variation can be expected to fall within the range ±5.6%, 68% of the time, and within the range ±11.2%, 98% of the time. In this study this is equivalent to ±134 ml·min^{-1} (±5.6%) and ±277 ml·min^{-1} (±11.2%). It can be seen from Table 2 that the variability between the two systems shown by the limits of agreement is well in excess of this. On inspection of individual test results, for ten of the thirteen subjects, the difference between the two systems was less than 125 ml min^{-1} which is acceptable for independent tests. For two subjects, however, the difference was approximately 350 ml·min^{-1}, and for one subject it was nearly 700 ml·min^{-1}.

Leakage from the face mask may account for the differences in $\dot{V}E$ observed, a factor identified as a potential source of error by Lothian et al. (1993). These differences in $\dot{V}E$, however, cannot fully account for the variability between the two systems since at $\dot{V}O_{2max}$ the K2 tends to overestimate $\dot{V}O_2$ despite the significantly lower $\dot{V}E$.

Several other factors in K2 design may also influence measurement. The mask may increase the re-inspiration of CO_2, and cold conditions appear to accentuate the drift in recorded values of $\dot{V}O_2$ (Crandall et al., 1994). Although environmental conditions in this investigation remained relatively constant, testing in an external environment can only add to doubts over the system.

There is an obvious need to assess the reproducibility of the K2. From the inconsistencies in measurement found in this and other studies, however, it must still be assumed that the accuracy and reliability of the K2 are in some doubt. The K2 is potentially a powerful tool in the assessment of $\dot{V}O_2$. Nevertheless, until the wide variation in the system's accuracy can be accounted for, the K2 should not be relied upon in detailed analyses.

5 References

Altman, D.G. (1991) **Practical Statistics for Medical Research.** Chapman and Hall, London.

Clausen, J.L. (1982) **Pulmonary Function Testing Guidelines and Controversies.** Academic Press, New York.

Crandall, C.G. Taylor, S.L. and Raven, P.B. (1994) Evaluation of the Cosmed K2 portable telemetric oxygen uptake analyzer. **Medicine and Science in Sports and Exercise,** 26, 108-111.

Dal Monte, A. Faina, M. Leonardi, L.M. Todaro, A. Guidi, G. and Petrelli, G. (1989) Maximum oxygen consumption by telemetry. **Sports Culture Review,** 15, 3-12.

Jones, N.L. (1984) Evaluation of a microprocessor-controlled exercise testing system. **Journal of Applied Physiology,** 57, 1312-1318.

Katch, V.L. Sady, S.S. and Freedson, P. (1982) Biological variability in maximum aerobic power. **Medicine and Science in Sports and Exercise,** 14, 21-25.

Kawakami, Y. Nozaki, D. Matsuo, A. and Fukunaga, T. (1992) Reliability of measurement of oxygen uptake by a portable telemetric system. **European Journal of Applied Physiology,** 65, 409-404.

Lothian, F. Farrally, M.R. and Mahoney, C. (1993) Validity and reliability of the Cosmed K2 to measure oxygen uptake. **Canadian Journal of Applied Physiology,** 18, 197-206.

Lucia, A. Fleck, S.J. Gotshall, R.W. and Kearney, J.T. (1993) Validity and reliability of the Cosmed K2 instrument. **International Journal of Sports Medicine,** 14, 380-386.

Peel, C. and Utsey, C. (1993) Oxygen consumption using the K2 telemetry system and a metabolic cart. **Medicine and Science in Sports and Exercise,** 25, 396-400.

35 Bioelectrical impedance equation for determination of body composition in athletes

V. Bunc and R. Dlouha

1 Introduction

The assessment of body composition is important as an indicator of the nutritional and/or healthy status of a subject (Deurenberg et al., 1994; Forbes, 1987; Lukaski, 1987). Depending on the subjects and the circumstances, different aspects of body composition can be assessed for which, generally, several methods are available. Although in recent years new information has been made available by the use of modern techniques such as neutron-activation and computer tomography-scanning, most of the generally used methods are still based on the results of the chemical and anthropological analysis of a few human cadavers (Widdowson et al., 1951; Clarys and Marfell-Jones, 1994). From these chemical and anthropological analyses, three basic methods have been derived which have been accepted as reference methods. These are the densitometric method, the dilution method for total body water, and the 40K method (Forbes, 1987). Each of these approaches has its own assumptions, which are in fact only valid for healthy adults at a group level and which are known to be invalid in many other groups of subjects (Slaughter et al., 1988; Deurenberg et al., 1989; 1994). From the reference method many "indirect" and "doubly indirect", techniques were developed, such as hydrostatic weighing- HW (Siri et al., 1961), skinfold thickness measurements - SF (Durnin and Womersley, 1974; Parizkova, 1977) and bio-impedance analysis - BIA (Lukaski et al., 1985).

The bio-impedance analysis seems promising for clinical use because it is non-invasive, takes only a few minutes, and requires no active collaboration of evaluated subjects. The analysers are portable and relatively inexpensive. The accuracy and thus use of BIA for body composition assessment are directly related together with a hardware that is even now stabilised, to the prediction equation used with them (Deurenberg et al., 1994). These equations for determination of body composition in athletes (when %BF is lower than 10%), in obese subjects (%BF is higher than 30%), and in older subjects (older than 60 years) are lacking.

The purpose of this study was to determine prediction equation for BIA in trained athletes and compare results determined by this equation to estimates from the derived by sum of 10 skinfolds (Parizkova, 1977) and by HW (Siri, 1961).

2 Methods

A total of 93 endurance trained male athletes (mean age= 24.7±4.3 years, height=176.1±3.7 cm, mass=65.2±4.7 kg) served as subjects. All these subjects were used to derive the BIA prediction equation by means of %BF which was determined by skinfold measurements. The ability of BIA to determine body fat was assessed in a group of 25 men (part of the whole samples) by means of HW.

Whole-body impedance was measured using a commercially available bioimpedance system Bodystat 500 (Bodystat Ltd., Isle of Man, British Isles) by a tetrapolar electrode configuration in a supine position on the right hand and foot. Four electrodes were placed on each subject as follows : one current-injecting electrode was placed on the dorsum of the right hand 1 cm proximal to the knuckle at the base of the middle finger and the second current-injecting electrode was placed on the dorsum of the right foot 2 cm proximal to the space between the large and second toe. The two voltage-sensing electrodes were placed midway between radial and ulnar tubercles and lateral and medial malleolli, respectively. Prior to positioning the electrodes, each electrode site was prepared by swabbing with alcohol and then allowing the site to dry. An excitation current of 800 uA at fixed 50 kHz frequency was introduced to the subject.

Skinfold measurements were taken by an investigator who had previously shown test-retest reliability of r>0.90 on the right side on the body using Harpenden calipers at the ten sites as described by Parizkova (1977). Body fat was calculated using the generalized equation of Parizkova (1977).

Body density was assessed from HW with correction for residual lung volume using the oxygen dilution method of Wilmore (1969). Residual volume was determined on land with the subject seated in a position similar to that assumed during HW. Percent body fat was estimated from body density using the revised formula of Brozek et al. (1969). Descriptive statistics were calculated. Multiple stepwise linear regression analyse was used to derive BIA prediction equations using percentage fat derived by SF measurement and/or HW as the dependent variable. For BIA prediction equations the variables allowed were anthropometric parameters (height, height2, mass, mass2, age) and bioimpedance (BI). Variables were entered automatically in the order in which they contributed to the prediction equation and were only included in the final equation if they resulted in a significant increase in the r2 values or a significant reduction in the SEE. Total error (TE) was calculated according to formula TE = (Σ(Predicted %BF - Actual %BF)2/n)1/2. The ANOVA test with repeated measures was used to test differences between methods. Significance was determined at the 1% level.

3 Results

The predictive equation for %BF estimation was in the form %BF(%) = 4.4649 + 0.0577*Age(yrs) - 9.2044*Height2(m) + 0.4077*Mass(kg) + 0.0084*BI(Ohms); r = 0.751, P<0.001, r2 = 0.564, SEE = 0.99%; TE = 1.10%.

The mean value of %BF determined according to this equation was 7.9±1.9% (93 subjects), the same values determined using SF measurements were 7.3±1.5%. The mean values of %BF according to BIA in 25 subjects were 7.6±1.9%, according to SF 7.3±2.0% and according to HW 7.2±2.3%. The differences in %BF were non-significant in all methods.

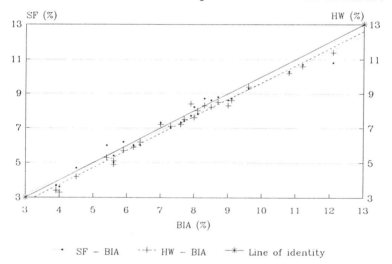

Fig. 1 The relationship between HW and SF determined percent body fat and %BF determined with BIA.

The values of percentage fat derived using the BIA prediction equation were compared with the values measured by SF in Fig. 1 - %BFSF = 0.982*%BFBIA - 0.221; r = 0.962; SEE = 0.54%; TE = 0.59%. In the same Figure was compared values of %BF determined by BIA and HW - %BFHW = 0.919*%BFBIA + 0.430; r = 0.919; SEE = 0.78%; TE = 0.82%. Mean values of FFM determined by BIA, SF and HW were 60.5±8.5, 60.3±8.9 and 60.2±9.1 kg, respectively. The differences were non-significant. Highly significant correlation coefficients

were found between values of FFM determined by SF and by BIA
(r = 0.894) and between HW and BIA (r = 0.874

4 Discussion

Measurement of the electrical impedance between the wrist and
ankle in human is used extensively as a method of assessing
body composition. The measured BI is frequency dependent and
the frequency dependence may be understood by considering the
reactive and capacitive components of the impedance. The cell
membranes act as capacitors with the intra- and
extra-cellular fluid contributing resistance to the overall
impedance. At low frequencies the cell membranes act as
insulators and current conduction occurs exclusively through
the resistive path in extracellular fluid. At higher
frequencies, the cell membrane impedance decreases and the
intracellular fluid resistance contributes to the overall
impedance (Smye et al., 1993). The two resistance terms may
be empirically related to the volumes of the extra- and
intra-cellular fluid. In this way it is possible to obtain
information on body fluid content and associated nutritional
status. Commonly a single-frequency measurement of BI at 50
kHz is made and this is then related empirically, using
previously derived regression equations, to total body water
and fat content (Lukaski, 1987). At 50 kHz the reactive
component of BI is small and the purely resistive term
dominates (Smye et al., 1984).

Elsen et al. (1987) pointed out that two basic sources of
error exist with BI measurements: 1) instrument error, the
instrument's accuracy for measuring resistance; 2)
measurement error, such as biological variation, electrode
placement, and inter-observer variation. Besides, the
hardware sources of errors, the electrode placement seems to
be main problem. Elsen et al. (1987) moved the sensor
electrode proximally in 2 mm increments up the arm, up the
leg and on both the arm and leg simultaneously until the
electrode had been displaced a distance of 1 cm from the
standard location. Changes in resistance were similar (2.1%)
when the electrode was moved on the arm and then the leg. At
a maximal displacement of 2 cm the change in resistance was
4.1%. When impedance was measured with the electrodes in
standard position, the coefficient of variation for repeated
measurements was 0.4%. Additionally, no effects were observed
for changes in the respiratory cycle. The authors concluded
that thermoregulation and skin temperature may play a role in
achieving accurate and precise impedance measurements. For
precise determination of BI it is important to define the
hydration state of the subjects.

The results of the analyses were evaluated on the
recommendations of Lohman (1981) and included the following :
1) the mean values for actual %BF (SF or HW) and predicted
%BF should be comparable; 2) a low SEE value is desirable and

is preferred over the correlation coefficient since the correlation is likely to be affected by inter-sample variability in %BF; 3) TE should be calculated because it reflects the true differences between the actual and predicted %BF values, whereas SEE only reflects error associated with regression between the variables; 4) the SD values for the actual and predicted %BF values should be in close agreement.

Both the SEE of 0.99% (SF) or 0.78% (HW) and the TE of 1.10% (SF) or 0.82% (HF) were lower than 3.8% which is conventionally an acceptable error for field applicable methods (Lohman, 1981). The differences between mean values of %BF determined by prediction equation for BIA and by SF and HW were non-significant. Additionally, values determined by means of BIA were highly correlated to SF and HW values. This finding is consistent with other studies (Eaton et al., 1993; Stout et al., 1994).

No indirect method currently exists to determine %BF that is error free. Indeed, the SEEs involved in the prediction of HW or SF %BF from body fat by BIA do not include the error associated with densitometry due to the variability in the density of the fat-free mass. The criterion method of HW has a reported error of 2.5% (Lohman, 1981). Thus, any method used is hampered by the lack of an accurate in vivo reference method. Each of the techniques used in this study can be affected by technical and biological errors. Although these errors were controlled for as much as possible, certain assumptions (e.g. absolute constancy of the chemical composition of the fat-free mass) are difficult to account for. The establishment of population-specific equations for BIA may further improve the accuracy of these methods.

In conclusion, BIA may be a valid method for assessing body composition in physically active subjects. The equations supplied by the manufacturers of the BIA devices must be adapted for specific groups of subjects. Any generally used formula for subjects with %BF in range of 3-30% do not exist.

5 References

Brozek, J., Grande, F., Anderson, J.T. and Keys, A. (1963) Densitometric analysis of body composition: revision of some quantitative assumption. **Annals of New York Academy of Sciences**, 110, 113-140.

Clarys, J.P. and Marfell-Jones, M.J. (1994) Soft tissue of the body and fractionation of the upper and lower limbs. **Egonomics**, 37, 217-229.

Deurenberg, P., Leenen, R., van der Kooy, K. and Hautvast, J.G.A.J. (1989) In obese subjects the body fat percentage calculted with Siri´s formula is an overestimation. **European Journal of Clinical Nutrition**, 43, 569-575.

Deurenberg, P., Westerterp, K.R. and Velthuis-Te Wierik,

E.J.M. (1994) Between-laboratory comparison of densitometry and biomedical measurements. **British Journal of Nutrition**, 71, 309-316.

Durnin, J.V.G.A and Womersley, J. (1974) Body fat assessed from total body density and its estimation from skinfold thickness: measurements on 481 men and women aged from 17 to 72 years. **British Journal of Nutrition**, 32, 77-97.

Eaton, A.W., Israel, R.G., O´Brien, K.F. and Hortobagyi, T. (1993) Comparison of four methods to assess body omposition in women. **European Journal of Clinical Nutrition**, 47, 353-360.

Elsen, R., Siu, M.L., Pineda, O. and Solomons, N.W. (1987) Sources of variability in bioelectrical impedance determinations in adults, in **In vivo body composition studies** (ed K.J.Ellis), Institute of Physical Science and Medicine, London, pp. 184-188.

Forbes, G.B. (1987) **Human Body Composition**. Springer Verlag, New York.

Lohman, T.G. (1981) Skinfold and body density and their relation to body fatness: A review. **Human Biology**, 53, 181-225.

Lukaski, H.C., Johnson, P.E., Bolonchuck, W.W. and Lykken, G.E. (1985) Assessment of fat-free mass using bioelectrical impedance measurements of human body. **American Journal of Clinical Nutrition**, 41, 810-817.

Lukaski, H.C. (1987) Methods for the assessment of body composition: traditional and new. **American Journal of Clinical Nutrition**, 46, 437-456.

Parizkova J. (1977) **Body Fat and Physical Fitness**. Nijhoff, Hague.

Siri, W.E. (1961) Body composition from fluid spaces and density: analysis of methods, in **Techniques for measuring body composition** (eds J. Brozek and A. Henschel A., National Academy of Sciences, Washington, pp. 223-244.

Slaughter, M.H., Lohman, T.G., Boileau, R.A., Horswill, C.A., Stillman, R.J., van Loan, M.D. and Bemben, D.A. (1988) Skinfold equations for estimation of body fatness in children and youth. **Human Biology**, 60, 709-723.

Smye, S.W., Sutcliffe, J. and Pitt, E. (1993) A comparison of four commercial systems used to measure whole-body electrical impedance. **Physiological Measurement**, 14, 473-478.

Stout, R.J., Eckerson, J.M., Housh, T.J., Johnson, G.O. and Betts, N.M (1994) Validity of percent body fat estimation in males. **Medicine and Science in Sports and Exercise**, 26, 632-636.

Widdowson, E.M., McCance, R. and Spray, C.M. (1951) The chemical composition of the human body. **Clinical Science**, 10, 113-125.

Wilmore, J.H. (1969) A simplified method for determination of residual lung volume. **Journal of Applied Physiology**, 27, 96-100.

36 The factor analysis of motor adjustment
Z. Waskiewicz

1 Introduction

One of the determinants of successes of movement activities is the ability regarded as "motor adjustment". It was defined, by Meinel and Schnabel (1987), as the ability to react (adjust) according to predicted or unpredicted changes of task circumstances. It can lead to little changes (modifications) of motor programs performed or to the creation of completely new ones. In their opinion reactions according to relatively predictable stimuli only need to involve little verification of previous activity. This correction resolves itself to adjustment of chosen space-time-force parameters of movement structure, simultaneously retaining a long term plan of activity (for instance change of pace during cross country running in relation to the terrain). Greater changes in the environemental surroundings can disturb the flow of movement which can produce temporary interruption of the program or force the initiation of a completely new one. What is more, it dose not possess the continuation of the previous movement phase.

Roth (1982) while emphasizing the dychotomous character of motor adjustment ability, asserted that the level of variability in external circumstances is a most important factor determining the character of human motor behaviour. Calling this ability "the general motor ability" (functionally located in frontal part of cortex), he set forth the hypothesis that a proper reconstruction of "movement model" conditions for the success of human movements. Phlmann and Kirchner (1979), in their concept of coordinational motor abilities, placed the motor adjustment in a group of superior abilities, emphasizing its complex character. Hirtz (1985) similarly underlined this ability, although he considered it elementary. He created from all the coordinational abilities three main complexes: control of movement, motor learning and motor adaptation. The last item can be identified with motor adjustment.

Experiments connected with motor adjustment are based mainly on tracking exercises. They are characterized by containing two elements in a task: the target (constant or moving independently from the reactions of the subject) and the cursor controlled by the subject. The subject tries to match the contact of this cursor and the target. The consequences are that it is possible to distinguish two main forms of motor adjustment: **disjunctive** (when the subject can not understand the structure of the stimuli) and **continuous** (when the reactions and stimuli are in logical relation). The second form can be divided into **simple** continuous adjustment (the movements of target are created by the device, and movements of the cursor are the function of the subject's behaviour) and **compensatory** (the target is constant, movement of cursor results from the device and subject activity). Despite the many studies on tracking adjustments, there are no research reports to explain how human control procesess function in gross motor (whole-body) activities.

The main aim of this study is to characterize the ability of motor adjustment and determine if it is homogeneous feature of human personality. If it becomes evident that it is heterogeneous, then an attempt to describe its specific elements and relations between them will be considered.

2 Methods

The research was conducted on 92 male and female students of the Academy of Physical Education in Katowice (Poland), aged 22-25. Nine subjects were excluded since they had great experience in work with computers (minimum 10-12 hours per week) and long contacts with professional sport.

They were subjected to 26 measurements using a computer program (substantially designed by the author and validated by a computer specialist) and laboratory tests. The MACS (Motor Adjustment Computer System) allows the diagnosis motor adjustment in four main tests (16 measurements) based on exploring motor coordination using tracking exercises i.e. disjunctive, pursuit, simple and complex compensatory (computer implementation of tasks described by Hartman and Fitts, 1955; Helson, 1945). The program posseses its own data management environment with a possibility of creating, supplementing, modifying and exporting personal data records. During the tests two main measurements are performed i.e. the integer of the difference between the ideal and performed track, speed of adjustment (time elapsed from any change of movement speed or direction to returning into contact with the target). The measurements are repeated each 0.001 s and are simultaneously saved in a database. It is possible to calculate all the recorded parameters for designated parts of the track.

The first trial is called "Point the target" and subjects have to point eight circles (the shape of the track resembles the envelope) appearing on the computer screen as fast and precisely as possible. Secondly - "Two triangles" is a computer implementation of Helson's idea (1947), measuring simple countinuous tracking abilities. It forces the subject to keep two equilateral triangles adjoining each other with angles. An upper triangle is moved from left to right side (and vice versa) by the computer and a lower one by the subject using a computer mouse. A third trial designed to diagnose the ability to adjust in a complex continuous task is called "Watch the circle". The subject has to point to the target (little circle) which moves on the computer screen on different tracks (envelope, elipse, eight) at different speeds (regularly or irregularly accelerated). The last trial is a computer implementation of Hartmann and Fitts' idea (1955) of diagnosing the compensatory adjustment. The subject is forced to keep the cursor in contact with a circle placed centrally on the screen. The movement of the cursor is a resultant of the activity of the device and the subject and only without any reactions of the subject is it possible to find out what is the character of the movement (all options i.e. tracks, speeds as in test described above).

In addition to tests previously described, 10 laboratory measurements were performed. The diagnosis of adjustment using a stabilometer (own construction) lasted 20 s for each repetition, during which two measurements were performed: the deviation of the platform from the horizontal plane and the number of changes of the platform's movements direction (2000 samples with 0.001 degree precision). The result of the test was the difference between the balancing on the platform in a frontal plane (having the axis of turning between the feet) and balancing in two planes (feet placed in quarters being the result of axis intersection). The second trial is called "The star in the mirror" and its result is the difference between the amount of errors (contacts with sides of 3 mm wide channel) electronically counted during drawing the shape of a star looking at it into the mirror and with closed eyes. The mirror is placed behind the star and stands perpendicular to it. The third laboratory test consisted the difference between measurements of time balancing on Fleishman's device (2 cm wide) placed on the ground and on a 1.50 m high box. Two coefficients connected with whole-body movements were also calculated. The first "Coefficient of running adjustment" is the effect of comparing the results in running, crawling and slalom (5 turns) on a 15 m distance, and 3x5 m run forward and backward. A second "Coefficient of jumping adjustment" was calculated as a difference between jumps forward, backward, left and right from a standing position.

3 Results and Discussion

The empirical data achieved during the measurements were subject to factor analysis and Hotteling's method of principal components, modified by Tucker (1955) and supplemented by Varimax rotation (Weber, 1980). The results of 26 measurements (51 variables) were grouped into 8 factors, explaining 87.26% of common variance were:

1. **Complex compensatory adjustment** - 19.26% (of common variance) contains 6 parameters describing the precision of tracking in compensatory exercises in all curves of the track (i.e. envelope, elipse, the figure eight shape) in different circumstances. It is clearly the most complex factor and simultaneously it explains the greatest amount of motor adjustment.

2. **Pursuit adjustment** - 17.21%, includes 6 measurements of pursuit tracking which could be described as an attempt to trace a target moving on different tracks, and at different speeds.

3. **Adjustment in translational movements forward and backward** - 10.21%, includes four measurements - the difference between broad jumps forward and backward, the difference between running at 15 m distance and 3x5 m shuttle run, the 15 m dash and crawling over this distance and one measurement of precision of simple tracking on the envelope track.

4. **Adjustment in running and balancing** - 9.99%, includes four measurements characterised by one great similarity, existence of movements toward both sides (left and right). The first parameter arises from the difference between 15 m sprint performance and

slaloming over the same distance, second, from the difference between jumps to the left and right side from a standing position.

5. **Speed of adjustment** - 8.24%, includes nine measurements of duration of reactions to changing circumstances i.e. speed or direction of movement. They are independent of   the kind of tracking exercise and came from pursuit and simple compensatory tasks. They were clearly excluded from measurements of precision of movements.

6. **Disjunctive adjustment** - 8.22%, includes four measurements of precision of adjusting in situations where there is no logical dependence (for the individual) on the order of stimuli.

7. **Retrospective adjustment** - 7.20%, includes seven measurements with relatively low factor loadings, characterized by the interval between two motor activities.

8. **Simple compensatory adjustment** - 6.94%, created by three   measurements of precision of motor adjustment in a task named "Two triangles".

The results show that there is a need to treat the motor adjustment ability as complicated. It is concluded that this ability is not homogeneous, and consists of 8 components, which should be diagnosed separately. It will help to characterise this specific area more precisely. In further investigations it should help during theoretical considerations and preparations to diagnose the ability of motor adjustment as accurately as possible.

4 References

Hartmann, B.O. and Fitts, P.M. (1955) Relation of stimulus and response amplitude to tracking performance. **Journal of Experimental Psychology** 49, 82-92.

Helson, H. (1949) Design of equipment and optimal human operation. **American Journal of Psychology**, 62, 473-497.

Meinel, K. and Schnabel, P. (1987)   Bewegungslehre-Sportmotorik. Berlin: **Volk und Wissen.**

Phlman, R., Kirchner, G. and Wehlgefahrt, K. (1979) Der psychomotorische Fhigkeitskomplex - seine kennzeichen und seine Vervollkomnung. **Theorie und Praxis der Krperkultur**, 28, 898-907.

Roth, K. (1982) Strukturanalyse koordinativer Fhigkeiten. Bad Homburg, **Limpert Verlag**.

Weber, H. (1980) Grundriss der biologischen Statistik. Jena: **VEB Gustav Fischer**.

37 Computer estimation of the visual aspect of space orientation
G. Juras

1 Introduction

The ability to orientate the body in space plays a fundamental role in the processes of motor control and learning (Farfiel, 1977). It allows for the determination of body position and its changes during movements in relation to the surroundings (Roth, 1982).

The state of knowledge about space orientation improved significantly after Kelley (1928) described for the first time the proccesses of visualization and orientation. Presently it is known that informations related to body position, comes from many receptores, yet the dominant role is probably played by vision (Schmidt, 1988).

Because of the great variety and frequent changes in situations requiring fast analysis, the proccess of orientation is among the most complicated processes co-ordinated by the nervous system. The problem presented by precise diagnosis of this ability may explain why it has not been researched and adequately described. It also justifies the goals of this work which are directed at answering the following questions: (i) is it possible to diagnose reliably the visual aspect of space orientation with the application of computer tests? (ii) does the visual aspect of orientation possess a homogenous inner structure or is it possible that independent factors exist which describe this phenomenon confirming its heterogeneous character? (iii) is the level and structure of space orientation sex-dependent?

2 Methods

The research was conducted on 37 female and 45 male students (aged from 20 to 23) of the Academy of Physical Education in Katowice. Subjects were selected according to athletic and computer experience. Only those that possessed minimal experience in the above mentioned areas were chosen to minimalize the influence of any factors which could disturb the inner structure. The following computer tests were applied to evaluate the visual aspect of space orientation:

- **length replication** - this test is based on the replication of the length of a segment placed horizontaly, verticaly or diagonally and is visible on the computer monitor. The segment

disappears after a certain period of time and the length must be reconstructed;
- **division of the segment** - this test is based on the division of the horizontal, vertical or diagonal segment into 2 or 3 parts;
- **replication of the angles** - this test is based on the reconstruction of angular patterns: options - closed or open angles, the visible or invisible pattern;
- **identification of shapes** - this test is based on pointing to one identically shaped figure from 8 similar ones: options - the model figure visible or invisible, identification of triangles, quadrangles and ellipses;
- **orientation of space**:
 - choosing the circles according to numbers - this test is based on indicating as quickly as possible 16 numbered circles of different dimensions;
 - finding points - this test is based on finding and indicating small points that appear in different parts of the screen;
 - subsequent choice of similar figures - this test is based on choosing particular shapes (triangles, quadrangles, circles and ellipses) according to the shape without considering size;
 - alternative choice of figures - this test is based on indicating the apropriate figure considering its size (from the smallest to the bigest) and not shape.

In all of the above tests precision was registered - the evaluation of relative and absolute mean values of the model and length created(dl0/l) or angles (dλ0/λ), absolute mean values of the model and distance created (dd0/d) between particular figures and the total amount of mistakes (ae) in identifying the figure. The time taken to complete particular tasks was also measured. In all, space orientation was diagnosed with 22 tests (different options of the 5 basic tests) which resulted in 86 variables. All of the above tests are components of a computer program named "Orientation", which posseses its own data management environment with ability to create, supplement, modify and export personal data records, by computer specialist was worked out. The concept of diagnosing the visual aspect of space orientation is based on analysis of the motor behaviour and experimental psychology and physiology literature and author ideas (Blume, 1984; Farfiel, 1977; Hirtz, 1985; Lindsay, Norman, 1972; Meinel, Schnabel, 1987; Puni, 1967; Roth, 1982; Schmidt, 1988).

The collected material was analysed statistically. Reliability was evaluated with the test-retest method, while the sex differences in relation to space orientation were evaluated by Student's test. Factor analysis was the primary statistical method used. From many variations the method based on Hotteling's main components with Tucker's modification supplemented by Varimax rotation was chosen (Weber, 1980).

3 Results and Discussion

Before analyzing the results of the factor analysis, it must be stated that the Pearson's correlation coefficients reached values from 0.74 to 0.92 and thus the overall reliability was at a acceptable level. The analysis of the distribution of results of the subjects in subsequent trials allowed exclusion of those variables that did not possess normal distributions. In case of the test that was presumed to evaluate the speed of perception of shapes, the distribution of results was not normal and though these results were eliminated from further analysis to avoid problems with the interpretation of Pearson's correlation coefficients which formed the background for factor analysis.

Before an attempt was made at determining the inner structure of space orientation with these methods, the differences between the results of male and female students were established. The differences in the level of this coordination ability were not significant (P>0.05). This permitted further analysis with the possibility of combining males and females into one group of 82 subjects.

The application of factor analysis also creates the possibility of determination the hierarchy of factors based on the percent of common variance explained.

The largest amount of variance was explained by the factor described as the **speed of orientation**. It explained 23.74% of the common variance (total common variance of all factors: 83.63%). This factor was created by almost all of the variables measuring time for completing different tasks besides those eliminated due to the non-normal distribution. The factor was composed of time for estimating length and angle (all options), segment division into 2 or 3 parts and orientation of space in four of the diagnosed situations. The times to conduct particular tasks possessed high factor loadings (up to 0.876), yet it was difficult to indicate the most representative tests.

The second factor was described as **length estimation** and explained up to 19.68% of common variance. It was composed of variables that determine the precision of tasks related to the evaluation of length. The estimation of length through its replication must be treated as compresing independent subfactors (during the replication task the model pattern is visible at all times and the pattern is not visible during the reconstruction time). The first of these subfactors explained 11.86% while the second explains 7.82% of common variance. The representative tests included: length replication (factor loading 0.856) and length reconstruction (0.782) evaluated in both cases by the consistency of the trial and model horizontal pattern.

The third factor that appeared from the factor analysis was named the **shape perception**. It was characterized by a group of tests in which the primary task is related to the proper identification of shapes of three types of geometrical figures (triangles, quadrangles and ellipses). The following tests appeared as independent subfactors: identification (visible pattern) and reconstruction (invisible) of different shapes (7.89% of common variance), the quadrangle reconstruction (4.65%) and the replication of ellipses (4.35%). This factor explained 16.89% of the phenomenon under investigation. The representative tests for that aspect of visual orientation (the last 2 subfactors) included the quadrangle reconstruction (0.701) and the ellipses identification (0.733) - variables determining the total amount of error made during the test. It is difficult to point out (because of the similar factor loadings) a representative test for the first of the subfactors named "shape perception".

The fourth factor was named the **angle evaluation**. It explained 11.42% of common variance. It was composed of tests requiring precision of replication (visible pattern) or reconstruction of angular alignment. The particular tasks describing this factor had loadings from 0.804 to 0.922 and can all be viewed as representative.

The fifth factor isolated by factor analysis was named **complex orientation**. It explained 9.8% of the total variance. This factor was created by tests of different specifications, requiring in general the conduct of highly complex task. It included tests related to arrangment of space according to shape, size or numbers placed inside the figures as well as the determination of aligment of suddenly appearing points or dividing segments into parts. The test based on subsequent indication of 16 numbered circles can be treated as the most representative (loading 0.657) for this complex factor.

The results clearly indicate a complex structure of the visual aspect of space orientation. It is justified to treat all factors (different aspects) of visual orientation as separate, independent components of coordination ability.

In attempting to describe the inner structure of space orientation, a certain resemblance can be noticed to Farfiel's (1977) hierarchical levels of coordination abilities. It thus seems worth considering if diagnostic methods should not be chosen according to these levels of coordination. The only doubts remain in relation to the fact that the largest amount of common variance was explained by the factor speed of orientation (second level of coordination according to Farfiel) while factors related to precision (first level) received secondary status.

At the same time this fact illustrates the complicated structure of orientation and diagnosis by means of computer programs and also indicates our further research perspectives.

4 Conclusions

(a) The evaluation of visual aspects of space orientation by means of a computer program is reliable and   precise.
(b) The visual aspect of space orientation possesses a complicated inner structure (five basic factors explaining 83.63% of common variance) which is not significantly influenced by sex. The main factor influencing visual orientation is speed of orientation.

5 References

Blume, D.D. (1984) Einige aktuelle Probleme des Diagnostizierens koordinativer Fhigkeiten. **Theorie und Praxis der Krperkultur**, 2, 122-124.
Farfiel, W.S. (1977) **Bewegungssterung im Sport**. Sportverlag, Berlin.
Hirtz, P. (1985) **Koordinative Fhigkeiten im Schulsport**. Volk und Wissen, Berlin.
Kelley, T.L. (1928) **Crossroads in the Mind of Man**. Stanford University Press, Stanford.
Lindsay, P.H. and Norman, D.A. (1972) **Human Information Processing. An Introduction to Psychology**. Harcourt Brace Jovanovich, Inc., New York.
Meinel, K. and Schnabel, G. (1987) **Bewegungslehre - Sportmotorik**. Volk und Wissen, Berlin.
Puni, A.C. (1984) **Psichofijologija**. Fizkultura i sport, Moskwa.
Roth, K. (1982) **Strukturanalyse koordinativer Fhigkeiten**. Limpert Verlag, Bad Homburg.
Schmidt, R.A. (1988) **Motor Control and Learning**. Human Kinetics Publ., Champaign.
Weber, H. (1980) **Grundriss der biologischen Statistik**. VEB Gustav Fischer, Jena.

38 Using notational analysis to create a more exciting scoring system for squash
M. Hughes

1 Introduction

Many sports go through the process of changing their playing rules, usually to alter performance parameters so that the game is more attractive to spectators and television audiences. On occasion the rule changes are made to make the game safer. It is difficult to establish whether any of these rule changes are made on the basis of accurate quantitative analyses of the sport. Despite the numbers of publications concerned with match analysis of sports, it seems that none of the respective governing bodies has referred to these databases before making changes in the rules of its sport.

In squash the scoring systems generally used in the game, English and point-per-rally, generate long periods of play without 'crisis' points. Point-per-rally (P-P-R) scoring was introduced with the intention of making the rallies more exciting, but research (Hughes and Knight, 1994) has shown that although this system generates more winners, there are no other significant changes in rally length or the number of errors. Many informal squash tournaments have been organised using different forms of tennis scoring in order to make the game more exciting. Recently the organisers of a top international tournament, the Grasshopper tournament in Zurich, Switzerland, March 17th-22nd, 1994, which included four of the top five players in the world, decided to use a form of tennis scoring for this very reason.

The aim of this analysis is to create models of the different scoring systems from data gathered from this tournament, and, with data previously gathered by Hughes and Knight (1994) and Hughes and Clarke(1994), create a model of a new scoring system.

2 Method

The whole of the Grasshopper tournament was video-taped. Five matches were selected to balance and match the data from elite players analysed in the previous studies (Hughes and Knight, 1994; Hughes and Clarke, 1994). These matches were analysed post-event from video, using a computerised notation system, written for an IBM compatible computer in a language that allowed use of a graphical user interface, to ease data entry. The analysis was orientated to defining a time base for the game, as well as detailed observations on rally length, shot, position and player. Both T-tests and chi-square tests were used to compare the data from each of the analyses.

3 Results and Discussion

Squash played under 'tennis rules' showed that the rally length was not significantly different to that played with English or point-per-rally scoring (P>0.05). It should be noted that in the slightly different rules in Zurich, a set was the first to win four games, no tie break, and so on. This accounts for the shorter set time length of the squash played under 'tennis' rules. The potential for spectator interest of the 'tennis rules' type of scoring is that there is a critical game point every 6 rallies (almost 3 min) on average - in English or P-P-R scoring this occurs every 17 and 12 min, on average, respectively. In this way critical points are generated over shorter time cycles. Coincidentally the rally cycle is almost the same for lawn tennis (see Table 1), but the play and rest times between rallies are greatly different.

Table 1. Time based models of tennis, on different surfaces, and squash, under different scoring systems

	Tennis		Squash		
	Wimbledon	Australian Open	English	P-P-R	'Tennis'
Rally (s)	2	4	18	18	18
Between rallies (s)	23	23	10	10	10
rallies/game	6	6	36	25	6
Between serves (s)	10	10	N/A	N/A	N/A
2nd Serves	2	2	N/A	N/A	N/A
Game (s)	**169**	**181**	**998**	**690**	**158**
Between games (s)	32	32	90	90	15
Change end	112	112	N/A	N/A	N/A
Rest - 3rd game (s)	N/A	N/A	N/A	N/A	60
Set (s)	**2378**	**2498**	**N/A**	**N/A**	**1495**
Match (s) **(min:s)**	**7134** **(118:54)**	**7494** **(124:54)**	**3992** **(66:32)**	**2760** **(46:00)**	**2990** **(49:50)**
Ball in Play	**7 min 12 s**	**14 min 06 s**	**43 min 12 s**	**30 min 00 s**	**28 min 48 s**
Av. Score	**6-4,6-4,6-4**	**6-4,6-4,6-4**	**3-1**	**3-1**	**5-3,5-3**

Another factor that restricts squash as a spectacle is that the serve is given to the player who wins the rally. This, in effect, handicaps the lesser player as the better player will then serve more. The analysis of English scoring, and P-P-R scoring, showed that the winner made 56% of all serves, on average, whilst the loser served for 44% of the game (see Table 2). Further, the match-winners gained points from 47% of their own serve, but the match-losers won only 41% of their serves (Fig. 1). In the Zurich tournament, this form of tennis scoring almost balanced out the distribution of the serves, but there is some other effect on serve-rally outcome, in so much as both the winners and the losers, in tennis scoring, won higher percentages of the rallies on their own serves.

- Each player serves for a whole hand irrespective of who wins the rally, the spin of a racket determines who commences, the players alternate serve for each hand. The winner of each rally receives a point whether serving or not, the same as in tennis scoring, or P-P-R in squash.

- There is a 60 s rest at the end of each third hand and at the end of each game.

In addition, two other minor modifications to the rules used at the Grasshopper tournament are suggested. In squash scoring systems to date, as players approach the conclusion of a game in a close match (8-8 in English scoring; 14-14 in P-P-R), the player receiving serve is given the choice of playing to 9 or 10 in English, 15 or 17 in P-P-R. This tactical decision does add interest to the game, and has been the subject of some research by Alexander et al. (1988). They found that, statistically, there were instances when probability favoured the player with lesser ability calling for 9 rather than 10, in English scoring. To make this tactical choice clearer it is recommended to retain, and strengthen, this feature.

- Each 'hand' is decided by who reaches 4 points first (i.e. best of seven points) - in the event of a 3-3 score, handout decides whether to play to 4, or whether the hand should be won by 2 clear points.

In the Grasshopper tournament, if the score reached 3-3 in a set, the 7th game decided the set, so the server in that set had an advantage. To balance out the advantage of the serve, and to create a more climactic end to a set (game in squash terminology), a tie-break is recommended. Again this is modelled on the tennis version, both for reasons of familiarity and the fact that it also nullifies lateral advantages, i.e. the advantage of continually serving to a player's backhand which is, at most standards, the weaker side of a player (Hughes, 1986).

- The tie-break is started by the player, whose turn it was to serve, making one serve, the opponent then makes two serves, followed by the first player for two serves and so on until one player reaches 4 points. In the case of a 3-3 score, the tie break must be won by 2 clear points.

4 Conclusions

It is concluded that the Grasshopper tournament did create an environment for squash that had more critical points, more frequently. It also balanced the frequency of serves betwen the players. Combining these features, with other aspects of matchplay from previous match analysis research, has enabled this system to be modified to a model of scoring in squash that should create a more interesting game for players and spectators. It is proposed that these forms of analyses should be adapted and applied to other sports when rule changes are proposed.

Table 2. Analysis of the importance of serve in squash under the different scoring systems

English and P-P-R scoring		
	Winners	**Losers**
Serves made	56%	44%
Rallies won with serve	47%	41%
Tennis scoring		
	Winners	**Losers**
Serves made	49.7%	50.3%
Rallies won with serve	54%	43%

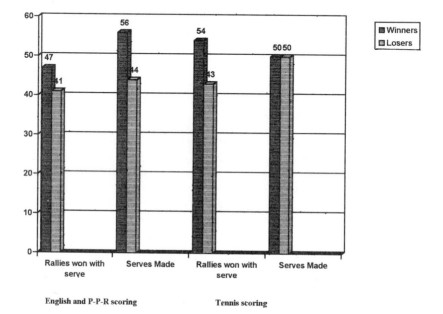

Fig. 1. Percentage of serves made by winners and losers, and respective rallies won, in squash under the different scoring systems.

The shape of the scoring system used in Zurich, with its cycle of 'critical' points every 3 min or so, and its potential for tactical developments, created an attractive template for squash tournaments in the future. Consequently, it is recommended that these features be adopted into a scoring system for squash, using squash terminology. The main points would be:

• Each match is the best of three 'games' (sets in tennis parlance) at elite level, the best of five 'games' at intermediate levels.

• Each 'game' (set) is the best of seven 'hands' (games) - in the event of a 3-3 score, the deciding 'hand' is decided by a 'tie-break' (see below).

5 References

Alexander, D., McClements, K. and Simmons, J. (1988) Calculating to win. **New Scientist,** 10th Dec., 30-33.

Hughes, M.D. (1985) A comparison of the patterns of play of squash. in **International Ergonomics '85** (eds I.D.Brown, R.Goldsmith, K.Coombes & M.A.Sinclair), Taylor & Francis, London, pp. 139-141.

Hughes, M. and Clarke, S.(1994) Surface effects on patterns of play of elite tennis players. in **Science and Racket Sports** (eds T. Reilly, M.Hughes and A. Lees) E.& F.N. Spon, London, pp. 272-277.

Hughes, M. and Knight, P. (1994) Playing patterns of elite squash players , using English and point-per-rally scoring. in **Science and Racket Sports** (eds T. Reilly, M.Hughes and A. Lees) E.& F.N. Spon, London, pp. 257-259

39 The use of notational analysis in support of the coach: a netball specific example

A. Borrie, C. Palmer, D. Whitby, L. Burwitz and L. Broomhead

1 Introduction

Notational analysis of sports performance has been recognised as having the capability to fill an important role in supporting the coaching process (Franks et al., 1983). Published notational analysis reports rarely give detail as to how the information generated has been used by a coach or demonstrate why the information is relevant to the coaching process. This study sought to demonstrate that notational analysis can produce relevant sport specific data on performance that can be used directly by the coach to support the coaching process. The context for the study was the England versus South Africa netball Test series in 1994.

2 Method

A netball specific computerised notational analysis system was developed at the request of the England netball coach to analyse play during the England v South Africa (South Africa) netball Test series in 1994. The analysis system itself was developed by the All England Netball Association Sports Science Support Programme whilst the parameters of play to be included in the system were decided upon by the England coach.

Netball is a court-invasive ball game, the rules of which do not allow players to move when in possession of the ball therefore the passing patterns that are adopted by teams are critical determinants of success. Two aspects of passing were therefore assessed using the analysis system; the passing pattern following a centre pass and the pattern of feeding the ball into the shooting circle. In notating centre pass play only the first three passes after the centre pass were recorded. It was felt that once play had progressed beyond the third pass, players were engaged in open play and the majority of predetermined passing patterns would be complete. The components of play recorded by the system were player in possession and court position utilising the court representation shown in Figure 1.

The system utilised real-time data input and was developed specifically so that it had potential for delivering information to the coach during matches. During this study quantitative data were only given to the coach post-match. The data were then used in tactical preparation for subsequent matches. The system was used during the England versus South Africa Test matches in 1994 and data were obtained from the first four Tests. South Africa beat England in all four matches.

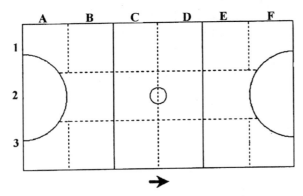

Figure 1. Court representation utilised in the notation system. In the analysis it is assumed that teams attack from left to right.

All players were included in the notation but data are only presented with respect to five players, goal attack (GA), wing attack (WA), centre (C), wing defence (WD) and goal defence (GD). The positional and player distribution of English and South Africa centre passes and feeds were compared using chi-squared analysis.

In addition to the quantitative data, a semi-structured interview was conducted with the England coach after the third Test. The interview explored the coach's perceptions of the third Test and also how the quantitative data had supported the coaching process in terms of tactical development and planning during the Test series.

3 Results

Table 1 shows a marked difference between England and South Africa in terms of the court position of the ball receiver at centre pass in all matches apart from the first Test. England played the forward from the centre pass, 94% of centre passes in the area D1-D3, whereas South Africa played 35% of passes back from the centre circle. The player analysis shows that England predominantly passed to WA, whereas South Africa made greater use of WD and GD as pass receivers (Table 2).

Table 1. Frequency distribution of first passes at Centre Pass according to court position for each individual Test match and for the Test series. (SA denotes South Africa)

			Passes received							
Court	1st Test		2nd Test		3rd Test		4th Test		Series	
Position	Eng	SA	Eng	SA	Eng	SA	Eng	SA	Eng	SA
C1-C3	4	8	3	16	2	10	1	16	10	50
D1-D3	25	21	37	19	40	27	44	26	146	93
χ^2	0.94		12.5		5.93		15.57		54.38	
p	0.33		<0.01		0.01		<0.01		<0.01	

Table 2. Frequency distribution of first passes at Centre Pass according to player for each individual Test match and for the Test series.

| | Passes Received | | | | | | | | | |
| | 1st Test | | 2nd Test | | 3rd Test | | 4th Test | | Series | |
Player	Eng	SA	Eng	SA	Eng	SA	Eng	SA	Eng	SA
GA	2	10	4	8	10	11	6	7	22	36
WA	20	5	29	2	29	8	34	7	112	22
WD	7	5	6	11	2	9	4	14	19	39
GD	0	9	1	14	1	9	0	14	2	46
χ^2	23.66		37.4		22.5		37.6		110.7	
p	<0.01		<0.01		<0.01		<0.01		<0.01	

The data in Table 3 were grouped into the two court areas, C1-D3 and E1-F2, because frequency values in individual cells were too low to allow meaningful analysis. The data showed that South Africa retained 57% of all second passes in centre court in contrast to 35% of England second passes. The same trend is apparent in the data for the third pass (Table 4.) although the difference between England and South Africa is not apparent from single match data because the frequency of completed third passes was low. The difference between England and South Africa on third pass only becomes clear when the cumulative data for the series are considered.

Table 3. Frequency distribution of second pass after Centre Pass according to court position for each individual Test match and for the Test Series.

| | Passes Received | | | | | | | | | |
| | 1st Test | | 2nd Test | | 3rd Test | | 4th Test | | Series | |
Court Area	Eng	SA	Eng	SA	Eng	SA	Eng	SA	Eng	SA
Centre (C1-D3)	4	11	14	20	13	19	16	18	47	87
Attack (E1-F2)	19	14	20	8	22	11	27	18	68	51
χ^2	2.8		4.51		3.44		0.13		11.5	
p	0.09		0.03		0.06		0.16		<0.01	

Table 4. Frequency distribution of third pass after Centre Pass according to court position for each individual Test match and for the Test series.

| | Passes Received | | | | | | | | | |
| | 1st Test | | 2nd Test | | 3rd Test | | 4th Test | | Series | |
Court Area	Eng	SA	Eng	SA	Eng	SA	Eng	SA	Eng	SA
Centre (C1-D3)	2	8	4	7	3	10	7	15	16	53
Attack (E1-F2)	8	7	10	8	13	15	22	10	40	40
χ^2	1.56		0.38		1.17		5.74		10.23	
p	0.21		0.53		0.2		<0.01		<0.01	

Table 5. Frequency distribution of feeds into the shooting circle according to court position for each individual Test match and for the Test series.

	Feeds Given									
Court	1st Test		2nd Test		3rd Test		4th Test		Series	
Position	Eng	SA	Eng	SA	Eng	SA	Eng	SA	Eng	SA
E1/F1	19	27	15	24	19	21	30	23	83	94
E2	16	20	24	14	17	18	15	18	72	70
E3/F2	17	11	12	11	20	13	21	24	72	59
χ^2	2.8		3.4		1.46		1.67		1.96	
p	0.24		0.18		0.48		0.43		0.37	

Table 6. Frequency distribution of feeds into the shooting circle according to player for each individual Test match and for the Test series.

	Feeds Given									
	1st Test		2nd Test		3rd Test		4th Test		Series	
Player	Eng	SA	Eng	SA	Eng	SA	Eng	SA	Eng	SA
GA	12	14	3	22	6	15	6	17	27	68
WA	21	16	28	13	46	14	29	31	124	74
C	27	46	36	28	16	38	43	30	122	142
χ^2	3.94		20.8		29.88		7.64		31.63	
p	0.13		<0.01		<0.01		0.02		<0.01	

In analysing the feed into the circle, the data were grouped as feeds from the left side of the circle (E1/F1 combined), the top of the circle (E2) and the right side of the circle (E3/F2). The analysis showed no differences between the feeding patterns of England and South Africa for individual matches or the series as a whole (Table 5.). The England and South Africa data sets were then analysed independently to assess differences within each teams' feeding pattern. The cumulative series data showed a significant difference in the balance of South Africa feeds with the left side of the circle being dominant (χ^2=5.62, P<0.01).

Assessment of the data on a match by match basis showed that the feeding pattern was not consistent. The percentage of South Africa feeds from the left side of the court declined from the second Test (49% of all feeds) to the fourth Test (34% of all feeds) whereas the right side feed increased throughout the series from 19%, first Test, to 38%, fourth Test. Analysis of the player giving the feed showed significant differences between the England and South Africa use of players (Table 6.). The predominant England feeders were WA and C, both with 45% of feeds, with a much lower contribution from the GA. In contrast, the South Africa feed depended heavily on their C, 49% of feeds, but with a more balanced use of WA and GA.

The semi-structured interview with the England netball coach after the third Test revealed three key points that enhanced interpretation of the data and identified the benefit of the system to the coach during the Test series. In relation to tactical preparation for the third Test the coach indicated that specific tactics had been pursued to force the South Africa first pass to the court area D1-D3. Defensive tactics had also been modified to disrupt the South Africa preference for feeding from the left side of the shooting circle. In relation to subjective perceptions of play during the third Test the coach had perceived that the South Africa WD and GD were receiving 80% of centre passes.

4 Discussion

The cumulative data for the Test series showed significant differences between the passing pattern of South Africa and England on centre pass and the subsequent second and third passes. The same pattern could be identified in the data from each individual Test for first and second passes but not third pass. The low frequency of completed third passes within each individual match obscured the overall trend in the data making it difficult for the coach to predict any pattern in the South Africa play from analysis of a single game. The cumulative data therefore expanded the understanding of the South Africa pattern of play providing additional information to support the coaching process.

The increase in the South Africa use of the area D1-D3 for first pass reception from the second to third Tests, 54% to 73% of first passes, suggested that England's tactical preparation to force greater use of D1-D3 had been successful. The decreased use of D1-D3 in the final Test raises the question of whether the variation in direction of the South Africa centre pass was being dictated by English tactics or was being deliberately varied. Examination of the trend over the series gave greater insight into this issue than consideration of individual games.

The greater use of WD and GD as first pass receivers by South Africa was apparent in all matches. This is unusual tactically and is in contrast to previously published data showing that successful teams play the first pass predominantly to WA and GA (Palmer et al, 1994). The use of WD and GD is interlinked with the data on court position. Both WD and GD enter the centre third from the defensive end of the court on centre pass. Therefore the use of these players in first pass reception determines the high frequency of pass distribution in the C1-C3 area of the centre third. The decreased use of these players during the third Test is concomitant with a decreased use of area C1-C3 for centre pass reception.

The England coach had perceived that WD and GD received 80% of the South Africa centre passes during the third Test. This is a marked overestimate with only 55% of passes going to these players. It is possible that the high frequency of pass reception by these players in the previous Test (71% of centre passes) and the unusual nature of the tactic had cued the coach into noticing the use of these players. The quantitative data were used to correct this misperception.

The cumulative data on feeds showed that South Africa had a preference for feeding from the left side of the circle. Consideration of the data from individual Tests showed a trend for decreasing frequency of South Africa feeds from the left side with a reduction from 46% of all feeds, first Test, down to 35%, fourth Test. In the fourth Test, the South Africa feed showed a relatively even balance between the three court areas with centre and right areas covering 28% and 37% feeds respectively. In this case the analysis of the cumulative data for the series masked an important trend. The England coach had indicated that specific defensive tactics had been developed in response to the preference for left side feeds. The quantitative data from the individual matches indicate that these defensive tactics were successful as the series progressed. This interpretation is not possible from consideration of the cumulative data alone.

In relation to the player making the feed, the cumulative data showed a significant difference between the English and South Africa play. Over the series England made equal use of the WA and C, both gave 45% of total feeds, and consequently made little use of the GA (10%). South Africa made similar use of the C in making feeds (49%) but made more use of the GA (24%) and less of the WA (26%). The individual match data, whilst showing significant differences between teams on all but the first Test, showed variation in the balance of players used by both England and South Africa. In terms of percentage of total feeds the use of the England C ranges from 23% (third Test) to 55% (fourth Test). Similarly the use of the South Africa centre fluctuates from range 60% (first Test) to 38% (fourth Test). The pattern of use was not consistent for either team however this was not apparent just from the consideration of the cumulative data.

The system provided the coach with in-depth quantitative data about the passing patterns adopted by both teams. The quantitative assessment clearly generated data relevant to the coach and the development of the coaching process. The information provided served to both confirm the success of tactical preparation and also challenge the coach's perceptions of particular aspects of performance. Both cumulative and individual match data can obscure important information that is relevant to the coaching process. The value of the quantitative assessment process is enhanced if a combination of both cumulative and individual match data is fed back to the coach.

5 Acknowledgements

The authors would like to acknowledge the support of the United Kingdom Sports Council in funding this research through the All England Netball Association Sports Science Support Programme.

6 References

Franks,I.M., Goodman, D. and Miller,G. (1983) Analysis of Performance: Qualitative or Quantitative . **Science Periodical on Research and Technology in Sport**, March, GY-1.

Palmer,C., Hughes,M. and Borrie,A. (1994) A comparative analysis of centre pass patterns of play of successful and non-successful international netball teams. **Journal of Sports Sciences**, 12, 181

Part Six

Health Benefits of Exercise and Workplace-based Programmes

40 Physical activity for a healthy workforce
N.T. Cable

1 Introduction

The concept of a healthy workforce has changed since the establishment of the Healthy and Safety at Work Act in 1974. This legislation required employers to ensure the adequate health, safety and welfare of their employees and was under the jurisdiction of the Health and Safety Executive (HSE). Over the past two decades, much attention has focused on the health risks associated with the working environment, controlling the use of known or suspected hazards, the establishment of safe working practices, provision of first aid and helping with the rehabilitation of workers following injury or sickness. These initiatives represent a philosophy geared towards the prevention of ill-health or injury. There has been very little emphasis placed on the use of the workplace to actively promote good health practices by employees.

Following the publication of a Government White Paper (The Health of The Nation Statement) in 1992, this situation is likely to change. This publication has produced specific targets for reducing the incidence of morbidity and mortality from various lifestyle-oriented diseases, and given that 22 million people are employed within the United Kingdom workforce, has suggested that the workplace represents a logical vehicle for the dissemination of health promotion policies.

The aim of this paper is therefore to discuss, briefly, the evidence suggesting that inactivity is a major cause of morbidity and mortality in society, and to establish a role for activity/fitness programmes in the work setting. This, of course, is not a new concept, and therefore the success of previous activity strategies is discussed in terms of cost benefit analysis for the employer and benefits gained by the employees. Finally the importance of need assessment and evaluation of such initiatives in the workplace will be discussed.

2 Health, Activity and Disease

There is much evidence from prospective surveys conducted both in the work setting and during leisure time that physical activity is protective against coronary heart disease (CHD) (for review see Morris, 1994). Evidence is also mounting that the incidence of various cancers (Lee and Paffenbarger, 1994) and type II diabetes (Helmrich et al., 1994) is also significantly reduced in a more active population. Hahn et al., (1990) established that the health implications of a sedentary lifestyle are significant by observing that 23.3% of deaths from nine chronic diseases occurring in the USA in 1986 were attributed to a lack of exercise alone. This risk factor accounted for a greater proportion of all deaths than those occurring from both hypertension and hypercholesterolaemia.

The importance of this observation is underlined by the fact that almost sixty percent of the United States population remains inactive (no activity versus three 20 min sessions per week)(Caspersen, 1987) in comparison with eighteen percent that present as smokers of one pack of cigarettes per day which represents the largest risk factor for chronic disease (32.8%) (Hahn et al., 1990).

Relatively few studies have been undertaken comparing the health benefits of an active lifestyle with increased physical fitness. However, Blair et al. (1989) have reported that higher levels of physical fitness appear to delay all cause mortality primarily associated with a reduction of cardiovascular and cancer mortality rates. These findings will assume new importance as our society enters the twentieth century, as the demographic shifts underway will result in 20% of the population being over the age of 60 years.

3 Health of The Nation Statement

In 1992 The Government published a White Paper on the Health of the Nation. This reported that cardiovascular disease and cancer represented the highest mortality rates of all disease. The Paper highlighted specific lifestyle factors that contributed to these high incident rates and targeted smoking, a reduction in dietary fat intake, reduced alcohol consumption and increased activity levels as areas requiring direct health promotion to reduce the incidence of such disease. The proposed mechanism of health promotion was to focus on a number of proposed "healthy alliances" as vehicles for disease reduction.

These alliances included healthy hospitals, healthy schools and healthy workplaces. The choice of the workplace appears appropriate given that 22 million individuals are "captured" in such a market. The government therefore recommend that the workplace be used as a medium for the delivery of health promotion messages in addition to its traditional role of protecting the worker from undue hazards.

4 Current provision of health promotion activities in the workplace

Of the 22 million individuals that comprise the total workforce of the United Kingdom, three million are self-employed. It is interesting to note that 45% of the total workforce are engaged by employers that have staffing levels in excess of 200 people, but that these 12000 businesses only represent a small fraction (0.5%) of the total number of companies. Some 96% of all businesses employ less than 20 people.

This segregation of the workforce between large and small employers is significant because it appears (from recent Health Education Authority Estimates) that the greatest health promotion activity occurs in the larger workplaces. For example the provision of health promotion activities for tackling heart disease risk factors are much more prevalent in larger organisations with 81% of major organisations (500+ employees) providing smoking advice compared with 30% of small businesses (11-24 people). In terms of the prevention of CHD, 31% of all workplaces have activities promoting smoking cessation, 14% educate about alcohol abuse, 6% instruct on healthy eating and 6% have specific exercise and fitness programmes.

It therefore appears that in terms of health in the workplace, the promotion of an active lifestyle or the improvement of fitness levels has a very low priority . Given the previous argument concerning the incidence of inactivity as a population risk factor for disease, such a low emphasis seems unjustifiable. However, it must be stated that in the United Kingdom very limited research has been conducted on the implementation of activity and fitness programmes in the workplace. The impact of fitness and activity programmes on worker health and performance have been investigated more extensively in the USA, Japan and Scandinavia, and it is therefore no accident that the implementation of such programmes in the United Kingdom has occurred predominately in multinational companies from these countries.

5 Traditional Philosophy of Worksite Health and Fitness Programmes

The traditional rationale for the promotion of fitness programmes in the workplace is based upon the premise that a fitter workforce will produce certain cost benefits for the employer. The company invests in fitness strategies because it expects to see an economic benefit in terms of enhanced productivity, reduced absenteeism and employee turnover, a reduction in health care costs and associated levels of sickness and an increase in the morale of staff. Any health benefit that the employees gain, appears to be of secondary importance. The philosophy has generally been to increase the fitness of the workforce to enhance economic efficiency of the company, rather than improving the health of the workforce directly and using this development to enhance the cost effectiveness of the company. However, claims of a clear association between the introduction of worksite wellness programmes and increase productivity lack rigorous scientific support (Pencak, 1991) and any evidence of a direct relationship between increased fitness and productivity appear to be tenuous. Worksite fitness and health promotion programmes are usually assumed to influence productivity by improving general endurance capacity and muscle strength. A fitter and stronger workforce can therefore perform tasks more efficiently and with a reduced incidence of fatigue.

Typically the improvements observed in endurance capacity in a laboratory setting are in the order of 20% following a training programme. However, the response at the worksite is much less. Routinely only 20% of the available workforce are recruited to the programme initially, and following the first few months only 10% remain actively involved (Leatt et al., 1988). Cox et al. (1981) observed a 13% improvement in predicted aerobic power in response to office fitness programmes, but the gains were restricted to frequent programme participants only. Blair et al. (1986) found gains of 10.5% across the workforce as a whole. However, in control subjects that only received a health screening, a 4.7% increase in fitness score was detected. The net programme effect was therefore of the order of a 5.8% gain in aerobic power.

Worksite strategies to improve muscle strength have produced mixed results. Slee and Peepre (1974) found a significant (4.6%) improvement in grip strength following the implementation of a resistance training programme as did Superko et al. (1983). The latter group also reported an associated reduction in the incidence of back injuries. However, Cox et al. (1981) and Danielson and Danielson (1982) observed decreases in muscle strength in response to similar programmes.

The lack of consistency between studies that have attempted to quantify the effects of such programmes is often complicated by the fact that these initiatives are not usually implemented in isolation, but as part of a multifaceted approach to health promotion that might include modules on smoking cessation, dietary advice and general health screening. In addition, it is a common observation in studies of worksite fitness programmes that participants are likely to have been enrolled in such programmes previously or represent a population that are currently exercising and were therefore of a higher fitness level initially. Thus any gains observed in such a group are only likely to be small, in comparison with increases in fitness that could be developed in more preferable target groups (i.e. a lower fitness group).

Assessment of the impact of exercise and fitness programmes on productivity is hampered by various measurement problems, the greatest of which is the difficulty in evaluating the impact of initiatives using a strict double blind controlled experiment. It is not possible to introduce a fitness and health promotion package into a company without either the employees or experimenters being aware of its existence. Furthermore those studies that have been conducted using non-participating control groups have reported an increase in productivity in both control and experimental groups of 4.3% and 7.0% respectively (Cox et al., 1981), which presumably reflects a Hawthorne-type response in the control individuals. Additionally, there is no evidence that subjects are routinely randomised into experimental and control groups, further indicating that recruitment to the exercise group is skewed in favour of fitter individuals.

In terms of the impact of these programmes on reducing the incidence of absenteeism, the picture is as unclear as above with some reports of a relationship between fitness and reduced absenteeism (Jones et al., 1990), and others observing no relationship (Cox et al., 1987). However, on a more positive note, programmes specifically designed to reduce the incidence of absenteeism resulting from back injury are successful with a reduction of at least 5 days per year per employee provided (Versloot et al., 1992).

6 The Future of Health promotion in the Workplace

Traditionally, activity and fitness programmes have been implemented without consulting the workforce of the requirements that the workers desire from such a process (Erfurt et al., 1991). Glasgow et al. (1991) have demonstrated that smoking cessation packages work more effectively if the programme is developed with strong input from employee steering groups that have combined representation from management and the shop floor. Glasgow et al. (1991) also suggested that continued success of the programme is more likely if progress is routinely evaluated and modifications made. In this manner the workforce not only perceives that it is benefitting from the health promotion strategy itself, but that it is actually in control of its development. Evaluation integrated with participation and intervention is therefore health enhancing in itself, and this process should be encouraged in the development of activity programmes. It is also important that such employee groups are given the support of top management, otherwise it is likely the programme will fail (Brennan, 1981). Generally international studies have shown that the most effective programmes, in terms of health benefits for the employees, are those that are comprehensive, with a high level of management and employee participation, reflecting the needs of the community and offering social support.

It is evident that the promotion of a more active lifestyle is probably the best community health promotion strategy given the links between mortality and a sedentary existence and the high incidence of inactivity as a risk factor in the population. However, it is also clear that little research exists that focuses on the relationship between activity promotion in the workplace and improvements in employee health, rather than improvements in productivity and absenteeism. This will be an important development in the future due to the fact that programmes are so complex and varied it is difficult to define which programmes will work in the United Kingdom.

7 References

Blair, S.N., Smith, M., Collingwood, T.R., Reynolds, R., Prentice, M.C. and Sterling, C.L. (1986) Health promotion for educators: Impact on absenteeism. **Preventive Medicine,** 15, 166-175.
Blair, S.N., Kohl, H.W., Paffenbarger, R.S., Clark, D.G., Cooper K.H. and Gibbons L.W. (1989) Physical fitness and all-cause mortality. A prospective study of healthy men and women. **Journal of the American Medical Association,** 262, 2395-2401.
Brennan, A.J. (1981) Health promotion in business: Caveats for success. **Journal of Occupational Medicine,** 23, 639-642.
Caspersen, C.J. (1987) Physical Inactivity and coronary heart disease. **The Physician and Sportsmedicine,** 15, 43-44.
Cox, M.H., Shephard, R.J. and Corey, P.N. (1981) Influence of employee fitness programme upon fitness, productivity and absenteeism. **Ergonomics,** 24, 795-806.
Erfurt, J.C., Foote, A. and Heirich, M.A. Worksite wellness programmes: Glasgow, incremental comparison of screening and referal alone, health education, follow-up, and plant organisation. **American Journal of Health Promotion,** 5, 438-448.
Glasgow R.E., Hollis J.F., Pettigrew L., Foster, L., Givi M.J. and Morrisette, G.

(1991) Implementing a year-long worksite based incentive programme for smoking cessation. **American Journal of Health Promotion,** 5, 192-199.

Hahn, R.A., Teutsch, S.M., Rothenberg, R.B. and Marks, J.S. (1990) Excess deaths from nine chronic diseases in the United States, 1986. **Journal of the American Medical Association,** 264, 2654-2659.

Helmrich, S.P., Ragland, D.R. and Paffenbarger, R.S. (1994) Prevention of non-insulin-dependent diabetes mellitus with physical activity. **Medicine and Science in Sports and Exercise,** 26, 824-830.

Leatt, P., Hattin, H., West, C. and Shephard, R.J. (1988) Seven year follow-up of employee fitness programme. **Canadian Journal of Public Health,** 79, 20-25.

Lee, I. and Paffenbarger, R.S. (1994) Physical activity and its relation to cancer risk: a prospective study of college allumni. **Medicine and Science in Sports and Exercise,** 26, 831-837.

Morris, J.N. (1994) Exercise in the prevention of coronary heart disease: today's best buy in public health. **Medicine and Science in Sports and Exercise,** 26, 807-814.

Pencak, M. (1991) Workplace health promotion programs. An overview. **Nursing Clinics of North America,** 26, 233-240.

The Health of the Nation: A Strategy for Health in England. (1992) **Department of Health, HMSO**

41 Efficacy of corporate health and wellness assessment programmes in the primary prevention of coronary heart disease

E.S. Wallace, F.A. Meenan, G.W.N. Dalzell and J.A. White

1 Introduction

Cardiovascular disease persists in being the leading cause of premature morbidity and mortality within the United Kingdom, with Northern Ireland holding the unenviable position of first in the league table of related deaths throughout the world (Vemura and Pisa, 1988). Screening has emerged as the ultimate tool in primary prevention strategies against coronary heart disease (CHD) and hence screening programmes in many formats have developed. While there is no universally accepted definition of screening, it has nonetheless been defined as "the systematic application of a test or enquiry, to identify subjects at sufficient risk of a specific disorder to benefit from further investigation or direct preventive action, among persons who have not sought medical attention on account of symptoms of that disorder" (Wald, 1994).

Screening has evolved since the late nineteenth century, with a recent model proposed (Calman, 1994) for national screening programmes that will only be introduced if there is good research evidence to prove that they will result in significant health gain. In times of scarce resource choice has to be made about health care provision, the sacrifices made through not taking up opportunities, and the benefits of those sacrifices (Donaldson, 1994). Economic considerations have led to the proposed screening of "high-risk" individuals only, yet any incurred benefits are limited to these individuals and not the community at large, since more than half of the future victims of CHD have risk factors below the high range and therefore remain unprotected (Epstein, 1993). This claim led to the proposal for a complementary community-wide strategy. Furthermore, the actual value of screening outcomes has been questioned, with the claim that tests perform badly in a screening environment leading to many false positive results (Arroll, 1990). Against this background, the present study was designed to evaluate the effectiveness of a corporate health and wellness programme in determining the level of CHD and other related illnesses in asymptomatic adults.

2 Methods

Informed consent was obtained from two hundred and fifty six volunteers (male=237, female=19) who participated in this study, all of whom were asymptomatic of any signs of CHD and were fit for work at the time of their assessment. The subjects were drawn from a diverse local industrial base within Northern Ireland and represented all sectors of the workforce. No age limitation was imposed; however, age was naturally limited by programme recruitment and retirement policies and ranged from 28-63 years.

The test procedures in the study were similar to those routinely used in the health and wellness programme, details of which have been reported previously (Wallace et al., 1993). The initial stage of assessment involved subjects completing an extensive health-risk appraisal questionnaire prior to attendance at the University of Ulster's "Positive Health Care" programme for a full health and fitness assessment. This included a medical examination by a consultant cardiologist, a 12-lead resting electrocardiogram (ECG), an exercise stress test ECG using a modified Bruce Protocol, measures of total serum cholesterol (Reflotron), blood pressure assessment both at rest and during exercise (auscultatory technique), urine analysis (for albumen, glucose and blood abnormalities), and lung function assessment. Anthropometric measures included height, body mass and estimated percentage body fat (skinfold thicknesses). Physical fitness measures included estimated aerobic fitness (treadmill test duration), muscular strength (Eurofit tests of grip strength and sit-ups) and flexibility (sit and reach).

All equipment employed was standardised and calibrated on a regular basis throughout the data collection period. All staff were trained in equipment use to avoid discrepancies in recorded results. Each subject was informed of their complete set of test results at the end of their test session. Guidelines were developed and adhered to regarding safe limitations of all tests employed. These safety measures were especially related to the exercise stress test where blood pressure and ECG indicators were agreed beyond which a test would no longer be safe for the subject to continue. The screening procedure normally took one hour to complete.

3 Results

Since the majority of the subjects were male (92.5%), a representative descriptive analysis was conducted by randomly selecting 50 male subjects and obtaining mean values (±SD) for the various parameters and variables under investigation (Table 1). Thus the voluntary health assessment programme mainly attracted individuals in their

Table 1. Parameters and results of tests for sample group

parameter/variable	mean	(±SD)
Age (years)	44.1	(±9.1)
Height (m)	1.75	(±0.57)
Body mass (kg)	80.2	(±10.1)
BMI (wt/ht^2)	26.1	(±2.9)
% body fat	24.2	(±6.4)
% overweight	6.2	(±7.6)
Systolic BP (mmHg)	133.2	(±16.3)
Diastolic BP (mmHg)	84.2	(±10.4)
Total cholesterol (mmol/l)	5.4	(±1.1)
Treadmill time (min)	12.2	(±4.9)
Grip strength (kgf)	39.8	(±23.8)
Sit-ups (no)	14	(±10.2)
Flexibility (cm)	- 0.5	(±8.0)

mid-forties, with height and weight values which may be
considered as being average for the population. The Body
Mass Index of 26.1 is slightly higher than the desirable
upper limit of 25, which is also reflected in the finding
that the group was 6.2% overweight according to the height
and weight recommendations of the Royal College of
Physicians (1983). Resting blood pressure was considered
normal for the group, while the mean value for total
cholesterol is similar to that for the age-related Northern
Ireland population, but above the recommended value of 5.2
mmol/l. Estimated aerobic fitness (treadmill time) and the
results of the other physical fitness tests are also
considered average for the age group.

Analyses of individual results yielded a total of one
hundred and forty subjects (54.7%) with a previously
undiagnosed medical/clinical condition which was deemed to
be worthy of clinical referral for further investigation or
treatment. These referrals were classified as cases
requiring further cardiac tests, cases for blood pressure
treatment or cholesterol treatment, and cases for other
analyses or treatments, with a summary breakdown of these
results given in Table 2. The number of subjects requiring

Table 2. Outcomes of initial health assessments (n=256)

Referral category	no. (% of total)
All types	140 (54.7%)
Cardiac tests	25 (9.8%)
Blood pressure treatment	36 (14.0%)
Cholesterol treatment	65 (25.4%)
Others	14 (5.5%)

some form of medical/clinical follow-up (ie over 50%) was unexpected, as were the numbers in each of the individual referral categories. In particular, the 9.8% referred on for further cardiac tests was concerning as was the number of previously undiagnosed cases of hypertension. The relatively high percentage of referrals for cholesterol-lowering treatment (ie individuals with values above 5.2 mmol/l) was not particularly surprising given the well-documented dietary habits within the Northern Ireland population. Those cases making up the "others" category were mainly comprised of individuals requiring repeated urine analyses or additional blood tests.

The high incidence of cardiac referrals required further investigation. As alluded to in the introduction, some authors have suggested that tests perform poorly when employed for screening purposes and hence a large proportion of false positive results may be obtained. To test this theory, all cardiac referrals were followed up at various intervals to obtain outcomes of further investigations and thereby test the validity of test results obtained in the screening environment. While the number of true positives was unexpectedly high, the ratio of true positives to false positives (Table 3) was interpreted as indicating acceptable levels of test validity and reliability.

It should be noted when considering the proportion of cases classified as false positives that these were largely determined by thallium scanning procedures during exercise stress tests which showed no significant evidence of CHD. If coronary arteriography had been performed on each of these cases the resultant number of false positive results may indeed be reduced. Of the 13 subjects classified as being true positives, 7 showed significant evidence of diseased coronary arteries. As regards surgical intervention, two subjects were referred on for coronary artery bypass grafting, whilst another had a successful angioplasty procedure. One subject suffered a myocardial infarction whilst on the waiting list for coronary arteriography but has since had an insertion of a permanent pacemaker and is currently undergoing rehabilitation. All other subjects within the group were treated medically and are under periodic review.

Table 3. Outcomes of cardiac referral tests (n=25)

Classification	No (% of total cardiac referrals)
True positive	13 (52%)
False positive	5 (20%)
Innocent murmur	4 (16%)
Awaiting investigation)	3 (12%)

4 Discussion

Any screening activity, like any other medical intervention, should be evaluated in terms of the costs it incurs and the benefits it produces. Coronary heart disease prevention strategies are necessarily reviewed and debated on a regular basis throughout the literature, with the majority of studies emphasizing the need for a consideration of the cost-effectiveness of prevention. Much debate also surrounds the methodological soundness of many of these studies, with problems arising from the estimation of costs and benefits, the definition of benefit and its measurement, and resolution of the equity principle in economic terms.

Results from the present study are interpreted as indicating the worthwhile nature of a corporate-based health and wellness programme in the prevention of coronary heart disease and related illnesses. While the primary goal of this programme is to assist individuals to make appropriate lifestyle modifications conducive to good health, an unexpected level of silent pathologies has emerged which prompted the present study. Over 50% of the individuals tested have been shown to require further tests or treatments, while the remainder were offered lifestyle advice only. Given that the subjects were all asymptomatic at the time of initial testing, this finding clearly supports the concept of screening beyond the known high-risk category.

The costs of the programme are usually borne entirely by the participating companies. A range of motivating factors have been advocated for the companies' sponsoring role and the employees' involvement in the programme, but the crucial fact remains that the individuals who avail of the programme have a screening opportunity which they otherwise would not have. However, the need to verify the outcomes of preliminary screening activities and the associated assessments has already been established. In relation to the present study, the outcomes of these activities, particularly in relation to the proportion of true positive findings, are considered to be encouraging and supportive of the effectiveness of the screening aspect of the wider programme.

The relevance of these findings to other screening programmes needs to be carefully considered. The University of Ulster's Positive Health Care programme is offered to a wide range of the workforce population which evidently includes individuals with unknown high-risk for coronary heart disease. The programme is multi-faceted in its approach and its scope, drawing upon a range of information obtained from detailed self-completed questionnaires and medical/clinical examinations and other lifestyle assessments, and utilising sophisticated testing equipment and highly trained professionals in each of the test procedures. The programme is complementary to existing company health-care schemes and NHS provision, with a clear strategy concerning the further investigation and treatment of individuals diagnosed as requiring some form of follow-

up. Finally, it should be borne in mind that the costs of
the programme, at approximately £200 per individual, are
almost entirely borne by the corporate sector, with the
common view that the workforce is its most important asset.

In summary, the proposal of a community-wide screening
strategy to operate on a complementary basis to the "high-
risk" strategy is supported. Such measures will have the
undoubted effect of widening the population field which may
draw benefit from the resultant screening activities. The
corporate sector is well positioned to play a significant,
though not exclusive, role in the primary prevention of
major illnesses such as coronary heart disease.

5 References

Arroll, B. (1990) Screening: the double edged sword! **New
Zealand Medical Journal**, 103, 346-348.

Calman, K. (1994) Developing screening in the NHS. **Journal
of Medical Screening**, 1, 101-105.

Donaldson, C. (1994) Using economics to assess the place of
screening. **Journal of Medical Screening**, 1, 124-129.

Epstein, F.H. (1993) Strategies for primary coronary heart
disease prevention. **Cor et Vasa**, 35, 16-19.

Royal College of Physicians (1983) Obesity: A Report of the
Royal College of Physicians. **Journal of the Royal College
of Physicians London**, 17, 5-65.

Vemura K. and Pisa, Z. (1988) Trends in cardiovascular
disease mortality in industrialised countries since
1950. **World Health Statistics Quarterly**, 41, 155-178.

Wald, N.J. (1994) Guidance on terminology. **Journal of
Medical Screening**, 1, 139.

Wallace, E.S. White, J.A. Downie, A. Dalzell, G.W.N. and
Doran, D. (1993) Influence of exercise adherence
level on modifiable coronary heart disease risk
factors and functional-fitness levels in middle-aged
men. **British Journal of Sports Medicine**, 27, 101-106.

42 Spiritual well-being, lifestyle and health
Li.I. Dreyer, S. Van der Merwe and G.L. Strydom

1 Introduction

Total health consists of a variety of components, notably the physical, mental, emotional, social and spiritual dimensions (Bensley, 1991). The spiritual dimension is seen by some researchers as the dimension that unifies, coordinates and facilitates the other dimensions (Banks et al., 1984). Spiritual Well-Being (SW) is also seen as something which gives meaning or purpose to life and which makes the other dimensions function better (Banks et al., 1984). Closely related to level of SW are values, norms, attitudes and self-concept (Banks et al., 1984; Sweeting, 1990).

According to Rokeach (1968) human behaviour is a function of attitudes, values, and self-concept. Spiritual Well-Being is thus considered to be the "catalyst of health" or the basis of a healthy lifestyle and good health (Banks et al., 1984; Sweeting, 1990).

The purpose of this study was, therefore to investigate the relationship between SW, lifestyle and health. Some evidence exists that physically active people are more health concious and less prone to develop physical or mental ailments (Sweeting, 1990). The relationship between physical activity and SW, as well as the influence of physical activity on the relationship between SW, lifestyle and health was also studied.

2 Method

The subjects of the study were 525 Caucasion male inhabitants of Potchefstroom, a city in the Northwest Province of South Africa. Subjects between the ages of 30-60 years were selected at rondom according to their street address. The response rate was 95% that is, 95% of the respondents that were approached and were of the correct age, completed the questionnaire. The questionnaire included measures of Spiritual Well-Being, a Seriousness of Illness Rating Scale, Lifestyle and a Physical Activity Index.

correlation was found between the medical and the lay samples, and a system of weights was accordingly constructed. This carefully developed scale of seriousness of illness has served as a frequent tool in stress and illness studies (Kobasa et al., 1981; Schroeder & Costa, 1984).

2.2 Measure of lifestyle

The Health Promoting Lifestyle Profile (HPLP) of Walker et al. (1987) was used to evaluate the respondents regarding their likelihood to engage in health-promoting behaviours. The HPLP is a 48-item summated rating scale which provides a measure of frequency of performance of specific health promoting behaviours. An overall measure of the health promoting component of lifestyle is obtained along with measures of six subscales: 1) Self-actualization, 2) Health responsibility, 3) Exercise, 4) Nutrition, 5) Interpersonal support, and 6) Stress management. The HPLP was developed from a 100-item checklist of positive health behaviours originally designed as a tool for clinical nursing. Item analysis, factor analysis, and a reliability analysis produced the 48-item instrument used in the current study. The total scale has high internal consistency reliability (alpha = 0.922) and subscale alpha coefficients are reported to range from 0.702 to 0.904. Stability as measured by a two-week interval test-retest of 63 adults produced a Pearson r of 0.926 for the total scale and subscale coefficients ranged from 0.808 to 0.905.

2.3 Measure of physical activity (PAI)

The quality of the respondents participation in physical activity was measured and quantified with the Physical Activity Index of Sharkey (1984).

2.4 Measure of spiritual well-being

Spiritual Well-Being was measured with the Spiritual Well-Being (SW) Scale of Ellison (1983). It consists of 20 items responded to on a six-point scale ranging from strongly agree to strongly disagree. Responses for each of the items are assigned a numerical value of 1-6. Ten of the items are designed to measure Religious Well-Being (RW) and 10 items measure Existential Well-Being (EW). Those items which contain a reference to God are summed to provide a RW subscale score, and the remaining ten are summed to attain EW. Scores for the two subscales are summed to provide an overall measure of SW. Test-retest reliability coefficients obtained from 100 student volunteers at the University of Idaho (Ellison, 1983) were 0.93 (SW), 0.96(RW) and 0.86 (EW). Coefficient alphas, an index of internal consistency, were 0.89 (SW), 0.87 (RW) and 0.78 (EW).

2.5 Statistical analysis of the data

The statistica computer software statistical analysis package was used to analyse the data. The relationship of SW, the HPLP and the PAI with the IRS was evaluated by means of one-way and two-way analyses of variance as well as a stepwise multiple regression analysis. For the purpose of the two-way analysis of variance the respondents were placed into three groups regarding SW, the HPLP and the PAI.

With regard to SW and the HPLP, the respondents were placed into groups (low, moderate and high) by using the group distribution. Those with values higher or equal to 80% of the group distribution were classified as high and those with values equal and lower than 20% were classified as low. Respondents with values between 21% and 79%

of the group distribution were classified as moderate. Individuals with a physical activity index value of higher than 45 were classified as highly active, while respondents with values lower than 16 were placed in the low activity group. Respondents with values between 17-44 were accordingly classified as moderately active. In cases where statistically significant ($P<0.05$) differences were found, intergroup differences were determined with the Newman-Keuls post-hoc test. Practical significance was determined by using Cohen's effect size (ES) calculation (Thomas & Nelson, 1990).

3 Results and Discussion

The relationship of SW with the HPLP, the PAI and the IRS as analysed with a one-way analysis of variance is presented in Table 1. The results of this analysis indicate that the higher the level of SW, the more likely individuals are of following a lifestyle that is health promoting in nature. Respondents classified as high regarding SW had statistically ($P<0.05$) and practically significantly ($ES\geq0.8$) higher values with regard to the HPLP subscales, self-actualization, interpersonal support and stress management as well as the total HPLP score. Only in the case of self-actualization were the differences between the three SW groups (low, moderate and high) practically significant ($ES>0.8$). In the case of interpersonal support, stress management and the total HPLP score practically significant ($ES>0.8$) differences were found between respondents classified as low and high with regard to their SW. Level of SW (high vs low) also showed a statistically ($P<0.05$) but not a practically significant relationship with quality of participation in physical activity as measured with the PAI of Sharkey (1984). Regarding the HPLP-exercise-subscale the differences were also only statistically significant ($P<0.05$). The difference between the two measuring instruments is that the PAI measures quality of participation and the HPLP subscale only measures whether or not the participant exercises and follows some other health related behaviours when exercising, like checking his/her pulse rate (Walker et al., 1987).

Level of SW also showed statistically significant ($P<0.05$) but not practically significant ($ES>0.8$) relations with the IRS of Wyler et al. (1968). The results of this analysis indicate that only the social-psychological aspects of the HPLP-questionnaire like self-actualization, interpersonal support and stress management showed practically significant relationships ($ES>0.08$) with SW. Lifestyle measures of the HPLP-questionnaire like health responsibility, exercise and nutrition as well as the PAI and a measure of health (IRS) did not show a practically significant relationship with level of SW.

This suggests that SW has some relationship with social-psychological well-being. The relationship of SW with health (IRS-score) and lifestyle aspects like participation in exercise, correct eating habits and health responsibility does not seem to be practically significant.

Table 1. The relationship of SW with the HPLP, the PAI and the IRS

		SPIRITUAL WELL-BEING						
		(a) Low (N=99)		(b)Moderate (N=323)		(c) High (N=103)		
		X	SD	X	SD	X	SD	F-value
Self-actualization	(RW)	56.0$^{b+,c+}$	4.1	62.0$^{a+,c+}$	3.9	68.4$^{a+,b+}$	4.5	$F_{(2,522)}$=64.2***
	(EW)	55.0$^{b+,c+}$	8.6	62.9$^{a+,c+}$	7.3	68.8$^{a+,b+}$	7.1	$F_{(2,522)}$=99.1***
	(SW)	55.1$^{b+,c+}$	9.3	62.3$^{a+,c+}$	7.4	69.4$^{a+,b+}$	7.0	$F_{(2,522)}$=85.6***
Health responsibility	(RW)	25.8^{b,c}	6.3	28.0^{a,c}	6.7	30.2^{a,b}	8.0	$F_{(2,522)}$=10.6***
	(EW)	25.8^{b,c}	6.9	28.4^{a}	6.6	29.5^{a}	7.8	$F_{(2,522)}$= 9.7***
	(SW)	25.2^{b,c}	6.4	28.4^{a,c}	6.6	30.0^{a,b}	8.2	$F_{(2,522)}$=13.5***
Exercise	(RW)	11.3^{b,c}	3.8	12.8^{a,b}	4.4	14.0^{a,b}	4.9	$F_{(2,522)}$=10.2***
	(EW)	11.4^{b,c}	3.6	12.9^{a,c}	4.4	13.9^{a,b}	5.2	$F_{(2,522)}$=10.6***
	(SW)	11.2^{b,c}	3.5	12.8^{a,c}	4.3	14.3^{a,b}	5.2	$F_{(2,522)}$=12.8***
Nutrition	(RW)	14.8^{c}	3.7	15.3^{c}	3.8	16.6^{a,b}	3.7	$F_{(2,522)}$= 7.0***
	(EW)	14.8^{b,c}	3.9	15.5^{a,c}	3.8	16.4^{a,b}	3.6	$F_{(2,522)}$= 6.8**
	(SW)	14.4^{b,c}	3.9	15.5^{a}	3.7	16.3^{a}	3.7	$F_{(2,522)}$= 6.1**
Interpersonal support	(RW)	38.3$^{b,c+}$	6.1	42.1^{a,c}	6.1	46.3$^{a+,b}$	6.1	$F_{(2,522)}$=46.4**
	(EW)	38.1$^{b,c+}$	6.4	42.6^{a,c}	5.9	46.2$^{a+,b}$	6.0	$F_{(2,522)}$=53.5***
	(SW)	37.7$^{b,c+}$	6.8	42.3^{a,c}	5.9	46.7$^{a+,b}$	5.9	$F_{(2,522)}$=55.8***
Stress management	(RW)	21.4$^{b,c+}$	4.1	22.9^{a,c}	3.9	25.1$^{a+,b}$	4.5	$F_{(2,522)}$=23.9***
	(EW)	21.0$^{b,c+}$	4.2	23.1^{a,c}	3.7	25.4$^{a+,b}$	4.1	$F_{(2,522)}$=36.6***
	(SW)	21.3$^{b,c+}$	3.7	22.9^{a,c}	3.7	25.5$^{a+,b}$	4.4	$F_{(2,522)}$=28.4***
Total HPLP-score	(RW)	167.5$^{b,c+}$	23.7	183.9^{a,c}	23.9	200.6$^{a+,b}$	8.0	$F_{(2,522)}$=50.2***
	(EW)	165.9$^{b+,c+}$	24.9	185.4$^{a+,c}$	22.9	200.0$^{a+,b}$	24.2	$F_{(2,522)}$=63.9***
	(SW)	164.8$^{b+,c+}$	25.4	184.1$^{a+,c}$	22.7	202.1$^{a+,b}$	25.0	$F_{(2,522)}$=62.7***
PAI	(RW)	13.3^{c}	23.1	18.1	24.1	21.9^{a}	28.9	$F_{(2,522)}$= 3.1*
	(EW)	10.8^{b,c}	19.5	18.3^{a,c}	25.3	25.1^{a,b}	28.3	$F_{(2,522)}$= 9.9***
	(SW)	10.8^{b,c}	19.8	17.8^{a,c}	25.1	26.0^{a,b}	27.7	$F_{(2,522)}$= 9.6***
IRS	(RW)	340.8^{b,c}	207.1	281.8^{a}	178.4	250.1^{a}	188.7	$F_{(2,522)}$= 6.5*
	(EW)	357.7^{b,c}	223.1	282.3^{a,c}	171.0	216.1^{a,b}	159.9	$F_{(2,522)}$=17.9***
	(SW)	338.1^{b,c}	218.9	292.9^{a,c}	177.0	213.4^{a,b}	170.3	$F_{(2,522)}$=12.2***

RW = Religious Well-Being; EW = Existential Well-Being; SW = Spiritual Well-Being.
a,b and c indicate intergroup statistically significant (P<0.05) differences (Newman-Keuls post-hoc test).
+ = practically significant differences (ES>0.8).   *** = P<0.001;   ** = P<0.01;   * = P<0.05

In order to determine the influence of physical activity on the relationship between SW and illness (IRS), a two-way analysis of variance was performed. The results of this analysis are presented in Figure 1 and Table 2. Independent of physical activity SW still showed a statistically significant (P<0.05) relationship with the IRS (a vs c, Figure 1). The relationship was, however, only moderately practically significant (ES>0.54). Groups a and b differed practically significantly (ES>0.8) from groups h,f and i with regard to their IRS score. No statistically significant (P>0.05) differences were found between respondents in groups g,d,e,h,f and i. The reason for groups d and g not differing practically significantly from groups a and b is probably because of the relatively low number of respondents in groups d (n=17) and g (n=7). These results suggest that physical activity has health benefits independent of level of SW.

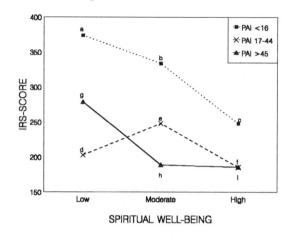

Figure 1. Relationship of SW and the PAI with the IRS asevaluated with a two-way analysis of variance

Table 2. Combined and individual relationship of SW and the PAI with the IRS

		SPIRITUAL WELL-BEING							
		Low			Moderate			High	
	N	X	SD	N	X	SD	N	X	SD
PAI<16	75	(a)374.1$^{c,d,e,f+,h+,i+}$	232.2	202	(b)333.8$^{c,d,e,h+,f+,i+}$	178.9	46	(c)247.8^{a}	185.7
PAI17-44	17	(d)203.4^{a,b}	96.4	73	(e)248.0^{a,b}	163.6	30	(f)185.6$^{a+,b+}$	154.2
PAI>45	7	(g)279.1	145.5	48	(h)189.3^{a+}	124.5	27	(i)185.9$^{a+,b+}$	154.4

Statistically significant (P<0.05) differences between groups are indicated with the alphabetical codes a,b,c,d,e,f,g and i. + = practically significant (ES≥0.8) differences.

The other lifestyle factors in the HPLP-questionnaire like self-actualization, health responsibility, nutrition, interpersonal support and stress management will probably also have an effect on SW's relationship with the IRS. The question thus arises as to whether SW would show any relationship with the IRS if the other HPLP-questionnaire subscales are taken into consideration. The contribution of the HPLP subscales, the PAI and SW to the variance of the IRS was consequently evaluated by means of a stepwise multiple regression analysis (Table 3). The results of the stepwise multiple regression analysis showed that physical activity contributed most, namely 10.7% to the variance of Wyler's Illness Rating Scale (IRS). Only two of the six subscales of Walker's HPLP-questionnaire, namely self-actualization (3.9%) and health responsibility (3.8%) had statistically significant (P<0.05) contributions to the variance of the IRS. Spiritual Well-Being also contributed statistically significantly (P<0.05) but least, namely only 0.9% to the variance of the IRS. The combined contribution of the PAI, the HPLP and the SW scale to the variance of the IRS was, however, only 19.3% indicating that health is influenced by other factors as well.

Table 3. Stepwise multiple regression analysis of PAI, SW and the HPLP relationships with an illness rating scale.

Predictor Variable	Cumulative R	Cumulative R^2	R^2	F-Value
Physical Activity	0.326	0.107	0.107	62.5**
Self-actualization	0.383	0.147	0.039	24.3**
Health responsibility	0.429	0.184	0.038	24.1**
Spiritual well-being	0.441	0.193	0.009	5.67*

** = $p \leq 0.001$ * = $p \leq 0.05$

4 Conclusion

Spiritual Well-Being showed a statistically (P<0.05) and practically significant (ES>0.8) relationship with social-psychological aspects of the HPLP-questionnaire. The relationship of SW with illness (IRS) and lifestyle measures like nutrition and exercise was, however, not practically significant (ES>0.08). Of all the measuring instruments used in this study SW contributed least (0.9%) and physical activity most (10.7%) to good health.

5 References

Banks, R.L., Poehler, D.L. and Russell, R.D. (1984) Spirit and human-spiritual interaction as a factor in health and in health education. **Health Education**, 15(5), 16-19.

Bensley, R.J. (1991) Defining spiritual health: a review of the literature. **Journal of Health Education**, 22(5), 287-290.

Ellison, C.W. (1983) Spiritual well-being: conceptualization and measurement. **Journal of Psychology and Theology**, 11(4), 330-340.

Kobasa, S.C., Maddi, S.R. and Courington, S. (1981) Personality and constitution as mediators in the stress-illness relationship. **Journal of Health and Social Behavior**, 22, 368-378.

Rokeach, M (1968) **Beliefs, Attitudes, and Values: a Theory of Organization and Change.** Jossey-Bass, San Francisco.

Schroeder, D.H. and Costa, P.T. (1984) Influence of life event stress on physical illness: substantive effects or methodological flaws. **Journal of Personality and Social Psychology**, 46, 853-863.

Sharkey, B.J. (1984) **Physiology of Fitness.** Human Kinetics, Champaign, IL.

Sweeting, R.L. (1990) **A Values Approach to Health Behavior.** Human Kinetics, Champaign, IL.

Thomas, J.R. and Nelson, J.K. (1990) **Research Methods in Physical Activity**. Human Kinetics, Champaign, IL.

Walker, S.N., Sechrist, K.R. and Pender, N.J. (1987) The health promoting lifestyle profile: development and psychometric characteristics. **Nursing Research**, 36(2), 76-78.

Wyler, A.R., Masuda, M. and Holmes, T.H. (1968) Seriousness of illness rating scale. **Journal of Psychosomatic Research**, 11, 363-374.

43 Adult physical activity patterns and lifestyle factors
J.A. White, H. Roberts, D. Weller and P. Davies

1 Introduction

The health benefits of physical activity are widely recognised and there is now considerable evidence that physical activity has a role to play in maintenance of good health as well as in the prevention of ill-health (Fentem, Bassey and Turnbull, 1988). Despite this evidence, it appears that individuals in western countries are resistant to public health messages aimed at encouraging physical activity and participation rates are generally low (Casperson, Christenson and Pollard, 1986; Eammons et al., 1994). Population based surveys in the UK have indicated the relatively sedentary nature of large numbers of the adult population (Allied Dunbar National Lifestyle Survey, Health Survey in England, 1993; Health Education Authority, 1993). Furthermore, the relationships between inactivity and lifestyle factors such as smoking (Conway and Cronan, 1992) alcohol consumption (Goldberg et al., 1994) and diet (Hallfrish et al., 1994) remain a cause for public health concern. The present study had two objectives: firstly, to compare a recent generalised activity target of 30 minutes accumulated activity on most days of the week for health maintenance (American College of Sport Medicine, 1993) with an alternative target of an age/sex "optimal" level of activity for health benefit (Allied Dunbar National Fitness Survey, 1993) and, secondly, to examine the relationships between extreme levels of physical activity (optimal activity versus sedentary status) and selected lifestyle factors which are known to influence health status.

2 Methods

Sample
A stratified random sample of 18,787 adults aged 16-70 years was drawn from eight Family Health Services Authorities (FHSA) registers to represent the Trent Regional Health Authority of England with a population of 3.5 million, within that age group. The sample was stratified by age (15-34, 35-54, 55-70 years) and gender. The response rate of 66% (11,427/17,430) after exclusions was reasonably representative of the population and all data were weighted by the size of each FHSA's population.

Questionnaire
Data were collected by a reliable postal questionnaire (Roberts and Dengler, 1994). This included items on general health, diet, physical activity, injuries, alcohol and tobacco

usage, health checks, stress and feelings, health perceptions as well as demographic information.

Data
The data were entered directly from the questionnaire using a pre-set format (SPSSPC) with double entry to check for anomalies which were corrected at source. All data were handled in accordance with the Data Protection Act (1984).

Physical Activity Levels
Data on physical activity participation were compared with both the Allied Dunbar National Fitness Survey (1993) and American College of Sports Medicine's (1993) criteria.

Allied Dunbar National Fitness Survey (ADNFS) Criteria
Questions from the Trent Lifestyle Survey were used to classify physical activity into three levels of intensity namely light, moderate and vigorous. The frequency and intensity of 20 minute sessions of activity per week were then used to derive the ADNFS physical activity according to the following activity scale:

Level 5:≥12 occasions of vigorous activity in the last 4 weeks
Level 4:≥12 occasions of mixed moderate and vigorous activity
Level 3:≥12 occasions of moderate activity
Level 2: 5-11 occasions of mixed, moderate or vigorous activity
Level 1: 1-4 occasions of mixed, moderate or vigorous activity
Level 0: = no occasions of activity (sedentary)

where "vigorous" and "moderate" activity were clearly defined by specific examples.

"Optimal" activity was defined according age/sex criteria:

Women 35-74 years, and men aged 55-74: Level 3, 4 or 5
Women aged 16-34, and men aged 35-54: Level 4 or 5
Men aged 16-34: Level 5

In addition to sedentary status (Level 0) a further category "sub-optimal" activity was derived between Level 0 (sedentary) and the optimal age/sex related levels.

American College of Sports Medicine (ACSM) Criteria
The ACSM classification is based upon epidemiological evidence for disease prevention with a target set for the USA population that:

"every American adult should accumulate 30 minutes or more of moderate physical activity over the course of most days of the week"

In the present study examples of various types of physical activity including both leisure and work related activities were provided. Total accumulated activity was further sub-divided into 3 categories >30, 15-30 and <15 minutes of daily activity. "Sedentary" status was defined as a combination of the latter two categories.

Lifestyle Factors

Questions on lifestyle habits which influence health included 3 categories of smoking status: never, ex-smoker and daily smoker, and 3 categories of alcohol consumption: teetotal (total abstinence), ≤ recommended limits and ≥ recommended limits, where the recommended limits of safe drinking are defined; men: ≤21 units, women: ≤14 units of alcohol per week. Dietary habits were classified according to the frequency of consumption (regularly - most days of the week, rarely - less than once a week) of each type of foodstuff from the following lists;

"Healthy" Foods

1 Skimmed/Semi-skimmed milk
  products
2 Fresh fruit, vegetables or salad
3 White meat or fish
4 Wholemeal, granary or high fibre
  bread
5 Rice or pasta
6 Low-fat/polyunsaturates as a
  spread or in cooking

"Less Healthy" Foods

1 Other types of milk products
2 Biscuits, cakes, puddings, sweatmeats
  sweet snacks, chocolate etc
3 Red meat or processed meats
4 Butter, hard margarine as a spread or
  cooked in food
5 Lard or dripping in fried, roasted
  or baked foods

Body Mass Index (BMI) was derived from height and weight measures according to the normal standards:

Underweight: < 20kg/m^2
Overweight: 25-30 kg/m^2

Ideal Weight: 20-25 kg/m^2
Obese: > 30 kg/m^2

3 Results

Physical Activity Levels

The findings of physical activity participation classified according to the ADNFS and ACSM criteria are presented in Table 1. Overall within both the ADNFS and ACSM classifications the respective levels of activity for males and females in each age group were similar, with little or no difference in participation rates between males and females. The ADNFS classification indicated relatively low but reasonably consistent percentages of males and females taking optimal levels of activity for their respective age groups. There was a progressive increase with age in the percentages of sedentary males and females, and a progressive decline in males and females achieving sub-optimal levels of activity with increasing age. In contrast, the ACSM classification indicated relatively high percentages of males and females taking more than 30 minutes of activity daily, with consistently lower percentages of males and females taking both <15 and 15-30 minutes of daily activity. The combined percentages of those taking <15 and 15-30 minutes accumulated daily activity, who may be considered as relatively inactive were still considerably lower in the middle and older age groups in the ACSM compared with the ADNFS sedentary classification.

Table 1   Physical activity levels (%) in the population

		Males			Females		
Age Groups		16-34 n=1877	35-54 n=2003	55-70 n=1371	16-34 n=2264	35-54 n=2399	55-70 n=1472
ADNFS Criteria	Optimal	15	13	19	13	18	14
	Sub-optimal	58	39	20	55	35	23
	Sedentary	27	48	61	32	47	63
ACSM Criteria	>30 min	71	62	63	61	63	72
	15-30 min	18	22	22	28	24	16
	<15 min	11	16	15	11	13	12
	Sedentary	(29)	(38)	(37)	(39)	(37)	(38)

Body Mass Index and Physical Activity

The results of the BMI classification for the respective ADNFS sedentary and optimal activity groups are presented in Table 2. Overall the findings indicated levels of "ideal" BMI to be higher in females (58%) compared with males (50%), but overweight was higher in males (37%) than females (23%). Similar levels of obesity were noted in males (9%) and females (9%), although underweight was more common in females (10%) than males (5%). There were consistently higher percentages of "ideal" BMI in each group of males and females associated with optimal activity compared with sedentary status. In contrast, the percentages of obese males and females in each age group were consistently higher in the sedentary compared with the optimal activity level, and, except at middle age for both sexes, a similar trend in the percentage overweight. There was no such clear trend in the underweight category associated with differential activity status except in younger females where higher percentages of underweight were associated with optimal activity levels.

Table 2   Body weight & activity Levels (%) in the population

	Males						Females					
Age	16-34		35-54		55-70		16-34		35-54		55-70	
Activity	Sed	Opt	Sed	Opt	Sed	Opt	Sed	Opt	Sed	Opt	Sed	Opt
Ideal	46	57	38	46	34	50	46	55	48	53	38	45
Overweight	33	26	39	45	45	42	17	12	26	27	33	31
Obese	8	2	13	6	14	3	7	3	14	9	18	11
Underweight	7	10	4	1	3	2	16	24	7	5	5	7

Smoking and Physical Activity

The results of smoking status classification for the respective ADNFS sedentary and optimal activity groups are presented in Table 3. Overall the findings indicated that the percentages of "never having smoked" were higher in females (44%) than males (39%). Smoking prevalence rates were 29% males and 24% of females. Consistently "never having smoked" was associated with optimal activity compared with sedentary status in each age group in males, but only in the oldest group of females. Similarly, there was a clear trend of lower percentages of smokers associated with the optimal activity level in males, but only in the older group of females.

Table 3   Smoking & activity levels (%) in the population

	Males						Females					
Age	16-34		35-54		55-70		16-34		35-54		55-70	
Activity	Sed	Opt	Sed	Opt	Sed	Opt	Sed	Opt	Sed	Opt	Sed	Opt
Never Smokers	45	63	29	41	20	33	56	54	34			33
		21	25									
	39	18	35		14	29	25	29	31		26	34
		30	25									

Alcohol and Physical Activity

Alcohol intake classification for the respective ADNFS sedentary and optimal activity groups are presented in Table 4. Overall the findings indicated that the percentages of alcohol consumption above recommended limits were higher in males (22%) than females (7%), while consumption below recommended limits was similar in males (47%) and females (46%), with abstinence (teetotal) levels higher in females (15%) than males (10%). There was a trend towards alcohol consumption at or below the recommended limits being associated with optimal activity compared with sedentary status in the middle and older age groups. However, in younger, middle age male and younger age female groups, alcohol consumption above the recommended limits was associated with optimal activity levels. Abstinence from alcohol consumption, except for the younger male group, showed a consistent trend of higher percentage of teetotallers associated with sedentary status in both males and females.

Table 4   Alcohol intake & activity levels (%) in the population

	Males						Females					
Age	16-34		35-54		55-70		16-34		35-54		55-70	
Activity	Sed	Opt	Sed	Opt	Sed	Opt	Sed	Opt	Sed	Opt	Sed	Opt
≤Recommended	37	35	45	50	41		56	40	38		43	49
≥Recommended		32		34								
Teetotal	26	32	23	26	15	14	9	16	8		6	
		3	3									
	12	13	10	7	17	7	15	14	18		14	
		34	22									

Diet and Physical Activity

The results of dietary intake classification for the respective ADNFS sedentary and optimal activity groups are presented in Table 5. Females generally had higher percentage intake of healthy food categories and lower percentage intake of less healthy food categories than males, although males and females showed a trend towards increased healthy food intake with increasing age. There were consistently clear patterns in the intake of healthy and less healthy food categories in both males and females across all age groups. Those eating a healthier diet were more likely to take optimal exercise and those eating a less healthy diet were associated with sedentary status. The percentage intake of healthy food categories associated with optimal activity levels were higher compared with sedentary status, and conversely, the percentage intake of less healthy food categories associated with sedentary status were higher compared with optimal levels of activity.

Table 5   Dietary pattern & activity levels (%) in the population

	Males						Females					
Age	16-34		35-54		55-70		16-34		35-54		55-70	
Activity	Sed	Opt	Sed	Opt	Sed	Opt	Sed	Opt	Sed	Opt	Sed	Opt
Healthy	22	29	27	39	27	36	27	45	38	52		
Unhealthy		36		52								
	24	20	20	13	24	17	17	9	14	14		
		18		14								

4 Discussion

In contrast with other studies (Allied Dunbar National Fitness Survey, 1993; Health Survey for England 1993, Health Education Authority, 1993) the finding that relatively large proportions of adults are sedentary (30% 16-34 years, 48% 35-54 years, 62% 55-70 years) is a cause for concern. Indeed only 19% of adults achieved optimal age/sex physical activity levels needed for health benefit. Furthermore, since overweight/obesity, smoking and less healthy dietary intake were associated with sedentary status, the potential cumulative health risk is considerable (Eammons et al., 1994). In contrast, however, 65% of adults usually achieved 30 minutes of daily activity which has the potential to confer some health benefits (American College of Sports Medicine, 1993). Moreover, if these large numbers of adults who achieved daily activity levels which are health protective, could be persuaded to make changes in the other lifestyle factors which influence health, the potential exists for population based health improvement. It is important therefore, to promote a clear, combined activity and lifestyle health promotion message in order to produce public health gain.

5 References

Allied Dunbar National Fitness Survey, Main Findings (1993) The Health Education Authority, The Sports Council, London.

American College of Sports Medicine (1993), **Position Statement on Physical Activity and Public Health**. ACSM, Indianapolis.

Casperson, C.J. Christenson, G.M. and Pollard, R.A. (1986) **Status of the 1990 Physical Fitness Objectives: evidence for the NHIS 1985**. Public Health Reports, 101, 587-92.

Conway, T.L. and Cronan, T.A. (1992) **Smoking, Exercise and Physical Fitness**. Preventive Medicine, 21, 723-24.

Eammons, K.M. Marcus, B.H. Linnan, L. Rossi, J.S. and Abrams, D.B. (1994) **Mechanisms in multiple risk factor interventions: smoking, physical activity and dietary fat intake among manufacturing workers**. Preventative Medicine, 23, 481-89.

Fentem, P.H. Bassey, E.J. and Turnbull N.B. (1988) **The New Case for Exercise**. The Sports Council and HEA, London.

Goldberg, R. Burchfiel, C.M. Reed, D.M. Wergowske, G. and Chiu, D. (1994) **A prospective study of the health effects of alcohol consumption in middle aged and elderly men: the Honolulu Heart Program**. Circulation, 89, 651-59.

Hallfrish, J. Drinkwater, D.T. Wuller, D.C. Fleg, J. Busby-Whitehead, M.L. Andres, R. and Goldberg, A. (1994) **Physical and training status and diet intake in active and sedentary older men**. Nutrition Research, 14, 817-27.

Health Survey for England (1993) Office of Population Census and Survey, Social Survey Division, London.

Health Education Authority National Survey of Activity and Health (1993) The Health Education Authority, London.

Roberts, H. Dengler, R. and Zamorski, A. (1994). **Technical Report to Trent Regional Health Authority, 1993/1994: Trent Health Lifestyle Survey**, 1994. Department of Public Health Medicine and Epidemiology, Medical Faculty, Queen's Medical Centre, Nottingham, NG7 2UH.

44 Exercise behaviour, physical fitness and coronary heart disease risk factors status: evidence from a worksite screening programme

J.P. Wyse and T.H. Mercer

1 Introduction

The health benefits attained from habitual physical activity are well documented and have been extensively reviewed (Bouchard et al., 1990, 1994; Powell et al., 1987). These reviews have identified, following analysis of numerous epidemiological studies, that physical inactivity appears to be an independent primary risk factor for coronary heart disease (CHD) of a magnitude similar to that of the more "traditional" risk factors (namely hypercholesterolaemia, hypertension and cigarette smoking) (Powell et al., 1987; Berlin and Colditz, 1990).

Paffenbarger et al. (1990) proposed the theoretical calculation of Community Attributable Risk of CHD, an estimate of the potential reductions in death rates in a population if the unfavourable behaviours had been converted to more favourable ones. These researchers estimated that had the subjects in their study expended 2000 or more kilocalories (8372 kJ) per week in physical activities (walking, stair-climbing, recreational activities), then the risk of first heart attack would have been reduced by 23%, whilst the risk of death would have been reduced by 16%. These figures are greater than those for other CHD risk factor behaviours, highlighting the significance of being physically inactive.

Physical (cardiorespiratory) fitness has also been proposed as a risk factor for CHD (Blair et al., 1989), suggesting that those individuals with lower levels of fitness are at higher risk for CHD. Although more recent evidence points towards a significant inverse relationship between physical fitness and CHD risk, physical fitness has not yet been clearly established as an independent risk factor for CHD (Barlow et al., 1993, 1994; Blair et al., 1993).

Despite the less clearly established role of cardiorespiratory fitness in delivering health benefits compared to physical activity (exercise behaviour) status, very few studies have examined these factors concurrently. Therefore the purpose of this study was to investigate the relationship between exercise behaviour, physical fitness levels and CHD risk factors in a worksite community.

2 Methods

2.1 Subjects
Subjects for this study comprised 117 male and 143 female university employees. Subject characteristics are displayed in Table 1. All subjects voluntarily presented themselves at a worksite CHD risk factor check. This service was offered free of charge on an annual basis to all employees. The sample in the present study represented approximately 17% of the total workforce.

2.1 Exercise Behaviour
Exercise behaviour was assessed via self-report using the Godin and Shephard's Leisure-Time Questionnaire (1985). Subjects reported their weekly frequency of participation (for a minimum of 15 minutes per session per week) in exercise behaviours deemed to be of "Strenuous", "Moderate", and "Mild" intensities.

2.2 Physical Fitness
Physical (cardiorespiratory) fitness was determined by means of submaximal cycle ergometry, according to the Young Men's Christian Association [YMCA] multi-stage protocol (Golding et al., 1988). This incremental test begins at an exercise intensity of 25 Watts for three minutes, with the intensity of subsequent stages being determined by heart rate responses, assessed using short-range radio telemetry (Polar Electro Sport Tester PE-3000, Kempele, Finland) during the last 15 s of the stage. Following the completion of three stages, an estimation of maximal oxygen consumption (VO_2 max) was calculated, by the visual extrapolation of heart rate responses against exercise intensity (Golding et al., 1988).

2.3 Risk Factors for CHD
The following CHD risk factors were assessed:
   (a) Serum cholesterol levels were assessed using blood samples drawn from subjects, analysed in a Reflotron Clinical Chemistry Analyser (calibrated daily and subject to external quality control bi-monthly).
   (b) Blood pressure (BP) was assessed at rest in the seated position, using a Accoson sphygmomanometer attached to the left upper arm. Both systolic BP (1st phase) and diastolic BP (5th phase) blood pressure were measured.
   (c) Body Mass Index (BMI: $kg.m^{-2}$) was calculated following the measurement of height (to the nearest cm, using a Seca Stadiometer), and body mass (to the nearest 100 g, using an Avery Electronic weigh scale).
   (b) Percentage Body Fat (BF%) was derived from the prediction formula of Durnin and Wormersley (1974), using the sum of skinfold measurements. The skinfolds were assessed using Harpenden skinfold calipers.

2.4 Data Analysis
Subjects were subsequently classified on the basis of their exercise behaviour scores into three groups. These sex-specific groups were formed on the basis of responses related to the "Strenuous", "Moderate", and "Mild" intensities enquired into by the Leisure Time Questionnaire. The groups were subsequently termed 'INACTIVE', 'IRREGULAR EXERCISERS' (less than three exercise sessions per week), and 'REGULAR EXERCISERS' (three or more exercise sessions per week).

Similarly, for physical fitness status, subjects were classified into three groups. These were termed 'LOW FITNESS', 'INTERMEDIATE FITNESS', and 'HIGH FITNESS', formed on the basis of sex-specific tertiles. Multivariate analysis of covariance (using a 3 x 3 design, with age as a covariate) was used to determine whether differences existed in terms of physical activity or physical fitness. Univariate follow-up tests (using ANCOVA, with age as a covariate) were employed to investigate further the nature of any differences.

3 Results

Subjects characteristics are displayed in Table 1 for males and females.

Multivariate analysis of covariance revealed that significant differences existed in terms of the CHD risk factors between groups according to fitness and exercise behaviour status. This was observed for both males (*Wilks' Lambda* > 0.70, F > 4.04, P < 0.001) and females (*Wilks' Lambda* > 0.75, F > 4.18, P < 0.001).

Univariate follow-up tests, for males, revealed significant differences (F > 4.10, P < 0.05) between fitness groups, with the highest risk factor scores observed in 'LOW FITNESS' versus 'HIGH FITNESS' groups. These differences were revealed for BF%, BMI, and both systolic BP and diastolic BP (see Table 2). Significant differences (F > 9.15, P < 0.001) were also revealed between females in 'LOW FITNESS' versus 'HIGH FITNESS' groups. However, these differences were only evident for BMI and BF% (see Table 2).

Table 1. Subject characteristics: Mean (S.D.).

Variable	Males		Females	
Age (years)	42.1	(10.6)	38.9	(9.6)
Height (m)	1.77	(0.07)	1.63	(0.06)
Body mass (kg)	75.8	(10.5)	62.5	(9.7)
Exercise Behaviour: (no. of 15 min sessions)				
"Strenuous" Exercise	1.23	(1.66)	1.05	(1.89)
"Moderate" Exercise	2.35	(3.40)	1.34	(1.46)
"Mild" Exercise	2.17	(3.28)	1.29	(1.75)
Physical Fitness:				
VO_2 max (ml.kg^{-1}.min^{-1})	42.8	(9.2)	35.3	(8.1)
CHD Risk Factors:				
Serum Cholesterol (mmol.l^{-1})	5.13	(1.01)	5.02	(1.02)
Systolic Blood Pressure (mm Hg)	118	(10)	113	(9)
Diastolic Blood Pressure (mm Hg)	77	(8)	72	(8)
Body Mass Index (kg.m^{-1})	24.3	(3.2)	23.5	(3.3)
Body Fat (%)	15.5	(4.7)	23.5	(5.6)

Table 2. CHD Risk Factor scores for cardiorespiratory fitness and exercise behaviour groups: Mean (S.D.).*

Males					Females			
			PHYSICAL FITNESS					
'LOW'		'HIGH'				'LOW'		'HIGH'
25.0	(2.5)	23.1	(2.3)	BMI (kg.m^{-2})	24.9	(3.8)	22.0	(3.5)
18.1	(4.5)	12.6	(4.0)	BF% (%)	26.5	(5.1)	20.9	(5.0)
121	(9)	116	(10)	SBP (mm Hg)	---		---	
80	(8)	75	(8)	DBP (mm Hg)	---		---	
			EXERCISE BEHAVIOUR					
'INACTIVE'		'REGULAR'				'INACTIVE'		'REGULAR'
			"Strenuous" Exercise:					
17.0	(4.3)	13.3	(4.7)	BF% (%)	25.2	(5.2)	21.7	(4.0)
			"Moderate" Exercise:					
119	(9)	115	(10)	SBP (mm Hg)	115	(9)	111	(8)

* Note: Only significant differences ($P < 0.05$) are displayed.

Analysis of data in relation to exercise behaviour status revealed similar results. The highest CHD risk factor scores were observed in those subjects categorised as 'INACTIVE' versus 'REGULAR EXERCISERS' (see Table 2). Specific differences were observed for BF% ($F > 5.68$, $P < 0.01$) at the "Strenuous" level of exercise behaviour, and systolic BP ($F > 3.01$, $P < 0.05$) at the "Moderate" level of exercise behaviour, as illustrated in Table 2.

4 Discussion

The results of this study imply that both physical activity (exercise behaviour) and physical fitness are important in terms of their relationship with individual risk factors for CHD. This evidence supports the findings of Rohm Young and Steinhardt (1993), who reported that both low physical activity and low physical fitness were associated with a higher CHD risk score. The present study further confirms the observations of these researchers, that it was cardiorespiratory fitness and not exercise behaviour or physical activity that was more closely related to single coronary risk factor scores (percentage body fat, smoking status, and high-density lipoprotein cholesterol). Similar results had been suggested previously by Lochen and Ramussen (1992), who reported that physical fitness had a stronger relationship than leisure-time physical activity with coronary risk factors. In addition, it has been suggested that vigorous physical activity may be more advantageous in reducing cardiac morbidity (Kaminsky et al., 1994) and mortality risk (Lee et al., 1993) than non-vigorous activity.

It thus appears that physical activity must be sufficient to influence cardiorespiratory fitness in order to produce statistically significant risk-reducing benefits. This conclusion seems both intuitively appealing and biologically plausible given the well-documented relationship between the two constructs (American College of Sports Medicine, 1990).

These data also provide tentative support for the existence of intensity-specific exercise-CHD risk factor relationships. In particular, these results suggest that percentage body fat might be related to "Strenuous" exercise behaviour. This seems surprising, in view of the reported relationship between body composition and low-to-moderate exercise, due to increased duration of lipid metabolism at the expense of exercise intensity (Bray, 1990). Furthermore, these results suggest that blood pressure might be linked to levels of "Moderate" exercise behaviour. This confirms the observations of Hagberg (1990) who suggested that moderate-intensity exercise training (40% to 60% of $\dot{V}O_2$ max) may be as effective as is higher-intensity training.

The findings of the present study are limited somewhat, since subjects were relatively healthy self-selected volunteers drawn from a predominantly white-collar (University-based) workforce (see Table 1).

In summary, this study has confirmed that both exercise behaviour and cardiorespiratory fitness appear to be important discriminators with regard to CHD risk. Moreover, these findings, in their support for the elevated importance of cardiorespiratory fitness in coronary risk factor development, have potentially significant ramifications for Public Health Promotion strategy. Such findings perhaps somewhat controversially may dilute existing Public Health advice, which advocates the importance of the process of exercise behaviour over the product of cardiorespiratory fitness.

5 Acknowledgements

The first author was funded by the Centre for Health and Exercise Research Scholarship from the School of Sciences, Staffordshire University.

6 References

American College of Sports Medicine. (1990) The recommended quantity and quality of exercise for developing and maintaining cardiorespiratory and muscular fitness in healthy adults. **Medicine and Science in Sports and Exercise**, 22, 265-274.

Barlow, C.E., Kohl, H.W., and Blair, S.N. (1993) Physical fitness and cardiovascular disease mortality in men with chronic disease. **Medicine and Science in Sports and Exercise**, 25, S75.

Barlow, C.E., Kohl, H.W., and Blair, S.N. (1994) Change in physical fitness and all-cause mortality in men with chronic disease. **Medicine and Science in Sports and Exercise**, 26, S60.

Berlin, J.A. and Colditz, G.A. (1990) A meta-analysis of physical activity in the prevention of coronary heart disease. **American Journal of Epidemiology**, 132, 612-628.

Blair, S.N., Barlow, C.E., and Kohl, H.W. (1993) Change in physical fitness and all-cause mortality in apparently healthy men. **Medicine and Science in Sports and Exercise**, 25, S75.

Blair, S.N., Kohl, H.W., Paffenbarger, R.S.,Jr., Cooper, K.H., and Gibbons, L.W. (1989) Physical fitness and all-cause mortality: A prospective study of healthy men and women. **Journal of the American Medical Association**, 262, 2395-2401.

Bouchard, C., Shephard, R.J., and Stephens, T. (1994) **Physical Activity, Fitness, and Health: A Consensus of Current Knowledge.** Human Kinetics, Champaign, IL.

Bouchard, C., Shephard, R.J., Stephens, T., Sutton, J., and McPherson, B. (1990) **Exercise, Fitness, and Health: A Consensus of Current Knowledge.** Human Kinetics, Champaign, IL.

Bray, G.A. (1990) Exercise and obesity, in **Exercise, Fitness, and Health: A Consensus of Current Knowledge.** (eds. C. Bouchard, R.J. Shephard, T. Stephens, J.R., Sutton, J., and B.D. McPherson), Human Kinetics, Champaign, IL, pp. 487-510.

Durnin, J.G.V.A. and Wormersley, J. (1974) Body fat assessed from total body density and its estimation from skinfold thickness: Measurement on 481 men and women aged 16 to 72 years. **British Journal of Nutrition,** 32, 77-85.

Godin, G. and Shephard, R.J. (1985) A simple method to assess exercise behaviour in the community. **Canadian Journal of Applied Sport Sciences,** 10, 141-146.

Golding, L.A., Myers, C.R., and Sinning, W.E. (1988) **Y's Way To Physical Fitness.** Human Kinetics, Champaign, IL, pp. 89-106.

Hagberg, J.M. (1990) Exercise, fitness, and hypertension, in **Exercise, Fitness, and Health: A Consensus of Current Knowledge.** (eds. C. Bouchard, R.J., Shephard, T., Stephens, J.R., Sutton, J., and B.D. McPherson), Human Kinetics, Champaign, IL, pp. 75-101.

Kaminsky, L.A., Whalley, M.H., Miller, C.R., and Getchell, L.H. (1994) Vigorous exercise program participation associated with reduced cardiac morbidity in men. **Medicine and Science in Sports and Exercise,** 26, S218.

Lee, I-M., Hseish, C-C., and Paffenbarger, R.S.,Jr. (1993) Vigorous physical activity, non-vigorous physical activity and risk of mortality in men. **Medicine and Science in Sports and Exercise,** 25, S167.

Lochen, M-L. and Ramussen, K. (1992) The Trosmo study: Physical fitness, self-reported physical activity, and their relationship to other coronary risk factors. **Journal of Epidemiology and Community Health,** 46, 103-107.

Paffenbarger, R.S.,Jr., Hyde, R.T., and Wing, A.L. (1990) Physical activity and physical fitness as determinants of health and longevity, in **Exercise, Fitness, and Health: A Consensus of Current Knowledge.** (eds. C. Bouchard, R.J. Shephard, T., Stephens, J.R., Sutton, and B.D. McPherson), Human Kinetics, Champaign, IL, pp. 33-48.

Powell, K.E., Thompson, P.D., Caspersen, C.J., and Kendrick, J. (1987) Physical activity and the incidence of coronary heart disease. **Annual Review of Public Health,** 8, 253-287.

Rohm Young, D. and Steinhardt, M.A. (1993) The importance of physical fitness versus physical activity for coronary artery disease risk factors: A cross-sectional analysis. **Research Quarterly for Exercise and Sport,** 64, 377-384.

45 Exercise prescription for cardiac rehabilitation
M.A. Cooke, J.H. Chapman and M.L. Fysh

1 Introduction

Exercise prescription based on age-predicted maximum heart
rate (APMHR) is both a practical and an effective method of
exercise programming (McArdle et al., 1994). To induce
cardiovascular benefits, aerobic activity of an intensity
of 70 to 85% APMHR is recommended three times per week, for
a duration of 20 to 30 min (American College of Sports
Medicine, 1991).

The various activities which make up rehabilitation
exercise programmes (REP) for cardiac patients are often
prescribed on the basis of a circuit (Stewart et al., 1988
and Haennel et al., 1991). Within REP, the resistive
exercises suggested by Verrill et al. (1992) can be
performed alongside the more dynamic exercises of cycling
and stair-climbing recommended by Williams (1994). For the
cardiac patient myocardial oxygen demand is an important
consideration. It increases during exercise due to an
interaction between changes in myocardial contractility,
increases in heart rate and changes in arterial blood
pressure (McArdle et al., 1994). Those activities with
associated high myocardial oxygen demand but low oxygen
uptake ($\dot{V}O_2$) need to be carefully monitored (Coplan et al.,
1986).

Previous physiological evaluations of REP (Greer et al.,
1980), have used bulky gas analysers and electrocardiograph
(ECG) systems with restrictive leads which have prevented
normal movement patterns. The Cosmed K2 is a miniaturised,
telemetric gas analysis system designed for measuring heart
rate and VO_2 in the field (Concu et al., 1992; Lucia et
al., 1993) and allows unrestricted movement during an
exercise programme.

Graded exercise testing (GXT) is commonly used to assess
the cardiorespiratory response and exercise capacity of
cardiac patients prior to inclusion in Phase II (early-
outpatient) REP (Fletcher et al., 1990). Such assessments
consist of continuous, multi-stage exercise tests,
performed on a treadmill or cycle ergometer which place
progressively greater demands on the cardiorespiratory

system. The end-point of continuous graded exercise tests is varied and includes muscle fatigue, angina, dyspnea, exercise hypotension, arrhythmias and S-T segment depression (Hellerstein and Franklin, 1984). If clinical symptoms do not appear, the test may be terminated on achieving a heart rate of 85% APMHR.

Graded exercise testing acts as a guide for setting the intensity of exercise for out-patient programmes (Hall, 1993). The validity of using heart rate information obtained from GXT as a tool for prescribing the exercise intensity for REP depends, to some extent, on the relationships between heart rate and $\dot{V}O_2$ during the continuous exercise of GXT and the intermittent activity of REP. By using the Cosmed K2 it is possible to compare the VO_2 and heart rate relationships during REP with the responses to the GXT.

The aims of this investigation were to use the Cosmed K2 to a) identify activities which might induce a greater myocardial oxygen demand with little concomitant increase in aerobic metabolism and b) assess the appropriateness of using heart rate information obtained from the GXT in the prescription of REP.

2 Methods

2.1 Subjects
Four healthy, non-smoking, female volunteers (mean age = 20.8 years, range 20-22 years) gave verbal informed consent prior to the investigation. Anthropometric data including height (mean height = 1.66 m, range 1.60-1.71 m) and body mass (mean body mass = 59.0 kg, range 50-65 kg) were collected. Age-predicted maximum heart rate was calculated for each of the subjects using the following equation (McArdle et al., 1994):

$$220 - \text{age in years} \tag{1}$$

2.2 Cardiac Rehabilitation Exercise Programme
Activities were chosen which would result in a range of cardiovascular and musculoskeletal demands and were typical of activities found in cardiac rehabilitation programmes. Cycling and step-ups are examples of dynamic activities which are non-weight bearing and weight bearing, respectively. Sit to stand and medicine ball passing involve muscle groups used in everyday activities whilst star jumps are classified as a whole-body activity. Each activity formed part of a circuit (Figure 1) which was continuously monitored. All activities were performed for 2 min, followed by a rest period of 30 s, before progressing to the next station. The range of intensities was achieved either through an increase in the number of repetitions or by an increase in work rate during cycling.

2.3 Graded exercise testing

A graded exercise test was performed on a treadmill (Ergo ES1, Woodway GmbH, Weil am Rhein, Germany) until a test end-point of 85% APMHR had been reached. The Bruce protocol, of an initial grade of 10% and 0.76 m.s^{-1} for 3 min, followed by increments in the grade and/or speed every 3 min, was adopted during the exercise test. The 0% and 5% grade were omitted in accordance with Bruce (1971) as all subjects originated from a healthy population.

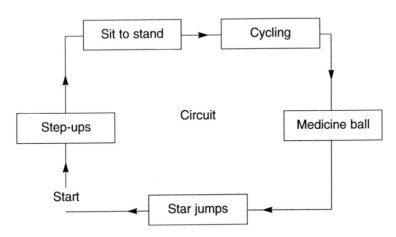

Figure 1. Activities performed during the circuit.

2.4 Metabolic Evaluation

Heart rate (beats·min^{-1}) and $\dot{V}O_2$ (l·min^{-1}) were measured throughout, using the Cosmed K2, (Cosmed, Rome, Italy). The system uses a face mask containing a 28 mm photoelectric gas turbine for volume measurement and an oxygen electrode for the determination of expired oxygen content. Signals were transmitted by radio-telemetry, from a light-weight portable transmitter unit worn around the chest and back.

3 Data analysis

For each activity, the mean heart rate, $\dot{V}O_2$ and oxygen pulse were calculated. A one-way analysis of variance (ANOVA) was used to evaluate inter-activity differences in HR, $\dot{V}O_2$ and oxygen pulse values recorded during the circuit. A post hoc Tukey test was then performed to identify differences between activities.

Heart rate and $\dot{V}O_2$ relationships during GXT and REP were expressed as linear regression equations for each subject. Heart rates corresponding to the upper and lower limits of an effective training zone (70 to 85% APMHR) were used to calculate the corresponding values of $\dot{V}O_2$ during these two different types of exercise. A one-way ANOVA compared $\dot{V}O_2$

values for GXT and REP at 70% and 85% APMHR.

4 Results

During REP, significant differences in heart rate, $\dot{V}O_2$ and oxygen pulse were observed between activities (Table 1). Star-jumps resulted in significantly higher heart rates ($P<0.001$) than all other activities. A significantly higher$\dot{V}O_2$ ($P<0.01$) was only observed when star-jumps were compared with medicine ball passing. Oxygen pulse was found to be significantly higher during sit to stand and star-jumps ($P<0.01$) when compared to step-ups and medicine ball passing, respectively.

Heart rates ranged from 111 to 179 beats·min^{-1} during the GXT and from 129 to 186 beats·min^{-1} during REP. Significantly higher values of $\dot{V}O_2$ were found to occur during GXT when compared to REP at 70% ($P<0.01$) and 85% APMHR ($P<0.005$) (Table 2.

Table 1. Heart rate, oxygen uptake and oxygen pulse (mean ± standard deviation) during REP

Activity	Heart rate (beats·min^{-1})	Oxygen Uptake (l.min^{-1})	Oxygen pulse (ml.beat^{-1})
Medicine ball	145 ± 10	0.76 ± 0.14	5.28 ± 0.99
Step-ups	151 ± 18	0.91 ± 0.22	5.92 ± 0.69
Cycling	143 ± 10	0.93 ± 0.10	6.49 ± 0.06
Sit to stand	143 ± 6	1.08 ± 0.25	7.35 ± 0.15
Star-jumps	175 ± 8	1.33 ± 0.17	7.60 ± 0.96

Table 2. Oxygen uptake (mean ± standard deviation) at 70% and 85% APMHR during REP and GXT

	Oxygen uptake at 70% APMHR (l.min^{-1})	Oxygen uptake at 85% APMHR (l.min^{-1})
REP	0.79 ± 0.07	1.11 ± 0.08
GXT	0.94 ± 0.09	1.45 ± 0.13

5 Discussion

According to Williams (1994) even seemingly innocent activities should be carefully considered before they are included in REP. By measuring $\dot{V}O_2$ during an unrestricted REP, more information can be gained about the relative benefits and risks of different components of the programme.

The low $\dot{V}O_2$ and oxygen pulse of medicine ball passing was as expected, due to the small muscle mass involved in this activity (Chapman and Elliott, 1988). Myocardial oxygen demand is further increased in arm exercise by the associated blood pressure rises which are greater than those observed during lower body exercise (Miles et al., 1989). The risks associated with medicine ball passing need to be balanced with the benefits of arm strengthening as part of the rehabilitation process (Stewart et al., 1988).

The dynamic activity of cycling is generally recommended for cardiac patients (Williams, 1994). The $\dot{V}O_2$ measured during this non-weight bearing activity was not significantly different from any other activity. The highest oxygen pulse was observed during star-jumps which also resulted in the most elevated heart rates. The strenuous nature of this activity needs careful monitoring by the exercise therapist.

The high heart rates which occurred during star-jumps represented 87% APMHR for these subjects. All heart rate and $\dot{V}O_2$ results from REP were compared to the heart rate and $\dot{V}O_2$ relationships from GXT to see if by prescribing exercise at a percentage APMHR, this would result in different oxygen uptakes. Significantly higher $\dot{V}O_2$ values were observed during continuous exercise at 70% and 85% APMHR. These results have implications for prescribing exercise heart rates to patients undergoing cardiac rehabilitation exercise programmes which are essentially intermittent in nature. It is possible that a target heart rate prescribed from a graded exercise test will result in lower $\dot{V}O_2$ values than expected while performing intermittent circuit-type activities.

6 Acknowledgements

Acknowledgement is given to the valuable assistance of Claire Kettlewell and Ceri-Lynne Williams during this investigation.

7 References

American College of Sports Medicine (1991) **Guidelines for Exercise Testing and Prescription.** Lea and Febiger, Philadelphia, p. 106.

Bruce, R.A. (1971) Exercise testing of patients with coronary artery disease. **Annals of Clinical Research,** 3, 323-332.

Chapman, J.H. and Elliott, P.W.R. (1988) Cardiovascular effects of static and dynamic exercise. **European Journal of Applied Physiology,** 58, 152-157.

Coplan, N.L. Gleim, G.W. and Nicholas, J.A. (1986)

Principles of exercise prescription for patients with coronary artery disease. **American Heart Journal**, 112, 145-149.

Concu, A. Marcello, C. Rocchitta, A. Ciutu, C. and Esposito, A. (1992) Telemetric measurement of heart-rate-matched oxygen consumption during volleyball games. **Medicine and Science Research**, 20, 243-245.

Fletcher, G.F. Froelicher, V.F. Hartley, L.H. Haskell, W.L. and Pollock, M.L. (1990) Exercise standards: A statement for health professionals from the American Heart Association. **Circulation**, 82, 2286-2321.

Greer, M. Weber, T. Dimick, S. and Ratliff, R. (1980) Physiological responses to low intensity cardiac rehabilitation exercise. **Physical Therapy**, 60, 1147-1151.

Haennel, R.G. Quinney, H.A. and Kappacoda, C.T. (1991) Effects of hydralic circuit training following coronary artery by-pass surgery. **Medicine and Science in Sports and Exercise**, 23, 158-165.

Hall, L.K. (1993) Exercise prescription for cardiac patients (ed L.K. Hall). **Developing and Managing Cardiac Rehabilitation Programs**. Human Kinetics, Champaign, Illinois, pp. 73-83.

Hellerstein, H.K. and Franklin, B.A. (1984) Evaluating the cardiac patient for exercise therapy:role of exercise testing. **Clinics in Sports Medicine**, 3, 317-393.

Lucia, A. Fleck, S.J. Gotshall, R.W. and Kearney, J.T. (1993) Validity and reliability of the Cosmed K2 instrument. **International Journal of Sports Medicine**, 14, 380-386.

McArdle,W.D., Katch,F.I.and Katch, V.L. (1994) **Exercise Physiology: Energy Nutrition and Human Performance**. Lea and Febiger, Philadelphia, p. 250 and 360.

Miles, D.S. Cox, and H. Bomze, J. (1989) Cardiovascular responses to upper body exercise in normals and cardiac patients. **Medicine and Science in Sports and Exercise**, 21, S126-S131.

Stewart, K. Mason, M. and Kelemen, N. (1988) Three year participation in circuit weight training improves muscular strength and self efficacy in cardiac patients. **Journal of Cardiopulmonary Rehabilitation**, 8, 292-296.

Verill, D. Shoup, E. McElveen, G. Witt, K. and Berhey, D. (1992) Resistive exercise training in cardiac patients. **Sports Medicine**, 13, 171-193.

Williams, M. (1994) **Exercise Testing and Training in the Elderly Cardiac Patient, Current Issues in Cardiac Rehabilitation Series**. Human Kinetics, Leeds, p. 31.

46 Isoinertial evaluation of low back fatigue in Belgian nursing personnel with and without a history of low back problems

D. Caboor, E. Zinzen, M. Szpalski, P. Van Roy and J.P. Clarys

1 Introduction

Physical fitness is a component of health and the overall functioning capacity is a parameter for the assessment of physical fitness. There is evidence to suggest that the functioning capacity and an individual's body type can have a moderating effect on job preferences or on the performance level. The parameters of musculo-skeletal operating capacity are torque, velocity, endurance and co-ordination. The velocity of the movement of the trunk is a very delicate variable in low-back problems (LBP) (Marras and Wongsam, 1986; Gomez et al., 1991; Szpalski et al., 1991). Endurance tests show a decrease of velocity and a loss of co-ordination (Parnianpour et al., 1989; Szpalski and Hayez,1992).

Nursing personnel show a very high frequency of LBP. This job population performs frequent and varied lifting tasks during their daily work. Complementary to the quality of loading, the effect of peak spinal compression and shear forces, the summation of repetitive submaximal loading, the effect of fatigue, all may influence the incidence of LBP.

The purpose of this study was to investigate which parameters during a fatigue test of low back function in the sagittal plane, are related to LBP in nursing personnel.

2 Methods

Eleven male (3 with and 8 without LBP) and twenty-one female nurses (7 with and 14 without LBP) from two different hospitals in Belgium, volunteered for the study. The history of LBP was based on life-time prevalence. The demographic description of these subjects is listed in Table 1.

Each subject performed twenty-five repetitions of forward and backward bending on the Isostation B-200®, a triaxial dynamometer (Isotechnologies, Hillsborough Inc., NC, USA). The velocity of performance was maximal, the range of motion was maximal in forward bending and limited at 15° backward bending. The resistance was 50% of the maximal isometric torque in forward bending.

Table 1. The population: demographic description

Population	n=32	Body mass (kg)	Height (cm)
female nurses	n=21	62.2 ± 5.3	167.2 ± 5.1
without LBP	n=14	61.8 ± 4.5	167.2 ± 5.2
with LBP	n= 7	63.0 ± 6.8	167.2 ± 5.4
male nurses	n=11	74.0 ± 8.5	176.4 ± 5.1
without LBP	n= 8	76.5 ± 7.5	177.2 ± 1.5
with LBP	n= 3	67.3 ± 8.3	174.3 ±10.7

The recorded parameters for each movement were: maximal torque, average torque, impulse, maximal velocity, average velocity, and power.

For each variable we compared the mean of the second to sixth performance (first 5) with the mean of the twenty-first to twenty-fifth performance (last 5), using a paired Student t-test ($p<0.05$).

Using a two-way ANOVA and a one-way ANOVA with the Scheffe-F post-hoc test, we examined the significant ($p<0.05$) differences between the groups with and without LBP.

3 Results

The mean values of the maximal isometric torque are described in Table 2.

Table 2. Average maximal isometric torque in forward and backward bending (N.m), and the Ratio backward/forward bending of the average maximal isometric torque

	Forward bending	Backward bending	Ratio
female nurses	75.1±21.5	-117.3±23.9	1.56
without LBP	72.2±25.1	-112.0±22.8	1.55
with LBP	80.8±10.7	-127.8±24.0	1.58
male nurses	125.5±33.8	-161.2±33.7	1.28
without LBP	136.6±33.1	-171.5±26.7	1.25
with LBP	95.7± 7.3	-133.9±40.6	1.39

For the female subjects (n=21) we found, regardless of LBP and only in forward bending, a significant decrease of torque (maximal and average), velocity (maximal and average) and power, and a significant increase of impulse (see Table 3).

Table 3. The results (mean values) of the performances of the female nurses

	Forward bending (1)	Forward bending (2)	Backward bending (1)	Backward bending (2)
Torque maximal (N.m)				
- LBP	54.0±16.3	52.8±12.3	48.9±12.1	47.0±12.0
+ LBP	56.1± 8,6	54.5± 8.0	51.0± 9.5	48.4± 9.9
Torque average (N.m)				
- LBP	44.4±10.9	43.8±11.4	36.7±11.0	36.6±10.7
+ LBP	46.6± 7.5	46.5± 7.8	39.2± 8.4	38.0± 8.2
Impulse (N.m.s)				
- LBP	44.2±13.5	49.7±15.3	31.8±11.0	33.5±11.3
+ LBP	45.4± 8.7	49.2±11.9	33.3± 7.0	36.9± 9.1
Velocity maximal (rad/s)				
- LBP	2.02±0.27	1.90±0.39	2.35±0.29	2.33±0.37
+ LBP	2.09±0.27	1.88±0.32	2.38±0.28	2.26±0.30
Velocity average (rad/s)				
- LBP	1.35±0.27	1.27±0.32	1.51±0.21	1.49±0.30
+ LBP	1.38±0.16	1.29±0.23	1.53±0.19	1.40±0.20
Power (N.m/s)				
- LBP	64.0±21.4	59.7±22.7	63.5±18.8	61.3±20.5
+ LBP	70.3±15.7	64.0±17.3	67.9±19.2	61.4±18.2

- LBP = without a history of LBP (n=14)
+ LBP = with a history of LBP (n=7)
(1) = the first 5 performances
(2) = the last 5 performances
± = standard deviation

The male nurses (n=11) showed different results for the subgroups: in the group with LBP none of the changes were significant. The subgroup without LBP indicated a significant increase of impulse both in forward and backward bending (see Table 4).

Table 4. The results (mean values) of the performances of the male nurses

	Forward bending (1)	Forward bending (2)	Backward bending (1)	Backward bending (2)
Torque maximal (N.m)				
- LBP	88.8±12.9	88.2±12.0	82.3±12.5	79.1±11.1
+ LBP	68.2± 7.2	71.0± 4.3	63.0± 7.0	63.2± 5.2
Torque average (N.m)				
- LBP	72.4±10.6	72.7±10.0	64.8±10.0	64.8± 9.8
+ LBP	56.9± 6.5	57.7± 3.7	49.5± 6.2	50.0± 4.4
Impulse (N.m.s)				
- LBP	59.3±11.2	62.5±14.3	48.7±11.9	51.5±13.7
+ LBP	48.4±13.6	54.3±17.4	38.9± 7.5	43.0± 9.2
Velocity maximal (rad/s)				
- LBP	2.89±0.43	2.77±0.48	2.95±0.57	2.93±0.61
+ LBP	2.39±0.59	2.49±0.57	2.47±0.65	2.60±0.57
Velocity average (rad/s)				
- LBP	1.81±0.28	1.79±0.33	1.94±0.39	1.91±0.51
+ LBP	1.53±0.41	1.60±0.41	1.57±0.42	1.65±0.44
Power (N.m/s)				
- LBP	141.9±32.7	140.3±35.2	138.6±35.6	138.6±47.9
+ LBP	87.3±20.7	94.8±20.8	86.3±27.7	94.3±29.2

- LBP = without a history of LBP (n=8)
+ LBP = with a history of LBP (n=3)
(1) = the first 5 performances
(2) = the last 5 performances
± = standard deviation

No significant differences between the groups with and without LBP were found.

Table 5. The Ratio backward/forward bending for average torque and average velocity at the begin- and end performances

Ratio	average torque (1)	average torque (2)	average velocity (1)	average velocity (2)
female nurses	0.82	0.82	1.12	1.16
male nurses	0.88	0.88	1.05	1.05

(1) = the first 5 performances
(2) = the last 5 performances

For the torque and velocity variables we found no significant differences between the level of fatigue of the forward bending muscles and the level of fatigue of the backward bending muscles, as shown by the ratio backward/forward bending in Table 5.

4 Discussion and Conclusion

The results of the isoinertial testing in this nursing population indicate a significant level of fatigue caused by the summation of repetitive submaximal performances during sagittal trunk movements, but we did not find a significant difference in torque and velocity between the fatigue of the flexor and extensor muscles of the trunk. These results confirm the hypothesis of Parnianpour et al. (1989) and the study of Szpalski et al. (1992), where they refuted the supposition that fatigue starts earlier and becomes greater in the flexors than in the extensors. This assumption is deduced from isokinetic studies, performed with a low velocity of 0.524 rad/s (Smidt et al., 1983; Langrana et al., 1984). The combination of the data of torque and velocity is necessary for a correct evaluation of low back fatigue.

The data of this sample suggest that none of the measured parameters seems to have an impact on the occurrence of LBP. An explanation can be found in the lifetime prevalence as an indication of LBP, a history of LBP. We can imagine that other studies, using a population with acute LBP, indicate significant differences for these variables. A group with acute LBP or a group with a history of LBP will show different attitudes and strategies at the moment of examination on the triaxial dynamometer.

The female data suggest that the subgroups with and without LBP have an almost identical pattern of back fatigue, and we find the same tendency in male nurses without LBP. The data of the male nurses with an LBP-history revealed a certain coping strategy concerning movements of the lower back by taking a more prudent start.

5 Acknowledgements

The authors would like to acknowledge the "Belgian Federal Services for Scientific, Technical and Cultural matters".

6 References

Gomez, T. Beach, G. Cooke, C. Hrudey, W. and Goyert, P. (1986) Normative database for trunk range of motion, strength, velocity and endurance with the Isostation B-200 Lumbar dynamometer. **Spine**, 16, 1, 15-21.

Langana, N. Lee, C.K. Alexander, H. and Mayott, C.W. (1984) Quantitative assessment of back strength using isokinetic testing. **Spine**, 9, 287-290.

Marras, W.S. and Wongsam P.E. (1986) Flexibility and velocity of normal and impaired lumbar spine. **Physical Medecine and Rehabilitation**, 67, 176-187.

Parnianpour, M. Li, F. Nordin, M. and Kahanovitz, N. (1989) A database of isoinertial trunk strength tests against resistance levels in sagittal, frontal and tranverse planes in normale male subjects. **Spine**, 14, 409-411.

Smidt, G.L. Herring, T. Amundsen, L. Rogers, M. Russel, A. and Lehmann, T. (1983) Assessment of abdominal and back extensor function, a quantitative approach and results for chronic low-back patients. **Spine**, 8, 211-219.

Szpalski, M. and Hayez, J.P. (1992) How many days of bed rest for acute low back pain? Objective assessment of trunk function. **European Spine Journal**, 1, 29-31.

Szpalski, M. Hayez, J.P. Debaize, J.P. and Spengler, D. (1991) Velocity of trunk movements: most sensitive variable of low back condition. A prospective study. in **Abstracts book** of **The International Society of the Study of the Lumbar Spine**, Heidelberg, p. 13.

Szpalski, M. Ray, J. Keller, T.S. Spengler, D. Hayez, J.P. and Debaize J.P. (1992) Evolution of trunk flexors and extensors fatigue during high velocity sagittal movements. in **Abstracts book** of **The International Society for the Lumbar Spine**, Washington.

47 The influence of leisure time physical activity on some coronary risk factors

D.C. van der Westhuizen, G.L. Strydom, L.l. Dreyer and H.S. Steyn

1 Introduction

It is difficult to ascertain directly the role of physical activity in the prevention of coronary heart disease (Robinson and Leon, 1994). Physical activity that complies with specific requirements facilitates positive changes in coronary heart disease risk factors, apparently reducing the overall risk of coronary heart disease and related deaths (Paffenbarger et al., 1994).

Several researchers (e.g. Leon et al., 1987; Paffenbarger, 1994) have indicated a marked decrease in coronary mortality risk among those who participate in physical activity demanding more than 6278 kJ.week^{-1}. Drygas (1988) and Slattery et al. (1989) have respectively proposed that 4186-6278 kJ.week^{-1} and 4186 kJ.week^{-1} might be sufficient to render protection against coronary heart disease (CHD).

There is a favourable association between certain levels of regular leisure-time physical activity (LTPA), blood lipids and certain anthropometric dimensions (Blair, 1992). The aim of the study was to examine the association between LTPA (independent variable) with selected exercise-related coronary risk factors (dependent variables) in 278 males.

2 Methods

Data were obtained from a systematic-stratified sample of 278 white male residents of two industrialized cities (Witbank and Vanderbijlpark, South Africa) between the ages of 35 and 54 years. Each subject was allocated to one of three LTPA-categories (low, moderate and high) (Sharkey, 1990). The participants were subjected to a battery of tests which included measurements of serum blood lipids and lipoproteins, waist/hip ratio, body mass index and PWC_{170}. Only subjects who were capable of completing a PWC_{170} test were included in this study.

The measurements were done in the following manner:

Body mass index (BMI)(kg.m^{-2}): This was calculated by dividing body mass (kg) by height (m^2) (American College of Sports Medicine, 1993).

Waist/hip ratio (WHR): The waist/hip ratio was measured in a horizontal plane at the narrowest portion of the torso and the largest hip circumference (American College of Sports Medicine, 1993) with a non-stretchable tape.

Serum blood lipids: Non-fasting venous blood samples (20 ml) were taken. Laboratory analyses consisted of total cholesterol concentration (TC), high density lipoprotein (HDL-

C) and low density lipoprotein (LDL-C) determinations, as described by Vermaak et al. (1991).

Physical working capacity (PWC): A multistage submaximal physical working capacity test up to 70-85% of the age-predicted maximal heart rate of the subject, was executed according to the protocol of Watson (1983). All subjects except those with absolute contra-indications (American College of Sports Medicine, 1993) underwent this test. Subjects using certain types of medication like beta-adrenergic blocking agents were also excluded. A Monark cycle ergometer (model 864) was used to execute the test.

Leisure-time physical activity index (LTPA): The physical activity index suggested by Sharkey (1990) was used. In this regard, a physical activity index of 36 implies, for example, that a particular person who took part in leisure-time physical activity consisting of 20-30 minutes (duration = 3) aerobic type activities, three times per week (frequency = 4) experienced it as moderately heavy (intensity = 3). The LTPA-index was based on a person's regular daily activity by multiplying each person's score for each category (score = intensity x duration x frequency) (Sharkey, 1990).

The World Health Organization (WHO) (Andersen et al., 1978) classified an energy consumption of <15.5 kJ.min^{-1} for men 40-49 years as light intensity physical activity, while moderate, heavy and high intensity physical activity respectively implies 15.9-29.7, 30.1-44.8 and >44.8 kJ.min^{-1}. A person who exercises to a high intensity (>44.8 kJ.min^{-1}) for 30 minutes, 5 days.week^{-1} consume approximately 6718 kJ.week^{-1} (44.8 kJ.min^{-1} X 30 min X 5 days.week^{-1}). Based on this, the cut-off points used in this study, were: Low active = <16 (±586 kJ.week^{-1}); moderately active = 17-63 ($\pm$ 586-6278 kJ.week^{-1}); high active = >64 (>6278 kJ.week^{-1}).

A one-way analysis of variance was used to ascertain any differences between the three levels of LTPA with respect to the dependent variables. Post-hoc comparisons were done according to Tukey's test. Finally, practical significance was determined by means of effect size measurements (ES) (Thomas et al., 1991).

3 Results

Table I represents a summary of the effect of low-, moderate- and high activity during leisure-time on some coronary risk factors as observed in this study.

It is clear that the high LTPA group showed a significantly higher level of HDL-C and PWC$_{170}$.kg^{-1} comparing to the moderate and low LTPA groups. In the case of TC/HDL-C ratio, the high LTPA group showed a significant lower ratio (5.3 mmol.l^{-1}) when compared with the moderate (5.9 mmol.l^{-1}) and low (6.5 mmol.l^{-1}) LTPA groups. When the practical significances of the above mentioned differences were calculated, the HDL-C and PWC$_{170}$.kg^{-1} between the high versus low LTPA groups were practically significant (HDL-C = ES 0.82; PWC$_{170}$.kg^{-1} = ES 0.93).

Table I also indicates that BMI and waist/hip ratio (WHR) show no practically significant difference with regard to effect size (ES) measurements. Analysis of covariance was applied to control for age. The only difference according to the results was found for the TC/HDL-ratio where the effect size declined from the initial 0.63 to 0.59 mmol.l^{-1} after controlling for age. However, this difference shows no practically significant difference (ES <0.8). The ES measurements for HDL-C (ES=0.82) as well as the PWC$_{170}$.kg^{-1} (ES=0.93) between the low and high active groups of both variables, were still practically significant and remained the same as before controlling for age.

However, the differences between high vs moderate (HvsM) active (ES=0.61) and the

Table I. Leisure-time physical activity index (LTPA-index) and some coronary risk factors in men aged 35-54

Variables	LTPA=0-16 (Low)			LTPA=17-63 (Moderate)			LTPA=>64 (High)			F-ratio P-value	ES
	n	X	SD	n	X	SD	n	X	SD		
Body mass(kg)	193	82.9	14.0	65	82.3	10.2	21	81.0	8.9	F(2:276)=0.23; P=0.7936	-
BMI(kg.m²)	191	26.6	3.8	65	26.5	2.7	21	26.3	2.9	F(2:274)=0.09; P=0.9128	-
WHR	194	1.0	0.6	64	0.9	0.1	21	0.9	0.1	F(2:276)=0.38; P=0.6833	-
TC (mmol.l^{-1})	187	6.1	1.1	63	6.0	1.0	21	5.9	0.9	F(2:268)=0.79; P=0.4549	-
HDL-C (mmol.l^{-1})[**]	187	1.0^a	0.3	63	1.1^a	0.2	21	1.2^b	0.5	F(2:268)=6.88; P=0.0012	HvsM=0.61 HvsL=0.82[***]
LDL-C (mmol.l^{-1})	187	4.0	0.9	63	4.1	1.0	21	3.9	0.9	F(2:268)=0.23; P=0.7935	-
TC/HDL-ratio[**]	187	6.5^a	2.0	63	5.9^{ab}	1.8	20	5.3^b	1.3	F(2:267)=5.13; P=0.0065	HvsL=0.63
PWC170 (watt.kg^{-1})[**]	194	2.0^a	0.5	65	2.2^b	0.7	21	2.5^b	0.3	F(2:277)=12.57; P=0.0001	HvsL=0.93[***] MvsL=0.51

[**]   Different symbols of group means e.g. a, b and c indicate statistically significant differences between group means (Tukey's test).
[***] Practically significant differences (ES ≥0.8)
      L = Low active; M = Moderate active; H = Highly active

moderate vs the low (MvsL) active groups (ES=0.51) of respectively the HDL-C and PWC170.kg^{-1} were not practically significant (ES <0.8).

4 Discussion

Exercise has major beneficial effects on lipid and lipoprotein metabolism that are, within limits, a function of intensity, duration and frequency of exercise (Berg et al., 1994). One of these benefits is the increase in HDL-cholesterol (Blair et al., 1992). There is a negative correlation between coronary heart disease and plasma HDL-C (Gordon et al., 1977). Generally, results show a 5-15% (0.07-0.20 mmol.l^{-1}) increase in plasma HDL-C levels following chronic exercise (Gordon and Cooper, 1988). The results of this study and the study by Gordon and Cooper (1988) are more or less consistent, showing that the differences between the low- and the moderate active groups compared to the high active group regarding HDL-C were respectively 0.23 (22% increase) and 0.06 mmol.l^{-1} (6% increase).
    Haskell (1994) has suggested that an increase of only 0.10 mmol.l^{-1} in a population

(which by most standards would be considered a relatively small change), might reduce CHD mortality by as much as 14%. Haskell (1991) postulated that 5023-6278 kJ.week^{-1} seems necessary to evoke favourable changes in plasma levels of HDL-C. A practically significant difference by means of effect size (ES >0.8) between the low (<586 kJ.week^{-1}) vs the high LTPA group (>6278 kJ.week^{-1}) regarding HDL-C (ES=0.82) most probably supports the dose-response effect which frequently exists between low- and high LTPA groups (Haskell, 1994).

A meta-analytic (Tran and Weltman, 1985) and review (Haskell, 1986) supports the notion that reductions in LDL-C and TC-concentration may occur and are the greatest when substantial weight loss or decreased dietary intake accompanies the exercise. This might be one of the reasons why no significant or practically significant reductions in LDL-C and TC-concentration occurred, as significant or practically significant differences regarding the BMI and/or WHR were absent. In this respect, Després et al. (1990) have shown a significant correlation between an increase in WHR and LDL-C. However, some conflicting results have been reported in a community study by Sallis et al. (1986) who showed significant differences in both TC-concentration (P<0.05) and BMI (P<0.01) between low and high physical activity groups of men (35-49 year). The authors believed that body mass differences alone accounted for the observed difference in TC-concentration.

It seems that a PWC$_{170}$.kg^{-1} value of 2.5 watt.kg^{-1} which coincides with the value proposed by Jones and Campbell (1992) seems necessary to produce a practically significant difference (ES=0.93) between the low and high LTPA groups (35-54 years).

5 Conclusions

Regular leisure-time physical activity of approximately 6278 kJ.week^{-1} probably contributed to a practically signficant increase in plasma HDL-C and physical fitness (PWC$_{170}$.kg^{-1}) levels, and had therefore a positive influence on some coronary risk factors. This is reason enough to implement various strategies encouraging sedentary people in a community to increase their leisure time physical activities as it may contribute significantly to primary prevention of coronary heart disease.

6 References

American College of Sports Medicine. (1993) **Resource Manual for Guidelines for Exercise Testing and Prescription.** Lea and Febiger, Philadelphia.

Andersen, K.L. Masironi, R. Rutenfranz, J. and Seliger, V. (1978) **Habitual Physical Activity and Health.** World Health Organization, Copenhagen.

Berg, A. Frey, I. Baumstark, M.W. Halle, M. and Keul, J. (1994) Physical activity and lipoprotein lipid disorders. **Sports Medicine**, 17, 6-21.

Blair, S.N. Kohl, H.W. and Gordon, N.F. (1992) How much physical activity is good for health? **Annual Review of Public Health,** 13, 99-126.

Després, J. Moorjani, S. Lupien, P.J. Tremblay, A. Nadeau, A. and Bouchard, C. (1990) Regional distribution of fat, plasma lipoproteins and cardiovascular disease. **Arteriosclerosis**, 10, 497-511.

Drygas, W., Jegler, A. and Kunski, H. (1988) Study on threshold dose of physical activity in coronary heart disease prevention. Relationship between leisure time physical activity and coronary risk factors. **International Journal of Sports Medicine,** 9, 275-278.

Gordon, T., Castelli, W.P., Hjortland, M.C., Kannel, W.B. and Dawber, T.R. (1977) High density lipoprotein as a protective factor against coronary heart disease: the Framingham Study. **American Journal of Medicine,** 62, 707-714.

Gordon, N.F. and Cooper, K.H. (1988) Controlling cholesterol levels through exercise. **Comprehensive Therapy,** 14, 52-57.

Haskell, W.L. (1986) The influence of exercise training on plasma lipids and lipoproteins in health and disease. **Acta Medica Scandinavica,** 711, 25-37.

Haskell, W.L. (1991) Dose-response relationship between physical activity and disease risk factors, in **Sport for all** (eds P. Oja and R. Telama), Elsevier Science Publishers, Amsterdam, pp. 125-133.

Haskell, W.L. (1994) Dose-response issues from a biological perspective, in **Physical Activity, Fitness and Health: International Proceedings and Consensus Statement** (eds C. Bouchard. R.J. Shephard and T. Stephens), Human Kinetics Publishers, Champaign, Illinois, pp. 1030-1039.

Jones, N.L. and Campbell, E.J. (1982) **Clinical Exercise Testing.** W.B. Saunders Company, Philadelphia.

Leon, A.S. Connett, J. Jacobs, D.R. and Rauramaa, R. (1987) Leisure-time physical activity levels and risk of coronary heart disease and death. **Journal of the American Medical Association,** 258, 2388-2395.

Paffenbarger, Jr., R.S. Kampert, J.B. Lee, I. Hyde, R.T. Leung, R.W. and Wing, A.L. (1994) Changes in physical activity and other lifeway patterns influencing longevity. **Medicine and Science in Sports and Exercise,** 26, 857-865.

Robinson, J.G. and Leon, A.S. (1994) The prevention of cardiovascular disease: Emphasis on secondary prevention. **The Medical Clinics of North America,** 78, 69-98.

Sallis, J.F. Haskell, W.L. Fortmann, S.P. Wood, P.D. and Vranizan, K.M. (1986) Moderate intensity physical activity and cardiovascular risk factors. **Preventive Medicine,** 15, 561-568.

Sharkey, B.J. (1990) **Physiology of Fitness.** Human Kinetics Book, Champaign, Illinois.

Slattery, M.L. Jacobs, D.R. and Nichaman, M.Z. (1989) Leisure time physical activity and coronary heart disease. The US Railway study. **Circulation,** 79, 304-311.

Thomas, J.R. Salazar, W. and Landers, D.M. (1991) What is missing in $P<0.05$? Effect size. **Research Quarterly for Exercise and Sport,** 62, 344-348.

Tran, Z.V. and Weltman, A. (1985) Differential effects of exercise on serum lipid and lipoprotein levels seen with changes in body weight. **Journal of the American Medical Association,** 254, 919-924.

Vermaak, W.J.H. Kotze, J.P. Van der Merwe, A.M. Becker, P.J. Ubbink, J.B. Barnard, H.C. Roux, F.G. Schoeman, J.J. and Strydom, G.L. (1991) Epidemiological reference range for low-density lipoprotein cholesterol and apolipoprotein B for identification of increased risk of ischaemic heart disease. **South African Medical Journal,** 79, 367-371.

Watson, A.W.S. (1983) **Physical Fitness and Athletic Performance.** Longman, Inc., New York.

Author index

Subject index